The Fantasy Principle

"Michael Vannoy Adams moves the field of psychoanalysis into the 21st century by turning the clock back to the main discovery of Freud and Jung: fantasy rules the psyche. *The Fantasy Principle* is a major serious researched work and yet a book of imagination and humor. It is also a book aimed beyond professional therapists, engaging everyone who is, will be, or has been in therapy."

James Hillman

Contemporary psychoanalysis needs less reality and more fantasy. It needs a new principle – what Michael Vannoy Adams calls the "fantasy principle."

Freud insists that we conform to the reality principle. He assumes that there is only one reality and that we all define it in exactly the same way. Reality, however, is not given. There are many "realities" and they are constructed from fantasies that occur in us continuously. Fantasy, Adams declares, is what transforms consciousness.

This book is distinctive: it radically affirms the centrality of imagination. Adams challenges us to exercise and explore the imagination. He shows us how to value vitally important images that emerge from the unconscious, how to evoke such images, and how to engage them decisively. *The Fantasy Principle* explains how to apply special Jungian techniques to interpret images accurately and to experience images immediately and intimately through what Jung calls "active imagination."

The Fantasy Principle argues for the recognition of a new school of psychoanalysis – the school of "imaginal psychology." As Jung says, "Image *is* psyche." The school of imaginal psychology emphasizes the transformative impact of images.

Michael Vannoy Adams is a Jungian psychoanalyst in New York City.

Michael Vannoy Adams is a Jungian psychoanalyst in New York City. He is a founding member of and director of admissions for the Jungian Psychology Association (JPA), a group of Jungian psychoanalysts who have developed a training program based on new models and formats of analytic learning. He is a clinical associate professor at the New York University Postdoctoral Program in Psychotherapy and Psychoanalysis. He is also a faculty member at the Object Relations Institute, the Blanton-Peale Institute, the C. G. Jung Foundation, and the New School University, where he was formerly associate provost.

Adams is the author of two previous books: *The Mythological Unconscious* (2001) and *The Multicultural Imagination: "Race," Color, and the Unconscious* (1996). He is the recipient of two Gradiva Awards from the National Association for the Advancement of Psychoanalysis. He has been a Marshall scholar in Britain and a Fulbright senior lecturer in India.

For information about Jungian analysis, visit Michael Vannoy Adams's website: www.jungnewyork.com

The Fantasy Principle

Psychoanalysis of the imagination

Michael Vannoy Adams

 Brunner-Routledge
Taylor & Francis Group

HOVE AND NEW YORK

First published 2004 by Brunner-Routledge
27 Church Road, Hove, East Sussex, BN3 2FA
Simultaneously published in the USA and Canada
by Brunner-Routledge
29 West 35th Street, New York, NY 10001

Brunner-Routledge is an imprint of the Taylor & Francis Group

© 2004 Michael Vannoy Adams

Typeset in Times by Regent Typesetting, London
Printed and bound in Great Britain by TJ International Ltd, Padstow, Cornwall
Paperback cover design by Lisa Dynan

This publication has been produced with paper manufactured to strict environmental standards and with pulp derived from sustainable forests.

British Library Cataloguing in Publication Data
A catalogue record for this book is available from the British Library

Library of Congress Cataloging-in-Publication Data
Adams, Michael Vannoy, 1947–
    The fantasy principle : psychoanalysis of the imagination / Michael Vannoy Adams.
        p. cm.
    Includes bibliographical references (p.   ) and index.
        ISBN 1-58391-818-3 (hbk) – ISBN 1-58391-819-1 (pbk.)
    1. Jungian Psychology. 2. Imagination. I. Title.

BF173.J85A33 2004
150.19'37–dc22

2003018977

ISBN 1-58391-818-3 (hbk)
ISBN 1-58391-819-1 (pbk)

For Una Chaudhuri,
who transforms all of my fantasies
into realities and pleasures.

Contents

Jung and Freud

Drawing by William Bramhall

Preface

The illustration opposite this page represents one of my attempts to acknowledge both Freud and Jung. In 1992, the New School University (then the "New School for Social Research") established a Psychoanalytic Studies program in the Graduate Faculty of Political and Social Science. The purpose of the program was to study psychoanalysis not as a clinical practice but as a cultural theory. (A number of students who graduated from the program did eventually train at psychoanalytic institutes.)

I was privileged to be the director of the Psychoanalytic Studies program for the first three years of its existence. The curriculum that I designed allotted equal time to both the Freudian and Jungian traditions (Adams 1993). In addition to courses on Freudian and post-Freudian analysis and Jungian and post-Jungian analysis, that curriculum included such courses as "Psychoanalysis and Gender Studies" and "Psychoanalysis and Social and Political Thought," as well as a lecture series of guest speakers from all of the different schools of psychoanalytic thought.

The cartoon of Jung and Freud sitting together, the one smoking his pipe, the other smoking his cigar, was my idea. The artist William Bramhall drew the image beautifully, brilliantly, with all the humor that I had imagined. (Free associate, if you will, to that *very* phallic cigar, with Freud's fingers so ready to flick red-hot ash right into Jung's lap!) For me, the cartoon is an especially apt illustration for this book because it evokes a fantasy of just how imaginative (and just how much fun) psychoanalysis might have been had Jung and Freud remained colleagues. Just imagine!

The New School University used the cartoon of Jung and Freud to promote the Psychoanalytic Studies program in advertisements with the headline "Earn the Degree of Your Dreams." Not everyone, however, appreciated my effort to establish a Freudian–Jungian program. Eventually, I was replaced as director of the program, and the curriculum was redesigned, effectively to exclude Jung. Sadly, the program has been defunct for the last few years. The Graduate Faculty offers occasional courses on psychoanalytic topics and now plans a psychoanalytic concentration in the Philosophy department, but it does not currently grant a degree in Psychoanalytic Studies. Perhaps one day it will again. As for me, I continue to teach psychoanalytic courses at Eugene Lang College of the New School University, and I very much appreciate the opportunity to do so.

Freud never taught at the New School University, nor did Jung, although many other analysts have done so over the years. Sandor Ferenczi was the first, in 1921. Alvin Johnson, the first president of the New School University, recounts the following anecdote, which includes an ironical commentary on the law-and-order priorities of that period in New York City:

> Anyway, Ferenczi proved to be a most charming, cultivated gentleman, and his course drew such a fleet of limousines to Twenty-third Street that the local police captain felt called upon the investigate. He was an upstanding young fellow, attended by half a dozen ordinary cops. He explained to me that, seeing such a lot of limousines, he wanted to know what was going on, perhaps a lecture on physics or – or –
>
> "Birth control," I suggested.
>
> "Yes, that is what I suspected."
>
> "Well, it's nothing of the kind, but a lecture on psychoanalytic psychology. Come in and hear it."
>
> Soon the police captain and his squad retired to the door. "Pity that old boy can't speak English. I couldn't understand a word he said."
>
> (Johnson 1952: 284–5)

A few of the many analysts who have taught at the New School University include: Alfred Adler, A. A. Brill, Fritz Wittels, Wilhelm Reich, Karen Horney, Erich Fromm, Clara Thompson, Ernst Kris, Melitta Schmideberg, Robert Waelder, Sandor Rado, Peter Blos, Gregory Zilboorg, Theodor Reik – as well as these Jungian analysts: Eleanor Bertine, Frances Wickes, Edward F. Edinger, and Edward C. Whitmont.

I am glad to say that in my personal experience many contemporary analysts in the Freudian tradition are pluralists who have a very positive, inclusive attitude toward Jungian psychology. It especially pleases me that I have many good friends who are Freudian analysts. Unfortunately, however, in many universities (all too often from either ignorance or prejudice) Jung is persona non grata. Jungian psychology remains marginal as an academic subject. (A new organization, the International Association for Jungian Studies, seeks, in part, to redress this situation.) In addition, very few psychoanalytic institutes in the Freudian tradition offer any courses in Jungian psychology. I hope that this book will encourage more psychoanalytic dialogues between Freudians and Jungians.

Although I am a Jungian analyst, I respect all of the other schools of psychoanalytic thought, including the Freudian school. As Michael Eigen says: "We all stand on the shoulders of the giants Freud and Jung" (1986: x). Eigen makes psychoanalytic use of an aphorism that many individuals – among them, most famously Isaac Newton – have used, usually as a demonstration of modesty. Robert K. Merton, who has written a marvelously ironical book that attempts to trace the origin of the aphorism, quotes Newton as saying: "If I have seen further it is by standing on ye shoulders of giants" (1965: 9). The aphorism itself, to which Newton alludes, may be rendered as follows: "Pigmies standing on the shoulders of giants see farther than the giants themselves." Other translations substitute "dwarfs" for "pigmies." In effect, Eigen says that in the history of psychoanalysis we are all pigmies or dwarfs in comparison with the giants Freud and Jung and that only by standing on their shoulders may we see farther than they did.

Merton lists 47 individuals who have used the aphorism for one purpose or another. The last individual on the list is Freud himself, who modifies the aphorism into a sarcastic retort against Wilhelm Stekel. Ernest Jones reports that Stekel felt that "he had surpassed Freud" in the ability to interpret symbols. Jones continues: "He was fond of expressing this estimate of himself half-modestly by saying a dwarf on the shoulder of a giant could see farther than the giant himself. When Freud heard this he grimly commented: 'That may be true, but a louse on the head of an astronomer does not'" (1955 2: 136). From a Jungian perspective, what is a louse? Marie-Louise von Franz says:

> The louse in symbolism usually carries the meaning of a completely autonomous thought; something that sticks in your mind, though you don't want it, and sucks your blood. It is a beautiful symbol for thought obsession: an idea that stays in your mind, obsesses all your other thoughts, and at the same time sucks your blood, takes away your psychic energy.
>
> (Von Franz 1995: 44)

Psychoanalytically, the louse is a small parasite (a "complex," Jungians would say) that consumes the "libido" of a larger host.

Are we all pigmies or dwarfs who see farther than the giants Freud and Jung? Or are we merely so many immodest lice? It seems to me that if we have any aspirations to be far-sighted analysts, we need properly to acknowledge the gigantic contributions of both Freud and Jung. Otherwise, we are just lousy analysts, whether we be Jungians or Freudians.

As the subtitle of the book indicates, this is a study in what I call *psychoanalysis of the imagination*. Among the various psychoanalytic psychologies, Jungian psychology is an *imaginal psychology*. What is unique about Jungian analysis is its emphasis on images, as well as its methods for interpreting and experiencing those images – the techniques of *explication*, *amplification*, and *active imagination*. Psychoanalysts who master these three Jungian methods and apply them with the necessary discipline are in an enviable position accurately to analyze the images that emerge spontaneously and autonomously from the psyche.

To me, the purpose of psychoanalysis (including Jungian analysis) is simply to *increase consciousness*. In that respect, this book is an attempt to demonstrate the practical value of contemporary Jungian psychology, both clinically and culturally. Among the topics that I discuss are fantasy, dream interpretation, archetypes and archetypal images, mythological knowledge, sex and gender, racism and multiculturalism, fathers and sons, cannibalism and suicide, and blasphemy. Some of these are issues that I have addressed in my previous two books, *The Mythological Unconscious* (Adams, 2001) and *The Multicultural Imagination: "Race," Color, and the Unconscious* (Adams, 1996). What is distinctive about this book, however, is its radical (and deliberately provocative) emphasis on the utter centrality of the *imagination* in psychoanalysis.

"A curious thing," James Hillman says, "is that there's never been a single piece of true doctrinal dispute, theoretical dispute, among the Jungians." He conjectures that Jungians are not disputatious (at least about doctrine or theory) because they are, instead, so stylistically imaginative. According to Hillman, the Jungian style is to imagine rather than dispute. "Imagination," he asserts, "does not argue" (1983b: 35). I myself, however, imagine Jungians arguing with other Jungians (as well as with non-Jungians) over doctrinal or theoretical issues – and doing so imaginatively. I do not consider imagination and argumentation to be mutually exclusive. Jungians do not need controversy merely for controversy's sake, but they could very much use some controversy over serious issues – as well as some criticism (if at least some of them could develop a capacity not to take that criticism personally). What interests me is the possibility of Jungians who are not sensitive to criticism and therefore defensive about it but who are receptive to criticism and reflective about it. A receptive, reflective ego in effective relation to a constructively (and deconstructively) critical unconscious is what I consider to be the sine qua non of any psychoanalysis. It is a necessary (if not sufficient) condition for each and every increase in consciousness.

Finally, I should emphasize that I apply the word "psychoanalysis" to all of the various schools of analytic thought, including the Jungian school. I do not consider myself an "analytical psychologist." I call myself a "Jungian psychoanalyst." Jungians are just as much psychoanalysts as Freudians or any other analysts.

Michael Vannoy Adams
New York City

Acknowledgments

I thank James Hillman, Andrew Samuels, Christopher Hauke, Paul Kugler, Yoram Kaufmann, Beverley Zabriskie, Luigi Zoja, Renos Papadopoulos, Thomas Singer, Thomas B. Kirsch, John Beebe, Robert Bosnak, Alan M. Jones, Laurel Morris, Sylvester Wojtkowski, Jeffrey Rubin Morey, Mark Kuras, Sherry Salman, Philip Zabriskie, Barbara Koltuv, Priscilla Rodgers, Susanne Short, Linda Carter, Joseph Cambray, Harry W. Fogarty, Richard C. Lewis, Marga Speicher, Melinda Haas, Kathleen Martin, Greg Mogenson, Michael Whan, Ginette Paris, Dennis Patrick Slattery, Mary Watkins, Karin Barnaby, Margot McLean, Tessa Adams, Jocelyne Samuels, Betty Sue Flowers, Kirkland C. Vaughans, Michael Moskowitz, James L. Fosshage, Lewis Aron, Bruce H. Bernstein, Michael Eigen, David Shapiro, Kathryn Madden, Susan Kavaler-Adler, Robert S. Weinstein, Blake Burleson, Laurence J. Kirmayer, Noel Cobb, Peter Carey, Deirdre Bair, Janet Careswell, Arnold DeVera, David Ward, Judith B. Walzer, Beatrice Banu, Elizabeth Dickey, Sekou Sundiata, Craig Harris, Lee Leatherwood, Bush Bowden, Harry Heleotis, Dick Benson, Tamara Glenny, Gad Alpan, Stacey Foiles, Wendy Kaplan, and Ben Goldberg.

I thank Kate Hawes, publisher, Brunner-Routledge, Taylor & Francis, for commissioning this book. I also thank Helen Pritt, Editorial Assistant and Imogen Burch, Managing Editor.

I especially thank those individuals who granted me permission to use dreams, fantasies, or other material in this book.

I should also like to remember Katrin Cartlidge, who as both an actor and a person exhibited so much intelligence, courage, and integrity. We first met after I had seen her perform in New York City in *Mnemonic*, a play about layers of collective unconscious memory, and had then written to her that the subject matter seemed to me very "Jungian." Over lunch in Greenwich Village, she told me that as a teenager she had struggled to read Jung's *Memories, Dreams, Reflections* but had managed to complete only two-thirds of it because she was so severely dyslexic and had such difficulty with words. At a cast party a week later, she told me that she had telephoned her mother in London and had told her that she had met "a Jungian analyst." Her mother had then told her that, as she remembered it, one of their relatives had been "one of Jung's associates." Who, we wondered, could that have been? None other than Aniela Jaffe, who had edited Jung's *Memories, Dreams, Reflections*! We laughed at the irony (and, of course, the "synchronicity"). Now I am both sad and happy to have an opportunity to honor, fondly, the memory of a friend.

A version of Chapter 1, "The Fantasy Principle: Imaginal Psychology and the Dethroning of 'Mr. Reality,'" was presented at the Jung Studies Day, Goldsmiths College, University of London, November 16, 2002.

A version of Chapter 2, "Compensation in the Service of Individuation: Phenomenological Essentialism and Jungian Dream Interpretation," was published in *Psychoanalytic Dialogues*, 10, 1 (2000): 127–42.

A version of Chapter 4, "Mythological Knowledge: Just How Important Is It in Jungian (and Freudian) Analysis?", was published in *Harvest: Journal for Jungian Studies*, 48, 1 (2002): 7–21. It was also presented at the New York Association for Analytical Psychology, April 28, 2002.

A version of Chapter 5, "The 'Womanning' of Schreber: Catastrophe, Creation, and the Mythopoeic Forces of Mankind," won a Gradiva Award at the National Association for the Advancement of Psychoanalysis Conference, New York, May 13, 2000. In a wonderfully funny Freudian slip, the psychoanalyst (a woman) who presented the award to me announced the title as "Womanizing!"

A version of Chapter 6, "Dreaming of the Ku Klux Klan: 'Race,' Culture, and History in Psychoanalysis," was presented at the Metropolitan Chapter Forum of the New York State Society for Clinical Social Work, New York, April 13, 1997; at The Relevance of Jungian Psychology for Cultural Psychiatry Conference, McGill University, Montreal, May 26, 2000, and at the International Federation for Psychoanalytic Education Conference, Fort Lauderdale, November 2, 2002.

A version of Chapter 7, "Jung, Africa, and 'Geopathology': Psychic Place and Displacement," was presented in the John N. Jonsson Peace and Justice Lecture Series, Baylor University, Waco, February 7, 2000, and at the C. G. Jung Institute of San Francisco, October 14, 2000.

A version of Chapter 8, "Refathering Psychoanalysis, Deliteralizing Hillman: Imaginal Therapy, Individual and Cultural," was presented at the London Convivium for Archetypal Studies Conference, Cumberland Lodge, May 28, 1994, and was published in Petruska Clarkson (ed.), *On the Sublime in Psychoanalysis, Archetypal Psychology and Psychotherapy*, London, Whurr Publishers, 1997, pp. 109–22. It won a Gradiva Award at the National Association for the Advancement of Psychoanalysis Conference, New York, April 23–24, 1999.

A version of Chapter 9, "A Baby Is Being Eaten: A Case of Cannibalistic Malpractice and Suicide," was presented at the International Federation for Psychoanalytic Education Conference, Fordham University, New York, November 8, 1998.

Finally, I thank the members of my family: Una Chaudhuri (to whom I have dedicated this book), Nathaniel Lee Grotowski Adams, Sonu Rita Jessie Adams, James Adams, Sandra Adams Leatherwood and George Leatherwood, Usha Baljit

Singh, Natasha and Surrinder Singh, Baldeep and Alka Singh, and Uma and Harsh Mahajan. Everyone should be so lucky to have such a loving family.

PERMISSIONS

Permission to reproduce or reprint the following material is gratefully acknowledged:

Drawing of Freud and Jung by William Bramhall, reproduced by permission of William Bramhall and the New School University.

Approximately 3,840 words from *Collected Works* by C. G. Jung, Princeton, NJ: Princeton University Press, Copyright Princeton University Press, reprinted by permission of Princeton University Press.

"Compensation in the Service of Individuation: Phenomenological Essentialism and Jungian Dream Interpretation," *Psychoanalytic Dialogues*, 10,1 (2000): 127–42, reprinted by permission of The Analytic Press.

"Mythological Knowledge: Just How Important Is It in Jungian (and Freudian) Analysis?", *Harvest: Journal for Jungian Studies*, 48,1 (2002): 7–21, reprinted by permission of *Harvest* (website: www.jungclub-london.org/frameset.htm).

Approximately 2,518 words from *Memoirs of My Nervous Illness* by Daniel Paul Schreber, translated and edited by Ida MacAlpine and Richard A. Hunter, Cambridge, MA: Harvard University Press, Copyright 1955 by the President and Fellows of Harvard College, reprinted by permission of Harvard University Press.

"Refathering Psychoanalysis, Deliteralizing Hillman: Imaginal Therapy, Individual and Cultural," in P. Clarkson (ed.), *On the Sublime in Psychoanalysis, Archetypal Psychology and Psychotherapy*, London: Whurr Publishers, 1997, pp. 109–22, reprinted by permission of Colin Whurr, Whurr Publishers.

"Dear Mr. Fantasy" (Capaldi/Wood/Winwood), copyright Universal Music Publishing (66.7%), used by permission of Music Sales Limited, all rights reserved, international copyright secured.

Chapter 1

The fantasy principle

Imaginal psychology and the dethroning of "Mr. Reality"

One of the concepts that I have attempted to introduce into psychoanalytic discourse is what I call the *fantasy principle*. I have advocated the concept as an alternative to the "pleasure principle" and the "reality principle." For some time, I have told myself that I should elaborate on what I mean by the fantasy principle, and I now propose to do just that.

For many years, I have felt that what Jung has to say about the imagination has been ignored or neglected. As long ago as April 25, 1986, I had a dream about this state of affairs and what I might do to rectify the situation:

> I'm in a library. There's a shelf of books on psychoanalysis. On the shelf is a volume by Jung on the imagination. I think that it may go unnoticed on the shelf. There are also a couple of volumes by Freud. I put them next to the Jung book, thinking that now the Jung book will have a chance of being seen.

In this dream, it occurs to me that what Jung has written on the imagination may never be seen unless I place what Freud has written next to it. People will be more likely to "check out" and read what Jung has to say about the imagination if I juxtapose it with what Freud has to say.

In 1911, Jung published the first part of *Wandlungen und Symbole der Libido* (*Transformations and Symbols of the Libido*). He entitled the first chapter "Concerning Two Kinds of Thinking." Jung noted that William James had identified two kinds of thinking: "directed thinking" and "non-directed thinking." Non-directed thinking, Jung says, "quickly leads us away from reality into phantasies," and "image crowds upon image" (*CW* B: 19). In short, directed thinking is reality thinking, while non-directed thinking is fantasy thinking.

Later that same year, Freud published an article entitled "Formulations on the Two Principles of Mental Functioning." The two principles were the "pleasure principle" and the "reality principle." In contrast to the reality principle, Freud defined the pleasure principle as fantasy thinking: "With the introduction of the reality principle one species of thought-activity was split off; it was kept free from reality-testing and remained subordinated to the pleasure principle alone. This activity is *phantasying*" (*SE* 12: 222).

As early as March 2, 1910, Jung had informed Freud that in a "lecture on symbolism" he had distinguished two kinds of thinking and had called one of them "fantasy thinking" (Freud and Jung 1974: 298). Subsequently, Jung sent Freud a copy of that lecture. On June 19, 1910, Freud wrote the following to Jung:

> Don't be surprised if you recognize certain of your own statements in a paper of mine that I am hoping to revise in the first weeks of the holidays, and don't accuse me of plagiarism, though there may be some temptation to. The title will be: The Two Principles of Mental Action and Education. It is intended for the *Jahrbuch*. I conceived and wrote it two days before the arrival of your "Symbolism"; it is of course a formulation of ideas that were long present in my mind.
>
> (Freud and Jung 1974: 332)

This letter was a defensive effort by Freud to preempt any criticism that he had stolen ideas from Jung. Freud both confesses to the crime ("Don't be surprised if you recognize certain of your own statements in a paper of mine.") and pleads not guilty ("I conceived and wrote it two days before the arrival of your 'Symbolism'; it is of course a formulation of ideas that were long present in my mind."). In effect, Freud admits to Jung that the "two principles" are virtually identical with the "two kinds of thinking." On the issue of originality, priority in discovery, and intellectual property rights, John Kerr comments: "In context, Freud's short paper ['Formulations on the Two Principles of Mental Functioning'] reads like nothing so much as an attempt to steal Jung's thunder" (1993: 336).

I should perhaps say that, for me, fantasy is an "F-word." In *A Critical Dictionary of Psychoanalysis*, Charles Rycroft says that the *Oxford English Dictionary* defines "fantasy" as "caprice, whim, fanciful invention" and "phantasy" as "imagination, visionary notion." As a result, he says, British analysts invariably prefer the "ph" spelling. He notes, however, that "few, if any, American writers have followed them in doing so" (1968: 50). In "The Nature and Function of Phantasy," Susan Isaacs provides a different explanation for the "ph" spelling. "The English translators of Freud," she says, "adopted a special spelling of the word 'phantasy', with the *ph*, in order to differentiate the psycho-analytical significance of the term, *i.e.*, predominantly or entirely unconscious phantasies, from the popular word 'fantasy', meaning conscious day-dreams, fictions, and so on" (1952: 80-1). It is a fact, however, that nowhere in Freud's *Standard Edition* is the word spelled with an "f"; it is always spelled with a "ph," even in reference to daydreams and other ostensibly conscious examples.

As in Jung's *Collected Works*, I employ the word "fantasy" as a synonym for "imagination," whether conscious or unconscious. "All the functions that are active in the psyche," Jung says, "converge in fantasy." He remarks that fantasy has "a poor reputation among psychologists," including psychoanalysts, but he asserts that "it nevertheless remains the creative matrix of everything that has made progress possible for humanity." Jung very much esteems fantasy, which he says "has its own irreducible value" (*CW* 7: 290, par. 490). According to Jung, "Developing fantasy means perfecting our humanity" (1977: 40).

Jung does note that alchemy, which he regards as a historical precursor of psychoanalysis, implores the alchemist to imagine "with true and not with fantastic imagination" (*CW* 12: 167, par. 218). In this alchemical context, "fantastic imagination" is equivalent to untrue, or false, imagination. Thus Jung says: "I really prefer the term 'imagination' to 'fantasy,' because there is a difference between the two which the old doctors had in mind when they said that 'opus nostrum,' our work, ought to be done 'per veram imaginationem et non phantastica'" (*CW* 18: 171, par. 396). Jung also mentions the classical distinction between *imaginatio* and *phantasia*. In contrast to *phantasia*, which has a pejorative connotation, he defines *imaginatio* as active imagination. "*Imaginatio*," he says, "is the active evocation of (inner) images" (*CW* 12: 167, par. 219). Although in these instances, Jung privileges true imagination over fantastic imagination and *imaginatio* over *phantasia*, in almost all other instances he equates imagination with fantasy, without prejudice, as I do.

When I began to consider what I might say about the fantasy principle, one of my very favorite novels came to mind – Philip Roth's *The Breast* (1980). It is a book that I have read several times and that I have assigned in an undergraduate course that I have taught off and on over the last 20 years. The title of that course is "Madness in Literature: Psychopathology through Case Fictions." In the novel, David Kepesh, a professor of literature, is overnight transformed into a breast. The book seems obviously to invite a Kleinian interpretation. Kepesh, in fact, confesses to having experienced breast envy before his transformation. As he sucks the breast of his girlfriend on the beach one day, his girlfriend fears that she is cutting off his air because Kepesh is turning green. "With envy," he says. Kepesh, however, rejects the Kleinian notion that he has now suddenly been transformed into a breast because of envy. "I assure you," he says to the reader, "that I have wanted things far less whimsically in my life than I wanted on that beach to be breasted" (1980: 37). Why, he wonders, would that one envious wish, out of all the others, have been fulfilled? "No, I refuse to surrender my bewilderment to the wish-fulfillment theory," he says. "Neat and fashionable and delightfully punitive though it may be, I refuse to believe that I am this thing because this is a thing that I wanted to be" (1980: 38).

The year before his transformation, Kepesh had ended five years of psychoanalysis. After Kepesh is transformed into a breast, his analyst, Dr. Klinger, visits him in the hospital. Dr. Klinger assures Kepesh that he is not insane but that he is, quite literally, a breast. Kepesh, however, believes that he is simply suffering from a delusion. In analysis, Kepesh attempts to interpret the meaning of what he calls "the fantasy of physical transformation" (1980: 66). He says:

> Now, with Dr. Klinger's assistance, I was trying to figure out just why, of all things, I had chosen a breast. Why a big brainless bag of dumb, desirable

tissue, acted upon instead of acting, unguarded, immobile, hanging, *there*, as a breast simply hangs and is *there*? Why this primitive identification with *the* object of infantile veneration? What unfulfilled appetites, what cradle confusions, what fragments out of my remotest past could have collided to spark a delusion of such classical simplicity?

(Roth 1980: 66–7)

Eventually, Kepesh accepts the fact that he has been transformed into a breast. He assumes that everyone knows about his transformation and that he is now famous. Dr. Klinger, however, assures him that "the case has been handled with the utmost discretion" (1980: 86). If hardly anyone knows, Kepesh says, then perhaps he himself should be the one to tell everyone. If he does that, Dr. Klinger says, then everyone will merely dismiss him as a "joke," a "freak," and a "charlatan." Kepesh says: "You're advising me to leave well enough alone. You're advising me to keep this all to myself." Like a good, neutral analyst, Dr. Klinger replies: "I'm advising you nothing, only reminding you of our friend with the beard who sits on the throne." Kepesh says: "Mr. Reality." Dr. Klinger says: "And his principle" (1980: 88). The allusion, of course, is to Freud: "Mr. Reality," our friend with the beard who sits on the throne of psychoanalysis with his principle.

Freud regarded Jung as heir to the throne of psychoanalysis. He called Jung his "crown prince." That, of course, implied that Freud was the "king," and, in fact, Freud ruled psychoanalysis like an absolute monarch and eventually disinherited Jung, with the result that Freud remains, to this very day, on the throne (although perhaps Melanie Klein is now his "queen"). This seems to me a "royal" problem, one to which the fantasy principle provides a solution – the dethroning of "Mr. Reality" and his principle.

Freud defines the reality principle in contrast (not in contradiction) to the pleasure principle. The exigencies of reality, Freud says, require the ego "to postpone the obtaining of pleasure, to put up with a little unpleasure and to abandon certain sources of pleasure altogether." Such an ego, he says, "has become 'reasonable'; it no longer lets itself be governed by the pleasure principle, but obeys the *reality principle*, which also at bottom seeks to obtain pleasure, but pleasure which is assured through taking account of reality, even though it is pleasure postponed and diminished" (*SE* 16: 357). As Freud defines the ego, it is "reason" (*SE* 19: 25) – or reason in the service of the reality principle. In short, for the ego to be reasonable is for it to be realistic.

Freud declares in no uncertain terms that "a happy person never phantasies, only an unsatisfied one" (*SE* 9: 146). "Mr. Reality" would probably have disapproved of rock-and-roll as just one more example of the vulgarities of popular culture, but he would certainly have approved of the lyrics of Steve Winwood, Jim Capaldi, and Chris Wood (1967):

Dear Mr. Fantasy, play us a tune,
Something to make us all happy.

Do anything, take us out of this gloom,
Sing a song, play guitar, make it snappy.

Like Freud, Winwood, Capaldi, and Wood assume that the purpose of fantasy is to make unhappy people happy.

Freud equates fantasies with daydreams and contends that they, like dreams, are without exception wish-fulfillments. "The motive forces of phantasies," he says, "are unsatisfied wishes, and every single phantasy is the fulfilment of a wish" (*SE* 9: 146). In effect, the pleasure principle is a "fantasy principle," but the only motivation of this fantasy principle is wish-fulfillment. The pleasure principle (or Freudian drive psychology) is, in philosophical terms, a variety of hedonism. When drives cannot be satisfied in reality, Freud says, they are repressed into the unconscious, where they are then fulfilled as wishes (for example, in dreams and daydreams), which, he acknowledges, are expressed as fantasies. What most interests Freud, however, is that drives are fulfilled as wishes, not that wishes are expressed as fantasies. That is, he emphasizes the drives and wishes, not the fantasies. Freud says that there is a certain "class of human beings" who find it necessary to recount their fantasies. Whom, exactly, does he have in mind? "These are the victims of nervous illness," he says, "who are obliged to tell their phantasies, among other things, to the doctor by whom they expect to be cured by mental treatment" (*SE* 9: 146). According to Freud, the purpose of analysis is to cure patients of their fantasies!

In contrast to Freud, I would say that not only unhappy persons but also happy ones fantasize (and do so continuously), that not all fantasies are wish-fulfillments, that some fantasies are pleasurable but that some are unpleasurable, and that the purpose of analysis is not to "cure illness" by correcting the fantasies of patients in conformity with reality but to *increase consciousness* by interpreting or experiencing the meaning of those fantasies. Jung says that fantasy is "a natural expression of life which we can at most seek to understand but cannot correct" (*CW* 18: 527, par. 1249). It is, he contends, "not a sickness but a natural and vital activity" (*CW* 18: 528, par. 1249). Rather than correct the fantasies of the patient, Jung says that "I even make an effort to second the patient in his fantasies." He says that he has "no small opinion of fantasy" and contends that "we can never rise above fantasy." Although Jung concedes that "there are unprofitable, futile, morbid, and unsatisfying fantasies whose sterile nature is immediately recognized by every person endowed with common sense," he insists that "the faulty performance proves nothing against the normal performance." He concludes: "All the works of man have their origin in creative imagination. What right, then, have we to disparage fantasy?" (*CW* 16: 45, par. 98).

"The psyche creates reality every day," Jung says. "The only expression I can use for this activity is *fantasy*" (*CW* 6: 52, par. 78). If, as Jung succinctly says, "image *is* psyche" (*CW* 13: 50, par. 75) and if the psyche creates reality, then what creates reality is the image. Rather than say that the psyche, or the image, "creates" reality (which might imply that the activity of fantasy creates reality ex nihilo), I myself prefer to say that it *constructs* reality. Thus I emphasize what I call the psychic construction of reality, or the *imaginal construction of reality*. "Every psychic process," Jung says, "is an image and an 'imagining'" (*CW* 11: 544, par. 889). He says that "the psyche consists essentially of images" (*CW* 8: 325, par. 618). I would say that the psyche is composed of images and that reality is constructed in and through those images. The psyche comprises an ego-image – as James Hillman says, the ego should acknowledge that "it too is an image" (1979a: 102) – and a vast variety of non-ego images. In addition, I would say that reality is not only constructed but also, as Jacques Derrida might say, *deconstructed* by the imagination. In this respect, *the imaginal deconstruction of reality is just as important as the imaginal construction of it*. Non-ego images spontaneously and autonomously manifest in the psyche in order to deconstruct (Jung would say "compensate") images that the ego-image has previously privileged.

"We live immediately," Jung says, "only in the world of images" (*CW* 8: 328, par. 624). He asserts that "the world itself exists only so far as we are able to produce an image of it" (*CW* 11: 479, par. 766). Does Jung believe that the world has no existence independent of our image of it? Jung is no solipsist, or "absolute imagist." He acknowledges that the world has an existence independent of our image of it, but he maintains that our image of it always mediates our experience of the world. For Jung, the image is not secondary and derivative from external reality but is primary and constitutive of it. The fantasy principle, I would say, is logically prior to the reality principle – or, as Hillman says: "first fantasy then reality" (1975: 23).

In *Jung and the Postmodern* (2000), Christopher Hauke cites Jean Baudrillard, who says that in contemporary America the question is one "of concealing the fact that the real is no longer real, and thus of saving the reality principle" (1994: 13). What Baudrillard says, however, itself conceals the fact that, for Jung, the "real" was never *real*, that reality was always, as Jung says, "so-called reality" (*CW* 11: 479, par. 766), because our experience of it is always mediated by our image of it. For Jung, there was never any question of "saving the reality principle." Jung was never, like Freud, "Mr. Reality." He was always, if I may say so, "Mr. Fantasy."

Before Jung ever even met Freud, when Jung was a psychiatrist at the Burgholzli Hospital in Zurich, he observed just how unpsychological the other psychiatrists were. "No one concerned himself with the meaning of fantasies," Jung says, "or thought to ask why this patient had one kind of fantasy, another an altogether different one" (1963: 127). For Jung, the purpose of analysis is to interpret or experience what distinctive meaning a quite specific fantasy has for the particular individual having the fantasy – not, like Freud, to correct that fantasy in conformity with the reality principle. As Hillman says: "If fantasy is to be restrained by reference to its relation to the outer world, to criteria of 'reality-testing' about what can be realized in direct action, then it loses the name and nature of fantasy altogether" (1984: 116).

In this respect, what interests – or should interest – every Jungian analyst is how patients imagine the world, how their psyches image it, not whether their image of if conforms correctly to so-called reality. In Jungian analysis, there is no criterion of "imaginal correctness." Analysts (whether Freudian, Kleinian, Jungian, or otherwise) do not have immediate access to the reality of patients. All that is available to analysts are the versions that patients recount of reality to them – and those versions of reality are images. These versional images are mediatory variables that intervene between patients and reality.

In addition to the four psychoanalytic psychologies that Fred Pine mentions – drive psychology, ego psychology, object relations psychology, and self psychology (1990) – there is a fifth, uniquely Jungian psychology. What is distinctive about Jungian psychology, especially in the Hillmanian rendition of it, is that it is an *imaginal psychology*. Jungian psychology is as much a psychology of the imagination as it is a psychology of the unconscious. Hillman even says: "I tend to use 'imagination' instead of that word 'unconscious' ... not that there isn't unconsciousness in us all the time" (1983b: 32). According to Edward S. Casey, "'Imagination' is a word which has come to promise more than it can possibly deliver" (1976: 1). In this respect, what I propose is to consider, from a Jungian perspective, exactly what the imagination does deliver.

Jungian psychology is what I would call *imaginology*, and Jungian psychologists are *imaginologists*. Mark C. Taylor and Esa Saarinen have introduced the term "imagology" in reference to the study of images in contemporary electronic media, but for Jungian psychology I prefer the term "imaginology." In contrast to Taylor and Saarinen, who say that "the real is imaginary" (1994: 3), I would say that the imaginal is real. I prefer "imaginal" rather than "imaginary" (which, for example, Lacanian analysts employ), because, as Henry Corbin says, "the term *imaginary* is equated with the *unreal*" (1972: 1). For me, the imagination is a reality just as real as any other reality. Jung says that "fantasy has a proper reality" (1977: 302). I also prefer "imaginal" rather than "imaginative," because the term *imaginative* is equated with the *creative* – and the imagination can be destructive as well as creative. For me, "imaginal" is a neutral term for the capacity of the psyche spontaneously and autonomously to produce images.

In a discussion of reverie (or what I would call fantasy), Gaston Bachelard distinguishes between the "reality function" and the "irreality function":

> The demands of our *reality function* require that we adapt to reality, that we constitute ourselves as a reality and that we manufacture works which are realities. But doesn't reverie, by its very essence, liberate us from the reality function? From the moment it is considered in all its simplicity, it is perfectly evident that reverie bears witness to a normal, useful *irreality function*.
>
> (Bachelard 1969: 13)

The function of reality is adaptation; the function of irreality is liberation from that very adaptation. According to Bachelard, the reciprocity between these two functions "multiplies and crisscrosses to produce the psychological marvels of human imagination." Reverie may be not only not pathological but also quite practical. "Man," Bachelard says, "is an imagining being" (1969: 81).

"Reality" is a problematic notion. I was once at a party in the presence of a physicist from the Argonne National Laboratory near Chicago. One of the guests happened to use the expression "external reality." The physicist, who was an incorrigible wag, mischievously said: "External to *what*?" For him, there was only one reality. For psychoanalysts, of course, there are at least two realities: external (or physical) reality and internal (or psychic) reality – or, as I prefer to say, imaginal reality. In fact, psychically, there is not just one reality, there are not just two realities – there are many realities, as many as we can (and do) imagine.

Reality is relative to fantasy, to how we imaginally construct it. This is what I might call the *theory of imaginal relativity*. J. H. van den Berg employs the example of an oak tree to demonstrate that reality is relative to the different images that individuals have of it: "To the hunter, the oak tree is a shelter for birds and an opportunity to find cover for himself. To the timber dealer, the oak tree is an object that can be measured, counted, and sold. To the young, romantic girl, it is part of her love-landscape" (1972: 37). There is one oak tree in external reality, but there are at least three (and potentially many more) imaginal realities. F. S. Perls employs the example of a corn-field to serve the same purpose. He acknowledges that the corn-field has an independent existence, or "objective reality," which he defines as "a piece of ground on which a cereal is cultivated" (1969: 39), but he also says that the very same corn-field may have quite different "subjective realities" to different individuals:

> A merchant, looking at the corn-field, will estimate the gain he may derive from handling the sale of the crop, while a couple of lovers, choosing the corn-field as a place in which to withdraw from the world, do not care at all about its monetary value. A painter may grow enthusiastic about its slowly moving harmonies of light and shade, but to the pilot, who is about to make a forced landing, the movement of the corn serves only as a wind indicator. To an agronomist, wind direction or colour harmonies are of no importance, as he considers the chemical composition of the soil. The nearest to the objective reality which we defined above is the subjective reality of the farmer, who cultivated the field and planted the corn.
>
> (Perls 1969: 39–40)

I would only argue that none of the realities that Perls calls "subjective" are any less (or any more) "objective" than any other reality. For example, a couple making love in a field is just as objective (and subjective) a reality as a farmer cultivating cereal in that same field. (Any reality that has been arbitrarily privileged as more "real" than other realities can be deconstructed, as can the very opposition "subjective–objective.") In contrast to Perls, who says that reality is relative to the "interests" of individuals (1969: 40), I would say that it is relative to the *fantasies* of individuals.

In a discussion of psychic reality, Heinz Hartmann concedes that all contents of the psyche are, in a sense, "real." For Hartmann, however, this does not entail that all contents are *realistic*. For example, he says that "fantasy activity also is real, though not realistic" (1964: 265). I would say that this begs the question. If, as I maintain, "reality" is a psychic (or imaginal) construction, just how unrealistic (or realistic) any fantasy may be cannot be prejudged in theory and always remains to be determined in practice. Who can say, in advance, whether a certain fantasy is realistic or not? "Realism," I would say, is also a psychic, or imaginal, construction.

Whereas Freud asserts that images mean something else than they say, Jung contends that images mean nothing else than they say. (These are what I call the *something else assumption* and the *nothing else assumption*.) Medard Boss notes that Ludwig Wittgenstein criticizes Freud for assuming that the manifest *appearance* of the image disguises a latent *reality*. As Boss quotes Wittgenstein, the Freudian assumption is: "This is *in reality* something else." Wittgenstein regards the Freudian method of interpretation as unscientific because it assumes that what the image really means is something else than what it apparently says. Boss again quotes Wittgenstein: "I am reminded of the wonderful saying that 'Every thing is what it is, not something else'" (1977: 3). In the lectures that Wittgenstein delivered on aesthetics, he says that "Freud does something which seems to me immensely wrong" (1967: 23). The wrong that Freud does, he says, is to assume that something is not what it apparently is but is really another thing. Thus Wittgenstein criticizes Freudian interpretations that say, "This is *really* this." In contrast to the Freudian assumption, Wittgenstein cites what he calls "that marvelous motto," which insists: "Everything is what it is and not another thing" (1967: 27). Similarly, Jung states: "There is no reason to believe that the unconscious does not say what it means; in sharpest contradiction to Freud, I say that the unconscious says what it means" (1984: 30). According to Jung, when Freud maintains that an image "means something other than what it says, this interpretation is a 'polemic'" (*CW* 17: 88, par. 162) – a tendentiously controversial opinion. Or, as Hillman says, Jungian analysis assumes that the image "cannot be otherwise" (1980: 9). In contrast, Freudian analysis employs an *otherwise* method of interpretation.

Freud *translates* images, often into sexual organs. For example, Hillman says that "long things are penises for Freudians" (1975: 8). This is what Alfred Adler calls "organ-jargon" (1916: 176). Thirty years ago, when I was a graduate student at the University of Texas at Austin, I called the Freudian method of interpretation "genitomorphic." From the perspective of the Freudian unconscious, reality has a genital morphology. In this respect, Sandor Ferenczi says: "The derisive remark was once made against psycho-analysis that, according to this doctrine, the unconscious sees a penis in every convex object and a vagina or anus in every concave one." Rather than rebut this characterization as a vulgar caricature, Ferenczi concurs! "I find that this sentence," he comments, "well characterises the facts" (1950: 227). (I would merely add that Kleinians see not only a penis but also a breast in every convex object.)

In contrast to Freud, Jung does not translate images but *defines* them. I might say that Jung respects the integrity of the image. Jung believes that the unconscious has the opportunistic capacity to select an especially apt image to serve a definite purpose. (This is what I call the *aptness condition*.) Thus Jung says that the decisive issue is why an image is "nothing else," why the image that "the unconscious has chosen" is that one image and no other. According to Jung, the question that demands an answer is "why would not anything else do equally well?" (1988 1: 259). In order to define what an image means, Jung says that analysts "must stick as close as possible" to the image (*CW* 16: 149, par. 320). As Hillman notes, Rafael Lopez-Pedraza has elevated "sticking to the image" to the status of a Jungian dictum (1979a: 194).

The Jungian method of defining images by sticking to them is radically different from the Freudian (and Kleinian) method of translating images. I would say that Kleinian analysts are in this respect the authentic continuation of the Freudian tradition. They tend to translate all images into sexual organs, usually the breast. They "out-Kepesh" David Kepesh. For example, in *Introduction to the Work of Melanie Klein*, Hanna Segal translates a pillow on the analytic couch into a breast (1974: 57). When I first read this, I was reminded of a former student of mine in my course "Madness in Literature." There were 25 students in the class, and he was the only young man among them; the rest were young women. We were reading Roth's *The Breast*. Before we began to discuss the novel, I decided to conduct a word-association exercise. I asked the students to associate to the word "breast." The young man said, "Pillow." (If a pillow on an analytic couch can be a breast, then, in a reversal of Kleinian translation, a breast can apparently also be a pillow.) "A breast," he said, "is a soft pillow on which I can lay my head." In unison, the young women in the room sighed: "Oh, that's *so* sweet!" I thought to myself: "What a *line*!" Segal does not just translate a pillow into a breast. She also translates a chamber-pot into a breast (1974: 61), three watches and two small drawers in a chest of drawers into breasts (1974: 79), a paint box into a breast (1974: 98), a bowl of porridge into a breast (1974: 105), and two glasses of beer into breasts (1974: 114). I do not know about Kleinians, but when I, a Jungian, order a pint in a pub, I do not expect to drink milk.

These Kleinian translations by Segal remind me of an anecdote that a friend of mine in New York once recounted to me. He had been toilet training his young son. One day, my friend was standing in the bathroom while his son was sitting on the toilet. His son stared for a while at the roll of toilet paper on the wall and then suddenly said: "You know what, Dad?" "What?" my friend replied. "That roll of toilet paper looks like a gun." My friend nodded impatiently and said perfunctorily, "Yes." His son then looked around the bathroom for a while and said, "You know what, Dad?" "What?" my friend again replied. "Everything in here," his son said, "looks like a gun." The only difference between Segal and that little boy is that, to her, everything looks like a breast.

The Freudian–Kleinian method employs what I might call a "conversion chart" by which analysts translate images into "something else," usually something sexual. On the left side of this chart is what Freud calls the "manifest content" (a virtual infinity of images); on the right side of this chart is what he calls the "latent content" (a variety of sexual organs: penises, breasts, and so forth). The Freudian–Kleinian method is to convert (or translate) the images on the left side into the images on the right side. By this method, Freudian and Kleinian analysts arbitrarily sexualize (or, I might say – if I may indulge in a pun – "organ-ize") the psyche into penises, breasts, and so forth.

In contrast, Jung rejects the distinction between manifest content and latent content. He says that "interpretation must guard against making use of any other viewpoints than those manifestly given by the content itself" (*CW* 17: 88, par. 162) – that is, by the image itself. Similarly, in a discussion of active imagination he says "don't let anything from outside, that does not belong, get into it, for the fantasy-image has 'everything it needs'" (*CW* 14: 526, par. 749). Jung believes that the image is sufficient unto itself and that if the psyche *means* penis or breast it has the purposive capacity to *say* "penis" or "breast," rather than something else.

For at least one Kleinian analyst, even the body politic of America has sexual organs. To Donald Meltzer, the White House is not so much the executive mansion (the residence of the president and the offices of the administration) as it is – guess what? – a breast.

Meltzer cites a dream that a patient apparently dreamed sometime after the Watergate scandal in 1973. (In that scandal, Richard Nixon was accused of authorizing a cover-up of a break-in by a Republican gang at the Democratic party offices in the Watergate complex in Washington, DC, during the election of 1972. Nixon resigned in 1974 rather than be impeached. The Watergate scandal was one of the "Dirty Tricks" of "Tricky Dick.") Meltzer recounts the patient's dream as follows:

> Richard Nixon, although not yet elected President, seemed to have been given full use of the White House and its facilities, which he proceeded to abuse to set up his gang.
>
> (Meltzer 1984: 86)

Meltzer emphasizes two images: Nixon and the White House. Although Meltzer is a Kleinian, in this instance he approaches the image of Nixon as a Jungian would. That is, he does *not* assume that the image *means something else than it says* and then *translate* the image into that other thing. Rather, Meltzer assumes that the image in the dream *says what it means* and *nothing else*. The assumption is that when the dream *says* "Nixon," it *means* Nixon. Like a Jungian, Meltzer attempts to *define* the image. Meltzer interprets the image of Nixon in the patient's dream as "a psychopathic bit of his infantile personality" (1984: 87). This interpretation is consistent with how David Abrahamsen, a psychobiographer, diagnoses Richard Nixon. "Nixon suffers from a character disorder," Abrahamsen says. "He can, in fact, be described as a *psychopathic personality*" (1977: 221). As Meltzer interprets the dream, if Richard Nixon is a psychopathic personality, then when a patient *dreams* of Nixon, the image of Nixon in the dream is *a personification of a psychopathic aspect of the dreamer's own personality*. This is an intrapsychic interpretation – or what Jungians call an interpretation on the *subjective level*. Jung says that such an interpretation regards all of the images in a dream "as personified features of the dreamer's own personality" (*CW* 8: 266, par. 509). In effect, this dream demonstrates that the psychic reality of this particular patient includes an "inner Nixon," which is (at least as Meltzer defines it) psychopathic.

When Meltzer interprets the image of the White House in the patient's dream, however, he approaches that image *not* as a Jungian would but as a Kleinian (or Freudian). That is, he assumes that when the dream says "White House," it means *something else* than the White House. He does not attempt to define what the White House is per se and then wonder what it might mean that the psychic reality of this particular patient apparently includes an "inner White House." Rather, Meltzer *translates* the image of the White House as "representing the breast" (1984: 87).

When I first read this Kleinian interpretation, I was so incredulous that I instantaneously visualized not the White House but the Capitol. The dome of the Capitol at least has a form (if not a function) similar to that of a breast. (Even a Jungian can comprehend how a Freudian might sexualize the Washington Monument and apply formalistic logic to interpret the obelisk as a penis – but the White House as a breast?) Surely, I exclaimed, Meltzer must mean the Capitol! What could he possibly mean by interpreting the White House as representing a breast?

As Meltzer translates the White House in the patient's dream, it is not just the breast. According to Meltzer, it is "the inside of the mother's breast," which, once Nixon "has organized his gang," then "may be turned into the delusional system of 'Watergate', paranoia" (1984: 93). Long before Nixon became president, he satisfied the criteria that the American Psychiatric Association in the fourth edition of the *Diagnostic and Statistical Manual of Mental Disorders* [*DSM-IV*] requires for a diagnosis of "paranoid personality disorder" (1994: 634–8). He did not suddenly become paranoid once he became president. "Nixon," Abrahamsen says, "exhibited all the signs of a *paranoid personality*" (1976: 226). From an intrapsychic perspective, the image of Nixon in the patient's dream is a personification of a paranoid aspect of the dreamer's own personality.

Why, however, does Meltzer translate the White House into "the inside of the mother's breast," which, he says, is turned into "the delusional system of 'Watergate', paranoia?" Is this translation an implicit reference to the "paranoid–schizoid position" (which Melanie Klein originally called simply the "paranoid position")? According to Kleinian developmental object relations theory, in the first few months of life the mother's breast is experienced as an object, is split into "good" and "bad," and then is experienced as a "bad object" by an infant in the paranoid–schizoid position. What, if anything, does the paranoid–schizoid position have to do with what Richard Hofstadter calls the "paranoid style in American politics" (1965)? Does Meltzer believe that American politics – or at least the paranoid style of Richard Nixon and the delusional system of Watergate – can be derived from and reduced to the inside of the mother's breast?

What is the consequence of this translation of the White House into a breast? The result, I would emphasize, is arbitrarily to sexualize what is an explicitly political dream and, in the process, to depoliticize the dream. This translation asserts that this patient has a Kleinian (or Freudian) "sexual psyche" rather than what Andrew Samuels calls a "political psyche" (1993). The essential function of the White House is, however, not sexual (notwithstanding the extracurricular activities of John Kennedy, Bill Clinton, and apparently many other presidents) but political – and radically different from the essential function of a breast. (It would, of course, be equally inappropriate arbitrarily to politicize what is an explicitly sexual dream and, in the process, to desexualize such a dream.)

If, as Jungians assume, images say what they mean, then when images in a dream say "politics," they mean politics. From this perspective, "manifest" political images in a dream are not a mere "derivative" of (or distortive allusion to) "latent" sexual (or any other) images. They simply are what they are: political images. Nixon is Nixon, the White House is the White House – *not a breast* – and a dream with political images is a political dream. Appearances are not deceptive; they do not belie reality. This is the Jungian position, which is in strict contradiction to (is logically incompatible with) the Freudian–Kleinian position.

In a discussion of political dreams, Kelly Bulkeley states that although such dreams are "*certainly* related" to the "personal lives," or "inner worlds," of dreamers, those dreams are "just as certainly related" to the "*political* lives," or "*outer world*," of those dreamers (1996: 188). What concerns Bulkeley is the tendency among psychoanalysts (both Freudians and Jungians) reductively to interpret images in dreams exclusively intrapsychically. He argues persuasively that dreams are (or may be) simultaneously about internal reality (the psychic reality of the dreamer) and external reality (for example, political reality).

I agree that psychoanalysts should interpret images in dreams both on what Jung calls the *subjective level* (which regards images as *correlatives of* aspects of the internal reality of the subject) and the *objective level* (which regards images as *references to* objects in external reality). Bulkeley acknowledges the practical value of interpretations on the subjective (or intrapsychic) level – for example, an interpretation that would regard the images of Nixon and the White House in a dream as correlatives of an "inner Nixon" and "inner White House" (aspects of the "inner world" of the subject). In addition, however, Bulkeley cautions that images in a dream may also be references to objects in the "outer world." For example, images of Nixon and the White House in a dream may also be references to the "outer Nixon" (Richard Milhouse Nixon, the thirty-seventh president) and the "outer White House" (the executive mansion, both the residence of the president and the offices of the administration, on Pennsylvania Avenue in Washington, DC).

Like Bulkeley, I have previously criticized psychoanalysts who tend to interpret images only intrapsychically. I would not retract that criticism, but I would qualify it. I would say that the more probable tendency is for individuals to commit a version of what Umberto Eco calls the *referential fallacy* (1976: 58) and simply to assume that images in dreams are references to objects in the outer world rather than correlatives of aspects of the inner world of the dreamer. (In addition, even if an image refers to an object in external reality – and not all images do – that does not necessarily imply, or entail, that the image corresponds accurately and exhaustively to that object. To assume that it does is to commit what I call the *correspondence fallacy*.)

That *the psyche is real* is still a radical proposition. That internal reality (or psychic reality) is a reality just as real as any other reality, including external reality, is an extremely difficult fact for many individuals to appreciate and accept. The "inner politics" of a dreamer are just as *real* a reality as any "outer politics" – and, I would emphasize, the "inner politics" of a dreamer are just as *political* a reality as any "outer politics." They are the *psychic politics* of the dreamer.

What is problematic about the Freudian–Kleinian translation method of interpretation is the assumption that images are not what they seem to be. I am hardly the first to criticize the translation method of interpretation. For example, 80 years ago a British psychologist, A. Wohlgemuth, published *A Critical Examination of Psycho-Analysis* in which he satirized the Freudian method of interpretation as arbitrary. In that book, Wohlgemuth criticizes what he calls the interpretative "license of the psycho-analysts." He says that in Freudian analysis "the number of interpretations is limited only by the interest of the interpreter" (1923: 137). To demonstrate what he means, Wohlgemuth presents a parodic conversion chart in five columns. In the first column are images from a fairy tale, the story of a king and his three sons, one of them a simpleton; in the second column are images from a "psycho-analytic" interpretation; in the third column, images from an "anagogic" interpretation; in the fourth column, images from an "oneirocritic" interpretation; and in the fifth and final column, images from a "kreopolic" interpretation. "Kreopolic," Wohlgemuth notes, is an English translation of a Greek word that means "butcher." Wohlgemuth proceeds to translate the images in the fairy tale into images from a butcher's shop! The king, he says, is an image of the butcher, and the three sons are images of the three meats the butcher sells: beef, mutton, and pork, with the youngest son, the simpleton, an image of pork. Three feathers are also images of the three meats; a trap-door is an image of the butcher's shop; a box is an image of the butcher's pie and sausage machines; the simpleton's carpet is an image of pork sausages and his brothers' shawls are images of beef and mutton sausages; rings are images of hams; the fairest woman is an image of a pork pie and peasant women are images of beef and mutton pies. As Wohlgemuth translates the fairy tale, the images in it illustrate a maxim: "The proof of the pudding (pies, sausages) is in the eating" (1923: 144). This kreopolic translation is a reductio ad absurdum, but is it any more preposterous than a phallocentric Freudian translation in which everything is a penis or a mammocentric Kleinian translation in which everything is a breast?

In reference to phallocentric Freudian translation, Jung notes that "you can say anything, you know." For example, Freudians can interpret "a church spire" phallically, "but," Jung asks, "when you dream of a penis, what is that?" Then he recounts an anecdote: "You know what an analyst said, one of the orthodox, the old guard, he said, 'In this case the censor has not functioned.' Now, you call that a scientific explanation?" (1977: 324).

The Jungian method of defining the image rather than translating it is what I call the method of *imaginal essentialism* – or what I have previously called the method of "phenomenological essentialism." Hillman says that the method is to "take a thing for what it is," not for something else, "and let it talk" (1983b: 14) – that is, to take a thing (an image) for what it says and to assume that it means nothing else than it says. (In effect, Hillman suggests that if psychoanalysis is in any sense a "talking cure," it is the *image* that talks – and that analysts should listen to what the image says.) Jungian analysts operate on the assumption that images have essences. In order to define what an image essentially means, Jungian analysts employ three special techniques. Two of these are interpretative techniques: *explication* and *amplification*. The third is an experiential technique: *active imagination*.

When Jungian analysts explicate an image, they interpret it in terms of what it essentially implies. In explication, the assumption is that an essence is implicit in the image and that the purpose of interpretation is to make that essence explicit. Jungian analysis assumes that the imagination has what David Bohm calls an "implicate order" (1981). By the method of imaginal essentialism, Jungian analysts render that implicate order into an "explicate order." I would emphasize that the distinction between the explicit and the implicit in Jungian analysis is not synonymous with the distinction between the manifest and the latent in Freudian analysis, for, contrary to what Freud says, images from the unconscious do not entail what Jung calls "a deceptive distortion" (*CW* 16: 149, par. 319), or covert operation in order to evade a putative censor. The "censor" that Freud posits in the psyche is, of course, also an image, and, like all images, it, too, has an essence. I might say that the censor is an image in the Freudian "theoretical unconscious." The essence of the censor is to repress drives that are ostensibly incompatible with the reality principle. In order to evade the censor, Freud says, drives manifest as wishes (or repressions return as symptoms) – images that, according to Freud, are deceptive distortions.

When Jungian analysts amplify an image, they interpret it *in comparison to the same or similar images* in other sources – for example, myths, fairy tales, folktales, art, literature, and culture – in order to identify parallels. I have noted that "amplification is only an extension of explication, for the purpose of the comparison is to identify parallels that establish a definition of the image *in essentia*" (Adams 2001: 114). (I have recently advocated that Jungian analysts should also interpret the image *in contrast to different images* in other sources. Amplification would then be both a comparative and a contrastive technique.)

In contrast to explication and amplification, active imagination is not an interpretation of the image but an experience of it. Active imagination is a deliberate induction of fantasy by the patient. Patients evoke images from the unconscious and regard those images as a reality just as real as any other reality. The technique entails both observation of the images and participation with them. Eventually, patients enter the fantasy and engage the images in conversations – or in what Mary Watkins calls "imaginal dialogues" (1986). Jung says that if the image "is a speaking figure at all then say what you have to say to that figure and listen to what he or she has to say" (1973 1: 460). In effect, *active imagination is interactive imagination*, in which the patient poses questions to the images, or figures, which then provide answers. "You must step into the fantasy yourself," Jung says, "and compel the figures to give you an answer." In short, he says, active imagination is "a dialectical procedure, a dialogue between yourself and the unconscious figures" (1973 1: 561). The patient does not interpret what the image means but experiences what it means.

Explication, amplification, and active imagination are three uniquely Jungian techniques. I would say that they are the pride of Jungian analysis. They are what make Jungian analysis different from and, if I may say so, superior to other varieties of psychoanalysis. All three of these techniques, I would emphasize, are dependent on *the fantasy principle: the conviction that fantasy is logically prior to reality, that the psyche, or the imagination, constructs reality, and that the image says what it means and means what it says.* To illustrate the application of these three techniques, I shall now present a dream:

> I'm in a house. A tiny red scorpion is chasing me around the house. That's the curse. The scorpion is poisonous or venomous. It's chasing me through a house with different floors. I can't do anything but run away. I'm paralyzed to take any other action. I'm afraid, and I call for help. My boyfriend is in the same house. He's somewhere on another floor, busy with other things. I think that if I were to ask my boyfriend for help he would answer, "Yes," but never come.
>
> Then I'm on the top floor in one of the rooms. I'm sitting on some furniture pretty high up and looking at the door. And here comes that tiny scorpion toward me. It's programmed to come after me. I throw two tennis balls at it. One of the balls hits the floor next to it; the other ball hits the scorpion. So the scorpion has to curl up. Before it has a chance to re-settle, I get the chance to jump off that furniture and run out the door.
>
> Then I'm in the same house but on a lower floor. Again, furniture is there. The scorpion is sitting on the furniture. And I'm calling for help. My boyfriend is next to the furniture, on the other side of it. On top of this furniture is stuff. A T-shirt is lying there. My boyfriend covers the scorpion with the T-shirt and then pushes it over toward the back of the furniture. (He doesn't kill it.) The scorpion crawls back out, toward me.
>
> There are also two audiotapes on the furniture. I'm trying to crush the scorpion between the two tapes. Then something weird happens that's never happened before in my life. As this scorpion is chasing me, I feel some kind of "power" that keeps me from taking action, that keeps me from killing this animal. When I'm trying to crush the scorpion between the tapes, I can't take it any more. It becomes too overwhelming. I'm screaming. I make myself exit the dream, and I wake up.

I assume that a Freudian–Kleinian interpretation of this dream would immediately sexualize the image of the scorpion. For example, a Freudian might translate the stinger on the tail of the scorpion as a penis, and a Kleinian might translate it as a breast (obviously, a very "bad" one). I am uncertain what would be gained by such translations, but I am very certain what would be lost: the scorpion qua scorpion, the essence of the scorpion, all of the qualitatively distinctive nuances of that specific image for this particular dreamer.

The patient who recounted this dream was a 35-year-old woman. She had been in analysis with me for three-and-a-half years when she had the dream. As a result, she had some knowledge of the three Jungian techniques. Over the course of five analytic sessions, she attempted to apply the techniques of explication, amplification, and active imagination to the dream. I would not say that she did so systematically and exhaustively, but the effort was sincere and serious.

Immediately after she recounted the dream, I asked the patient to define the essence of a scorpion. This was her initial attempt at explication: "I have never seen a scorpion. I know that in the tropics, you need to check your bed and your shoes for scorpions. Scorpions are sneaky. They go into places where you can't see them. They take you by surprise. They can inject you with their venom while you sleep. They're potentially dangerous. You have to watch out." In that first session, she also attempted an astrological amplification, a comparison of the scorpion in the dream to Scorpio in the Zodiac: "People who have Scorpio as their sign have in common secrecy. I could never figure out what those people were thinking, feeling, and doing. I couldn't get any idea of who those people were."

In the next session, the patient reported that she had attempted active imagination with the scorpion: "The first time I tried it without much success. I did, however, get the feeling that the scorpion was *not* trying to hurt me. (In the dream, I had felt that it was going to kill me.) But I didn't get anything else – just 'mind-chatter,' not anything else. I asked what the curse was, why it had been placed on me, but I didn't get an answer, I didn't hear anything."

In the third session, the patient reported that she had again attempted an amplification. Between sessions, she had read about scorpions in a book on myths. She said that in Greek mythology Orion and Scorpio engage in a battle between the forces of light and the forces of dark. "The scorpion," she said, "is always pictured as a demon." On the basis of that mythological amplification, she interpreted the scorpion as an aspect of her own psyche: "The scorpion is an image of my shadow side (though not necessarily in a negative way). And in the dream, I'm running away from that. In my life, I have spat venom words. I have been able to hurt some people – men and women. When I was a child, I had fights with my brother. I once hit him with the branch of a tree. Later on, looking back, I was shocked. I could see in those moments what I can do. Some people have been afraid of me. I have thought, how could anyone be scared of *me*?"

In the fourth session, the patient reported that she had gone on a trip to Maine with her boyfriend. While there, she had bought a scorpion in a store. The scorpion had served as the point of departure for a fantasy rather like an instance of spontaneous active imagination: "It was from Vietnam, a scorpion embedded in plastic (it looked like something preserved in amber). I had it in our room. I started getting so scared. I thought: 'Who knows where that thing came from? It might come out of there. It might come alive.' The woman who sold it to me said that someone had left one of those scorpions in the sunshine, and the plastic had melted and the thing had come out. 'Not alive,' the woman said. I thought: 'Maybe there's a curse on it. Maybe my dream was a prophecy. What's the intention of the scorpion?'" The patient had taken action to defend herself against the scorpion: "I put it in a plastic bag. I tied a knot in the bag. I thought, 'Maybe I should lock it in the car outside.'" She realized that this was "an irrational fear." As she interpreted the scorpion, she was "running away from things I'm afraid of, without really knowing what they are." She said that she had eventually "calmed down, let the scorpion stay in the room, and forgotten about it." Then the patient described the scorpion in detail: "It looks really terrifying. It has two pincers in front. Since the scorpion's dead, the tail curls around – it doesn't stand up. The scorpion looks evil. It's very powerful. It doesn't look like a 'sweet' animal, even though it's dead. I could understand why I was so terrified in my dream. Scorpions are not only powerful but also 'wise' or intelligent in their way of sneaking up and surprising you."

In the fifth session, the patient again commented on the scorpion that she had bought: "I've had the scorpion out of the bag for a couple of weeks. It's starting to feel better and better. I had been sitting there looking at it, terrified. My boyfriend had a great idea: he gave me a knife, and that helped." Then she mentioned that she had been reading the book *On Active Imagination*, the compilation that Joan Chodorow has edited of writings by Jung on active imagination (1997). "I hadn't realized," she said, "the extent to which you could have an *active* dialogue with the unconscious." What especially pleased her was, she said, that "the woman who brought out this book is a *dance* therapist." (The patient herself is a professional dancer and dance instructor.) Reading about active imagination had radically altered her attitude toward the scorpion: "I'm not afraid of the scorpion any more. I feel as though I'd like to engage it, make it 'come alive.' Whatever comes up that might be scary, I don't have to act on." I asked her what aspect of her psyche she now felt the scorpion was an image of. She replied: "Not always having to be nice. Standing up for myself. Defending myself when necessary. Letting myself be who I want to be, not repressing that. The scorpion has a lot to do with my sexuality. Taking risks. Being able to express myself when I have strong or passionate feelings. Daring to be loud. Being seductive. The scorpion's an image of my shadow side." With that, the patient concluded her analysis of the scorpion.

I would add only a few more remarks, which I believe are entirely consistent with what the patient says about the scorpion. The dream is a "mythological dream," a dream from what I call the *mythological unconscious* (Adams 2001). It is an imaginal variation on the archetypal theme of the "monster-slaying hero." In the dream, the ego-image first tries to escape a non-ego image (the scorpion) that pursues it; then another non-ego image (the boyfriend) tries to cover the scorpion (repress it); finally, the ego-image tries to crush the scorpion (kill it) because the ego-image assumes that the scorpion intends to kill it. All of these defensive efforts prove futile. The scorpion insistently, persistently pursues the ego-image. The image is irrepressible. From a Jungian perspective, the scorpion is a non-ego image (or, as the patient says, a shadow-image) that functions as an unconscious compensation for a certain ego attitude. In the dream, the ego-image attempts to be a "scorpion-slaying hero." Ultimately, however, after the patient applies the Jungian techniques of explication, amplification, and active imagination, she concludes that the scorpion is a helpful, not a harmful animal (or instinct), that because it does not intend to kill her she should not try to kill it, that she should engage it in dialogue, that she should talk to it and listen to it (or perhaps dance with it).

The scorpion is what I would call an *image of transformation*. Jung does not have much to say about scorpions. He does, however, amplify the scorpion by reference to alchemy. Jung cites the *Rosarium Philosophorum*, which says: "The living Mercurius is called the scorpion, that is, venom; for it slays itself and brings itself back to life" (*CW* 13: 79, par. 105n). In this amplification, the scorpion is an image of what I might call the "self-slaying monster." The scorpion is the very epitome of a *transformative image*. There is no need for a hero to slay the scorpion, for, as Jung says, it slays itself in order to bring itself back to life. In essence, the scorpion exemplifies how the ego-image might, if it were receptive rather than defensive, experience the same or a similar transformation: the death of an old ego attitude as the necessary condition for the birth of a new ego attitude. In this respect, the scorpion contains the *pharmakon*, a venom that is simultaneously and paradoxically also a medicine. As Derrida says, this is a substance that "acts as both remedy and poison" (1981: 70). To the defensive ego-image, the scorpion as a non-ego image seems only toxic, but to a receptive ego-image, it is also curative – or, as I prefer to say, transformative.

How this patient reimagines the scorpion serves as an example of how we, too, may apply the fantasy principle for transformative purposes. The methods of imaginal psychology demonstrate that what seems so obviously to the ego to be "reality" is a *fantasy* – and that other fantasies are immediately available as effective alternatives to the unimaginative attitudes of the ego.

Chapter 2

Compensation in the service of individuation

Phenomenological essentialism and Jungian dream interpretation

In the year 2000, *Psychoanalytic Dialogues* conducted a dream interpretation experiment to commemorate the one-hundredth anniversary of the publication of Freud's *The Interpretation of Dreams*. A psychoanalyst, Hazel R. Ipp, provided a clinical presentation that included three dreams. Four psychoanalysts from different schools of thought then interpreted those dreams. Lewis Aron, an associate editor of the journal, and James L. Fosshage, a member of the editorial board, invited me to represent the Jungian school and to interpret the dreams from that perspective.

I was pleased and honored to participate in and contribute to the experiment, especially because I so admire and respect Fosshage. Several years ago, I read *Dream Interpretation: A Comparative Study*, a book that Fosshage and Clemens A. Loew edited (1987). In that book, Fosshage and Loew present a case that includes five dreams of a patient whom they call "Martha." Six psychoanalysts and psychotherapists from different schools of thought – Freudian, Jungian, culturalist, object relational, phenomenological, and gestalt – interpret those dreams. Fosshage and Loew then compare and synthesize those six interpretations. The issue is whether – and, if so to what extent – different theories about dreams produce, in practice, what Paul Ricoeur calls a "conflict of interpretations" (1974) or, alternatively, a *consensus of interpretations*. Over the years, I have assigned *Dream Interpretation: A Comparative Study* as a text in a number of dream interpretation courses that I have taught at the New School University, and I have attended presentations by Fosshage at dream interpretation conferences that the C. G. Jung Foundation of New York and the Association for the Study of Dreams have organized and sponsored.

The format of the dream interpretation experiment in *Psychoanalytic Dialogues* was virtually identical with that of the comparative study by Fosshage and Loew, except that in this case the presentation included three dreams of a patient by the name of "Barbara." Because of space limitations, I had to abridge the draft of the article that I submitted to the journal. In this chapter, I have now restored certain sections that I had to delete from the original version, and I have revised and augmented the article that *Psychoanalytic Dialogues* finally published.

The title of this chapter is the same as the title of the article: "Compensation in the Service of Individuation: Phenomenological Essentialism and Jungian Dream Interpretation." Jungian psychology is a phenomenological psychology. "In view of the enormous complexity of psychic phenomena," Jung says, "a purely phenomenological point of view is, and will be for a long time, the only possible one and the only one with any prospect of success" (*CW* 9,1: 182, par. 308). Although "phenomenological essentialism" accurately describes the Jungian method of dream interpretation, if I were to write the article today, I would say *imaginal essentialism* rather than "phenomenological essentialism." As I employ the terms "imaginal" and "phenomenological," they are synonyms, but I prefer *imaginal* because it emphasizes that the phenomena in question are *images*. To me, Jungian psychology is a variety of phenomenological psychology – or, as I prefer to say, an *imaginal psychology*.

Unlike Freud, Jung never wrote a book on dream interpretation. Instead, he wrote a number of articles that demonstrate how his theory of dream interpretation evolved over time. These have now been collected in a book published under the title *Dreams* (1974). In addition, from 1928 to 1930, Jung conducted a dream interpretation seminar published under the title *Dream Analysis* (1984). If I were succinctly to state what Jung considers the primary function of dreams, I would say that it is *compensation in the service of individuation*.

Jungians have written many books on dream interpretation. Among the books that I personally consider especially valuable and that I have assigned as texts in the dream interpretation courses that I have taught over the years are the following: James Hillman's *The Dream and the Underworld* (1979a); Robert Bosnak's *A Little Course in Dreams* (1988) and *Dreaming with an AIDS Patient* (1989) – recently reentitled, revised, and republished as *Christopher's Dreams: Dreaming and Living with AIDS* (1994); Edward C. Whitmont and Sylvia Brinton Perera's *Dreams, A Portal to the Source* (1989); Frazer Boa's *The Way of the Dream: Conversations on Jungian Dream Interpretation with Marie-Louise von Franz* (1992) – a transcript of 20 half-hour films in which von Franz interprets dreams on camera. These books illustrate the variety of ways that contemporary Jungians interpret dreams.

In "General Aspects of Dream Psychology," Jung classifies dreams in three basic categories: (1) reactive, (2) compensatory, and (3) prospective (*CW* 8). Reactive dreams simply reproduce an experience that has had a traumatic emotional impact on the psyche. According to Jung, however, most dreams are compensatory. They are either positive compensatory dreams or negative compensatory dreams (what Jung calls reductive, or deflationary, dreams). What they compensate are the attitudes of the ego in the present. The attitudes of the ego are always partial and prejudicial; in the extreme case, they may be utterly defective.

In contrast to Freud, who defines the ego as rationality (or rationality in the service of the reality principle), Jung defines the ego as identity. According to Jung, the ego is identified with certain attitudes and is disidentified from other, alternative perspectives of which it is unconscious. That is, the ego may – but need not – be identified with rationality. "Ego" simply means "I," and the specific content of our "I-ness" is not invariant. The content varies considerably. The ego is a variable, not a constant. I would say that *the ego is an empty place holder* in our personal equation. Since the Enlightenment, or Age of Reason, however, it has seemed to some individuals – including Freud – that the content of our "I-ness," our very identity, is or should be identical with "reason." Thus Freud arbitrarily privileges reason over all other possible contents of the ego. Anything else, everything else, is "unreason," which we repress, relegate to the unconscious, and exclude from consideration. What, however, do we mean by "reason?" Is it rationality, or is it mere rationalization? Jung notes that even "rational judgment" may be partial and prejudicial:

> The very rationality of the judgment may even be the worst prejudice, since we call reasonable what appears reasonable to us. What appears to us unreasonable is therefore doomed to be excluded because of its irrational character. It may really be irrational, but may equally well merely appear irrational without actually being so when seen from another standpoint.
>
> (*CW* 8: 70–1, par. 137)

Similarly, Max Weber says that it is important to acknowledge that "what is rational from one point of view may well be irrational from another" (1992: 26).

Compensatory dreams confront the ego and challenge it to relate to alternative perspectives to which it has previously been unrelated or ineffectively related. The ego may then seriously entertain, critically evaluate, and either accept or reject these perspectives. There is no imperative for the ego to integrate these perspectives. What Jung advocates is not an uncritical capitulation by the ego to the unconscious but a relational dialogue between the ego and the unconscious. This dialogue is a dialectic, in which the thesis of the ego and the antithesis of the unconscious have an opportunity through conversation to produce a synthesis, or a new relation, a third position that transcends the original two different or even opposite positions of the ego and the unconscious. Jung calls this the "transcendent function":

> Once the unconscious content has been given form and the meaning of the formulation is understood, the question arises as to how the ego will relate to this position, and how the ego and the unconscious are to come to terms. This is the second and more important stage of the procedure, the bringing together of opposites for the production of a third: the transcendent function.
>
> (*CW* 8: 87, par. 181)

Compensatory dreams present alternative perspectives that have been repressed, dissociated, or otherwise defensively excluded from consideration by the ego, or that have been ignored or neglected, or that are merely undeveloped or unknown and therefore unlived. If the ego is receptive rather than defensive, it may then integrate these perspectives. Jung says that compensatory dreams "add to the conscious psychological situation of the moment all those aspects which are essential for a totally different point of view" (*CW* 8: 245, par. 469).

Prospective dreams are anticipatory dreams. They anticipate some possibility in the future. They are not prophetic, although they may be prognostic. Jung says that prospective dreams "are merely an anticipatory combination of probabilities" (*CW* 8: 255, par. 493). He cautions against any supposition that a prospective dream "is a kind of psychopomp which, because of its superior knowledge, infallibly guides life in the right direction" (*CW* 8: 256, par. 494). Only when an attitude of the ego radically "deviates from the norm" does the compensatory function become "a guiding, prospective function capable of leading the conscious attitude in a quite different direction which is much better than the previous one" (*CW* 8: 257, par. 495).

Jung defines the unconscious differently from Freud, as essentially purposive. The unconscious functions as if it were an intelligent agent, with a compensatory or prospective intentionality. It actively selects certain especially apt images to serve a quite specific purpose. (This is what I call the *aptness condition*.) According to Jung, the purpose of the vast majority of dreams is a compensation of the attitudes of the ego by the unconscious, which presents to the ego alternative perspectives for consideration. Freud asserts that all dreams, without exception, are "*a (disguised) fulfilment of a (suppressed or repressed) wish*" (*SE* 4: 160). For Freud, dreams are essentially wish-fulfilling; for Jung, they are primarily attitude-compensating. In contrast to Freud, who asks what instinctual (usually sexual) wish has been fulfilled, Jung asks what ego attitude has been compensated.

Freud tends to interpret dreams on what Jung calls the *objective level*. That is, he interprets the images in dreams as indirect references, or wishful allusions, to objects in external reality. Jung interprets dreams mainly on what he calls the *subjective level*. According to Jung, the images in dreams are mostly correlatives of factors in the internal reality of the subject – dramatizations and personifications of aspects of the psyche of the dreamer. As Jung says:

> The whole dream-work is essentially subjective, and a dream is a theatre in which the dreamer is himself the scene, the player, the prompter, the producer, the author, the public, and the critic. This simple truth forms the basis for a conception of the dream's meaning which I have called *interpretation on the subjective level*. Such an interpretation, as the term implies, conceives all the figures in the dream as personified features of the dreamer's own personality.
>
> (*CW* 8: 266, par. 509)

This conception of the dream as a drama is similar to what W. R. D. Fairbairn means by "state of affairs" dreams. In contrast to Freud, Fairbairn believes that "dreams are essentially, not wish-fulfilments, but dramatizations" of states of affairs in internal reality (1990a: 99). He maintains that the figures in dreams personify either the ego or internal objects and that dreams dramatize dynamic relations between them. As an example, Fairbairn presents a case in which the dreamer tended "to personify various aspects of her psyche" (1990b: 216), and he says that the dreams "in which these personifications figured thus provided the scenes of a moving drama" (1990b: 217). Both Jung and Fairbairn agree that dreams are basically dramatizations and personifications of subjective states of affairs. They also agree that dreams are not essentially wish-fulfilling. They differ only in that Jung also believes that dreams are primarily attitude-compensating. That is, Fairbairn regards dreams as a representation of a state of affairs in internal reality; Jung regards them also as a rectification of that state of affairs.

Jung does solicit what he calls "associations," but they are *not* what Freud means by "*free* associations." What Jung requests from the dreamer are "associations objectively grouped round particular images" (*CW* 16: 148: par. 319). Both Freud and Jung employ the same term ("association"), but what they mean by it is very different. It would have been preferable had Jung employed an entirely different term. For example, rather than "association," he might have employed the term *adherence* – for what he advocates is that the dreamer *adhere* to the image. As an alternative to free associating to an image, he proposes *sticking to the image*. "To understand the dream's meaning," Jung says, "I must stick as close as possible to the dream images" (*CW* 16: 149, par. 320). The method is to instruct the dreamer to suppose that Jung has "no idea" (*CW* 16: 149, par. 320) what the image means and then to ask the dreamer to describe the image in such a way that, Jung says, "I cannot fail to understand what sort of a thing it is" (*CW* 16: 150, par. 320). In contemporary Jungian dream interpretation, this is the method that Hillman says Rafael Lopez-Pedraza "felicitously calls 'sticking to the image'" (1979a: 194). To the extent that Jungians stick to the image, they employ a phenomenological, or imaginal, method. In this respect, Jungian psychology is a fifth psychoanalytic psychology in addition to the four psychologies that Fred Pine mentions (1990). Jungian psychology includes drives, ego, objects, and self, but, as an *imaginal psychology*, it emphasizes images.

In contrast to Freud, who believes that the images in a dream mean something else (usually something sexual) than they say, Jungians believe that the images mean nothing else than they say. (These are what I call the *something else assumption* and the *nothing else assumption*.) That is, Jungians reject the distinction between manifest content and latent content. Jung protests that there is no disguise to the dream and that what Freud calls the manifest content is nothing but "the dream itself and contains the whole meaning of the dream" (*CW* 16: 149, par. 319).

The phenomenological method is a descriptive method that respects the integrity of the specific dream image. In contrast, Freudian dream interpretation is reductive. It assumes, Jung says, that a dreamer "could just as well have dreamt that he had to open a door with a key, that he was flying in an aeroplane, kissing his mother, etc." He says that from the Freudian perspective "all those things could have the same meaning" (*CW* 8: 245, par. 470). He notes that "the more rigorous adherents of the Freudian school have come to the point of interpreting – to give a gross example – pretty well all oblong objects in dreams as phallic symbols and all round or hollow objects as feminine symbols" (*CW* 8: 246, par. 470).

Jung observes that a dreamer "may dream of inserting a key in a lock, or wielding a heavy stick, or of breaking down a door with a battering ram." A strict Freudian might interpret all of these images phallically. Key, stick, and battering ram are, however, qualitatively quite different images, irreducibly distinctive. They are the images "of choice" that the unconscious on this occasion has selected to serve a quite specific purpose. That the unconscious of the dreamer "has chosen one of these specific images – it may be the key, the stick, or the battering ram – is also of major significance," Jung says. "The real task is to understand *why* the key has been preferred to the stick, or the stick to the ram." He says that "sometimes this might even lead one to discover that it is not the sexual act at all that is represented, but some quite different psychological point" (1964: 29). Rather than *translate* the dream image, as Freud does, from what it apparently says into what it presumably really means – into instinctual or sexual terms, into sexual acts or sexual organs, into what Alfred Adler calls "organ-jargon" (1916: 176) – Jungians stick to the specific dream image and attempt to *define* it through a precise phenomenological description. They try to ascertain what the "essence" of the image is – that is, what the image essentially means. Jungians apply what I call the method of "phenomenological essentialism" (or *imaginal essentialism*).

Phenomenologists distinguish between different kinds of essentialism. For example, P. Erik Craig and Stephen J. Walsh distinguish *ontic essentialism* from *ontologic essentialism* (1993: 129). The former is the "being" of a phenomenon in particular; the latter, the "being-ness" of a phenomenon in general. As an example of a phenomenon, Craig and Walsh mention a 1957 Chevrolet convertible (1993: 128). To define this phenomenon ontically is to describe the being of a quite specific automobile in particular (a singular car that an individual owns and drives). In contrast, to define it ontologically is to describe the being-ness of that variety of automobile in general (by year, brand, model, and so forth) – "1957-ness," "Chevrolet-ness," "convertible-ness," "automobile-ness," and so forth. One level of essentialism emphasizes what is unique about a phenomenon; the other level, what is universal about it.

Douglas Medin and Andrew Ortony distinguish *metaphysical essentialism* from *psychological essentialism*. The former is "the view that *things* have essences"; the latter, "the view that people's *representations* of things might reflect such a belief (erroneous as it may be)" (1989: 183). According to Medin and Ortony, whether a phenomenon *has* an essence is irrelevant; in fact, it is indeterminable, because the process of determination is infinitely regressive. What is relevant and what is determinable is what people correctly or incorrectly *believe* the essence of a phenomenon to be. Medin and Ortony eschew any attempt to describe and define the absolute essence of a phenomenon metaphysically. What they advocate is a description and definition of the essence of the phenomenon relative to what people believe psychologically. I would quarrel (or quibble) with this account only because it emphasizes belief. Psychologically, the issue is not belief but projection.

What is of decisive importance is what essence people *project*, consciously or unconsciously, onto the phenomenon in question.

When Jungians stick to the image and attempt to describe and define it, they combine both ontologic and ontic essentialism, as well as both metaphysical and psychological essentialism. They believe that images do have essences, both universal being-ness and unique being, independent of what people may project onto them. That is, they believe that a specific image possesses both general and particular qualities intrinsic to it – attributes independent of what people may attribute to it. (Whether general qualities are ever utterly universal and particular qualities are ever utterly unique is, I would argue, quite problematic. The "universal" and the "unique" seem to me idealizations at the extremes of a continuum. I prefer to say that the qualities of images are only ever *more or less typical or atypical*.) Jungians believe that these essences are necessarily implied in, or entailed by, the image – and that these essences can, in principle (if not always in practice), be accurately (if not always exhaustively) described and defined. In addition, they believe that essences are projected both collectively and personally onto a specific image (erroneous or controversial as these projections may be). There may, of course, be a considerable discrepancy between: (1) the essence that is necessarily implied in, or entailed by, a specific image; (2) the essence that is collectively projected onto it; (3) the essence that is personally projected onto it. Such disparities may be pathologically symptomatic or utterly innocuous (they may be deviant from some ideological norm or incongruous with some popular consensus, or they may simply be idiosyncratic or eccentric).

The Jungian theory of dream interpretation is consistent with the revisions that Fosshage so persuasively proposes to the Freudian theory. Fosshage argues: (1) that the function of dreams is not primarily to fulfill wishes but to regulate, maintain, develop, restore, or creatively reorganize the internal reality of the dreamer; (2) that the Freudian notion of disguise and the distinction between manifest content and latent content are untenable; (3) that a phenomenological description and definition of dream images is preferable to a reductive translation of them into other terms. Fosshage says: "The primary dream interpretive task from the vantage point of this model is to remain with, as closely as possible, the phenomenology of the dream: to understand the meanings of the particular images and experiences as they are presented in the dream" (1987: 32). Or, again, as Jung says: "To understand the dream's meaning, I must stick as close as possible to the dream images." Virtually the only difference between Fosshage and Jung is that Fosshage uses the verb "remain," while Jung uses the verb "stick." Both advocate "close" phenomenological interpretation by strict adherence to the specific dream images. Fosshage would "remain with" the image; Jung would "stick to" it.

When I received the clinical presentation on Barbara, I quite deliberately decided to read immediately only the three dreams and to interpret them without prior recourse to the biography of the patient, the history of the analysis, or the associations of the dreamer. Only after I had interpreted the three dreams did I then read the clinical presentation. Clinical presentations comprise such information as the age, sex, sexual orientation or preference, gender identity, ethnicity, history of the family of origin, biography of the patient, diagnosis, presenting problem, history of the analysis, prognosis, process notes, a case vignette, and a dream or dream-series. In my experience, when analysts preface dream interpretations with clinical presentations that include extensive information about the patient, this material often prejudices the dream interpretations. From such information, analysts tend to form a preconception of what the patient is like, and then they interpret the dreams in ways that conveniently validate that preconception. In order to preclude any such bias, I wanted to do a "cold" reading of Barbara's three dreams, conduct a "blind" experiment in Jungian dream interpretation, and engage the dream images in pristine condition. I adopted this procedure in the belief that the dream images per se would disclose an enormous amount of valuable data about the dreamer, including diagnostic and prognostic information, defensive strategies and tactics, direct or indirect transference representations, indications about appropriate or inappropriate analytic interventions (what to say or not to say to the dreamer), the compensatory or prospective functions – and what Jung calls the individuation process.

I wanted to ascertain whether such an experiment could have any predictive value. Could I, by interpreting the three dreams from a Jungian perspective, without first reading the clinical presentation, "predict" (simply by inferring from the dream images as such) what Barbara was like (at least as Ipp portrays her)? To what extent would my dream interpretations be identical with, similar to, or different from Ipp's clinical presentation? If my dream interpretations differed considerably from Ipp's clinical presentation, what would that mean? Who – Ipp or I – would be right or wrong about Barbara? If my dream interpretations were accurate, and if they were substantially different from Ipp's clinical presentation, I would argue that this ought to oblige Ipp to entertain seriously the possibility that she should significantly revise the portrait that she provides of Barbara.

The three dreams that Ipp includes in the clinical presentation constitute a dream-series. They are not just three random dreams. "These dreams," Ipp says, "occurred chronologically but not sequentially" (2000a: 89) over a twice-a-week, six-year analysis. What was the principle of selection? Ipp says that she selected these specific dreams in order to demonstrate how she utilizes dreams clinically and how she comprehends the function of dreams in analysis. The three dreams, she says, exemplify "certain specific themes" that the analysis of Barbara addressed (2000a: 92). Any selection of only a few dreams from the many dreams that a patient recounts over the course of an analysis of several years is, of course, arbitrary – whatever the criteria may be (clinical, thematic, or otherwise).

Jung says that it is preferable to interpret several dreams in a series rather than a single dream in isolation. He says that "the basic ideas and themes can be recognized much better in a dream-series, and I therefore urge my patients to keep a careful record of their dreams and of the interpretations given" (*CW* 16: 150, par. 322). The value of a longitudinal dream-series is that it delineates a trend over time. Jung says that when an analyst "observes a series of dreams often running into hundreds, there gradually forces itself upon him a phenomenon which, in an

isolated dream, would remain hidden behind the compensation of the moment."
According to Jung, "This phenomenon is a kind of developmental process in the
personality itself." He says that the "apparently separate acts of compensation" in
isolated dreams "arrange themselves into a kind of plan." The dreams in a series,
he says, "seem to hang together and in the deepest sense to be subordinated to a
common goal, so that a long dream-series no longer appears as a senseless string
of incoherent and isolated happenings, but resembles the successive steps in a
planned and orderly process of development" (*CW* 8: 289, par. 550). Jung calls
"this unconscious process spontaneously expressing itself in the symbolism of a
long dream-series the individuation process" (*CW* 8: 289–90, par. 550). Thus he
emphasizes "the individuation process, which, according to all we know, lies at the
base of psychological compensation" (*CW* 8: 290, par. 553). (This is what I mean
by compensation in the service of individuation.)

Dream 1
Dan and I were at the club dancing around the fountain downstairs. I had
cooked dinner for my friends Sarah and Jacques – he's a French chef. I had
made a big white fish and felt proud of my efforts. When we sat down to eat,
Jacques announced the fish was still frozen in the middle. I was so embarrassed. I wanted to take it from him and put it in the microwave and nuke it.
Instead, I just stood there wanting to disappear – wishing I was invisible …
like I often felt when I was a child.

(Ipp 2000a: 94)

The first sentence of this dream sets the scene. That Barbara dances with Dan
around a fountain at the club immediately establishes a quite specific, intimately
emotional mood. The attitude of the ego is, in a word, "romantic" (in contrast, I
would conjecture, to a realistic attitude).

Then the scene shifts to a dinner party. Barbara has cooked dinner for a woman
friend and a French chef. Although I assume that the French chef is an actual
acquaintance, I also regard this image, on the subjective level, as a personification
of an aspect of the psyche of the dreamer. Phenomenologically, what is the essence
of a French chef? Necessarily implied in, or entailed by, and collectively projected
onto this image is haute cuisine. As a *New York Times* article, an invidious comparison of the English with the French, says so succinctly: "In France, cuisine. In
England, food" (Grimes May 9, 1998: B9). A French chef is not just a cook; he is
a master of the culinary arts, a connoisseur, the very epitome of sophistication in
taste. That Barbara presumes to cook dinner for a French chef suggests a certain
ego inflation – diagnostically, a rather grandiose narcissism.

Barbara has cooked a big white fish. A fish necessarily implies water, and, as
Jung says, "Water is the commonest symbol for the unconscious" (*CW* 9,1: 18, par.
40). Logically it follows that the image of the fish is a content of the unconscious,
an emergent phenomenon from the depths of the psyche of the dreamer. That
Barbara is proud of her efforts to cook the fish suggests a certain satisfaction with

mere attempts rather than results. Traditionally, pride goes before a fall, and hubris is the tragic flaw of the hero.

The French chef announces that the fish is still frozen in the middle. In spite of her proud efforts, Barbara has served an uncooked or incompletely cooked fish. In this respect, Claude Lévi-Strauss says that the "cooked" is the result of a cultural process that transforms natural phenomena, or the "raw" (1970). Long before Lévi-Strauss, Jung employed the image of the raw and the cooked. "The unconscious seizes upon the cooking procedure as a symbol of creation, transformation," Jung says. "Things go in raw and come out new, transformed" (1984: 332). Hillman says: "The fantasy of the 'raw and the cooked' (Lévi-Strauss) begins in the psyche's dream, which is not mere nature but elaborated nature, *natura naturata*" – that is, culture – or "cooking of psychic stuff that goes on in the night" (1979a: 135).

A raw content of the unconscious cannot be metabolized; it has to be cooked. In this instance, the fish goes in frozen and comes out not "well-done" but "half-baked," not thoroughly transformed. The content of the unconscious has not been properly processed, and therefore it cannot be "swallowed" or "stomached." It is inedible. As symbolic "food for thought" (or food for feeling), it cannot be digested and assimilated by any of the aspects of the psyche at this "inner dinner party." A competent cook would, of course, thaw a frozen fish before she ever tried to cook it. This ego, however, is apparently inept in this respect; it evidently has little or no capacity to test reality. Apparently, Barbara does not check the fish to be certain that it is well enough done before she serves it. Barbara may be at dinner, but she is also "out to lunch." In addition, anyone who realistically hoped to impress a French chef would cook for him only a fresh fish, never a frozen fish. It is simply a fact, of course, that this content of the unconscious is not fresh but frozen. In spite of all efforts, this content (perhaps an emotional content) remains frigid and is therefore indigestible and unassimilable by the ego or any other aspect of the psyche. The implication would be that Barbara is, in some respect, a "cold fish."

Barbara is embarrassed by this state of affairs. She then reacts with a psychotic style that, in regressive sequence, demonstrates the defensive strategies and tactics that she characterologically employs. Initially, the ego reacts with borderline anger and aggression. Barbara wants to take the fish from the French chef and "nuke" it in the microwave. There is no evidence in the dream to indicate that the French chef has been critical; he does not complain; he merely announces a fact – that the fish is still frozen in the middle. The ego, however, immediately reaches critical mass and produces a chain reaction of explosive radiation. This is an example of what Joseph Redfearn calls an "exploding self" (1992). In this respect, the microwave attains the status of a nuclear reactor with what Michael Eigen calls a "psychotic core" (1986) that is utterly out of control. Apparently, this ego unrealistically expects the French chef and the other aspects of the psyche to swallow and stomach, in a pretense of polite silence, any indigestible and unassimilable contents that it serves. This is all a fantasy that Barbara momentarily entertains but does not execute. Instead, the ego reacts passively and magically. Finally, Barbara just stands there, wants to disappear, wishes that she were invisible. The ego reacts defensively with a desperate desire simply to vanish in utter denial of the situation, as Barbara says she often felt like doing as a child.

A more normal adult with an ego that was not so romantic, so grandiosely narcissistic, borderline, passive, and magical, but that was more realistic, would be responsive rather than reactive, receptive rather than defensive, and would, in a word, improvise. She might put the fish back into the oven and cook it until it was done. She might, with a sense of humor, throw away the fish and telephone for Chinese. Or she might do the obvious and consult the expert, the French chef, who might offer a creative solution to the problem. (A Jungian might suggest that Barbara conduct an exercise in "active imagination," an imaginal dialogue, on the subjective level, between the ego and the French chef as a personification of an aspect of the unconscious. Barbara would regard the French chef in the dream as if he were a real person and would ask the image for whatever advice and assistance it could offer. As it is, however, I would not recommend active imagination, for Barbara does not seem to me yet to have an ego with the capacity to engage this image from the unconscious in serious, nondefensive conversation.)

At this point, the prognosis does not seem to me very optimistic for a truly effective relation between the patient and the analyst, much less between the ego and the unconscious. The French chef is not a direct transference representation of the analyst, but as an indirect transference representation the image does suggest several quite predictable projections by the ego of the dreamer onto the analyst (or manipulative projective identifications into the analyst). If I were the analyst, I would infer from this dream that Barbara would narcissistically regard herself as my equal if not my superior, that she would be competitively presumptuous in an effort to impress me, and that she would "cook up" and "serve up" various unconscious contents, frozen rather than fresh images, that would be difficult if not impossible for me to digest and assimilate analytically. There is potential for transformation and individuation in Barbara, for in the dream she does aspire to be a great cook. Currently, however, her reach exceeds her grasp of the culinary arts. This aspiration is, at present, not a proficiency but just a pretension, a narcissistic conceit that may, in future, become an actual capacity. Ultimately, of course, a sense of equality (or even superiority) in relation to the analyst may be perfectly realistic and absolutely necessary. In this respect, Marie-Louise von Franz says that "it can happen – and it is not at all rare – that a patient grows beyond one, that is, progresses further in the inner process than one has gone oneself" (1993a: 280). In such an instance, the patient is finally, really and truly, superior to the analyst.

As for indications about appropriate and inappropriate analytic interventions, the dream demonstrates that if the analyst were to offer any interpretation, even the most moderate observation, about these unconscious contents, Barbara would immediately regard it as severe, judgmental criticism and react to it with narcissistic, borderline anger and aggression and then with regressively passive and magical disappearance and invisibility. The dream indicates that, at this point, the analyst should engage Barbara primarily with a sensitively empathic silence that respects this resistance and that swallows and stomachs, or "contains," these unmetabolizable contents until she is eventually in a position to process them. In this respect, Harold E. Searles notes that "silence between persons is not necessarily a gulf, a void, but may be a tangibly richer communion than any words could constitute" (1979: 26–7). A Jungian would regard this dream as negatively, or reductively, compensatory. That is, the purpose of the dream is deflationary. The indication is that – not now but later – the analyst should address with Barbara the fact that she suffers from an inflation of the ego but that she has within her, in her own unconscious, a valuable imaginal, even archetypal resource, a "French chef" who might teach this bad cook to become a good enough cook, a good cook, or even a great cook, if only she would condescend to learn the culinary arts from a real expert.

I would predict from this dream that Barbara had an emotionally frigid mother who was a bad cook, with no competence or interest in the kitchen, and who neither nourished nor initiated her daughter into that vitally important function. In the clinical presentation, Ipp confirms this prediction. She says that Barbara's mother "had always hated cooking" (2000a: 98). A daughter with such a mother would never have developed the ability to cook, serve, swallow, stomach, digest, and assimilate symbolic food. As a result, Barbara suffers from a symbolic (cooking and) eating disorder.

Barbara associates the big white fish with Catholicism, which is the religion of Dan, her husband. In the clinical presentation, Ipp remarks, with no further elaboration, that this topic has been a source of tension in the marriage. She never says whether Barbara has another religion or any spiritual interest at all. Is Barbara a Catholic, a Protestant, a Jew, an atheist, an agnostic, or what? As an article in the *New York Times* reports, the fish is a Christian symbol that can excite considerable conflict and even involve the American Civil Liberties Union in legal controversy over the Constitutional issue of separation of church and state (Goodstein June 23,1998). Another article in the *New York Times* describes how by the 1980s the "Jesus fish," a silver, small, plastic, adhesive plaque formed simply with two curved lines, began to appear on the rear ends of automobiles as a Christian symbol and then how, satirically, other non-Christian symbols began to appear – among them, the "Darwin fish," the "Truth fish" (which devours a Darwin fish), the "Evolve fish", the "Gefilte fish," the "Sushi fish," and even a "Satan fish" (Yoon February 11, 2003: F1 and F7). Jung wrote a book that includes an extensive discussion of the fish as a symbol in Christianity, in a variety of other religions, and in alchemy (*CW* 9,2). With additional information about the association that Barbara provides, a Jungian might interpret the big white fish as an unconscious content that epitomizes a quite specific religious or spiritual issue in the psyche of the dreamer.

In the clinical presentation, Ipp also mentions that Barbara associates the cooking theme in the dream with a cookbook that she had previously given as a birthday present to Jacques, the French chef. In retrospect, Barbara regrets the gesture

because it seems a sheer absurdity to give a cookbook to a French chef. This association confirms the diagnosis of a preposterously presumptuous narcissism.
When Ipp suggests to Barbara that the frozen fish might be a representation of
emotionally frozen aspects of her self (spontaneity, sexuality, and vitality),
Barbara associates the image with several frigidly traumatic experiences both
recent and remote. The analysis then proceeds on the assumption that these frozen
aspects of her self should be thawed. The dream indicates that they should also be
properly cooked, served, eaten, digested, and assimilated, but Ipp and Barbara do
not directly address this issue, at least in the clinical presentation that Ipp provides.

Dream 2

I was traveling on a plush train with Mark – it felt like the train between
Geneva and Lausanne. We were traveling all over the continent together. At
the beginning of the dream, Mark's mother asked why we were traveling
together. I felt or said, "It doesn't matter." Mark was so nice and polite, and it
felt okay, like it did from time to time when he wasn't being sexual with me or
trying to win me over. In Cologne, Mark got off the train and was gone. He
had left some of his luggage behind, and I thought maybe he hadn't left after
all. Later, through the fog, I saw him returning. As he got closer, I saw it
wasn't him – it was Dan. Mark had become Dan. I felt shocked and woke up
shouting, "I don't believe it!"

(Ipp 2000a: 97)

The scene of this dream is a journey. The dream is a grand tour on a plush train,
which suggests indulgence in luxury, perhaps a holiday or vacation trip. Barbara is
traveling together with Mark all over Europe. Mark's mother asks why they are
traveling together. This "why" might be a question about whether it is appropriate
for Barbara and Mark to be together, or it might be a question about whether there
is any particular purpose to this traveling. On the subjective level, the ego of the
dreamer and a personification of some other aspect of the psyche are on a journey
evidently with no definite destination. The attitude of the ego is that of a tourist.
That Barbara replies that it does not matter that she and Mark are traveling together indicates that appropriateness and purposiveness are not questions that this ego
takes seriously; they just seem immaterial, and the ego is dismissive of them.

Barbara is able to relate to Mark in the dream because he is nice and polite, not
being sexual and not trying to win her over. These are the relational terms that the
ego apparently prefers. The ego can relate comfortably to this personification only
when that aspect of the psyche conforms to certain expectations about manners
and is strictly platonic, neither seductive nor competitive, so that Mark is not the
winner and Barbara does not feel that she is a loser.

The first part of the dream begins between Geneva and Lausanne and ends at
Cologne. In the history of Europe, Switzerland remains neutral and avoids conflict,
while Germany starts world wars. Phenomenologically, these are the essences that
are collectively projected onto these two nations, which can be regarded as two

different "states" of mind. It is perhaps relevant that the platonic behavior of Mark in the dream is similar to the neutral behavior of Switzerland. In this respect, this dream may be about possibilities for peace of mind.

When Mark gets off the train, he leaves behind some of his luggage, and Barbara thinks that maybe Mark has not left after all. I infer that this part of the dream is a dramatization of a real, external relation that ended in a separation – perhaps a marriage that ended in a divorce – with Mark being the one who left Barbara. I also conclude that Barbara feels that Mark left her with emotional baggage that enables her to perpetuate a fixation, an erroneously nostalgic fantasy in which she remains in that previous relation with him. If Mark is indeed Barbara's ex-husband, then Mark's mother would be Barbara's ex-mother-in-law. An ex-mother-in-law who asks why Barbara and Mark are traveling together might be posing to the ego, for critical reflection, a serious question as to whether such a relation is legal, licit, or legitimate.

Later in the dream, Barbara sees Mark returning through the fog. Mark is a rather literal image of what Freud calls the "return of the repressed." Atmospheric conditions are phenomena with essences that are indicative of states of consciousness. In this respect, the psyche of Barbara is "in a fog," a state of unconsciousness that can occasion misperceptions of reality and projections onto it. As Mark gets closer to Barbara, she sees that it is really Dan. The ego demonstrates that it has a capacity for sight, or insight, and for the retraction of a projection. Then, however, with a shock of recognition, Barbara awakens and shouts that she does not believe it. The reversal evidently traumatizes the ego into utter incredulity and denial. Barbara either cannot or will not believe her own eyes.

This dream confirms the diagnosis from the previous dream. Mark is a mere extension of Barbara; in the dream, he strictly conforms to the preferences of the ego. The ego desexualizes Mark in order to relate comfortably – that is, narcissistically – to him. The image of baggage suggests separation–individuation issues that this ego has yet to resolve. For this ego to individuate, it must eventually separate from any sentimental fantasies that it still entertains about an ideal Mark who is radically out of character with the real Mark, and it must acknowledge that Mark has departed, never to return. At this point, the attitude of the ego remains romantic rather than realistic.

Again, there is no direct transference representation of the analyst. If, however, Mark is an indirect transference representation, the analyst might anticipate that Barbara would have the attitude of a mere tourist who considers analysis a luxury, not a real necessity, with no purposive sense that the journey would terminate at any particular destination. In this scenario, the analysis would be a process parallel to the dream and would abruptly stop, not end with effective closure. The projection would be a fantasy that the analyst, like Mark, would not only leave Barbara but also leave her with emotional baggage that she would then sentimentally misconstrue as evidence that there had really been no termination. This dream indicates just how important it would be for this particular analytic process eventually to conclude with a sense of real finality. Freud believes that it is difficult if not impossible to analyze a narcissist because such a patient ostensibly has no capacity to form an effective transference. That the Mark in the dream is a mere extension of Barbara, or of what she ideally prefers a companion to be, suggests that she would project this same idealization onto the analyst. This projection would be a transference, but it would be a narcissistic transference, with all the difficulty of such an unrealistic relation to the analyst.

The dream indicates that the analyst should engage Barbara with strict "Swiss" analytic neutrality. That is, the analyst should simply adopt a nice, polite, platonic approach in order to accompany her on the analytic journey. At this point, Barbara would tend to resist any interpretation incompatible with the narcissistic attitude of the ego as a seductive, competitive attempt to win her over. What is contra-indicated is any suggestive attempt by the analyst to allure, entice, or otherwise unduly influence her.

This dream is more prognostically optimistic than the previous dream. Barbara effectively tests reality when she recognizes that it is Dan, not Mark, who emerges from the fog of unconsciousness. The ego demonstrates that it has the capacity to rectify a misperception. As Barbara awakens from the dream, however, the ego protests in disbelief. No sooner has the ego retracted a projection than it suddenly – and regressively – attempts to reinstate it. This ego is conservative, even reactionary. In this instance, the defensive strategy and tactic is denial. For Barbara, reality is evidently still too traumatic for the emergent, compensatory function of the dream to have a permanent, transformative effect on the narcissistic attitude of the ego. This ego is unable to tolerate and then integrate the alternative perspective that the unconscious presents for consideration. What is apparently impossible in the present may, of course, be possible in the future. In this respect, there may be a prospective function to this dream.

The clinical presentation by Ipp confirms the prediction that Barbara was indeed married to Mark and divorced by him. Ipp interprets the incredulity that Barbara exhibits when she recognizes that Mark, her ex-husband, is really Dan, her husband, as evidence that Barbara is still unconsciously attached to rather than consciously separated from Mark. Barbara denies to Ipp that the reversal of Mark into Dan is a disappointment to her. Rather, she insists that the dominant emotion is a fear that Dan could become Mark or become someone (sexually and competitively) like Mark. As Ipp comments, "Maybe but maybe not" (2000a: 98). The dream does not, however, say that Dan might become Mark; it unambiguously states that Mark becomes Dan. The disbelief that the ego registers at this reversal suggests that Barbara does indeed project onto Mark a romantically narcissistic (nonsexual, noncompetitive) ideal image of a husband – an image that the real Mark is inadequate to or incommensurable with. In the dream, Barbara feels "okay" about Mark because he does not attempt to win her over. In the associations to the dream, however, she acknowledges that "he had more winning ways about him" (2000a: 97) – ways of relating that were pleasing to her (perhaps more pleasing than some that Dan has about him).

Dream 3

There was a whole group of us – friends and family – floating on mats down this beautiful river. It had a feel of some of our better times when we were young and spending our summers at the lake with lots of people around. I was on a mat with my mother. … I felt very uncomfortable … I couldn't stretch my legs or find my own position. I didn't feel angry with my mother … I just felt that I had to do something different. My mother was quite distant but pleasant. She was a younger version of herself … not the frail self of her last few years. I felt a need to break away and find my own independence but in a gentle way this time. I looked around and saw you [Ipp, Barbara's psychoanalyst] floating on your own mat – separate from the group. You smiled at me. It felt reassuring. I found my own mat and continued to float down the river alongside my mother … together, but separate. It felt very peaceful.

(Ipp 2000a: 100)

The scene of this dream is, again, a journey without any definite destination. Barbara is not with Mark traveling in a train on land; she is with a group, friends and family, floating on mats down a river. Emotionally, the scene is reminiscent of the past – summers at a lake, better times than the present, when Barbara was a youth, not an adult. If, as Jung says, water is a symbol of the unconscious, what kind of water, what kind of unconscious, is this? Hillman notes that "many psychotherapists identify bodies of water in dreams, e.g., bathtubs, swimming pools, oceans, as 'the unconscious'" (1979a: 18). He advocates that analysts should stick to the image, to "the *kind* of water in a dream" (1979a: 152), and specify phenomenologically the distinctive qualities of the water. In this dream, the specific image is not a lake; it is a river. In this respect, William James is famous for the metaphor the "stream of consciousness." He says that consciousness "flows." According to James, "A 'river' or a 'stream' are the metaphors by which it is most naturally described" (1983: 233). Similarly, Jung says: "Water in motion means something like the stream of life" (*CW* 16: 13, par. 15). Von Franz says: "In mythology, a river is usually associated with the stream of time, the flow of life" (1993b: 9). Hillman, however, again recommends that analysts should exercise caution – and not "merely assume that rivers always mean the flow of life" (1979a: 152).

In the dream, Barbara is adrift on a river. The ego is not actively paddling a canoe or rowing a boat; it is passively carried along on the current, on a mat. Nor is the ego alone; rather, it is together, on the same mat, with a certain image of the mother, which, on the subjective level, is a personification of an aspect of the psyche. The dream says that Barbara's mother "cramps her style." The image of the mother simply occupies too much space in the psyche of the dreamer. It prevents the ego from stretching its legs or finding its own position. The ego feels uncomfortable but not angry. That is, the ego acknowledges the state of affairs in the present and actively assumes responsibility for it; it feels that it must do something different in the future (which would be to stretch its legs and find its own position).

The image of the mother is distant but pleasant. This emotional relation is apparently in contrast to how Barbara has previously experienced the mother. The dream says that this is a younger image of the mother, not a frail image. In short, this image of the mother is not old, weak, brittle, or fragile. The ego can relate to the image, break away from it, without anxiously feeling that the image might break. This image of the mother can evidently endure a new and different kind of relation to the ego. Barbara feels that she needs to find her own independence. For her to individuate, she must separate from a certain image of the mother. The ego feels that it can do so in a gentle way this time, evidently in contrast to a rougher way that it has previously employed in a futile effort to find its own independence from this aspect of the psyche – or, as the dream has already said, to find its own position.

Barbara then looks around and sees her analyst, Ipp, floating on her own mat separate from the group of friends and family. In the dream, the image of Ipp is a direct transference representation, which indicates how her analyst has engaged her or perhaps how Barbara expects or prefers her analyst to engage her. The image of Ipp serves the ego as a model of separation from the collective trend that the group epitomizes. Ipp goes her own way. She smiles at Barbara, who then feels reassured – apparently that perhaps she, too, can go her own way. In the dream, the analyst does not interpret but models; Ipp relates empathically and communicates silently, with only a smile that the ego construes as reassurance. On the subjective level, the image of Ipp is also a projection of the "inner analyst," an internal analytic capacity potentially available to the ego as a valuable resource (if the ego is able effectively to relate to this image from the unconscious). The dream offers a compensatory (or perhaps prospective) solution to the separation–individuation problem. Barbara finds her own mat, her own position, her own independence, and then floats down the river alongside the image of the mother, together but separate. Finally, Barbara attains peace of mind.

Diagnostically, this dream suggests that Barbara is not the narcissist that she once was – at least in relation to the image of the mother. The prognosis is much more optimistic than in the previous two dreams. The ego is not angrily defensive but gently receptive. There is no evidence of any grandiose inflation of the ego; there is no evidence of narcissistic and borderline defenses or of denial. That Barbara looks around and sees Ipp floating on her own mat suggests that the ego now has a capacity for sight – that is, analytic insight into the separation–individuation issue in relation to the image of the mother. The ego is receptively responsive rather than defensively reactive to the compensatory or prospective function of the dream. Barbara is now able actively to utilize a certain model of analysis through the direct transference representation of Ipp, to begin to appreciate on the subjective level her own internal analytic capacity, and to integrate from the unconscious an alternative perspective on the previously maladaptive, dysfunctional, or pathological attitudes of the ego. The dream does not end with Barbara at any definite destination (or with any definite destiny), but it does end with her on her own mat, with her own position and her own independence, going her own way. Her style is no longer cramped by the image of the mother; Barbara evidently now has plenty of legroom comfortably to stretch to her full length. Barbara is at least now on her own journey on the stream of time, in the flow of life, wherever she may ultimately end up.

Barbara's three dreams beautifully illustrate the transformative function of the unconscious as it compensates the partial, prejudicial, or defective attitudes of the ego. They demonstrate how, over the course of the analysis, Barbara becomes more able to integrate the alternative perspectives that the unconscious presents for consideration. The dreams compensate the maladaptive, dysfunctional, or pathological attitudes of the ego, and through active participation in the analytic process Barbara gradually begins to develop a capacity to separate and individuate. This is what a Jungian would mean by compensation in the service of individuation.

After the other three psychoanalysts and I had interpreted Barbara's dreams, Ipp wrote a commentary on the four interpretations. If I may summarize what she has to say about my Jungian perspective, she dislikes my interpretations of Barbara's first and second dreams and likes my interpretation of Barbara's third dream. Ipp considers my interpretations of the first and second dreams too diagnostically negative (or pathological) and too prognostically pessimistic. "I found little of Barbara that was recognizable in Adams's initial portrayal of her," she says. "By interpreting her dreams without recourse to her associations or clinical material, he seems to foreclose on critical elements that spoke to her initial feelings of vitality in the first dream" (2000b: 164). My interpretation of the third dream is more congenial to Ipp because it is positive and optimistic. "Although I agree with Adams's sensitive and incisive interpretation of the third dream and its implications in terms of Barbara's development through the treatment," Ipp says, "her transformation seems to be remarkable in terms of his earlier pessimism" (2000b: 164). (Ipp does not say at what points in the six-year analysis any of these three dreams occurred. If there was, however, a considerable interval between the first and third dreams, it might not be at all "remarkable" that they would document a radical transformation.)

What most perplexes Ipp is the Jungian method that requires the patient to *stick to the image*, in contrast to the Freudian method that requires the patient to *free associate to the image*. Jung eschews "unlimited 'free association,' starting from any and every image in the dream" (*CW* 16: 148, par. 319). He says: "Free association will get me nowhere." In fact, it *does* get Jung *somewhere*, but only to the complexes of the dreamer, not to what a particular dream means specifically. Jung says: "Free association will bring out all my complexes, but hardly ever the meaning of a dream. To understand the dream's meaning I must stick as close as possible to the dream images." The Jungian method, he says, is to insist that the dreamer "keep on returning to the image" (*CW* 16: 149, par. 320).

Jung describes the method of returning to the image as a *circumambulation*, or circling around the image. There came a point, Jung says, when "I no longer followed associations that led far afield and away from the manifest dream-statement." He says: "I concentrated rather on the actual dream-text as the thing which was intended by the unconscious, and I began to circumambulate the dream itself, never letting it out of my sight, or as one turns an unknown object round and round in one's hands to absorb every detail of it" (*CW* 18: 190, par. 430).

In the Freudian method, the image serves as a point of departure for free associations that may ultimately be quite tangential to the image. Jung abjures free association because it may result in a digression from the image and culminate at a very far remove from what the image means. In contrast, sticking to the image ensures that the dreamer remains with the image (as Fosshage says) and does not, under any circumstances, depart from it tangentially. The Jungian method guarantees that the attention of the dreamer converges on the specificity of the image, "zeroes in" on it, and does not diverge from it. Jung declares in no uncertain terms:

> We must put a check on limitless "free" association, a restriction provided by the dream itself. By free association, we move away from the individual dream-image and lose sight of it. We must, on the contrary, keep close to the dream and its individual form. The dream is its own limitation. It is itself the criterion of what belongs to it and of what leads away from it. All material that does not lie within the scope of the dream, or that oversteps the boundaries set by its individual form, leads astray.
>
> (*CW* 18: 191, par. 433)

The method of free association, Jung says, is, ironically, a method of *dissociation*:

> Only the material that is clearly and visibly indicated as belonging to the dream by the dream-images themselves should be used for interpretation. While free association moves away from the theme of the dream in something like a zigzag line, the new method, as I have always said, is more like a circumambulation, the centre of which is the dream-image. One concentrates on the specific topics, on the dream itself, and disregards the frequent attempts of the dreamer to break away from it. This ever-present "neurotic" dissociative tendency has many aspects, but at bottom it seems to consist in a basic resistance of the conscious mind to anything unconscious and unknown.
>
> (*CW* 18: 191–2, par. 434)

From a Jungian perspective, free association is often just a defensive dissociation that the ego employs to avoid the compensatory, transformative impact of images from the unconscious. "It is chiefly and above all fear of the unexpected and unknown that makes people eager to use free association as a means of escape," Jung says. "I do not know how many times in my professional work I have had to repeat the words: 'Now let's get back to your dream. What does the *dream* say?'" (*CW* 18: 192, par. 434). Thus Jung demands that the patient stick to the dream, stick to the text, stick to the image – and *not* free associate to them.

When I wrote my article for *Psychoanalytic Dialogues*, I anticipated that the method of "sticking to the image" would be the most difficult for non-Jungian analysts to comprehend, much less accept, because free associating to the image is such a shibboleth of the Freudian method of dream interpretation. It therefore did not surprise me in the least that this Jungian method nonplussed Ipp. She does accurately describe the method: "Adams, drawing from a Jungian model, views dreams as serving ego-compensatory functions. He emphasizes the Jungian approach of 'sticking to the image,' which, I assume, entails a close and detailed exploration between patient and analyst of each particular image." Then, however, she says: "Surprisingly, having emphasized the importance of this method, Adams then chooses to interpret the three dreams in isolation – separate from any of the associations or clinical material provided." The result of "this departure" (from the Freudian method of free association), she says, is that "he achieves a particularly negative and pathological view of Barbara" (2000b: 163). What Ipp does not comprehend is just how radically critical Jungian method is of Freudian method: that, from a Jungian perspective, the free associations of the patient may be not only utterly irrelevant but, worse, digressive, tangential, divergent.

I have one final remark to make. Ipp criticizes my interpretation of Barbara's second dream. I argue that the material in the dream indicates that the analyst should maintain strict neutrality in relation to Barbara (on an analogy with the neutrality of Switzerland), rather than seductively or competitively "allure, entice, or otherwise unduly influence her." Ipp does not address the issue of whether there is any such indication implicit in the material. She merely asserts (with an exclamation mark) that analytic neutrality is nonexistent – "as if there were such a thing and as if the Swiss were strictly neutral!" (2000b: 163). It is a historical fact that during World War II Switzerland did remain neutral, in contrast to Germany. Neutrality may be difficult (for some analysts), but it is *not* impossible. Analysis should not be a license to indulge in countertransferential projections. It is a *discipline* that requires analysts to exercise restraint (*especially* when the material indicates that they should do so).

Chapter 3

Jungian post-structural theory

Structures versus constructs, concepts versus images

In the Freudian tradition of psychoanalysis, the "structural theory" is one of six metapsychological perspectives. In addition to the structural theory, David Rappaport and Merton M. Gill list the topographic theory, the dynamic theory, the economic theory, the genetic theory, and the adaptive theory (1967). Freud introduced the structural theory as an alternative to the topographic theory (Arlow and Brenner 1964). In contrast to the topographic theory, which describes conflicts between the conscious and the unconscious, the structural theory describes conflicts between the "id," the "ego," and the "superego." Freud defines the ego as "reason and common sense" and the id as "the passions" (*SE*: 19: 25). The superego he defines as "conscience" (*SE* 21: 123).

The Jungian tradition also has a structural theory. Jungian structural theory describes relations between the "persona," the "ego," the "shadow," the "anima" or "animus," and the "Self" (with a capital "S" to distinguish it from ordinary usage). Jung defines the persona as the appearance that the ego presents in adaptive deference to conventional social expectations, the ego as identity, the shadow as the ostensibly negative or inferior aspects in the psyche, the anima as the feminine aspects in the psyche of a man, the animus as the masculine aspects in the psyche of a woman, and the Self as the totality of the psyche.

"Structural concepts," Charles Rycroft says, "seem unavoidable in psychological theories" like psychoanalysis (1968: 158). It is precisely this assumption that I would question. Does Jungian analysis need a structural theory? Or can it do very well without one? I maintain that there is little to be lost and much to be gained if Jungian analysis dispenses entirely with the structural theory of the persona, ego, shadow, anima or animus, and Self – and relies instead on a *post-structural theory*. In order to delineate what I regard as the limitations of the structural theory and the advantages of a post-structural theory, I shall argue:

1   that the *structures* that are ostensibly "in" the psyche are actually *constructs* "about" the psyche;
2   that these constructs are *concepts*;
3   that these concepts are *abstract generalizations* and therefore *content-poor in information* in contrast to *images*, which are *concrete particularizations* and therefore *content-rich in information*.

In place of a structural theory, what I propose is a post-structural theory that is an *imaginal theory* of the psyche. The *relative poverty of the structural theory in terms of both the quantity and quality of information* is why I consider it expendable.

Before I consider what the consequences would be if Jungians were to implement a post-structural theory, I shall discuss the structural theory in contemporary object relations psychology as W. R. D. Fairbairn articulates it. Although there are significant differences between object relations psychology and Jungian psychology, there are also important similarities. Fairbairn reaches certain conclusions that, to me, radically subvert the putative value of *any structural theory whatsoever*, including Jungian structural theory.

In 1955, Fairbairn published an article entitled "Observations in Defence of the Object-Relations Theory of the Personality." It was a response to an analyst who had criticized Fairbairn's theory of object relations. Fairbairn says that the criticism "is essentially that of the Jungian school of thought" (1994a 1: 111). The analyst had contended:

> (1) that, in so far as my conclusions are in conflict with those of Jung, they are largely in error; and (2) that, in so far as they turn out to have something in common with Jung's views, I should have been better advised if I had adopted these in the first instance instead of somewhat misguidedly making the views of Freud the starting-point of my struggle towards the light.
>
> (Fairbairn 1994a 1: 111)

Fairbairn eschews debates over whether one school of psychoanalytic thought is superior and another inferior. "Personally," he says, "I have always been inclined to deprecate controversies which assume a 'Freud versus Jung' complexion, on the grounds that considerations of truth should take precedence over scholastic argument." He does, however, acknowledge that theoretical differences do exist: "At the same time it must be recognized that between the tradition of Freud and that of Jung there are disparities which it is hard to reconcile." Fairbairn adopts a conciliatory position. He says that if "my views have the effect of to some extent mitigating such disparities and providing a measure of common ground upon which the two traditions may meet, then it seems to me a very happy circumstance" (1994a 1: 111). Then Fairbairn expresses, in no uncertain terms, a preference for Freud over Jung:

> I cannot say, however, that I entertain any regrets over the fact that my researches have been conducted under the auspices of the Freudian rather than the Jungian tradition. When I first became interested in problems of psychopathology, I had no controversial axe to grind; and if, on reaching the crossroads of thought, I chose to follow the path mapped out by Freud instead of that mapped out by Jung, this was certainly not because I considered Freud invariably right and Jung invariably wrong. It was because, on comparing Freud's basic conceptions with those of Jung, I found the former incomparably more

illuminating and convincing, and felt them to offer an infinitely better prospect of solving the problems with which psychopathology is concerned. If some of the conclusions which I have subsequently reached involve no inconsiderable divergence from Freud's views, I still feel that, in taking Freud's views as my starting-point, I was building upon a more solid foundation than would otherwise have been the case.

(Fairbairn 1994a 1: 111–12)

Harry Guntrip notes that "Fairbairn has stated that it was out of definite personal conviction that he followed the line of Freud and not that of Jung" (1961: 247).

There are, however, some rather obvious similarities between Jung and Fairbairn. (I do not mean to imply that when Fairbairn reached conclusions that diverged considerably from those of Freud he derived them from Jung. That *may* be the case, but it is quite possible that Fairbairn independently arrived at certain conclusions that just happen to resemble those of Jung.) For example, both Jung and Fairbairn believe that dreams are not, as Freud says, invariably fulfillments of wishes but are essentially dramatizations and personifications of various aspects of the psyche of the dreamer. They both employ what Joyce McDougall calls "the theater as a metaphor for psychic reality" (1991: 3). The dream, Robert Bosnak says, "is a product of what used to be called the *theatrum psychicum*, the theater of the inner world" (1988: 38).

When Jung discusses what he calls the *subjective level* of interpretation, he says:

> The whole dream-work is essentially subjective, and a dream is a theatre in which the dreamer is himself the scene, the player, the prompter, the producer, the author, the public, and the critic. This simple truth forms the basis for a conception of the dream's meaning which I have called *interpretation on the subjective level*. Such an interpretation, as the term implies, conceives all the figures in the dream as personified features of the dreamer's own personality.
>
> (*CW* 8: 266, par. 509)

As early as 1916, Jung had defined interpretation on the subjective level as an interpretation that "connects every fragment of the dream (*e.g.* all the persons who do anything) with the dreamer himself" (1916: 421). That is, dreams are dramatizations of the personality of the dreamer, and the persons in dreams are personifications, the dramatis personae of the psyche.

Jung does not describe the process by which he reached this conclusion. Fairbairn, however, does provide an account of how he concluded that dreams are primarily dramatizations and personifications of aspects of the psyche of the dreamer. It was, he says, a particular patient who prompted him eventually to relinquish the wish-fulfillment theory of dreams:

> Many years ago I had the opportunity to analyse a most unusual woman, who was a most prolific dreamer. Among the dreams recorded by this woman were

a number which defied all efforts to bring them into conformity with the 'wish-fulfilment' theory, and which she herself came to describe quite spontaneously as 'state of affairs' dreams, intending by this description to imply that they represented actually existing endopsychic situations. Doubtless this made an impression on me.

(Fairbairn 1990a: 98–9)

Subsequently ("much later," Fairbairn says), he "tentatively formulated the view that all the figures appearing in dreams represented either parts of the dreamer's own personality (conceived in terms of ego, superego, and id) or else identifications on the part of the ego." Eventually, he concluded that "dreams are essentially, not wish-fulfilments, but dramatizations or 'shorts' (in the cinematographic sense) of situations existing in inner reality" (1990a: 99). Although Fairbairn continued to regard dreams on an analogy with the theater (or cinema), he ultimately conceived the figures in dreams not in terms of Freud's structural theory of id, ego, and superego but in terms of his own structural theory of ego and object relations.

Fairbairn announces that "so far as the figures appearing in dreams are concerned, I have now modified my view to the effect that such figures represent either parts of the 'ego' or internalized objects." He says that "the situations depicted in dreams represent relationships existing between endopsychic structures." This additional revision is the logical product, he says, of object relations theory "in conjunction with a realization of the inescapable fact that internalized objects must be regarded as endopsychic structures if any theoretic significance whatever is to be attached to them" (1990a: 99). In short, Fairbairn regards dreams as dramatizations and the figures in dreams as representations of aspects of either the ego or internalized objects, which he regards, I would emphasize, as evidence of *structures* that are *in* the psyche.

Like Jung, Fairbairn calls the representations of these aspects of the psyche "personifications." In this respect, he mentions another patient who tended "to personify various aspects of her psyche." He says that the tendency "first manifested itself in dreams." According to Fairbairn, "The most striking and the most persistent of these personifications were two figures whom she described respectively as 'the mischievous boy' and 'the critic'." The former was "a pre-adolescent boy, completely irresponsible, and for ever playing pranks and poking fun," while the latter was "essentially a female figure" (although occasionally "a headmaster" or "some other male figure of a similar character"), "a serious, formidable, puritanical and aggressive woman of middle age" (1990b: 216).

Fairbairn says that "it is interesting to note from their descriptions how closely 'the mischievous boy' and 'the critic' correspond to the elements in the psyche described by Freud as 'the id' and 'the super-ego.'" A third figure in the dreams of this patient Fairbairn calls the "I," which he regards as a personification of the ego. "The dreams in which these personifications figured," he says, "thus provided the scenes of a moving drama in which the leading actors played parts corresponding significantly to those ascribed by Freud to the ego, the id, and the super-ego in the economy of the human mind." According to Fairbairn, "The conformity between the three leading actors in this patient's dreams and Freud's tripartite division of the mind must be regarded as providing striking evidence of the practical validity of Freud's scheme" (1990b: 217).

Fairbairn then says that "the dream-figures so far mentioned" – that is, the "mischievous boy," the "I," and the "critic" – "by no means exhaust the personifications appearing in this patient's dream life." He mentions two additional personifications: "the little girl" (a child "about five years of age," whom he describes as "charming" and "full of vivacity") and "the martyr" (1990b: 217). Fairbairn says that "although 'the little girl' and 'the martyr' played relatively subordinate roles, their validity as personifications seemed in no sense inferior to that of 'the critic' and 'the mischievous boy'" (1990b: 217–18). That is, secondary as these two additional personifications may be in terms of roles, they have a validity equal to that of the three primary personifications.

According to Fairbairn, "The data provided by the case under discussion seem to leave no doubt about the existence of functioning structural units corresponding to the ego, the id and the superego." Freud's tripartite division of the psyche, he says, is an accurate description of "a characteristic functional grouping of structural elements in the psyche." It is, however, hardly an exhaustive description. That the id, ego, and superego are "characteristic" structural elements does *not* entail that they are *the only three* structural elements in the psyche. As Fairbairn says: "That the ego, the id and the super-ego do represent characteristic functioning structural units seems to be indicated by the facts of the case before us; but the facts of the case also indicate the possibility of other functioning structural units arising" (1990b: 218). Other structures besides the id, ego, and superego may develop in the psyche and manifest as personifications.

In effect, even as Fairbairn endorses the id, ego, and superego as three structures in the psyche, he repudiates the tripartite division that Freud espouses. As an alternative, he proposes what I would call a *multipartite division* of the psyche. For Freud, the psyche is structurally triple; for Fairbairn, it is structurally multiple. It would be difficult to exaggerate just how radical a theoretical departure this is. The implication is that there are at least two more – and possibly *many* more – structures in the psyche than the three that Freud specifies. In fact, there would seem to be as many structures in the psyche as there are personifications in dreams!

In this respect, Fairbairn says that "the study of the personifications appearing in this patient's dreams" would seem "to throw some light upon the phenomenon of multiple personality." The personifications, he says, "all presented the appearance of separate personalities." He says that "this fact suggests the possibility that multiple personality may be merely an advanced product of the same processes that created such personifications in the present case" (1990b: 218). That is, the multiple personalities in what the American Psychiatric Association in the fourth edition of the *Diagnostic and Statistical Manual of Mental Disorders* [*DSM-IV*] now calls "dissociative identity disorder" (1994: 484–7) may only be a psychopathological exaggeration of the multiple personifications in dreams.

Fairbairn notes that Freud speculates that "multiple personality may have its origin in the various identifications of the ego" (1990b: 218–19). In this respect, Fairbairn says that "'the critic' as a characteristic personification in the dream life of the patient under discussion provides evidence in favour of this possibility." The other personifications "do not, however, seem capable," he says, "of being explained in a similar way" (1990b: 219). He proposes an alternative explanation:

> As a whole, the personifications seem best interpreted as functioning struc-
> tural units which, for economic reasons, attained a certain independence with-
> in the total personality; and it seems reasonable to suppose that the mental
> processes which give rise to multiple personality only represent a more
> extreme form of those which produced 'the mischievous boy', 'the critic', 'the
> little girl' and 'the martyr' in this patient's dreams.
>
> (Fairbairn 1990b: 219)

Fairbairn concludes with the remark that evidence for such multiple structures "is found so consistently in analytical work that their presence must be regarded, not only as characteristic, but as compatible with normality" (1990b: 219). Multiple structures in the psyche are perfectly normal; they only become abnormal in cases of multiple personality.

Like Fairbairn, Jung says that although dissociation "is most clearly observable in psychopathology, fundamentally it is a normal phenomenon." He says that the phenomenon "need not be a question of hysterical multiple personality." Like Fairbairn, Jung mentions that the products of dissociation "behave like independ-ent beings" (*CW* 8: 121, par. 253). Like Fairbairn, Jung notes that these products may "appear in personified form" – although he adds that these personifications appear "especially as archetypal figures" (*CW* 8: 122, par. 254). (In this respect, Jung would presumably regard the personifications of the "mischievous boy," the "critic," the "little girl," and the "martyr" as just such archetypal figures.) The psy-che, he asserts, has an intrinsic capacity (or tendency) to dissociate. Like Fairbairn, Jung states that the result is "multiple structural units" (*CW* 8: 122, par. 255).

In short, both Fairbairn and Jung discuss the normality of dissociation, multiple personality, the independence of personifications, and multiple structural units – and they do so in virtually identical terms. The only difference – and it is a major theoretical difference – is that Fairbairn explains the structures on the basis of an *internalization of objects* from external reality, whereas Jung explains them on the basis of an *externalization of archetypes* from internal reality. In contrast to Fairbairn, who is an object relations psychologist, Jung is an *archetypal psycholo-gist*. Object relations psychology (at least in the version that Fairbairn advocates) is what I call an *outside-in* psychology, while Jungian psychology is what I call an *inside-out* psychology. For Jung, the *structures are archetypes* always already *internal to the psyche*, prior to experience. These a priori structures ("archetypes") appear in dreams as archetypal figures ("archetypal images"). Fairbairn is like Hans W. Loewald, who regards internalization "as the basic way of functioning of

the psyche, not as one of its functions" (1980: 71). In contrast, Jung regards externalization as the basic way the psyche functions.

Fairbairn says of the "critic" in his patient's dreams that sometimes this personification "was a fanciful individual" (1990b: 216) – that is, apparently a figure that
was a figment of the imagination, a figure that could not be accounted for as a
product of internalization, a figure that could neither be derived from nor reduced
to an object in external reality, a figure that did not refer to an object in external
reality (much less correspond accurately and exhaustively to any such object). The
"critic" was more often, he says, "represented by some actual female personage to
whose authority the patient had been subject in the past, e.g. the matron of a
students' hostel, or a senior teacher" (1990b: 216–17). Sometimes, Fairbairn says,
it "was represented by the mother of a friend." Finally, he says that "not uncom-
monly the patient's own actual mother played the part without any disguise"
(1990b: 217). Fairbairn concludes that "the figure of 'the critic' is obviously based
for the most part upon an identification with the dreamer's mother" (1990b: 219).
Although he does not explicitly say so, he implies that the dreamer identified with
her mother as an external object, internalized her as a structure, and personified her
as the "critic." Fairbairn attempts to explain the personification of the "critic" as
the result of an identification with an external object and then an internalization of
that object as a structure.

What, however, of the personification of the "critic" as "a fanciful individual?"
Fairbairn offers no explanation for the appearance of this personification. He
identifies no object to which it either refers or corresponds in external reality. It is
evidently a pure figment, not an internalization. Apparently, the psyche of this
dreamer has the intrinsic capacity spontaneously and autonomously to imagine "a
fanciful individual" with no basis whatsoever in external reality. Is this figment
evidence of a "structure" in the psyche of the dreamer? Although Fairbairn does
not explicitly say so, he implies that it is a structure, for he does not state that "a
fanciful individual" is an exception to the rule that personifications are structures.
Of course, it is possible that Fairbairn believes that previous internalizations of
various external objects (the headmaster, hostel matron, senior teacher, friend's
mother, and the patient's own mother) have established a "structure" that subsequently enables "a fanciful individual" to appear as the "critic," but he does not
explain the figment on that basis.

Fairbairn regards the imagination as developmental preparation for "life's great
task of adaptation to reality" (1994b 2: 204). That is, he ultimately privileges external reality over the imagination. In this respect, he criticizes Melanie Klein, who
he says has never offered a satisfactory explanation of how "phantasies" of the
internalization of external objects can establish "internal objects as endopsychic
structures – and, unless they are such structures, they cannot be properly spoken of
as internal objects at all, since otherwise they will remain mere figments of phantasy" (1990c: 154). (With that one word "mere," Fairbairn succinctly expresses a
certain attitude toward the imagination.) Whereas Fairbairn (like Freud) regards
the imagination as secondary and derivative in relation to external reality (and

believes that it must ultimately "adapt" to external reality), I regard the imagination as primary and constitutive in relation to internal reality. This is what I mean by the *fantasy principle* in contrast to the "reality principle."

It seems obvious to me that *personifications* are *images*. (What else could they possibly be?) When, however, Fairbairn disavows that he is in any sense a "Jungian," he explicitly repudiates the notion that what he means by internal objects are images. He declares that "the 'internal objects' which I describe are in no sense images." He acknowledges that "images *of* internal objects are common enough" (does he mean that personifications of internal objects are images?). Such images, he says, are "part of the stock-in-trade of dreams and phantasies." He notes that he defines "'an internal object' as 'an endopsychic structure other than an ego-structure'" and says that "this can in no sense be regarded as a definition applicable to an image." In conclusion, he reiterates that "far from being mere images," internal objects "are specific structures established within the psyche under the influence of the vicissitudes of personal relationships during the most formative period of life" (1994a 1: 117). (Again Fairbairn employs that word "mere!")

What Fairbairn calls personifications, John Rowan calls "subpersonalities." As Rowan defines the "critic," it is the subpersonality that "tells us we have got it wrong," that "notices everything which could make us feel rotten about ourselves" (1990: 91). He says that the "critic" is a "standard" subpersonality that exists "in all people at all times." Such standard subpersonalities, Rowan says, appear "so often that they may be universal" (1990: 107). (I would note that from a Jungian perspective, the function of the unconscious in dreams is intrinsically *critical* – or, as Jung says, "compensatory." The unconscious exists to offer constructive criticism to the ego. Non-ego images emerge from the unconscious and criticize the ego-image in an effort to compensate the partial, prejudicial, or defective attitudes of the ego-image and to increase consciousness. The ego-image of a particular patient may, of course, regard these criticisms as excessive and may then react defensively – repress, dissociate, ignore, neglect, or otherwise exclude them from consideration – rather than respond receptively. In effect, for Jung, the entire unconscious is, at least functionally, the "critic!")

Fairbairn notes that the "critic" appears in the dreams of his patient as a fanciful individual, a headmaster, a hostel matron, a senior teacher, a friend's mother, and the patient's own mother. That all of these personifications criticize the dreamer does not necessarily mean, however, that *the* "critic" (in the singular) exists as a *structure* in the psyche of the patient. A fanciful individual, a headmaster, a hostel matron, a senior teacher, a friend's mother, and the patient's own mother are "critics" (in the plural) who appear as *personifications* in the dreams of the patient, but they are all obviously very *different* images. Presumably, they do not just utter "criticism" but criticize the dreamer in different ways and for different reasons in very different dreams that serve quite different purposes. It is precisely these *differences* that interest me, because they provide the *details* that are both necessary and sufficient for an accurate interpretation or experience of the specific images in the dreams of this particular patient.

Fairbairn acknowledges that the "critic" appears in the dreams of his patient as a variety of personifications, from a figure that is purely fanciful to figures that he maintains are derivative from and reducible to several different actual persons that he assumes the dreamer internalized as objects from external reality. Although he says that one of these objects was "the patient's own actual mother," who appeared "without disguise," he apparently regards the other objects (with the exception of "a fanciful individual") as actual persons who appeared in the patient's dreams *in disguise*. In effect, Fairbairn concedes that there is often a discrepancy between the personifications in dreams and the external objects from which he assumes they derive. That is, he admits that there may be little or no mimetic isomorphism between personifications, internal objects, and external objects (there may, in fact, be no identifiable external object at all, as in the case of a personification like "a fanciful individual"). Like Freud, Fairbairn attempts to explain this discrepancy as a disguise, the consequence of an effort to evade the "censor" that Freud posits as a function of "repression."

Other object relations psychologists offer an alternative explanation for the frequent discrepancies between internal objects and external objects. For example, in a discussion of the "bad object," Jeffrey Seinfeld says: "The internal bad object is based upon both the actual attributes of the original external parental object and the level of cognitive, psychosexual, and ego development at the time of internalization." That is, as Seinfeld attempts to explain the discrepancy between the internal object and the external object, it may not be the result of an effort, through "disguise," to circumvent repression but may merely be a function of the developmental level of the patient, which he says "played a part in how the child understood or fantasied about the actual external object" (1990: 19) at the age when the child presumably internalized that object.

Jung presents a radically different explanation for the discrepancy. In a discussion of the disparity between "actual others" (external objects) and "imaginal others" (internal objects), Mary Watkins notes that psychoanalysts in the Freudian tradition have attempted to explain "differences between actual and imaginal others through a theory of distortion and disguise." Jung regards this effort as an exercise in futility. He rejects the Freudian notion that objects are internalized from external reality and then distorted and disguised. Jung, Watkins says, "noticed that one cannot account for the particularity of the imaginal others and their scenarios even by a very detailed examination of the person's experience in the social and external world." As a consequence, she says, he realized that "it was necessary to posit some other factor apart from internalization." (That "other factor" is what I call the *externalization of archetypes*.) To explain "the deviations between the real" – by which Watkins means external reality – "and the imaginal," Jung proposed "his notion of archetypes" (1986: 69).

Watkins notes that Jung defines an archetype as a structure, or "form" (not an image, or "content"), "distinct from and prior to experience, although dependent on experience for its expression as a particular image." By this account, structures are not the result of an incremental accretion of experiences, or the internalization of objects from external reality. Rather, they are a priori factors intrinsic to the psyche. An archetype is "dependent on experience for its expression as a particular image" only in the sense that the archetype has the capacity opportunistically to appropriate from external reality an especially apt image and exploitatively adapt it to serve a quite specific purpose. (This is what I call the *aptness condition*.) Otherwise, an archetype is *independent of experience*, for in both the selection and modification of images from external reality, it exercises a quite decisive autonomy. In short, Watkins says, Jung introduces "a factor, logically prior to experience in the external world, which attempts to account for the fact that imaginal others are not always representations of 'actual' others" (1986: 69). Any incongruity between imaginal others and actual others is the result not of distortion and disguise but of purposive alteration of actual others by archetypes.

However much Fairbairn and Freud may differ, they both affirm the existence of structures in the psyche. In contrast to Freud, who says that there are three structures in the psyche, Fairbairn says that there are five structures in the psyche of one of his patients. (How many, I wonder, would there be in the psyches of other patients – and how different would they be from those in the psyche of Fairbairn's patient?) Jung says that there are many structures, or archetypes, in the psyche: not only the persona, ego, shadow, anima or animus, and Self but also the great mother, great father, divine child, eternal youth, wise old man, hero, trickster, and so forth. According to Jung, the number of such structures is virtually infinite. "There are as many archetypes," he says, "as there are typical situations in life" (*CW* 9,1: 48, par. 99).

That Freud, Fairbairn, and Jung each reckon a different number of structures (and different structures) indicates to me that they do not so much *infer* structures empirically as *posit* them theoretically – and that these structures are *arbitrary*. The procedure is deductive rather than inductive. *Personifications* (like the "mischievous boy," the "I," the "critic," the "little girl," and the "martyr" *are* empirical, but *structures*, I would argue, are theoretical. *Structures* do not appear in dreams; *personifications* do. Personifications are psychological; structures are *metapsychological*. That is, what Freud, Fairbairn and Jung call *structures* "in" the psyche are, in fact, *constructs* "about" the psyche (or, in the sense of *meta*, "above and beyond" the psyche).

Constructs are *concepts*. Freud, Fairbairn, and Jung *conceptualize* personifications as "structures." Or, as I prefer to say, they conceptualize *images* (only *some* of the images in dreams, I would emphasize, are in the strict sense "personifications" – that is, images of persons). What is the effect of this conceptualization of the imagination? I would argue that *concepts tend to obliterate the distinctive qualities of the specific images that manifest in the psyche of a particular patient – and it is precisely those distinctive qualities (the nuances of specific images) that are the only basis for any interpretation or experience that purports to be accurate.* In short, concepts (or "structures") are abstract, whereas images (or "personifications") are concrete.

For example, consider the concept of the "anima." (I should emphasize that all that I have to say critically about the "anima" as a concept applies equally to other concepts such as the "persona," "ego," "shadow," "animus," and "Self.") Jung defines the "anima" as "femininity" – or, more exactly, as the "feminine" aspects in the psyche of a man. The "anima," he says, is the "woman within me." Jung remarks that "this inner feminine figure plays a typical, or archetypal, role in the unconscious of a man" (1963: 186). When a woman appears as an image in the dream of a man, Jungians tend immediately to conceptualize that woman as an image of the "anima." As a theoretical concept, the "anima" (or the "feminine") is what I call an *abstract generalization*. The "feminine" is a grossly unspecific form without definite qualities. A woman who appears in a dream, however, is a specific content with quite definite qualities. As an empirical image, such a woman is what I call a *concrete particularization*. (When I employ such Jungian concepts as "persona," "ego," "shadow," "anima" or "animus," and "Self," I tend to *hyphenate* them as "persona-image," "ego-image," "shadow-image," "anima-image" or "animus-image," and "Self-image," in order to emphasize that *the psyche never manifests except as images*. I would, however, acknowledge that this hyphenation is a compromise, for it does perpetuate the perhaps untenable notion that concepts like the "anima" have at least some practical value, and I am uncertain that they do.) I would also say that abstract concepts like the "anima" (or the "feminine") are *content-poor in information*, in contrast to concrete images (for example, a specific woman who appears in the dream of a particular patient), which are *content-rich in information*. What does the "feminine" *inform* an analyst about in a particular patient? Nothing, I would argue. Or at least *nothing of any practical (that is, interpretative or experiential) value.*

"Femininity" is, for all practical purposes, an *empty form*. What "femininity" means is so vague, elusive, and controversial as to be virtually devoid of any definite content (and therefore any practical value). In recent years, some Jungians – for example, some of the contributors to a Jungian book about gender (Schwartz-Salant and Stein 1992) – have acknowledged just how problematic the "anima" (as well as the "animus") is as a concept. (Jungians have not applied the same intense scrutiny to other concepts such as the "persona," "ego," "shadow," and "Self," although these concepts are just as vulnerable to the same critical criteria that they apply to the "anima.") Some feminist Jungians have argued that, when Jung attempts to define the "anima" (or "femininity") – that is, to endow the form with content – the result is an exercise in misogyny: just a list of sexist (or "genderist") clichés, whether they be honorific or defamatory (for example, the "feminine" as receptive or passive in contrast to the "masculine" as penetrative or active).

The "anima" is hardly unique in this respect. Other concepts are equally dubious, *just because they are concepts*. "Instead of the language we use drawing us closer to the experiences it attempts to describe," Watkins says, "we too often use it to lead us the other way – away from direct experience of an image, towards a concept" (1984: 135). As an example of such a concept, Watkins mentions the "anima." She says:

If we have an experience and compare it to a concept, several things can happen. We can say, "Oh that was my anima talking" and we then think not of the experience but of whatever constructs the word "anima" symbolizes for us. Once we compare, we often too easily equate, and the "anima" (which was Jung's word) the concept, becomes what we are left with.

(Watkins 1984: 135)

Watkins privileges concrete imaginal experience over abstract conceptual language, as I do. When individuals speak in conceptual language, she asks, "do you not try to find out *what* they are talking about, i.e., what experience moved them?" Watkins says that a concept is intrinsically less complex (or, as I would say, much less informative) than a specific image that individuals experience: "One often finds that a very complex image, full of shades and depth, has struck them. They then dilute it through the language of psychology. It becomes an 'anima experience' and every man has an anima" (1984: 136). That is, when they employ such language, they reduce the complexity of the image (a specific woman in the dream of a particular patient) to the "anima," which is a relatively simplistic (and uninformative) concept.

Because concepts are simple and images complex, James Hillman says, the substitution of a concept for an image is psychologically reductive. "Then complexities become simple," he says, "the rich becomes poorer." (This is what I mean when I say that the image is *content-rich in information*, while the concept is *content-poor in information*.) Conceptualization of the imagination is a typification. "We begin," Hillman says, "to regard things typically: in types, then stereotypes." By means of concepts, we type-cast images. "Only the image," Hillman says, "can free us from type-casting, since each image has its particular peculiarity" – or distinctive quality. He then discusses the danger of concepts (or "ideas"). "When we neglect the image for the idea, then archetypal psychology can become a stereotypical psychology," Hillman says. "Then the precise detail of an image, just as it is, is replaced by a general idea of it" (1975: 144). (This substitution is, of course, what I call an *abstract generalization*. In contrast to Hillman, however, I would argue that it is quite problematic whether an archetypal psychology is, in this respect, preferable to a stereotypical psychology – for both psychologies equally reduce images to *types*, or general ideas.)

Hillman cautions that "each younger woman in each dream is not the anima." (Why, I would ask, is it at all advantageous to say that even *one* younger woman in a dream *is* the "anima?") When in a dream we see a younger woman "wading at the river bank, beckoning," that image, Hillman says, may enable us to "recognize" the younger woman as the "anima." He says, however, that although "we even gain insight through this archetypal recognition, we do not literally see the anima." (That is, in the dream we *see* only the *image* of the younger woman, not the *concept* of the "anima." If so, then what "insight," I would ask, do we gain if we reduce the image to a concept, whether it be an archetype or a stereotype?) Hillman says that concepts like the "anima" are "psychological ideas by means of which we see and which tend to cast what we see inescapably into molds." Thus, he concludes: "Ideas are inevitably dangerous for psychologizing" (1975: 144).

Like Hillman, I believe that "concepts are neither sufficient nor necessary for making sense of dreams" (1979b: 132) – and, I would add, for making sense of any images in the psyche. Images are sufficient unto themselves; they make perfect sense without concepts. In this respect, a *post-structural Jungian theory* would be a *post-conceptual theory*. It would be an *imaginal theory* of the psyche. Hillman says that it would be "a psychology that's not conceptual" (1983b: 2). Such a psychology, he says, would employ "the language of qualities" (1983b: 43). That is, it would emphasize the distinctive qualities of specific images. Hillman says that "*the image is always more inclusive, more complex* (it's a complex, isn't it?) *than the concept*" (1983b: 54). (What he means by "more inclusive" is what I mean by *richer in content, or information.*) Hillman does not propose to dispense entirely with concepts. "Sure, I think in concepts ... we're modern civilized people, we need our concepts," he says. "Of course, I don't mean throw out all conceptual language." He also says, however, that, in general, conceptual language is "where the images can't reach us" (1983b: 56–7).

I, too, of course, think in concepts (as we all do). I wonder, however, what the practical consequences would be if Jungian analysts threw out *some* conceptual language – notably, the "structural" (or "archetypal") language that they routinely employ and, as an alternative, relied entirely on the *imaginal* language that the psyche so obviously prefers. The concrete image of a younger woman "wading at the river bank, beckoning," *informs* me much more about a patient who dreams that image than an abstract concept like the "anima" (or "femininity") does. Images provide me with a wealth of information for either interpreting or experiencing the psyche of a particular patient.

Andrew Samuels says that in "the contemporary debate over gender, the focus seems to be on the question of essentialism" (1993: 186). Is there, for example, an *essence* to the "feminine" (or to the "anima")? "Anatomy," Freud declares, "is destiny" (*SE* 11: 189). In contrast to Freud, who asserts that the *feminine* (gender) is a function of the *female* (sex) – that is, that femininity is *given naturally* – Samuels notes that some critics contend that femininity is "constructed culturally." Samuels eschews any effort to resolve this dispute. "I feel it is important," he says, "to resist any attempt to settle the many questions associated with essentialism" (1993: 186).

I shall, however, attempt to address one question associated with essentialism, because I believe that it is an issue that "engenders" a great deal of quite unnecessary confusion. I distinguish between two varieties of essentialism. These are *conceptual essentialism* and *imaginal essentialism*. By the former, I mean the effort to define the essence of a concept (for example, the "anima," or the "feminine"). By the latter, I mean the effort to define the essence of an image (for example, a younger woman "wading in a river, beckoning"). I consider conceptual essentialism an exercise in futility, for it results in incessant, vain conflict over whether what is an empty form has any definite content. The "feminine" can mean almost anything, and therefore it means almost nothing. In contrast, imaginal essentialism can result in a rather immediate consensus as to what a specific image means, for all images always already have very definite contents. They are not forms, much less empty forms.

In contrast to a concept like the "anima" (or the "feminine"), the image of a younger woman "wading in a river, beckoning," has quite distinctive qualities. "Wading" is essentially different from "swimming"; a "river" is essentially different from an "ocean"; "beckoning" is essentially different from "rebuffing" – and, of course, a "younger woman" is essentially different from an "older woman" (not to mention a "man"). In short, a *contrastive* method that emphasizes essential differences between distinctive qualities ("wading" versus "swimming," "river" versus "ocean," and "beckoning" versus "rebuffing") effectively *restricts* what a specific image means. It is not immediately obvious what the image of a younger woman "wading in a river, beckoning," means. If I were to apply the method of *imaginal essentialism*, I would attempt meticulously and systematically to define what each image means.

"Wading" is a very specific activity. When a younger woman wades in a river, she is not just getting her toes wet; she is getting her feet, her ankles, her calves, perhaps even her knees, thighs, and waist wet. (I would ask the dreamer to describe the wading in detail.) A river, of course, may be quite deep, but wading in a river is essentially a shallow experience.

"Water," Jung says, "is the commonest symbol for the unconscious" (*CW* 9,1: 18, par. 40). In this respect, Hillman notes that "many psychotherapists identify bodies of water in dreams, e.g., bathtubs, swimming pools, oceans, as 'the unconscious'" (1979a: 18). The "unconscious" is, of course, an abstract concept, not a concrete image like a specific river. Hillman cautions that psychotherapists should consider "the *kind* of water in a dream" (1979a: 152). For example, wading in water necessarily implies that this kind of water is shallow (at least as the younger woman experiences it), however deep the river may be. A river is also a very specific kind of water. (I would ask the dreamer to describe in detail what kind of river this is. Is it deep or shallow, fast or slow, turbulent or placid, wide or narrow, muddy or clear, and so forth?) "Water in motion," Jung says, "means something like the stream of life" (*CW* 16: 13, par. 15). Similarly, Marie-Louise von Franz says: "In mythology, a river is usually associated with the stream of time, the flow of life" (1993b: 9). In contrast to Jung and von Franz, Hillman insists that we must not "merely assume that rivers always mean the flow of life" (1979a: 152). Immediately to interpret a specific river as the "unconscious," "time," or "life" is to indulge in the futile exercise that I call *conceptual essentialism*. ("Time" and "life" are not concrete images but concepts that are just as abstract as the "unconscious." It is impossible, I would argue, to define the essence of "time," "life," or the "unconscious.")

What of the image of "beckoning?" Or, more precisely, exactly *how* does the younger woman beckon – and *why*? Does she crook her finger, does she wave the dreamer toward her with her whole hand (or both her hands)? Apparently, the younger woman wants the dreamer to join her in the river. Does she want him to go wading with her in the water? Does she want him to go swimming with her? Does she want to bathe him, baptize him, dunk him, drown him? (I might ask the dreamer to engage in "active imagination" – that is, in a dialogue with the younger woman – in an attempt to ascertain what the essence of "beckoning" is in this specific instance.) The dreamer is evidently on the bank of the river. What if he were to enter the water and get wet? Is the image of the younger woman perhaps a compensation for a too high-and-dry attitude of the dreamer? What would the result be if this dreamer had what Gaston Bachelard calls "a hydrous psyche" (1983: 190)?

Hillman does not say that the image of the younger woman "wading in a river, beckoning," is an image from an actual dream. It is, however, an image that might plausibly be from an actual dream; in fact, it might be the entire dream. I might imagine a more elaborate dream:

> A pretty younger woman sits on a rock in a river and washes clothes. She wears a dress that is so transparently wet from the water that her undergarments are visible. She stands up, walks toward me, embraces me, runs her hands through my hair, caresses my face and body, and urges me to drink moonshine whiskey from a jug. As she does so, she sings a song. One of the lines is: "Go to sleepy little baby. Come lay your bones on the alabaster stones and be my ever-loving baby."

This is not a dream but a scene that I have adapted from the movie *O Brother Where Art Thou*. (In the movie, there are three younger women and three men, not just one younger woman and a dreamer.) Joel and Ethan Coen, who wrote the script, based the movie on the *Odyssey*. This scene is an allusion to the sirens who sing so sweetly and so seductively that they lure sailors to death on the rocks at sea. A Jungian analyst might interpret the scene intertextually by reference to the epic as Homer recounts it. That is, an analyst might "amplify" it in comparison to the relevant episode from the *Odyssey* in order to identify a mythological parallel and interpret the three younger women as "sirens." In this respect, Jung mentions the "feminine being whom I call the *anima*" and says that she "can also be a siren" (*CW* 9,1: 25, par. 53). Among images of "the feminine nature of the unconscious," Jung says, sirens are women "who infatuate the lonely wanderer and lead him astray" (*CW* 12: 52, par. 61).

It does not satisfy me merely to say that the younger woman in the "dream" that I have contrived for illustrative purposes is a "siren" who personifies the "anima" (an image that personifies an archetype) – or, in the object relations terminology that Fairbairn employs, an "exciting object" that personifies an "endopsychic structure" (1990a). Even if I were to call the younger woman a "seducing object" (which would be more adjectively adequate because it is a more precise description of the younger woman), this would still not satisfy me. What interests me are the distinctive qualities of all of the specific images in the "dream." Thus I emphasize the importance of what I call the *content-specific* interpretation or experience of images. What I advocate is a *psychoanalysis of the imagination* that is a *psychoanalysis of specificity*.

In this respect, the three Jungian methods of *explication, amplification*, and *active imagination* are all *content-specific* techniques. Explication and amplification are interpretative techniques, while active imagination is an experiential technique. Jungians who employ these methods: (1) interpret an image by "explicating" what it implies – that is, by defining it in terms of the distinctive qualities intrinsic to the image; (2) interpret an image by "amplifying" it – that is, by comparing it to the same or similar images in other sources (for example, myths, fairy tales, folktales, art, literature, and culture) and defining it in terms of parallels; (3) experience an image by actively imagining a dialogue with it. All of these methods are examples of what I call *imaginal essentialism*. They are all designed either to interpret or experience the essence of specific images.

All of these techniques require what Jungians call *sticking to the image*. When Hillman says that "*the image is always more inclusive, more complex* (it's a complex, isn't it?) *than the concept*," he also says: "Let's make that a rule. That's why 'stick to the image' is another rule" (1983b: 54). Or, as Jung says: "To understand the dream's meaning I must stick as close as possible to the dream images" (*CW* 16: 149, par. 320). Jungians who stick to the image have no interest in an abstract concept like "femininity" (whatever *that* might mean), but they have a great deal of interest in all the details intrinsic to the concrete image of a pretty younger woman who sits on a rock in a river, washes clothes, wears a dress that is so transparently wet from the water that her undergarments are visible, stands up, walks toward me, runs her hands through my hair, caresses my face and body, urges me to drink moonshine whiskey from a jug, and sings a song. *That* is an image that an analyst and a patient can interpret and experience the very essence of.

Bachelard says that "the psychology of imagination cannot even begin until these true, natural images have been examined in detail." The basis of any accurate interpretation or experience of an image is the distinctive qualities of that image. It is not a "form," "concept," or "structure" but the specific *content* that suffices to define what an image means. As Bachelard says:

> The only power of a general image, which exists only through one of its particular features, is in itself sufficient to show the limitations of a psychology of the imagination entirely absorbed in the study of forms. Many psychologies of the imagination, due to the exclusive attention they give to the problem of form, are condemned to be only psychologies of concept or structure. They are scarcely more than psychologies of the *image-filled* concept.
>
> (Bachelard 1983: 85)

To the extent that Jungian psychology and object relations psychology employ images as just so much "filler" for concepts (archetypes or endopsychic structures), they are not what Bachelard calls "psychologies of the imagination."

A post-structural theory would require a revolution in Jungian psychology. I am not so naive as to imagine that very many Jungian analysts will relinquish the structural theory of archetypes and never again employ such concepts as the "persona," "ego," "shadow," "anima" or "animus," "Self," "great mother," "great father," "divine child," "eternal youth," "wise old man," "hero," "trickster," and so forth. (There are, of course, many *typical* images, but whether they are *archetypal* in a structural sense is quite problematic.) The very word "archetype" is so impressive to Jungians that it is extremely improbable that they would ever consider it expendable, even if I demonstrated conclusively that the practical value of an imaginal psychology is obviously superior to that of a conceptual psychology. It does seem to me, however, that if they do retain the archetypal theory, Jungian psychology will continue to be only one of those "psychologies of concept or structure" that Bachelard mentions – and not a true psychology of the imagination.

Chapter 4

Mythological knowledge

Just how important is it in Jungian (and Freudian) analysis?

After Jung resigned as president of the International Psychoanalytical Association in 1914, most analysts – even most Swiss analysts – sided with Freud against Jung. Even so, for several years afterwards Freud remained wary of the psychoanalysts in Switzerland. Were they committed to him, or were they still more influenced by Jung than they were prepared to acknowledge? One of those who sided with Freud was Oskar Pfister, a Protestant pastor in Zurich. In a letter to Pfister in 1919, Freud said in reference to the Swiss analysts that some Freudians might well wonder whether " 'Jungification' has left a deeper mark on you than you are willing to admit to yourselves and others" (1963: 70).

Earlier, in *The Psychoanalytic Method*, originally published in 1913, Pfister had noted that both Freud and Jung had developed a special interest in the relation between psychology and mythology. Freud had discerned "in dreams and similar products of mental life" the recurrence of structures comparable to "the mythological creations of primitive periods." Similarly, Jung had identified "in the delusional structures of dementia praecox [schizophrenia]" the recurrence of "the old mythology" (1917: 243). Pfister said that Freud and Jung had conducted "extraordinarily keen investigations, executed with great sharpness of vision and astounding scholarship" (1917: 244).

Subsequently, in a letter in 1922, Pfister declared to Freud: "I have completely finished with the Jungian manner." What *was* the "Jungian manner?" Apparently, it was arbitrarily to "mythologize" the psyche and, by extension, psychoanalysis. According to Pfister, the Jungian manner was to perpetrate "high falutin interpretations" that "try to smuggle a minor Apollo or Christ into every corked-up little mind" (1963: 86–7).

What, I wonder, would Pfister have made of the following dream of one of my patients?

> Apollo is being buried in very light dry land, or soil. It's a wide open field that looks as if it may have been tilled or used for agriculture. Apollo has dark curly hair. He's being buried standing up so that the essence of Apollo will be absorbed by this earth.

Had I, in the "Jungian manner," surreptitiously imported "a minor Apollo," like so much contraband, into the psyche of my patient? Or do "gods," including Apollo, emerge spontaneously and autonomously from what I call the *mythological unconscious*?

Prior to the dream, this particular patient and I had never discussed Apollo – or, for that matter, any gods – and, I would emphasize, he was utterly unaware that I had written a book entitled *The Mythological Unconscious* (Adams 2001). He did know that Apollo was one of the Greek gods (he mentioned that he had studied myths "in school"), but that was the extent of his knowledge. He had never read Nietzsche's description of the "Apollinian" and "Dionysian" styles; nor had he ever read Jung's account of these styles as different "psychological types." This patient had no knowledge (or at least no *conscious* knowledge) of the "essence of Apollo." I shall not attempt an exhaustive interpretation of this dream, but I will state unequivocally that I believe that, in such instances, mythological knowledge on the part of the analyst is indispensable to any interpretation that purports to be accurate.

What *is* the essence of Apollo? As Nietzsche describes Apollo, he is the god of dreams, in contrast to Dionysus, who is the god of intoxication. Nietzsche notes that in dreams "the glorious divine figures first appeared to the souls of men" (1968: 33). Of what value are dreams? Nietzsche says that "the aesthetically sensitive man stands in the same relation to dreams as the philosopher does to the reality of existence; he is a close and willing observer, for these images afford him an interpretation of life, and by reflecting on these processes he trains himself for life" (1968: 34). No psychoanalyst – neither Freud nor Jung – presents a more cogent affirmation than Nietzsche does of the reality of the psyche and the existential value of interpreting the images that manifest in dreams. He says that "our innermost being, our common ground, experiences dreams with profound delight and joyous necessity" (1968: 35).

According to Nietzsche, "This joyous necessity of the dream experience has been embodied by the Greeks in their Apollo." Like a scrupulous psychoanalyst, Nietzsche cautions, however, that "we must also include in our image of Apollo that delicate boundary which the dream image must not overstep lest it have a pathological effect" (1968: 35). Apollo, he says, is the "glorious divine image of the *principium individuationis*" (1968: 36) – the very "apotheosis of individuation." For Apollo, individuation entails "measure" (or moderation, in contrast to the extremism of Dionysus). The maxims of Apollo, Nietzsche emphasizes, are "know thyself" and "nothing in excess" (1968: 46).

The Apollinian, Jung says, is a certain psychological type: "The comparison with dreaming clearly indicates the character of the Apollinian state: it is a state of introspection, of contemplation turned inwards to the dream world of eternal ideas, and hence a state of introversion" (*CW* 6: 144, par. 236). That is, psychologically, the Apollinian type introverts in order to ponder archetypal images.

One of those "glorious divine figures" appears in a dream to my patient. The god is being buried standing up so that "the essence of Apollo will be absorbed by this earth." As I would interpret this dream, a particular "god" has spontaneously and autonomously emerged from the mythological unconscious. The dream depicts the process by which the absorption of what is essential to a quite specific archetypal image ("Apollo") occurs compensatorily (or perhaps prospectively) in what Jung calls the "chthonic portion of the psyche" (*CW* 10: 31, par. 53).

If the essence of Apollo is dreams, images, interpretation, individuation, the maxims "know thyself" and "nothing in excess," and introversion, then this dream is a very "psychoanalytic" dream indeed. In this respect, it succinctly poses to my patient a number of issues for him seriously to consider in analysis. Is he absorbing (or will he eventually absorb) psychologically all that an "Apollinian" analysis has to offer? (This particular patient is a 30-year-old gay man who in appearance, attitude, and behavior is "Dionysian.")

Although James Hillman criticizes Apollo, he does acknowledge that there are times when the Apollinian style is "utterly essential, for example, when you need form, when you need distance, when you need an ideal image for orientation" (1983b: 25). Hillman elaborates on the necessity of Apollo:

> Sometimes the soul needs discipline and wants sunshine, clear and distinct ideas. If you resist Apollo completely, consistently, then he can't come in and there is no sense of form, no clarity, no prophetic deeper insight. You are always confusing everybody and keeping things emotional. There's no detachment, not even from the waiter in the restaurant, from the car in front of you – it's all involvement all day long.
>
> (Hillman 1983b: 25–6)

The decisive issue, Hillman says, is negligence: "which God, just now, has been neglected, and in which way neglected" (1983b: 26) – or, in analytic terminology, which "god" (or archetypal image) has been repressed, dissociated, or otherwise excluded from serious consideration. If a patient emphasizes emotions, involvement, and confusion to the neglect of ideas, detachment, and clarity, then "Apollo" may suddenly manifest to compensate "Dionysus."

I would add that Gregory Nagy has recently attempted to demonstrate by etymological derivation that Apollo is the "god of authoritative speech." Nagy argues that Apollo is "the word waiting to be translated into action." He concludes: "That is the essence of Apollo" (1994: 7). There could be no more accurate definition of psychoanalysis than the translation of words into actions.

The "gods" appear not only in dreams but also in everyday life. At the very moment that I begin writing this article, as I sit at my laptop computer in my living room in New York City, the mythological unconscious suddenly makes its presence felt. "Nightline" on ABC television presents a program on current scientific research into lightning. The program features a scientist from the Lightning Center at the University of Florida at Gainesville. The man's nickname is "Mr. Lightning." He is a man, the television commentator says, who can get lightning to strike exactly where he wants it to, in order to study it scientifically. The man, he says, "has made a deal with Zeus, the Greek god of lightning." According to the commentator, lightning is "a symbol to all cultures of the realm of the gods." When lightning strikes "from miles up," he says, "the gods reach down." Although the program presents the most recent scientific discoveries about lightning, it also contextualizes these discoveries mythologically, in terms that are archetypal and implicitly "Jungian." In this instance, the reference to Zeus is, of course, a journalistic appeal to "divine intervention" that augments – or, to use a Jungian term, "amplifies" – what would otherwise be strictly a factual report.

Examples of mythology in everyday life abound in New York City. Take Hermes, for instance. By far the most impressive example is the monumentally imposing statue of Hermes that stands atop the enormous gilded clock on the façade of Grand Central Terminal at 42nd Street, just three blocks from the C. G. Jung Foundation. That particular Hermes holds the caduceus in his left hand and extends his right arm in an appropriately grand gesture. Another Hermes, this one a large tile relief, greets commuters who emerge from underground at tracks 20–21 in Pennsylvania Station at 34th Street. Just two blocks from where I live in Greenwich Village, a colorfully painted Hermes protrudes, exactly like the figurehead of a ship, under a stars-and-stripes flag, from the building that houses Fire Patrol 2. These three images of Hermes all wear the winged cap or winged sandals to speed either train passengers or firefighters on their way.

Of course, Florist Transworld Delivery has for many years used Hermes as a logo, and the Ford Motor Company has used Hermes under the name "Mercury" as the brand of a car – and, more recently, another automobile manufacturer has used Hermes in a television commercial, racing against (and ultimately losing to) a Mercedes, a machine fast enough to defeat a god. If these corporations were so sure that the public is archetypally illiterate and that mythology is obsolete and therefore irrelevant on the contemporary scene – as, for example, Wolfgang Giegerich argues (1999) – then they would not, I assume, use Hermes to advertise. Apparently, they believe that today, as much as ever, they can sell their services or products by an appeal to the mythological unconscious.

Some mythological images serve as the very symbol of an entire city. For example, Pegasus scrapes the sky in Dallas, Texas. This image is a 30-foot-by-40-foot, 15-ton "Flying Red Horse," a neon sign that rotates and glows at night. The Flying Red Horse is, of course, the trademark of the oil company Exxon Mobil, but it is also the symbol of Dallas. The Pegasus was installed in 1934, 400 feet above street level, atop the Magnolia Building, which, when it was erected in 1922, was the tallest structure south of Washington, DC. Until recently, the Pegasus had not rotated in nearly 25 years, and it had not glowed since 1997. Thanks to a fund-raising campaign by the Dallas Institute of Humanities and Culture, a "Jungian" organization founded two decades ago by faculty (including James Hillman) who had resigned from the University of Dallas to protest a violation of academic freedom, the Pegasus has been restored and is once again rotating and glowing. The project was completed in time for the Pegasus to be relighted when the Y2K millennium was celebrated at midnight on New Year's Eve.

In 2003, Birmingham, Alabama, completed a similar restoration of a mythological image. The image is a 56-foot-tall, 71-ton iron statue of Vulcan, originally built for the 1904 World's Fair in St. Louis as a monument to the Alabama iron industry, and then returned to Birmingham. For many years, the statue was exhibited at the Alabama State Fair, where Vulcan was subjected to a variety of indignities:

> Not only was his right arm assembled upside down and his left arm propped up with a wooden pole, but Vulcan became a pitchman. Coca-Cola put a bottle in his hand. Heinz 57 pickles hung its logo on his arm. An ice-cream seller put a plaster-and-chicken-wire ice cream cone in his hand.
>   Liberty overalls, once made in Birmingham, sewed its largest pair and placed them on Vulcan.
>
> (Tomberlin June 14, 2003: 1A)

Eventually, in 1936, the statue was placed atop a 124-foot pedestal in a public park on Red Mountain. Originally, Vulcan held in his right hand a spear and in his left hand a hammer, resting on an anvil. In 1946, as part of a safety campaign, the Junior Chamber of Commerce in Birmingham replaced the spear with a neon torch – whenever a fatal traffic accident occurred, the police would switch the light from green to red as a warning to drivers. The statue was famous (or notorious) for bare buttocks, which were apparently a major tourist attraction. Over the years, the condition of the statue gradually deteriorated. In 1999, out of concern that the statue might break apart and fall down the mountain, it was dismantled. It then lay in pieces, awaiting reassembly. The US House of Representatives and Senate approved an appropriation of $1.5 million to aid in the restoration of the statue. Senator John McCain protested: "While the federal surplus is rapidly dwindling, why should federal dollars pay for a face lift of a statue of a Roman god in Alabama?" A Baptist minister in Birmingham retorted: "The senator is a little misinformed. No one thinks of it as a pagan symbol. It's the symbol of our city, and with the economy the way it is, we need our symbol back" (Firestone July 19, 2001: A14). A Christian fundamentalist denies that Vulcan is effectively a pagan symbol (at least to the citizens of Birmingham) and condones the presence of the mythological image by an appeal to a civic interest that is strictly materialistic!

At the 2001 Congress of the International Association for Analytical Psychology at Cambridge University, I noticed on a table just outside the bookstall room free offprints of a recent article from *Psychoanalytic Psychology*, the journal of Division 39 (the psychoanalytic section) of the American Psychological Association. The article, "What Freudians Can Learn from Jung," was co-authored by three prominent Jungian analysts – John Beebe, Joseph Cambray, and Thomas B. Kirsch – good friends of mine whose work I admire and respect. I took one of the offprints and read the article. At the same time, inside the bookstall room were 50 copies of *The Mythological Unconscious*, which my publisher had express mailed, hot off the press, from America to Britain. By the time the IAAP Congress ended, my book, I am pleased to say, had sold out, and postal orders were being taken.

I mention these two events because of a certain irony. I had just published a new book reaffirming the importance of mythological knowledge in Jungian analysis, and virtually simultaneously my colleagues Beebe, Cambray, and Kirsch had published an article advising Freudians that mythological knowledge is relatively unimportant in contemporary Jungian analysis!

Beebe, Cambray, and Kirsch contend that "Jung's decision to research comparative symbolism to understand clinical material has given rise to a number of misunderstandings, especially with regard to analytical technique" (2001: 216). Among these is "the mistaken assumption that Jungians believe dream images have fixed meanings, which can be looked up in books on mythology and then communicated, dogmatically, to the dreamer" (2001: 217). It should go without saying that *no* meanings should *ever* be communicated "dogmatically" to any patient. Whether – and if so, to what extent – "dream images have fixed meanings, which can be looked up in books on mythology" is, however, quite another matter.

As for the question of whether dream images have fixed meanings, Freud is apparently a strict contextualist. Thus he says that "the same piece of content" – that is, the same dream image – may have "a different meaning" when it appears "in various contexts" (*SE* 4: 105). Freud also, however, acknowledges that, at least in regard to sexual symbols in dreams, "the question is bound to arise of whether many of these symbols do not occur with a permanently fixed meaning." He continues: "On that point there is this to be said: this symbolism is not peculiar to dreams, but is characteristic of unconscious ideation." He notes, for example, that such symbols occur in "popular myths" (*SE* 5: 351). Freud entertains the possibility that at least *some* dream images *do* have fixed meanings and that the same images in myths may have the same fixed meanings.

One of the distinctive techniques of Jungian analysis is *amplification*, which is a comparative method. Jung conducted research in "comparative symbolism" for a quite specific purpose, which was in order to amplify images. A Jungian analyst who amplifies dream images compares them to the same or similar images in other sources, including myths, on the assumption that these images *may* have the same or at least very similar meanings.

Amplification is a very valuable technique that Freudians (and other psychotherapists) could learn from Jung. In *The Mythological Unconscious*, I do, however, criticize the manner in which some Jungians have applied the technique. I argue that amplification should be not only a comparative but also a contrastive method. I say that when Jungians amplify images "they should also *contrast them with* images from other sources in order to demonstrate not only how *similar* the images are but also how *different* they may be" (Adams 2001: 249). I also note that "when Jungians have employed the method of amplification, they have tended to emphasize comparison at the expense of contrast (similarity at the expense of difference)." The tendency has been "to neglect or even ignore the fact that *similarity entails difference*" (Adams 2001: 376). I would add, with emphasis, that an image in a dream may have a very different meaning from the very same image in a myth. The extent to which the meaning is the same, similar, or different cannot simply be assumed in advance but must be ascertained in process, through meticulous scrutiny of the images.

As for the question of whether meanings "can be looked up in books on mythology," in *The Mythological Unconscious* I quote with approval Marie-Louise von Franz, who says that "it is important to educate the prospective analyst so that he does not interpret dreams off the cuff but continually takes the trouble to look things up in the specialist literature on symbols, and he must be trained so that he knows where to look" (1993a: 272). I emphasize: "That is, analysts unacquainted with the mythological implications of a particular image must be prepared to conduct research, and analytic candidates should be trained to consult pertinent sources" (Adams 2001: 10–11). Beebe, Cambray, and Kirsch assert that a mistaken assumption about Jungians is "the idea that in order to be a Jungian analyst (or even a Jungian patient) one needs to have a background in mythology" (2001: 217). I do not believe that Jungian patients need such a background, but I do believe that Jungian analysts – and Freudian analysts – need it. Otherwise, I would never have written *The Mythological Unconscious*.

Beebe, Cambray, and Kirsch may (or may not) be right to say: "Although many analysts in Jung's intimate circle also became students of mythology, that is much less prevalent today" (2001: 217). The implication is that contemporary Freudians and Jungians are not so different after all – that because Jungians no longer either study or use mythology in clinical practice as much as they once did, Freudians need not do so. The effect (if not the intent) of what Beebe, Cambray, and Kirsch say is to "demythologize" Jungian analysis and to minimize one of the fundamental differences between Freudians and Jungians. In *The Mythological Unconscious*, I state that "it is by no means a misnomer" to call the Jungian school of analysis the " 'mythological school'" (Adams 2001: 244). s von Franz says: "In a Jungian analysis, mythological knowledge is significantly more important than in the analysis of other schools" (1993a: 272). The emphasis on mythological knowledge is one of the distinctive contributions of the Jungian school, and it is among the most valuable lessons that Freudians could learn from Jung, if only they would.

To learn this lesson, however, would require Freudians to go back to school and do some homework. They would have to study mythology seriously (and not only the Oedipus myth), conduct research in comparative symbolism, and master the technique of amplification as a clinical method. Freud envisaged founding a "college of psycho-analysis" (*SE* 20: 246) that would include as an integral part of the curriculum the study of mythology. To my knowledge, no Freudian institutes today offer courses in mythology. (For 16 years, a monthly study group, the Interdisciplinary Colloquium on Mythology and Psychoanalysis, has been chaired by William M. Greenstadt and sponsored by the New York Psychoanalytic Institute – but only as a public education program through the extension division.) In contrast, during my six years as a candidate, the Jungian institute where I trained in

New York offered courses in Greek, Egyptian, Hindu, Buddhist, Celtic, Norse and Teutonic, Jewish, and Christian mythology.

An analyst from one of the Jungian institutes in Britain recently remarked to me that even if his institute wanted to offer courses in mythology like those, none of the analysts at his institute would be competent to do so. If this is true – and I do not know whether it is or not – it is, in my opinion, a most peculiar state of affairs. Similarly, during the question-and-answer period following a talk that I recently gave at another Jungian institute in America, an analyst in the audience asked me to repeat aloud the list of courses, because she said that her institute does not provide such an extensive education in mythology, and she hoped to influence her colleagues to do so.

If Freudians (and apparently even some Jungians) were to appreciate the value of mythological knowledge, they would have to revise quite radically the curriculum of their institutes and provide for their candidates what would now amount to a "remedial" education in mythology. Jungian analysis, at least as I define it, is a discipline that demands erudition, an "encyclopedic" knowledge of mythology – or, if not that, a resolve on the part of analysts to conduct research in comparative symbolism in order adequately to comprehend the mythological images that emerge from the unconscious in the dreams, fantasies, and everyday lives of patients.

In *The Mythological Unconscious*, I quote Michael Fordham, who says: "So that there can be no ambiguity, I must state that I do not use mythological knowledge in analytic sessions" (1974: 282). He unequivocally repudiates mythological knowledge in clinical practice. Fordham, of course, is a proponent of what Andrew Samuels (1985) calls the "developmental school" of Jungian analysis (in contrast to what I call the mythological school).

David Shapiro, my dear friend and colleague at the New School University and author of the great book *Neurotic Styles* (1965), once sardonically remarked to me: "The only problem with developmental psychology is that it doesn't develop." According to Shapiro, the irony is that developmental psychology is *non-developmental* to the extent that it emphasizes arrest, fixation, and regression.

The developmental school, whether Jungian or Freudian, employs what I call a "derivative–reductive" technique. It derives present difficulties from past experiences and reduces the former to the latter. (Freudian technique is also derivative–reductive in another sense, in that it derives a "manifest content" from a "latent content" and reduces the former to the latter.) Under the influence of Melanie Klein, D. W. Winnicott, and other "Freudian" analysts, Jungian analysts in the developmental school tend to privilege the personal unconscious over the collective unconscious, internal objects over archetypal images, causality (or what I might call the "retrospective function") over the compensatory and prospective functions, and the dynamics of transference and countertransference over the techniques of amplification and active imagination.

The developmental school is, in fact, not so much developmental as it is causal. In developmental psychology, Hillman notes, "what happened to you earlier is the cause of what happened to you later" (1992: 17). This is what Erik H. Erikson criticizes as "*originology*," which he defines as "the habitual effort to find the 'causes' of man's whole development in his childhood conflicts" (1969: 98). Although Daniel Stern, perhaps the most influential contemporary developmental psychologist, says that psychopathology "may, but does not have to, have a developmental history that reaches back to infancy," and although he says that psychological development "is going on all the time" (1985: 260), most developmental psychologists continue to be originologists.

By and large, contemporary analysis is a developmental psychology that assumes that experiences of bad parenting (or bad mothering) in the past are the cause of difficulties in the present. By analogy (and in Kleinian–Winnicottian terms), the analyst is a ("good enough") mother and the patient a baby. The analyst-mother holds the patient-baby at the good breast and nurses the patient-baby with good milk. Analysis entails reparenting (or remothering). What is problematic about this paradigm is that it "maternalizes" the analyst and "infantilizes" the patient.

Historically, the demographics of psychoanalysis have shifted radically over the past century. For example, the group photograph of the participants in the Weimar Congress of 1911, in which Freud and Jung appear in the very center of the picture, includes 40 men and only 8 women. Today, the majority of analysts (and certainly the vast majority of therapists) are women, not men. Is it just a coincidence that Kleinian–Winnicottian developmental psychology (and analysis as remothering) is so popular, or does contemporary analysis implicitly countenance certain sexist stereotypes? One Jungian analyst, a man, remarked to me at the 2001 IAAP Congress, "If I had one of those, I would want to have babies too." By "one of those," he meant a womb, but he might as well have meant a breast. In the last half century or so, analysis has experienced a "feminization" that is a "maternalization."

Psychoanalysis was once a patriarchal activity that emphasized either the technique of interpreting under the penetrative image of the penis or the technique of interpreting under a castrative image (a Freudian analyst once recounted to me how the New York Psychoanalytic Institute had rejected the application of a prospective candidate because he had had a finger on one of his hands amputated in an accident and therefore could not be castrated symbolically because he had already been castrated literally!). In contrast, psychoanalysis now tends to be a matriarchal activity that privileges the technique of holding under the receptive image of the breast. Analysis is no longer phallocentric; it is now "mammocentric." Of course, the most responsible proponents of the developmental school combine both "paternal" interpreting and "maternal" holding, as, for example, Jeffrey Seinfeld advocates (1993).

The developmental school, as both a theory and a practice, is by and large unconscious of the fact that it is under the influence of a myth, the archetype of the "great mother," or, more specifically the archetypal image of the "Madonna and Child." The dominant ideology (or bias) in contemporary analysis is a variety not only of maternalism but also of what Hillman calls, provocatively and pejoratively, "Christianism" (1983b: 84). The tacit iconography is the Virgin Mary and the Baby Jesus.

The archetypal image of the Madonna and Child is a covert myth in the theory of developmental psychology. It behooves analysts to become conscious of any myth that implicitly informs (and prejudices) theory and practice – and some myth always does. In addition, the iconography of the Virgin Mary and the Baby Jesus is not so "innocent" after all, as the art historian Leo Steinberg so ably demonstrates in *The Sexuality of Christ in Renaissance Art and in Modern Oblivion* (1983), a book that the Freud of "infantile sexuality" would have found utterly hilarious. Samuels may advocate "resacralization" (1993), but Steinberg prefers what I might call "reprofanation" (or the "genitalization" of Christ). As Hillman says: "Imagine a culture whose main God-image has no genitals and whose Mother is sexually immaculate, whose Father did not sleep with his Mother" (1983b: 75).

A vulgarly literal and uncritical application of remothering can result in egregiously gross malpractice, such as the atrocities that the Boston psychiatrist (and psychoanalytic candidate) Margaret Bean-Bayog perpetrated in the late 1980s, when she remothered a depressive Harvard Medical School student, Paul Lozano (McNamara 1994). Bean-Bayog, who hypothesized that Lozano's mother had sexually molested him as a baby, encouraged him to call her "Mom" and himself the "baby." In role-playing sessions, they acted out those parts together. Bean-Bayog gave Lozano a "baby blanket" to use as a transitional object. Lozano also used for the same purpose a teddy bear, which he and Bean-Bayog named "Dr. Bean Bear." This remothering eventually resulted in Bean-Bayog's writing sado-masochistic sexual fantasies, which she apparently read to Lozano while masturbating in his presence during sessions. Ultimately, Bean-Bayog had sexual intercourse with Lozano. Under the rubric of the analyst-mother and the patient-baby, this was "incest." Finally, Lozano committed suicide. This is, of course, an extreme, perverse example of remothering. I am not a "purist" who believes that the developmental school is inherently non-Jungian (or even anti-Jungian) or that, under the paradigm of remothering, it is necessarily more prone to malpractice than other schools. Sexual intercourse and suicide are hardly necessary consequences of remothering, but this case is a cautionary tale that should give all analysts pause for serious reflection, both ethically and technically.

Although I am personally ambivalent about the word "clinical," because it tends restrictively to define analysis as a "medical" discipline, I do continue to use the word "patient" rather than "client." (The word "analysand" has always seemed to me an ugly neologism, and I never use it.) Analysis is clinical (or medical) in part – but, I would emphasize, *only* in part. The purpose of analysis is not so much to "cure illness" as it is to *increase consciousness*.

I believe that it is accurate to say that the developmental school considers itself to be the most "clinical school" of Jungian analysis. In contrast to Fordham, I believe (as Jung did) that mythological knowledge is absolutely essential in clinical practice. *The mythological school of Jungian analysis is just as clinical as the developmental school, and it is clinical in a uniquely "Jungian manner"* that Freudians (and other psychotherapists) could learn.

Why did I write *The Mythological Unconscious*? Since early childhood, when my parents bought me a 78 rpm record of the Greek myths, I have loved mythology. In high school in Texas I had a very serious (and difficult) Latin teacher who taught mythology. While a Marshall scholar at the University of Sussex from 1972 to 1975, I wrote a doctoral dissertation on *Moby-Dick*. For three years, I spent hours and hours in the Reading Room at the British Museum studying books in "comparative mythology" that British antiquarians (rather like the Rev. Edward Casaubon in George Eliot's *Middlemarch*) wrote in the late eighteenth and early nineteenth centuries and that Herman Melville used as a source of symbols for *Moby-Dick*. During that time, I met Kathleen Raine, who shared and discussed with me the mythological knowledge that William Blake used poetically. She also mentioned to me the name "James Hillman." I had never heard of Hillman, but she said that he was a Jungian analyst with a special interest in the relation between psychology and mythology. I finally met Hillman in 1981, and ever since he has been both an influence and an inspiration. He has always been kind, generous, and supportive. Although I have said that I became a psychotherapist "for love of the imagination" (Adams 1998a), I eventually became a Jungian analyst in large part because doing so afforded me the opportunity to apply mythological knowledge psychologically to serve an eminently practical purpose.

I also wrote *The Mythological Unconscious* in order to make a "statement." Some of the greatest analysts of all time declare emphatically that the unconscious is mythological. Freud speaks of "endopsychic myths" – or, in a word: "Psychomythology" (1985: 286). Jung refers to the "mythopoeic imagination" (1963: 188) and the "'myth-forming' structural elements" of the psyche (*CW* 9,1: 152, par. 259). (That is, both Freud and Jung argue that the psyche possesses an intrinsic capacity spontaneously and autonomously to generate myths.) Similarly, Bion asserts that the psyche extends into the "domain of myth" (1977: 12), and Hillman contends that "the *essence of psyche is myth*" and that "psychology is ultimately mythology" (1972: 16).

Although Hillman is still very much alive, Freud, Jung, and Bion – as well as others such as Joseph Campbell, Edward C. Whitmont, Edward F. Edinger, and Marie-Louise von Franz – have passed on. It seemed to me that the time was now right to reaffirm, in the most insistently declarative terms, the practical value (including the clinical value) of mythological knowledge. The "Jungian manner," at least as I define it, is not an indulgence in pretentious interpretations that attempt to "smuggle" gods into the psyches of patients but a serious effort to comprehend the spontaneous, autonomous emergence of "gods" (or archetypal images) from what I call the mythological unconscious.

Addendum

At the New School University, I teach an undergraduate course entitled "Psychoanalyzing Greek and Roman Mythology." Students in the course read Sophocles's *Oedipus Rex* and *Oedipus at Colonus* (and watch a videotape of Lee

Breuer's *Gospel at Colonus*, a musical version of the classical play with an entirely African-American cast), Ovid's *Metamorphoses*, Homer's *Iliad* and *Odyssey*, Virgil's *Aeneid*, and my book *The Mythological Unconscious*. The purpose of the course is to teach students how to analyze Greek and Roman myths psychologically. When they read *The Mythological Unconscious*, they also learn how ancient myths manifest in modern dreams, fantasies, and experiences in everyday life.

Occasionally, a student develops a special, very personal interest in the relation between mythology and psychology. Erol Cichowski was one such student. Jungian psychology interested him enough that he spent a considerable number of hard-earned dollars from his summer job as a construction worker in order to attend the Summer Study Program at the C. G. Jung Foundation of New York. A literature major, he proposed as his senior project at the New School University a Jungian interpretation of Kafka's *Metamorphosis* and Philip Roth's *The Breast*. (I might add that he had no idea that over the years I have taught those two books in tandem as examples of psychic transformation in my course "Madness in Literature: Psychopathology through Case Fictions.") He first took my course "Psychoanalyzing Greek and Roman Mythology" and then took my course "Dream Interpretation." In the latter course, he applied to his own dreams what he had learned in the former course. With his permission, I now present one of the essays that he wrote:

Cloven Psyche and Bull-Head: Two Mythological Dreams

By Erol Cichowski

Over the course of this semester, we have examined various approaches to dream interpretation. We have read Freud's *The Interpretation of Dreams*, Jung's *Dreams*, and Hillman's *The Dream and the Underworld*. We have discussed Freud's wish-fulfillment theory, Jung's attitude-compensation theory, and Hillman's criticism of those theories. What has interested me personally the most is the relation between dreams and myths. At least some modern dreams seem to be "mythological." That is, they seem to employ characters and plot-elements from ancient myths. How does this occur, and what does it imply about the unconscious?

In *The Mythological Unconscious*, Adams presents a Jungian method of dream interpretation that involves recognizing that the unconscious is "structured like a myth – or like myths, in the plural" (2001: 1). Although this is a conception held by many Jungian analysts, Adams emphasizes and illustrates the importance of "archetypal literacy" through references to mythological dreams in his clinical experience and even one of his own mythological dreams.

After being subjected to an entire semester filled with theories of dream interpretation and applications of those theories to certain "model" dreams, I have decided that it might be interesting to attempt an honest interpretation of two of my own "mythological dreams." In other words, I shall attempt to put theory into practice.

The first of the dreams is actually my earliest recollection of a dream. It is one that inspired my initial interest in dreams. I believe that I was about six or seven years old when I had the dream, as my mother remembers my telling it to her around that time. I call this dream "Cloven Psyche":

> I am in my house with my mother. Something evil is in the house and is chasing us. Although I have not seen our pursuer, I feel its presence. We run down a narrow hallway to a bathroom. Once inside, I lock the door, and we are sitting on the floor. I am very frightened. In the bathroom there is a small window that looks out into the hall. I hear something outside the window and get up to look out. At that moment, two cloven feet (somewhat resembling those of a goat) break through the glass and come into the room.

After having this dream, I woke up in a terror. It's actually the last "nightmare" that I can recall waking me so abruptly.

At the time, I had been enrolled in Bible study classes. This matriculation had been my own decision, which I had made after learning that a little girl whom I happened to have a "crush" on was taking these classes at a nearby church. My first real encounter with Christianity or organized religion of any kind coincided with my first interest in the opposite sex. I was raised in a house of mixed faith – my mother, a Muslim, and my father, a Catholic. They both agreed that they would let me choose whatever religion I liked rather than impose one on me themselves. I'm sure that my father was delighted when he learned that I regarded Catholicism as my faith. Little did he know that I had made the choice with prurient rather than pious intentions.

Before enrolling in the classes, I hadn't paid much attention to religion. Although my mother, a potter, was a Muslim, she was not practicing or devoutly dedicated to its preaching. Rather, she had always instilled in me a love and respect for all creatures of the earth and for the earth itself. I guess that I would define her religion as "pottery," which had always been her true passion. My interests at the time were similarly "earthy." I enjoyed playing with worms, salamanders, and other creatures that I would dig up in my back yard. I also had a large number of pets, which occupied most of my free time. This free time was drastically reduced when I began taking the bus to church, rather than to my house, every day after school.

Suddenly, I found that those objects that I had, in a sense, regarded as "magical," or worthy of worship, were actually the creation of an Almighty Being that I was to revere in their stead. To make matters worse, I learned that worshipping a being other than the "Almighty" was, in itself, a sin. You can imagine my terror in coming to such a realization. It was around this time that I had my dream.

I am in my house with my mother. Something evil is in the house and is chasing us. Although I have not seen our pursuer, I feel its presence. We run down a narrow hallway to a bathroom. Once inside, I lock the door, and we are sitting on the floor. I am very frightened. In this part of the dream, I am being pursued by my former ideals, whose nature I now question and fear to be sinful, or evil. My mother, who accompanies me in my attempt to escape, is an image of the "anima" that I wish to retain and protect from what I fear is an evil being (or evil ideals). As an image, a bathroom has many meanings. It is where one might go to clean up (or, in a sense, to "cleanse" oneself), to examine oneself in the mirror (or to "reflect"), or to expel unnecessary elements from one's body. As a little boy, I spent a great deal of time in the bathroom, reading. Rarely did I just use it for its intended purposes. The bathroom was where I did my best thinking. It is therefore natural that in the dream I seek refuge there. By hiding in the bathroom, I am avoiding what I fear would be a painful encounter. It is obvious, however, that according to the dream, I must confront and reckon with my former, now "evil" ideals.

In the bathroom, there is a small window that looks out into the hall. I hear something outside the window and get up to look out. At that moment, two cloven feet (somewhat resembling those of a goat) break through the glass and come into the room. The window in the dream was an actual small window that existed in our bathroom. When using the bathroom at that age, I methodically ensured that the blinds were completely closed, as I feared that someone might watch me through the window. The image of the cloven feet was what resonated most strongly with me at the time, and it continues to do so. Traditionally, the cloven hoof has been associated with Satan as an image of evil temptation – and of what is split, divided, or conflicted against itself. As a student of Catholicism, I had similar feelings of inner discord. Part of me wanted to remain in the Bible class – not for the religion but for the girl. At the same time, another part of me didn't enjoy or have any real interest in what I was learning. In this sense, the cloven feet breaking through the glass were an image of the conflict of ideals that had recently invaded my reflective sanctuary. In my dream, the cloven feet resembled those of a goat. In retrospect, I now realize that they were an image of Pan, the Greek goat-god. Eventually, I grew tired of the girl, realized that she wasn't worth the sacrifice, returned to my former ideals, and embraced a sort of "pantheistic" view of the world.

The following is a short dream that I had this semester, in mid-October of 2001, seven days after my twenty-first birthday:

> A door opens, and I see a headless figure, without a shirt, standing in the doorway. In his left hand, he holds a large wine glass filled with what appears to be red wine. In his other hand, he holds the severed head of a bull on a silver platter. I am sure that the head on the platter belongs to the figure.

Although this dream does not contain a direct mythological reference, in *The Mythological Unconscious* Adams says that "there may not be a direct reference to a god or hero but only an indirect reference, or allusion" (2001: 57). In this case, the allusion is to the Minotaur, a mythological creature with the body of a man and the head of a bull.

A door opens, and I see a headless figure, without a shirt, standing in the door-way. While pondering this image for some time, I began considering recent events that had been troubling me in my life. A week before the dream, in celebration of my birthday, I had gone to Las Vegas with five of my childhood friends. The trip was fun, and I had enjoyed the opportunity to "get crazy" with old friends. The downside was that I had drunk a lot of alcohol and had ended up losing $700 playing blackjack. As a result, I was financially compromised and morally conflicted. After returning to New York and emerging from my drunken stupor, I began to realize the magnitude of what I had done. I did not, however, consider why I had done it. Rather, I just kept lamenting the loss of the $700.

The dream presented another perspective. I had been unwilling to admit fault and had instead blamed my gambling losses on "bad luck" and the "fucking casinos." The headless figure in the dream forced me to redirect my anger. Having a faint acquaintance with Greek mythology – or, as Adams would say, having some degree of "archetypal literacy" – I began researching various images of bulls and the Minotaur specifically. I began considering how and to what extent I had a tendency to act "bullish" and "lose my head."

Traditionally, bulls have been defined as impulsive and difficult to control. If one waves a red flag in front of a bull, it will charge at the stimulus. I therefore began questioning my own impulsivity and the manner in which I often reacted to a stimulus without reflection or conscious consideration. The trip to Las Vegas was certainly an occasion when I had been guilty of a lapse of consciousness. Rather than consciously considering the consequences of drinking and gambling I had reacted impulsively like a bull and had lost control ("lost my head").

In Greek mythology, the Minotaur acts similarly, demanding every ninth year a sacrifice of seven Athenian youths, whom he devours impulsively. I began considering whether my own "inner Minotaur" was "devouring" certain positive aspects of my own youthful psyche, such as my ability to introspect, reflect, and *use* rather than *lose* my head. The Minotaur is imprisoned within the labyrinth and must be slain to avoid further sacrifice. In *The Mythological Unconcious*, Adams says: "To be 'bull-headed' means to be stupidly stubborn or headstrong. It is a certain attitude, and if the Minotaur 'embodies' it, then to slay the Minotaur would be for the ego-image quite consciously – and heroically – to repudiate that attitude" (2001: 284).

In his left hand, he holds a large wine glass filled with what appears to be red wine. In his other hand, he holds the severed head of a bull on a silver platter. I am sure that the head on the platter belongs to the figure. The dream may be regarded as "compensatory" in that it presents an alternative point of view of which I (my ego) was unconscious. The implication is clear. Not only was I guilty of losing my head in Las Vegas, I was aided in doing so by the alcohol, the wine that the figure holds in his hand. The specificity of the image is what interests me most about the dream. The figure of the Minotaur in the dream is not whole. Rather, its head, or thinking capacity, has been severed and is being presented on a silver platter, rather than used. The body of the Minotaur continues to function, however, without the use of its head. I began to question to what extent I functioned without a genuine "use" of my own head. The dream seemed to be saying that I had to "sever" my bullish tendencies from my body, or "slay" my impulsive attitudes. I had previously read T. S. Eliot's "The Love Song of J. Alfred Prufrock," which describes Prufrock as having seen his head (which has grown slightly bald) brought in upon a platter. The dream combines that image of a head on a platter with the image of the bullhead of the Minotaur.

In place of the bull-head, I must afix a human, "thinking" head to my body so that I might, in future, exercise some faculty of reflection between stimulus and response. I engaged the Minotaur through what Jung calls "active imagination." I asked the Minotaur what the meaning of the dream was for me. This was his exact reply: "Stimulus-reflection-response" as opposed to "stimulus-response." In order to rid myself of bullish impulses, I had, like Theseus in the labyrinth, to hold on to the reflective thread that would guide me on the path of conscious and deliberate decision.

Recognizing the mythological allusions in both of these dreams was integral to an accurate interpretation of the dreams. If I had not "amplified" the image of the cloven feet by reference to Pan (and Satan), I would have been unable to relate the image to my psychic conflict over my former ideals. Similarly, I would not have appreciated the specificity of the image of the headless figure as an allusion to the Minotaur. Without these amplifications, I might simply have passed the dreams off as "weird" or "strange," rather than understanding exactly what it was they had to offer me. This realization was, in itself, the most valuable aspect of these dream interpretations. Without it, I would never have had the opportunity to alter my consciousness and apply these two dreams to my waking life.

Commentary

This essay demonstrates how seriously an individual may attempt to put Jungian theory into practice in order to analyze himself psychologically and increase his own consciousness. If I were to summarize the two interpretations, I would say that the first dream presents a "pantheistic" (or "satanic") compensation for a Christian attitude, while the second dream presents a "reflective" compensation for a "minotauric" attitude. Both dreams are what Jung calls "mythological dreams." They differ, however, in that the first dream occurred when the dreamer was only six or seven years old, before he could have had much knowledge of Satan or probably any knowledge of Pan (in addition, it is *possible* but, I would argue, *quite improbable* that at that age he had any knowledge of the "cloven hoof"), and the second when he was 21 years old, after he had taken my course "Psychoanalyzing Greek and Roman Mythology" and did, as he says, have some knowledge of the Minotaur.

From a certain perspective, only the first dream approximates a "pure" mythological dream – that is, one in which a mythological image spontaneously and autonomously (I might say, *naively*) emerges from the unconscious without the dreamer having had prior knowledge of the relevant myth. Jung says that "in relation to their archetypal background, banal dream-images are usually more instructive and of greater cogency than 'mythologizing' dreams, which one always suspects are prompted by reading" (1975 2: 19). Presumably, Jung would be suspicious of the second dream, because of the possibility that reading *The Mythological Unconscious* "prompted" the dreamer to "mythologize" the dream. Does it really matter if individuals dream about myths that they have read about? What difference, if any, does it make? Such dreams would not prove the existence of archetypes, for the immediate source of the images in them would not be the unconscious but a book. Would, however, one dream be less "mythological" than the other?

The contrast between the first and second dreams (by the criterion of whether the dreamer had any prior knowledge of mythology through reading) seems to me a distinction without (much of) a difference. From a strictly pragmatic perspective, both dreams seem to me equally mythological. *Images* in dreams do not – in fact *cannot* – prove the existence of archetypes. As Jung says, the archetypes are "forms," *not* "contents" (or images). The archetypal unconscious is a purely *formal* unconscious. Archetypes "inform" dreams. The unconscious simply has the formal capacity to select especially apt contents, quite specific images that "conform," more or less, to archetypes. (This is what I call the *aptness condition*.) All that exists intrinsically and a priori in the unconscious are *forms*, or archetypes. There are *no innate images* in the unconscious. As I have previously said: "If Herman Melville had never been in a position to acquire any direct or indirect experience of a whale, he could never have written *Moby-Dick*. Melville could not have inherited that specific image" (Adams 1997a: 102). The same restriction applies to dreamers. The only source of the *contents*, or images, in any dream is the *experience* of the dreamer – and what dreamers have experienced includes what they have read.

Dreamers who have no experience (whatsoever) of bulls (for example, dreamers who have never even heard of bulls, much less read about them) *cannot possibly* have a dream with the image of a bull in it. If, however, they do have direct or indirect experience of bulls, then they can have a dream of a headless figure presenting its bull-head on a silver platter. Then a dreamer with sufficient mythological knowledge – one who happens to know that the Minotaur is a creature with the body of a man and the head of a bull – may amplify the image by reference to the relevant myth and logically conclude that the image in the dream is that of the Minotaur.

In *The Mythological Unconscious*, I quote Robert Graves, who says that Theseus slays the Minotaur either with "a sword," "his bare hands," or "his celebrated club" (Adams 2001: 267). In none of these versions of the myth does Theseus *behead* the Minotaur. In the "Bull-Head" dream, however, it is as if the unconscious of the dreamer has spontaneously and autonomously produced an *original, imaginal variation* on an archetypal theme: that the slaying of the Minotaur was a beheading. In a discussion of "poetic images," Gaston Bachelard says that phenomenology requires "grasping the very essence of their originality and thus taking advantage of the remarkable psychic productivity of the imagination." He says that we should be "able to find an element of originality even in the variations at work on the most strongly rooted archetypes." Minotaur-slaying is an image of the archetype of "monster-slaying" – and in the dream, the image of Minotaur-beheading is a variation on the image of Minotaur-slaying (with sword, hands, or club). "Since it has been our intention to delve more deeply into the psychology of wonder from the phenomenological point of view, the least variation in a wonder-filled image ought to help refine our inquiry," Bachelard says. "The subtlety of an innovation revives the source, renews and redoubles the joy of wonder" (1969: 3). What Bachelard says about poetic images also applies, I would argue, to oneiric images – that is, to images in dreams.

As I say in *The Mythological Unconscious*, mythological dreams do not monotonously repeat "myths in every detail" (Adams 2001: 38). Rather, they opportunistically appropriate bits and pieces from myths and exploit them to serve a certain purpose. I would now emphasize that, to the extent that the unconscious is innovative, dreams may also subtly vary these bits and pieces – these images – in the most original ways, with truly wonderful results, so that, for example, beheading suddenly seems not only a plausible but also a most cogent variety of slaying in a dream about the Minotaur (and about "losing one's bull-head"). We might even wonder why no one ever previously dreamed it, because the image now seems so obvious and so persuasive.

The dreamer says that he "lost his head" in Las Vegas. Christine Ammer defines the cliché to "lose one's head" as "to become so agitated that one cannot act sensibly." She continues: "This expression, which at one time meant literal decapitation and was used figuratively from the mid-nineteenth century on, differs from the more recent catchphrase, 'You'd lose your head if it wasn't screwed on,' addressed to an extremely absentminded person" (1992: 221). Von Franz says that "a person who does not dissociate in a moment of conflict and does not fall into an affect is a higher personality and always wins out in the end." Such a person, she says, is "the one who can keep his head" (1995: 176). According to von Franz, "With the help of the head we have the key to the solution of inner problems." She says that "the hero's acquisition of the head is the solution of his problem, because possessing it, he is then able to understand his inner psychic processes" (1996: 153).

The "headless figure" in the dream is also "without a shirt." When the dreamer lost his head in Las Vegas, he also lost a lot of money. That is, he not only lost his head but also "lost his shirt." In this respect, Ammer says that the cliché to "lose one's shirt" means to "lose everything." According to Ammer, "The term alludes to betting or investing everything one owns on some venture" (1992: 221). That is exactly what the dreamer did in Las Vegas – he bet $700 on blackjack, and he lost everything.

In the "Bull-Head" dream, the figure "holds the severed head of a bull on a silver platter," as if to present it to the dreamer. This is a quite specific image. In this respect, Ammer defines the idiom *"hand to on a silver platter"* as follows:

"Provide with something valuable for nothing, or give an unearned reward to; also, make it easy for" (1997: 279). More generally, Daphne M. Gulland and David Hinds-Howell say that "to *be handed* something *on a plate*" means "to obtain an important advantage without having to work for it in the usual way" (1986: 153). In this dream, the image of the silver platter essentially implies that the unconscious is offering to the ego a *value* ("something valuable") and making it easy for the ego to accept that value, if only it will.

Chapter 5

The "womanning" of Schreber

Catastrophe, creation, and the mythopoeic forces of mankind

I first read Daniel Paul Schreber's *Memoirs of My Nervous Illness* more than 20 years ago after reading Freud's interpretation of the book. I found Schreber's auto-biographical account far more interesting than Freud's psychoanalytic comment-ary. In fact, it would be no exaggeration to say that I was utterly fascinated by Schreber's *Memoirs*. It immediately became one of my very favorite books – and it continues to be so.

When Jung began work as a psychiatrist at the Burgholzli Hospital in Zurich in 1900, he was motivated by a desire "to know how the human mind reacted to the sight of its own destruction" (1963: 112). He says that "the pathological variants of so-called normality fascinated me, because they offered me the longed-for oppor-tunity to obtain a deeper insight into the psyche in general" (1963: 113). Reading Schreber's *Memoirs*, which is a reflection on just such a mentally destructive spec-tacle, was opportune for me in exactly the same way.

Schreber's *Memoirs* had been published in English translation in London in 1955 but had long been out of print. The copy that I had read was borrowed from a library. I liked the book so well that I wanted to own a copy myself. I searched – but to no avail – for a copy at virtually every used book store in New York City, including the Strand, which advertises an inventory of "eight miles of books." The staff in the rare book room at the Strand advised me that they had had many inquiries for Schreber's *Memoirs* but that the book was absolutely unavailable.

At some point, it occurred to me that I might be able to arrange to have Schreber's *Memoirs* reprinted. In the spring of 1983, I wrote to William Dawson & Sons in London. They were the firm that had published the English translation in 1955. They forwarded my inquiry to Thea M. Hunter, who shortly wrote to me from Cambridge. A mother and son, Ida Macalpine and Richard A. Hunter, had collaborated on the translation of Schreber's *Memoirs*. Mrs. Hunter informed me that both Macalpine and Hunter had died – the one in 1974, the other in 1981. She said that she would welcome a reprinting, provided that the text remained un-altered and that she retained the copyright. Mrs. Hunter added an intriguing remark: "My husband's views changed considerably during the years following publication and he intended to write a new introduction if a new edition was ever contemplated." It is a pity that we do not know what those views were, for both

Macalpine and Hunter were formidable psychoanalysts and historians of psychology. For example, in addition to translating Schreber's *Memoirs*, they wrote a beautiful and brilliant book, *George III and the Mad Business* (1969). Mrs. Hunter suggested that I get in touch with her solicitor, whom I subsequently met at Gray's Inn in London in the summer of 1983 to discuss a possible publishing agreement.

After I returned to America, I wrote to James Hillman and asked him whether Spring Publications might be interested in reprinting Schreber's *Memoirs*. Hillman said that he would, indeed, like to reprint the book but that the costs would need to be defrayed with a subsidy. I contacted the solicitor, who replied that since Mrs. Hunter was "a widow with three very young children," it would be impossible for her to subsidize the reprinting. With that, my attempt to have Schreber's *Memoirs* reprinted came to an end. I turned to other projects that seemed to me, at the time, more pressing. A few years later, Harvard University Press reprinted Schreber's *Memoirs* (1988). I regretted not having accomplished that myself, but I was pleased that the book was finally in print again. Now I and others could own a copy.

Over the years, I occasionally entertained the idea that eventually I would write something on Schreber's *Memoirs*. I knew that Jung had brought the book to Freud's attention but that Jung himself had never written his own interpretation of it. I thought that I myself might attempt a study of the book from a Jungian perspective. Now I have finally done so. I hope that the result honors the memory not only of Schreber but also of Macalpine and Hunter.

The End of the World

This is a Jungian study of one of the most extraordinary cases in the history of psychoanalysis, that of Daniel Paul Schreber (1842–1911). The case is also one of the most sensational, because Schreber believed that the world was coming to an end and that, as a consequence, he was being transformed into a woman – or, as I prefer to say, was being *womanned*.

Why is Schreber important? Not because he was (or was not) a paranoid schizophrenic, a homosexual (as Freud claimed), or a prophet (as Schreber claimed), but because he was the author of the most impressively instructive, candidly intimate autobiographical account of mental illness (or, as Schreber called it "nervous illness") and also because – through his experience of "womanning" – he was the "feminist" harbinger of the possibility of a new empathic relation between men and the *feminine* (especially the feminine aspect in the male psyche, or what Jung calls the "anima") and, by extension, between men and the *female*. Schreber, however, understood his "womanning" as if it were a physical, not a psychic, transformation, with the result that a visionary experience became only a psychopathological experience.

The case is a curious one because Freud, who in 1911 published a commentary on Schreber, "Psycho-Analytic Notes upon an Autobiographical Account of a

Case of Paranoia (Dementia Paranoides)," never had Schreber as a patient in analysis. He never even met the man (although he could have, because Schreber was still alive, and Freud knew that for a fact before writing the commentary). That Freud was not personally acquainted with Schreber did not, however, deter him from diagnosing Schreber as a paranoid schizophrenic and "psychoanalyzing" him in absentia. He interpreted not a person but a text, the *Memoirs* that Schreber had published in 1903 about his nervous illness. Freud asserts that paranoiacs "possess the peculiarity of betraying (in a distorted form, it is true) precisely those things which other neurotics keep hidden as a secret." As a result, he contends, "this is precisely a disorder in which a written report or a printed case history can take the place of a personal acquaintance with the patient" (*SE* 12: 9). This rationale for a departure from conventional analytic practice is, of course, a rationalization. Thus Freud converts an apparent liability into an asset.

I do not agree with Freud that paranoid schizophrenics are more transparent than "other neurotics." In my experience, they are no less secretive and no less effective in keeping things hidden – they are, in fact, notoriously suspicious and circumspect. It is arguable that the unconscious of paranoid schizophrenics is much more opaque and therefore much more inaccessible than that of other patients. In any event, to claim, as Freud does, that paranoia is a condition in which a text can conveniently replace a person seems to me a facile and dubious proposition. I believe that it would be preferable simply to concede that analyzing a text is very different from analyzing a person, that it is contrary to analytic practice, and that it is not at all unproblematic. Any study of Schreber's *Memoirs* – Freudian, Jungian, or otherwise – should include that caveat.

Who was Daniel Paul Schreber? A member of an eminent German family and the son of a famous father (a physician, educator, and social reformer who promoted health for the masses through physical exercise and gymnastics), Schreber pursued a career in the law. He was a candidate for the Reichstag in 1884. By 1893 he was president of a panel of judges at the supreme court of Saxony. He had a wife but no children (except, finally, for the adoption of a daughter in 1906).

Schreber suffered three periods of nervous illness. He was committed to and treated in asylums the first time from 1884 to 1885, then, after a respite of eight years, a second time from 1893 to 1902, and finally a third time from 1907 to 1911, the year he died.

In 1903 Schreber published *Denkwurdigkeiten eines Nervenkranken*, the title of which is translated into English as *Memoirs of My Nervous Illness*. (This is an account of his second period of nervous illness.) Zvi Lothane contends that a more accurate translation would be *The Great Thoughts of a Nervous Patient* (1992: 1–2). Whether the translation "great thoughts" is by the letter or not, it is at least consistent with the spirit of Schreber's grandiose opinion that, even if he were to "succeed only in arousing in other people a serious doubt whether it had not been granted me to throw a glance behind the dark veil which otherwise hides the beyond from the eyes of man, my work would certainly still belong to the most interesting ones ever written since the existence of the world" (1955: 289).

The book had two purposes. The first was to present the "great thoughts" that Schreber believed he had received by divine revelation. These were, Schreber said, "the most sublime ideas about God and the Order of the World" (1955: 80). The second was to question, as the subtitle of the book asks, "Under what premises can a person considered insane be detained in an asylum against his own declared will?" In the history of psychoanalysis, Schreber is remembered for neither of these two reasons. Instead, he is known as a schizophrenic who became paranoid because he experienced homosexual wishes, for that is how Freud characterized him.

Notwithstanding what Freud says, whether Schreber was, in any sense, a homosexual is quite problematic. (There is no evidence that Schreber ever engaged in any homosexual acts. As Freud interprets his *Memoirs*, Schreber was, in effect, a "latent" homosexual.) It is also controversial whether Schreber was a schizophrenic. He describes himself as suffering from melancholy, or depression. Although Schreber did exhibit delusional and hallucinatory symptoms, these symptoms do not restrictively and exhaustively define schizophrenia. For example, they also accompany what the American Psychiatric Association in the fourth edition of the *Diagnostic and Statistical Manual of Mental Disorders* [*DSM-IV*] (1994) calls schizoaffective disorders and mood disorders such as bipolar (or manic-depressive) disorder with psychotic features. Nevertheless, Schreber also satisfies the diagnostic criteria for paranoid schizophrenia (to the exclusion of a schizoaffective disorder or a mood disorder with psychotic features): at least two characteristic symptoms (in this case, persecutory and grandiose delusions and hallucinations), social/occupational dysfunction, duration of the disturbance for at least six months, exclusion of a substance/general medical condition, and non-relation to a pervasive developmental disorder. I believe that the evidence indicates that Schreber was a schizophrenic, but whether he was or not, he certainly had a plethora of psychotic symptoms – paranoid, delusional, and hallucinatory, as well as melancholic, or depressive.

In 1893 Schreber dreamed several times that he had relapsed into nervous illness. Each time on waking he was relieved to realize that this was not a fact but only a dream. Then while still in bed one morning – whether half asleep or fully awake, he could not recall – a quite curious idea occurred to him. "It was," he said, "the idea that it really must be rather pleasant to be a woman succumbing to intercourse" (1955: 63). This was Schreber's first thought of what he later called the experience of "female voluptuousness." It was also the beginning of his second period of nervous illness.

Everything that follows in Schreber's *Memoirs* is an elaboration of this moment, an attempt to make sense of that one idea. The thought of female voluptuousness was the beginning of Schreber's experience of his soul being murdered and his body being unmanned (that is, transformed into the body of a woman). Because the word "unmanning" does not accurately describe the ultimate purpose of his experience (at least as Schreber understood it), I prefer to say that he underwent a *womanning*.

Schreber believed that he was being transformed into a woman in order to be impregnated through transsexual intercourse with God and then delivered of a new world. Conception was to occur not the natural way but by supernatural contact between his nerves and God's nerves – or God's rays. What Schreber believed was being divinely revealed to him was that the old world was coming to an end, and that he had been selected to be the vehicle for a renewal of mankind through a miraculous irradiation. This was what he called his experience of the end of the world, a catastrophe of cosmic proportions that he compared to the Twilight of the Gods.

Freud alludes to the relation between Schreber's experience and "cosmic myths" (*SE* 12: 54). In this respect, Jung says that schizophrenics frequently have "terrifying dreams of cosmic catastrophes, of the end of the world and such things" (*CW* 3: 259, par. 559). As Anton T. Boisen describes his own schizophrenic experience, "there came surging in upon me with overpowering force a terrifying idea about a coming world catastrophe" (1936: 3). In a study that Boisen conducted of 173 patients in 1931, one-third of them reported "an impending world change of some sort" (1936: 33). He says that "ideas of death, of cosmic catastrophe, or of cosmic identification" were present in patients who suffered "the profounder panic reactions." Boisen notes that "ideas of cosmic catastrophe and cosmic identification" occur in clusters that also comprise "ideas of rebirth" (1936: 39).

Karl Jaspers says that the question is: "why is schizophrenia in its initial stages so often (though not in the majority of cases) a process of cosmic, religious or metaphysical revelation?" What impresses Jaspers are "these peculiar experiences of the end of the world or the creation of fresh ones, these spiritual revelations and this grim daily struggle in the transitional periods between health and collapse." These phenomena, he argues, cannot be understood "simply in terms of the psychosis which is sweeping the victim out of his familiar world, an objective symbol as it were of the radical, destructive event attacking him." To speak of the disintegration of "existence or the psyche," he says, is merely to speak in "analogies." According to Jaspers, "We observe that a new world has come into being and so far that is the only fact we have" (1946: 284). Like Jung and Boisen, he states that schizophrenic experience frequently entails a "cosmic experience" (1946: 294). He describes that experience as follows:

> The end of the world is here, the 'twilight of the gods'. A mighty revolution is at hand in which the patient plays the major role. He is the centre of all that is coming to pass. He has immense tasks to perform, vast powers. Fabulous distant influences, attractions and obstructions are at work. 'Everything' is always involved: all the peoples of the earth, all men, all the Gods, etc.
>
> (Jaspers 1946: 294–5)

In just this way, Schreber believed that he had been specially chosen to be the means to an end, the recreation of a new world after the destruction of an old world.

From the perspective of psychopathology, Schreber's experience was simply a delusion – an example of what Christian Scharfetter calls "complete personal and general catastrophe (cataclysmic, with the end of the world)" (1980: 168). In this respect, Medard Boss mentions a patient who feared immediate "annihilation of the world" (1963: 16). The patient experienced "intolerable dread of inchoate disaster and nameless cataclysmic doom." Boss quotes a therapist as having said to the patient that she had committed "the error of believing one's own neurotic egocentric world to be the sole possibility of existence and that when this shows signs of cracking, it means the crack of doom." The therapist then offered this interpretation to the patient: "For the real, essential being that is you, what is happening now is very far from being an end. It is merely a change taking place in its way of appearing" (1963: 20). According to Boss, the doomsday delusion was only apparently a cataclysmic end of the world. In actuality, it was an indication of the possibility of a profound existential change. In Schreber's case, cataclysm was the necessary precondition for the beginning of a world – nothing less than the renewal of mankind. Schreber had not only what Frank Kermode calls "the sense of an ending" (1967) but also the sense of a new beginning.

In a discussion of images of the end of the world, Robert J. Lifton contrasts theology as a "shared spiritual experience" with psychopathology as an "isolated delusional system" (1985: 162). He notes that millennial visions predict a world that will be annihilated and then renewed or revitalized. In schizophrenic delusional systems the world is also renewed or revitalized after it has been annihilated, but this "revitalization is radically literalized." Lifton says that "the 'thought-disorder' of schizophrenia" is nothing more nor less than "static literalization." In short, schizophrenics tend to be literalists. It is extremely difficult, often apparently impossible, for them to construe an image such as the "end of the world" metaphorically rather than literally. An image may indicate the possibility or the necessity of *something* coming to an "end," but what exactly that might be is the question. Lifton says that "when a millennial vision becomes so literalized that it is associated with a prediction of the actual end of the world on a particular day on the basis of biblical images or mathematical calculation applied to such images or whatever, we become aware of a disquieting border area of theology and psychopathology" (1985: 163).

The alternative to static literalization, whether in schizophrenic delusional systems or in millennial visions, would be what I would call *dynamic metaphorization*. The *image of the end of the world* would be *deliteralized* and understood as a metaphor for the *end of an image of the world*. Metaphorically, what would "end" would not be the world but only a certain image of it. Schizophrenics like Schreber, however, are virtually incapable of deliteralization. Psychopathologically, this incapacity is a failure of imagination – a failure to distinguish between world and image. In this respect, Eugen Bleuler (who coined the word "schizophrenia") says that schizophrenics often fail to understand an image as "a mere metaphor." He says that "they frequently think of these metaphors in a literal sense" (1950: 429).

James Hillman says: "Nothing is literal; all is metaphor" (1975: 175). This aphoristic remark is a deliberate exaggeration, for provocative effect. With this hyperbole, Hillman emphasizes just how important metaphor is in psychoanalysis. As I have previously said, "The unconscious is structured like a rhetoric – that is, it is structured in and through metaphors" (Adams 1997c: 36). The unconscious has a metaphorical structure not only in psychotic patients like Schreber but also in neurotic patients and in "normal" persons. What is exceptional about paranoid schizophrenics is that they tend to literalize the metaphors of the unconscious. They have little or no capacity for metaphorical understanding – and, as Hillman says, "Without metaphorical understanding, everything is only what it is and must be met on the simplest, most direct level" (1979a: 115). From this perspective, to make the unconscious conscious is to make the literal metaphorical. Thus I have said that "with metaphorical understanding, everything is different from and more than what it seems to be and can then be met on a more complex, indirect level" (Adams 1997c: 38). The tragedy of Schreber is that he was unable to understand his experience of the "end of the world" and of "womanning" metaphorically.

Delusion, revelation, or homosexual wish

From the perspective of psychopathology, the first part of Schreber's experience (his soul being murdered and his body being unmanned) was a delusion of persecution; the second part (being impregnated and being delivered) was a delusion of grandeur. Schreber anticipated that readers of his *Memoirs* might "be inclined at first to see nothing but a pathological offspring of my imagination in this" (1955: 33), but he hoped that they would ultimately see that the experience was not a delusion but the truth, the "great thoughts" that he had been miraculously vouchsafed. Freud says at the very end of his interpretation of Schreber's *Memoirs*: "It remains for the future to decide whether there is more delusion in my theory than I should like to admit, or whether there is more truth in Schreber's delusion than other people are as yet prepared to believe" (*SE* 12: 79).

As for Schreber, he believed that he had "come infinitely closer to the truth than human beings who have not received divine revelation" (1955: 41). He expected that "the spread of my religious ideas and the weight of proof of their truth will lead to a fundamental revolution in mankind's religious views unequalled in history" (1955: 215). In this respect, Jaspers argues that it is an error to reduce the religious experience of schizophrenics to a psychopathological phenomenon, as if it were nothing more than a mere symptom:

> The shattering of the self is said to be mirrored in the schizophrenic experience of the end of the world. This is not sufficiently explicit. Experiencing the end of the world and all that this implies involves a deep religious experience – of a symbolic truth that has served human existence for thousands of years. We have to regard this experience as such and not merely as some perverted psychological or psychopathological phenomenon if we really want to under-

stand it. Religious experience remains what it is, whether it occurs in saint or psychotic or whether the person in whom it occurs is both at once.

(Jaspers 1946: 108)

Likewise, Schreber did not want readers to dismiss his experience – his divine revelation of religious truth – as mere delusion, sheer fantasy, the figment of a morbid imagination.

This, of course, is exactly what Freud did. He pathologized what he called Schreber's "theologico-psychological system" (*SE* 12: 21). Freud used the case to illustrate his theory of paranoid schizophrenia as a defense against a homosexual wish. In effect, he applied his method of dream interpretation to Schreber's *Memoirs*. Freud believed that every dream, without exception, was "*a (disguised) fulfilment of a (suppressed or repressed) wish*" (*SE* 4: 160). He distinguished between what he called the "manifest content" and the "latent content" of the dream. The manifest content comprised the "dream elements" (or dream images); the latent content, the unconscious "dream thoughts." The interpretation of the dream reduced the manifest dream elements to the latent dream thoughts – and ultimately to the unconscious wish that motivated the formation of the dream. According to Freud, this was an instinctual, usually sexual wish. Because the wish had been repressed, it had to be disguised in order to be fulfilled in the dream.

Freud interpreted Schreber's experience as a fantasy that, like a dream, was a disguised fulfillment of a repressed wish – in this case, a repressed homosexual wish. He asserted that the cause of Schreber's nervous illness was "the appearance in him of a feminine (that is, a passive homosexual) wishful phantasy" (*SE* 12: 47). According to Freud, behind Schreber's fantasy of having transsexual intercourse with God was a wish to have homosexual intercourse with his psychiatrist and, behind that, a wish to have homosexual intercourse with his father. Being unmanned (or transformed into a woman) was equivalent to being castrated. As Freud wrote in a letter to Jung, the "father complex" and the "castration complex" were behind the fantasy (Freud and Jung 1974: 368–9). He concluded: "The enormous significance of homosexuality for paranoia is confirmed by the central emasculation fantasy, etc. etc." (Freud and Jung 1974: 369).

For Freud, Schreber's experience was a sexual (or homosexual) fantasy on the level of what Jung eventually called the "personal unconscious" – that is, on the level of complexes (in this case, the Oedipus complex). In another letter to Jung, Freud wrote that although he had not "even read half the book," he had already "fathomed the secret," which was that Schreber's fantasy was "easily reduced to its nuclear complex" (Freud and Jung 1974: 358). Because Schreber's wish to have homosexual intercourse with his father was unthinkable, it was repressed and disguised as a wish for homosexual intercourse with his psychiatrist. That wish, however, even though displaced, was also unthinkable and, in turn, was repressed and disguised as a fantasy of transsexual intercourse with God. Thus what was consciously unthinkable became thinkable unconsciously: the wish that was repressed could be fulfilled but only if it was disguised as a fantasy of divine revelation.

Since Freud, many studies of Schreber's *Memoirs* have been published. Among them are studies in psychobiography, literary criticism, philosophy, and cultural and intellectual history. The following are representative:

1   *Psychobiography.* William G. Niederland (1974) and Morton Schatzman (1973) argue that, etiologically, Schreber's fantasy is a distortion of memories of traumatic events in his childhood, that his delusion of persecution as an adult is a psychopathological derivative of and allusion to his experience of actual persecution as a child by his father. They depict Schreber's father as a child rearing fanatic who advocated absolute obedience, strict discipline, and corporal punishment and invented iron mechanical devices to restrain the body and head in order to ensure rigidly perfect posture both while waking and sleeping. Lothane (1992) rebuts this characterization as a caricature and a calumny. He argues that Schreber's father was not a torturer who applied sadistic gadgets to his son but a responsible, humane advocate of progressive orthopedic and pedagogic practices – and that if anyone persecuted Schreber, it was his psychiatrist and his asylum attendants.
2   *Literary criticism.* C. Barry Chabot (1982) argues that Freud's commentary on Schreber's *Memoirs* is a model of interpretative discourse for the hermeneutic disciplines and for reciprocal relations between psychoanalysis and literary criticism.
3   *Philosophy.* Louis A. Sass (1994) argues that Schreber's schizophrenic delusion is a self-referential, reflexive, and private experience of the sort that figures so prominently as a strictly philosophical issue in Wittgenstein's discussion of solipsism.
4   *Cultural and intellectual history.* Eric L. Santner (1996) argues that Schreber's *Memoirs* is an exemplary document in the cultural and intellectual history of modernity and that his delusion is an alternative to twentieth-century totalitarian ideology.

These studies are all valuable contributions to a more complete interpretation of Schreber's experience. It is both notable and curious, however, that Jung never wrote an interpretation of Schreber's *Memoirs*; nor, subsequently, have Jungians written much on the case.

Two Jungians, Alan Edwards and James Hillman, have commented on Schreber's experience. Edwards asserts that Schreber's paranoid delusion was a "disorder of the deintegrative–reintegrative processes," a regressive attempt in the second half of life to reconstitute the whole of the psyche from parts, or "archetypal self-objects" – an ultimately futile effort at compensation for dissociation in the first half of life (1989: 235). In order to account for Schreber's unmanning, or transformation into a woman, Edwards cites what Jung calls the "demon-woman of mythology." According to Jung, this is the anima, the contrasexual archetypal image of the feminine, "the woman in the man, who unexpectedly turns up during the second half of life and tries to effect a forcible change of personality." This

change of personality, Jung says, "consists in a partial feminization of the man."
Jung remarks: "A perfect example of this type of psychology is Schreber's account
of his own psychosis, *Memoirs of My Nervous Illness*" (*CW* 5: 300, par. 458).
(Schreber, however, believes that he is not partly feminine but wholly female, that
his man's body has been literally transformed into a woman's body.) Hillman
(1988) contends that Freud's sexualizing of this paranoid delusion is a defense
against Schreber's theologizing of a divine revelation. For Hillman, Schreber's
schizophrenic experience is one of the varieties of religious experience; it is an
apocalyptic prophecy, an eschatology. Neither Edwards nor Hillman, however,
formulates a systematic, comprehensive, Jungian interpretation of Schreber's
Memoirs.

What is so peculiar about the dearth of Jungian interpretations is that it was
Jung, not Freud, who initially recognized the unique value of Schreber's autobiographical account of his nervous illness. Jung first mentioned the case in 1907 in
The Psychology of Dementia Praecox, his study of schizophrenia. It was Jung in
fact who in 1910 drew Schreber's *Memoirs* to Freud's attention. After Freud
obtained a copy of the book, he wrote to Jung that he planned to read it on holiday.
He said that Schreber "ought to have been made a professor of psychiatry and
director of a mental hospital" (Freud and Jung 1974: 311). Later, Jung wrote to
Freud that he "was touched and overjoyed to learn how much you appreciate the
greatness of Schreber's mind." The book, he said, "deserves the place of honour in
every psychiatric library" (Freud and Jung 1974: 356). Freud replied: "I share your
enthusiasm for Schreber; it is a kind of revelation." For Freud, however, what was
revealed was not the "divine," as with Schreber, but the *unconscious*. Although so
far Freud had read less than half the book, he believed that after only one more
reading "I may be able to resolve all the intriguing fantasies." He acknowledged
that "I didn't quite succeed the first time" (Freud and Jung 1974: 358). Perhaps on
just a second reading, Freud would have the ability to interpret everything fantastic in Schreber's *Memoirs*.

Shortly thereafter, Freud began to write his interpretation. By 1911 it was typeset and ready to be published in a journal of which Jung was the editor. Jung proof-
read the interpretation and then wrote to Freud: "Only now that I have the galleys
can I enjoy your Schreber. It is not only uproariously funny but brilliantly written
as well." Although Jung expressed a high opinion of the interpretation, he con-
fessed to Freud that he also felt envious that he had not written his own interpretation of Schreber's *Memoirs* first. "If I were an altruist I would now be saying how
glad I am that you have taken Schreber under your wing and shown psychiatry
what treasures are heaped up there," Jung said. "But, as it is, I must content myself
with the invidious role of wishing I had got in first, though that's not much of a
consolation" (Freud and Jung 1974: 407).

The irony was that Jung had in fact got in first but now rued the day that he had
shared such a trove of valuable material with Freud, who had immediately seized
the opportunity to interpret it. By 1952, when *Symbols of Transformation*, the
revised version of *Transformations and Symbols of the Libido*, was published,

Jung expressed a different and much lower opinion of Freud's interpretation. He said: "This case was written up at the time by Freud in a very unsatisfactory way after I had drawn his attention to the book" (*CW* 5: 300, par. 458n.).

The redefinition of libido

Although Jung never wrote his own interpretation of Schreber's *Memoirs*, Freud's interpretation played a decisive role in his *Transformations and Symbols of the Libido*, the book whose publication in 1911–12 was a factor in the decision by Freud and Jung in 1914 to end all personal and professional relations. Freud's cases in his private practice in Vienna were hysterics; Jung's cases at the Burgholzli Hospital in Zurich were schizophrenics. In deference to Freud, Jung had accepted his explanation of the etiology of hysteria as sexual, but he had expressed reservations about his extension of that sexual etiology to schizophrenia. The issue for Jung was how to define libido. Should it be defined as sexual energy in particular, as Freud had defined it? Was all energy *libido sexualis*? By 1911 Jung concluded that libido should be redefined as psychic energy in general, only one manifestation of which was sexual energy.

Perhaps the split between Freud and Jung, between Freudians and Jungians, was inevitable. It may be that it was just a matter of time before certain irreconcilable theoretical differences emerged. It is also possible, however, that had Schreber not published his *Memoirs* and Freud not interpreted the book, Freud and Jung would have remained friends and colleagues. Although Jung had been consistently skeptical that the etiology of schizophrenia was sexual, it was the publication of Freud's interpretation of Schreber's *Memoirs* – and, in particular, one especially provocative passage in the book – that finally encouraged him to challenge that theory and, as a consequence, to redefine libido.

That passage provided Jung with all the opportunity he needed: he quoted the passage at length and employed it as a point of departure for his redefinition of libido. In that passage Freud himself raised the question of whether a loss of libido, defined as a loss of sexual interest, was a sufficient explanation for what both he and Jung believed was a loss of general interest in external reality by paranoid schizophrenics. (Paranoid schizophrenics might seem to exhibit no loss of interest in external reality but, quite to the contrary, an especially keen interest in it. This interest is, however, an excessively suspicious attention only to selective, quite particular aspects of external reality in an effort to confirm a delusion *about* external reality. In that sense, paranoid schizophrenics have an interest in external reality only to the extent that it serves as an apparent confirmation of the internal reality that so preoccupies them.)

Should we, Freud wondered, simply suppose that the withdrawal "of the libido from the external world would be an effective enough agent to account for the 'end of the world'?" (*SE* 12: 73). He said that one possible answer to this question would be "to assume that what we call libidinal cathexis (that is, interest emanating from erotic sources) coincides with interest in general" (*SE* 12: 74). That is,

Freud himself asked whether libido ought to be redefined as psychic energy in general. Suddenly he was expressing the very doubt that all along had so vexed Jung. As a paranoid schizophrenic, Schreber had withdrawn his interest from the external world and invested it in his internal world, what Freud and Jung called his fantasy or his delusion. Was this dynamic of withdrawal and investment the result of a loss of sexual interest, or was it the result of a loss of general interest?

Freud conceded that in the current state of knowledge this was a problem "which we are still quite helpless and incompetent to solve." The question could be answered, he said, "if we could start out from some well-grounded theory of instincts," but he admitted that "in fact we have nothing of the kind at our disposal." At present the theory of the instincts comprised "only hypotheses, which we have taken up – and are quite ready to drop again – in order to help us to find our bearings in the chaos of the obscurer processes of the mind" (*SE* 12: 74). Freud explicitly acknowledged that there was insufficient evidence for a conclusive answer. All that was available were surmises, which he said he was perfectly prepared to abandon.

Freud represented himself not as a dogmatist but as a scientist, willing and able to entertain what Karl R. Popper (1962) calls refutations of conjectures and to revise his theory accordingly. In spite of his doubt, Freud ultimately expressed a definite preference for an explanation consistent with his theory of sexual etiology. Although it was possible that the loss of interest in external reality in paranoid schizophrenics was the result of a loss of general interest, rather than a loss of libido defined exclusively as sexual interest, it seemed to Freud "far more probable that the paranoic's altered relation to the world is to be explained entirely or in the main by the loss of his libidinal interest" – that is, by the loss of his sexual interest (*SE* 12: 75).

To Jung, Freud seemed to have invited others, himself included, to engage in a theoretical debate about the definition of libido, especially as it applied to schizophrenia, or dementia praecox. In a letter to Freud in 1911, while writing *Transformations and Symbols of the Libido*, Jung said:

> As for the libido problem, I must confess that your remark in the Schreber analysis, p. 65, 3, has set up booming reverberations. This remark, or rather the doubt expressed therein, has resuscitated all the difficulties that have beset me throughout the years in my attempt to apply the libido theory to Dem. praec. The loss of the reality function in D. pr. cannot be reduced to repression of libido (defined as sexual hunger). Not by me, at any rate. Your doubt shows me that in your eyes as well the problem cannot be solved in this way.
>
> (Freud and Jung 1974: 471)

Freud's doubt had breathed new life into what had never really been a dead issue for Jung.

Subsequently, in *Transformations and Symbols of the Libido*, Jung asserted that "Freud, as well as myself, saw the need of widening the conception of libido." It was Freud's interpretation of Schreber's *Memoirs* that "seemed to compel Freud to enlarge the earlier limits of the conception" (*CW* B: 126, par. 219). Jung proceeded to argue that in the schizophrenic "not only the erotic interest but the interest in general has disappeared" (*CW* B: 127, par. 220). He noted that in *The Psychology of Dementia Praecox* he had already employed the concept "psychic energy" because he had been unable to base the etiology of schizophrenia on a loss of libido defined as sexual energy. The loss of reality in schizophrenia, he maintained, was "much more than one could write down to the account of sexuality in a strict sense." Jung declared in no uncertain terms: "The sexual character of this must be disputed absolutely, for reality is not understood to be a sexual function" (*CW* B: 128, par. 221). In contrast to Freud, he contended that schizophrenia "produces a loss of reality which cannot be explained by the deficiency of the libido defined in this narrow sense" (*CW* B: 129, par. 221). He then said that it was to him an "especial satisfaction that our teacher" – by whom he meant Freud – "was forced to doubt the applicability of the conception of libido held by him at that time" (*CW* B: 129, par. 222).

It did not take Freud long to protest that Jung had misrepresented his position. In 1914, in "On Narcissism," he said that Jung's desexualization of the libido theory was "to say the least of it, premature." The evidence for such a conclusion was "scanty." Freud noted that in *Transformations and Symbols of the Libido* Jung had appealed "to an admission of my own that I myself have been obliged, owing to the difficulties of the Schreber analysis, to extend the concept of libido (that is, to give up its sexual content) and to identify libido with psychical interest in general." This was simply an "erroneous interpretation" of what Freud had said in his interpretation of Schreber's *Memoirs*. "I have never," Freud stated emphatically, "made any such retraction of the libido theory" (*SE* 14: 80). Freud had expressed a doubt, but he had immediately declared that he believed that it was more probable that in paranoid schizophrenia the libido, defined as sexual interest, had been withdrawn from external reality only to be invested in the ego, which had then become grandiosely inflated. The paranoid schizophrenic was, in effect, a psychotic narcissist.

"Another argument of Jung's, namely, that we cannot suppose that the withdrawal of libido is in itself enough to bring about the loss of the normal function of reality," Freud complained, "is no argument but a dictum" (*SE* 14: 80). It was mere question-begging. Freud noted that Jung himself in 1913, in *The Theory of Psychoanalysis*, had expressed his own doubt about whether it was necessary to redefine libido as psychic interest in general. Jung had said: "Another thing to be considered – as Freud also pointed out in his work on the Schreber case – is that the introversion of sexual libido leads to an investment of the ego which might conceivably produce that effect of loss of reality. It is indeed tempting to explain the psychology of the loss in this way" (*CW* 4: 121, par. 276). Jung, however, resisted this temptation and insisted instead that schizophrenia "shows a loss of reality which cannot be explained solely by the loss of erotic interest" (*CW* 4: 122, par. 277). Both Freud and Jung doubted their respective positions but, in the end, affirmed them against the opposition of the other. As Jung said: "I think there is nothing for it but to abandon the sexual definition of libido" (*CW* 4: 118, par. 269).

In the history of psychoanalysis, Jung was not the only one to redefine libido. Wilhelm Reich also widened the concept – not just to psychic energy but to cosmic energy comparable to the irradiation that Schreber imagined as a divine emanation. The sexual energy in the organism, Reich concluded, was "bio-electrical energy," which was identical with what he called the "orgone energy" in the universe (1948: 300). Orgone energy even had a color – "*blue* or bluish gray" – which Reich believed he could render visible under experimental conditions in the laboratory. There were "three different kinds of radiation" in orgone energy: "bluish gray," "deep blue-violet," and "whitish" (1948: 302). In an effort to concentrate and collect cosmic energy from the atmosphere, Reich invented an apparatus, the orgone energy accumulator. W. Edward Mann and Edward Hoffman describe the orgone energy accumulator as "a rectangular box about 5 feet by 2½ feet by 2½ feet in size, made of alternating layers of sheet metal and an organic substance such as wood" (1980: 158).

Reich attempted "to understand the *cosmic* phantasies of the schizophrenic in terms of the functions of a truly *cosmic* orgone energy which governs his organism" (1945: 434). According to Reich, "The functions which appear in the schizophrenic, if only one learns to read them accurately, are COSMIC FUNCTIONS, that is, functions of the cosmic orgone energy within the organism in undisguised form" (1945: 449). Symptoms develop when the schizophrenic either intellectually realizes or directly experiences that organismic energy is identical with "*cosmic (atmospheric) orgone energy.*" For the schizophrenic, "the awareness of these deep functions is great and overwhelming." The schizophrenic, Reich said, "is not equipped or is too split up to accept and to carry the great experience of this identity of functions inside and outside the organism" (1945: 450).

Schreber's experience of divine rays, Freud declared, was "in reality nothing else than a concrete representation and external projection of libidinal cathexes" (*SE* 12: 78). The same could be said of Reich's theory of cosmic rays. Like Schreber, Reich eventually became a paranoid schizophrenic and suffered delusions of persecution and grandeur. In 1955, the Food and Drug Administration obtained a court order to destroy all of Reich's orgone energy accumulators and all of the Orgone Institute Press's publications that ostensibly advertised quack medical cures. Reich died of a heart attack in prison two years later.

The interpretation of schizophrenia

Jung put Schreber's *Memoirs* to a number of other uses besides the redefinition of libido. For example, in 1914 in "On Psychological Understanding" he used it to discuss the distinction between what he called the "reductive" and the "constructive" methods of interpretation. Jung noted that in order to analyze Schreber's delusional system Freud had, "in a very ingenious manner," reduced Schreber's experience to his psychobiographical relation with his father (*CW* 3: 179, par.

389). According to Jung, Freud's application of the reductive method "did not, however, furnish such enlightening results in regard to the rich and surprising symbolism" in Schreber's and other schizophrenics' delusional systems (*CW* 3: 179–80, par. 389). Jung concluded that the reductive method "does not altogether do justice to the almost overpowering profusion of fantastic symbolization" in schizophrenia, "illuminating though it may be in other respects" (*CW* 3: 180, par. 390).

The problem was that the reductive method derived extremely complex delusional systems from simpler components (causes in the past). In contrast, the constructive method elaborated them into even more complex components (purposes in the future). In short, the reductive method was causal and retrospective; the constructive method, purposive and prospective. Thus a constructive interpretation of Schreber's delusional system would require an answer to the question: "What is the goal the patient tried to reach through the creation of his system?" (*CW* 3: 180, par. 408). The delusional systems of schizophrenics are, Jung said, "aiming at something" (*CW* 3: 186, par. 410).

Schizophrenics like Schreber amassed as evidence "an immense amount of comparative material," Jung said, in an attempt to prove the truth of their delusional systems (*CW* 3: 186, par. 410). The constructive method was also a comparative method. It elaborated delusional systems into "*typical* components." No delusional system was "absolutely unique." Every delusional system was to a certain extent typical. By comparing delusional systems to "many systems" – by which Jung meant many mythological systems – "the typical formations can be discovered" (*CW* 3: 187, par. 413). These typical components or typical formations were what Jung was ultimately to call "archetypes," and this comparative method was what he was to call "amplification." In contrast to the Vienna school, the Zurich school had discovered in delusional systems "countless typical formations" that demonstrated parallels with "mythological formations." According to Jung, "These parallels have proved to be a new and exceedingly valuable source for the comparative study of delusional systems." Delusional formations could be compared to mythological formations because "both are fantasy-structures which, like all such products, are based essentially on the activity of the unconscious" (*CW* 3: 188, par. 414). The implication was that the typicality of these delusional and mythological fantasy-structures was a result of the universality of the unconscious, or of what Jung was eventually to call the "collective unconscious." As an alternative to the reductive method, the constructive method interpreted the symbolism of the schizophrenic unconscious by a purposive, prospective, comparative method that discovered just how typical (or archetypal) the delusional system was.

Jung also used Schreber's *Memoirs* to discuss the distinction between the external, objective world and the internal, subjective world of the schizophrenic. According to Jung, the problem with schizophrenics like Schreber was a difficulty in an objective adaptation to the external world. Instead, they created an internal world – a *Weltanschauung*, or world-view – to which they were only subjectively adapted. This subjective adaptation to an internal world was an attempt by schizophrenics to prepare for an eventual objective adaptation to the external world. Unfortunately, in all too many cases this transitional effort ultimately proved to be an exercise in utter futility. Because schizophrenics could not think objectively and understand themselves, they remained incorrigibly and uncommunicatively attached to the internal world that they had subjectively created as a substitute for the external world. Thus Jung said:

> Closer study of Schreber's or any similar case will show that these patients are consumed by a desire to create a new world-system, or what we call a *Weltanschauung*, often of the most bizarre kind. Their aim is obviously to create a system that will enable them to assimilate unknown psychic phenomena and so adapt themselves to their own world. This is a purely subjective adaptation at first, but it is a necessary transition stage on the way to adapting the personality to the world in general. Only, the patient remains stuck in this stage and substitutes his subjective formulation for the real world – which is precisely why he remains ill. He cannot free himself from his subjectivism and therefore does not establish any connection with objective thinking and with human society. He does not gain any real understanding of himself because he understands himself merely subjectively, and this precludes intelligible communication.
>
> (*CW* 3: 189, par. 416)

In this respect, the mode of analysis that Jung practiced at the Burgholzli Hospital was an effort to help schizophrenics understand themselves objectively and detach themselves from the internal world that they had subjectively created and substituted for the external world. Schreber, of course, was neither Jung's, Freud's, nor any other psychoanalyst's patient but a psychiatrist's patient. He was committed to an asylum and treated by other methods, which were ultimately ineffective. He never had an opportunity to experience psychotherapy of the unconscious.

Jung had previously used Schreber's experience as an example of how schizophrenics replaced the external world with an internal world. In *Transformations and Symbols of the Libido* he called this substitute not just subjective but archaic. By "archaic," Jung meant what he was eventually to call "archetypal." He noted that in schizophrenia "the phantastic substitution products which take the place of the disturbed function of reality bear unmistakable traces of archaic thought" (*CW* B: 135–6, par. 233). He contrasted hysteria and its sexual etiology with schizophrenia. In hysteria, he said, "where merely a part of the *immediate sexual* libido is taken away from reality by the specific sexual repression, the substituted product is a phantasy of individual origin and significance." That is, fantasy in hysteria was at the level of the repressed, sexual, personal unconscious. In schizophrenia, however, "a portion of the general human function of reality organized since antiquity has broken off," with the result that it "can be replaced only by a generally valid archaic surrogate" (*CW* B: 136, par. 233). That is, fantasy in schizophrenia was at the level of the dissociated, archaic (or archetypal), collective unconscious.

In effect, according to Jung, schizophrenic experiences like Schreber's should not be interpreted personally and sexually but collectively and archetypally.

In *The Theory of Psychoanalysis* Jung cited Schreber's experience as an example of what he was eventually to call the "compensatory function" of the unconscious. He said that the schizophrenic's "lack of adaptation to reality is compensated by a progressive increase in the creation of fantasies, which goes so far that the dream world becomes more real for the patient than external reality." Schreber's experience was a graphic illustration of this process. According to Jung, "Schreber found an excellent figurative description for this phenomenon in his delusion about the 'end of the world.'" He had portrayed "the loss of reality in a very concrete way." It was simple, Jung said, to explain the process dynamically. Libido, defined as psychic energy or general interest, withdrew "more and more from the external world into the inner world of fantasy," where it then created, "as a substitute for the lost world, a so-called reality equivalent" (*CW* 4: 120, par. 272). Such a reality equivalent, or fantasy world, was an attempt at compensation by the unconscious but one that went tragically awry when it completely dominated and permanently supplanted the real world, as it had done in Schreber's case.

One other comment by Jung in 1934 in "Archetypes of the Collective Unconscious" specifically addressed Schreber's experience of unmanning, or being transformed into a woman. The emergence of archetypal images from the unconscious, Jung said, "is by no means a question of fictitious dangers but of very real risks upon which the fate of a whole life may depend." The archetypal images posed such a threat because they exerted a "fascinating influence." It was even possible that the archetypal images, "which are endowed with a certain autonomy anyway on account of their natural numinosity, will escape from conscious control altogether and become completely independent, thus producing the phenomena of possession." By "possession," Jung meant compulsive, unconscious identification with an archetypal image – such as the "anima," the contrasexual, archetypal image of the feminine in a man. Jung said: "In the case of anima-possession, for instance, the patient will want to change himself into a woman through self-castration, or he is afraid that something of the sort will be done to him by force. The best-known example of this is Schreber's *Memoirs of My Nervous Illness*" (*CW* 9,1: 39, par. 82). Although Jung did not say, as Freud had, that paranoid schizophrenics experienced a problem with homosexual identity, he did say that Schreber had experienced a problem with contrasexual identity, and like Freud, he called Schreber's unmanning a castration.

These remarks on the constructive method, symbolism, the purposive and prospective functions, typical delusional formations and mythological formations, adaptation, subjective, archaic, or archetypal substitutes, fantasy, the end of the world, the compensatory function, and anima-possession are indicative of how Jung would have proceeded to interpret Schreber's *Memoirs* had he done so. They constitute the methods that he would have employed, the concepts that he would have applied, and the issues that he would have emphasized. As such, they schematize what a Jungian interpretation of Schreber's *Memoirs* might comprise.

Mythopoesis and metabiography

When Freud attempted to interpret Schreber's *Memoirs*, Jung finally considered the analysis to be too reductive and, as he said, "very unsatisfactory." What alternative possibility did Jung represent? The Vienna school led by Freud specialized in the repressed, sexual, personal forms and contents of the hysterical unconscious. In contrast, the Zurich school led by Jung concentrated on the dissociated, archetypal, collective forms and contents of the schizophrenic unconscious. The distinctive contribution of Jung and the Zurich school was to elaborate, by the comparative method, parallels between delusions and myths.

In 1914, in "The History of the Psycho-Analytic Movement," Freud said that this "elaboration (which, though open to criticism, was none the less very interesting) at the hands of Jung" was an attempt at a correlation between nervous illnesses and "mythological phantasies" (*SE* 14: 36). In "On Narcissism," Freud noted that the researches of the Zurich school had shown in schizophrenia "the similarity of the phantasies that occur in it to popular myths" (*SE* 14: 81). In effect, the Zurich school was the "mythological school."

Previously, in his interpretation of Schreber's *Memoirs* Freud had said that "Jung had excellent grounds for his assertion that the mythopoeic forces of mankind are not extinct, but that to this very day they give rise in the neuroses to the same psychical products as in the remotest past ages" (*SE* 12: 82). Harry Schlochower defines mythopoesis by recourse to etymology: "Mytho-*poesis* (from the Greek *poiein*, meaning to make, to create) *re*-creates the ancient stories" (1970: 15). Mythopoeis is, in a word, "myth-making." When Freud said that Jung had demonstrated that "the mythopoeic forces of mankind" still survive, he meant that Jung had proved that one of the essential functions of the unconscious, especially in schizophrenics, was to make myths. This is what I call the *mythological unconscious* (Adams 2001).

When Jung first began to experiment with the technique that he was eventually to call "active imagination," he encountered "the same psychic material which is the stuff of psychosis and is found in the insane." Although what he discovered was "the fund of unconscious images which fatally confuse the mental patient," Jung emphasized that it was "also the matrix of a mythopoeic imagination which has vanished from our rational age" (1963: 188). For Jung, the Age of Reason had superseded the Age of Myth, with the result that the myth-making imagination had all but disappeared except in schizophrenics like Schreber.

In a discussion of Schreber's experience, Michael Eigen notes that "Jung emphasized parallels between psychotic imagery and mythology that could not simply be understood in terms of repressed sexual conflicts" (1986: 252). Then Eigen mentions the paucity of Jungian interpretations of Schreber's *Memoirs*: "It is an oddity in the history of the depth psychologies that Jungians did not explore the Schreber case to the extent Freudians did. Schreber's basic movement from a male position to death and rebirth through the feminine seems made for Jungian analysis" (1986: 254).

If the Schreber case is indeed made for Jungian analysis, then what would such an interpretation entail? It would, as Eigen indicates, be an inquiry into the parallels between mythology and Schreber's own imagery. It would be an interpretation of the mythopoeic, or myth-making, function of Schreber's unconscious. Schreber may be one of those "sick souls" who William James says "must be twice-born in order to be happy" (1929: 163), but, if so, the process of death and rebirth does not occur for him in the most prevalent way. Contrary to what Eigen says, Schreber's experience is not a movement in which he himself dies and is then reborn through the *feminine*. Rather, by being unmanned (or being transformed into a woman) Schreber himself becomes a *female* through which a world that has been destroyed can be recreated. In short, Schreber's mythopoeic experience is not so much an example of what John Weir Perry calls "death and rebirth fantasies" as it is an example of what he calls "world destruction and recreation fantasies" (1976: 8) – or what he calls the "world catastrophe motif" (1987: 31).

Freud emphasizes two aspects of Schreber's experience: the "*assumption of the role of Redeemer*" and the "*transformation into a woman.*" According to Freud, "The Redeemer delusion is a phantasy that is familiar to us through the frequency with which it forms the nucleus of religious paranoia." In contrast, the precondition of unmanning, "which makes the redemption dependent upon the man being previously transformed into a woman, is unusual and in itself bewildering, since it shows such a wide divergence from the historical myth which the patient's phantasy is setting out to reproduce" (*SE* 12: 18). As Freud says, Schreber's nervous illness does not assume "the everyday form of Redeemer phantasy, in which the patient believes he is the son of God, destined to save the world from its misery or from the destruction that is threatening it, and so on" (*SE* 12: 28). He notes that Schreber "took up a feminine attitude towards God." Schreber was not God's son but "God's wife" (*SE* 12: 32). It is not a dead Schreber who is reborn through the feminine but a destroyed world that is recreated through him – or "her." The contrast between a death and rebirth fantasy and a world destruction and recreation fantasy is not a distinction without a difference; nor is it a mere quibble. Schreber does not imagine that he himself is being reborn. He believes that he is being transformed into a woman in order to give birth – that is, in order for a destroyed or dead world mythically to be recreated or "reborn" from his female body.

Only in one sense is Schreber's recreation a rebirth. In "Concerning Rebirth," Jung describes ten different types of rebirth. Schreber's experience might seem to be an example of the type that Jung calls *immediate experience* – that is, "spontaneous, ecstatic, or visionary experience" (*CW* 9,1: 118, par. 210). It is, however, more an example of the type that he calls *change of internal structure*, which he compares to "the phenomenon of possession." Jung says that in such cases "some content, an idea or a part of the personality, obtains mastery of the individual for one reason or another." The result is "peculiar convictions, idiosyncrasies, stubborn plans, and so forth," which tend to be utterly incorrigible. Jung says that there is no "hard and fast line of demarcation between possession and paranoia" (*CW* 9, 1: 122, par. 220). He defines possession as the unconscious identification of the ego with another aspect of the psyche. For instance, change of internal structure can be the consequence of identification with, or possession by, the anima, "in man the feminine traits" (*CW* 9,1: 124, par. 223). In such a state, the ego is unconsciously identified with the anima rather than consciously – and therefore effectively – related to it.

Schreber experiences what Jung calls a change of internal structure as a catastrophe, the end of the world. If this external catastrophe is a projection of Schreber's internal catastrophe, then in a certain sense he experiences the destruction of his own "world" as a "death," and the attempt at recreation an effort at "rebirth." In effect, Schreber displaces his own death and the possibility of his own rebirth onto the destruction and recreation of the world. Because Schreber is identified with the anima, he believes that he is literally being transformed into a woman, so that the world that has died can be reborn through him. For Schreber to be possessed by the anima is for him to be unmanned, or "womanned," in order for mankind to be renewed. In Schreber's experience the change of internal structure is a literalization of the feminine as the female. The anima, or soul, literally becomes the body of Schreber – at least as he imagines it.

Schizophrenics like Schreber "mythologize" their changes of internal structure. The myths that they make are among those that Henry A. Murray says "are chiefly concerned with internal, or endopsychic, occurrences or states." This mythopoeic process results in "*intrapsychic individual* myths," which deal with "the invisible but intimately experienced transformations of the psyche, self, or personality" (1960: 332). In just this way, Schreber's individual intrapsychic myth is an imaginative attempt to document "consequential subjective experiences, states of being or becoming, mutations of emotion and evaluation, interior conflicts and their resolutions" (1960: 332–3). Schreber's *Memoirs* is not just an exercise in autobiography but an example of what Murray calls "metabiography of an individual" (1960: 334).

In this respect, Schreber's mythopoeic account of his nervous illness is comparable to Jung's own memoirs, *Memories, Dreams, Reflections*, in which Jung recounts his own "personal myth" (1963: 3). Jung means that the life of a person may (and often does) have a mythic dimension. In this idiosyncratic sense, "myth" is not only the expression of a culture but also the expression of an individual who "makes" a personal myth and lives it.

When intrapsychic individual myths are cogent enough to gain pervasive acceptance, they have an opportunity to become what I would call *interpersonal cultural* myths. In such instances, a culture adopts the myth of an individual. For individually made myths to become culturally accepted myths, Murray says that they "are more likely to be formed unconsciously by slow degrees in many contemporary minds" (rather than in just one mind, as with Schreber). These myths "must wait for their acceptance and propagation until the psyches of others are prepared for their reception" (1960: 344). Then a personal myth may become a collective myth, what Murray calls a "vital" myth. He says that "the creative imaginations which participate in the formation of a *vital* myth must be those of people

– often alienated and withdrawn people – who have *experienced* in their 'depths' and on their own pulses, one or more of the unsolved critical situations with which humanity at large or members of their own society are confronted" (1960: 344–5). Murray concludes that "suffering in 'representative men' may be one of the necessary determinants of an adequate response to challenge" (1960: 345).

The term "representative men" is a reference to Ralph Waldo Emerson's *Representative Men*. In that book Emerson discusses what he calls the "uses of great men." He includes chapters on six representative men: Plato, the philosopher; Swedenborg, the mystic; Montaigne, the skeptic; Shakespeare, the poet; Napoleon, the man of the world; and Goethe, the writer. "Other men," Emerson says, "are lenses through which we read our own minds" (1987: 4). That is why biographies of great men are useful. In this respect, Schreber's *Memoirs* would be a lens for the mind-reading of our suffering selves, and the representative man would be Schreber, the psychotic – or perhaps Schreber, the prophet.

Schreber's alienation and withdrawal from external reality and his deep experience of internal reality constituted what Jung calls a "confrontation with the unconscious" (1963: 178). From that encounter, which did indeed entail enormous suffering, Schreber imaginatively created a personal myth that enabled him to endure his nervous illness. His personal myth has not been adopted as a collective myth. It remains to be seen whether Schreber's mythopoeic, metabiographical account of his change of internal structure is just an intrapsychic individual myth or whether it will eventually become an interpersonal cultural myth. The question is: Was Schreber merely a schizophrenic, or was he also a representative man – a great man with "great thoughts" of use to us all?

Schreber's nervous illness

Schreber was 51 years old when his world abruptly came to an end and he suffered a radical break with reality. The thoughts, great or otherwise, that he recounts in his *Memoirs* were a desperate attempt to understand what was happening to him, to make sense of his profoundly bewildering experience. Schreber says that what precipitated his psychotic breakdown was the intolerable stress that he experienced when he was appointed in June 1893 to the position of president of a panel of five judges at the supreme court of Saxony. It was then that he began to dream several times that his previous nervous illness had returned. It was also then that the thought occurred to him that it "must be rather pleasant to be a woman succumbing to intercourse" (1955: 63).

In October 1893 Schreber assumed his judicial duties. The responsibilities were a "heavy burden." He was "driven, maybe by personal ambition," but certainly by a desire to earn "all the necessary respect" of his colleagues "by unquestionable efficiency" (1955: 63). Almost all of the five judges over whom he presided were much older and more knowledgeable. Within a few weeks, he says, "I had already overtaxed myself mentally." In late October or early November he began to have difficulty sleeping. At night he also heard noises in the walls of the bedroom. Later he understood these noises to be the effects of divinely miraculous "interferences" caused by voices of souls talking to him (1955: 64). Eventually he developed several techniques in a frantic effort to defend himself against the constant influence of these intrusive voices.

Schreber's nervousness increased until the "menacing character" of it compelled him to consult the psychiatrist who had treated him successfully for his first, hypochondriacal illness in 1884–1885 (1955: 64). On this occasion the psychiatrist attempted to cure him "through one prolific sleep." When sleeping drugs like camphor failed, the psychiatrist prescribed chloral hydrate. During one sleepless night Schreber "left the bed in an attack of anxiety in order to make preparations for a kind of suicidal attempt by means of a towel or suchlike" (1955: 65). He continued to experience "endless melancholy." He became preoccupied with "thoughts of death." Then he developed the notion that his psychiatrist's plan "consisted in intensifying my nervous depression as far as possible, in order to bring about a cure all at once by a sudden change of mood" (1955: 66).

In the middle of one night two asylum attendants suddenly pulled Schreber out of bed and took him to "a cell fitted out for dements (maniacs) to sleep in." He was excited and terrified, and he resisted by fighting the attendants, who overpowered him and removed him to the cell. He felt "totally lost." During a mostly sleepless night he attempted unsuccessfully to commit suicide, trying "to hang myself from the bedstead with the sheet." Without sleep there was nothing to do for him "but to take his life." He knew that suicide was impermissible in an asylum, so he "laboured under the delusion that when all attempts at cure had been exhausted, one would be discharged – solely for the purpose of making an end to one's life either in one's own home or somewhere else" (1955: 66).

Schreber did not have a psychoanalyst like Freud or Jung but a psychiatrist who attempted to treat him with conventional asylum techniques such as sleep, drugs, baths, and games like billiards, jigsaw puzzles, and patience (solitaire). None of these techniques was effective, and Schreber's condition continued to deteriorate. As Schreber says, "My will to live was completely broken; I could see nothing in the future but a fatal outcome, perhaps produced by committing suicide eventually" (1955: 68). His suicidal ideation variously included starving himself by refusing food, being buried alive, poisoning himself with cyanide or strychnine, and throwing himself on train tracks or drowning himself in a river. Schreber's world had ended, and all that he could think was also to end his own life. The problem was dire, and the only solution was drastic.

At some point, Schreber began to formulate another answer to the question of what was happening to him – and why – and whether there was an alternative to suicide. He developed an explanation of the invasive voices that spoke to him incessantly and a notion about "the tendency innate in the Order of the World, according to which a human being ('a seer of spirits') must under certain circumstances be 'unmanned' (transformed into a woman) once he has entered into indissoluble contact with divine nerves (rays)" (1955: 69). By "a seer of spirits," Schreber meant "a man who sees, and is in communication with, spirits or departed souls." When voices spoke to Schreber, he understood them to be those of spirits or departed souls. The voice of his psychiatrist's soul, he says, "used to refer to me as 'the greatest seer of spirits of all centuries.'" Schreber's ironically grandiose rejoinder was that "one ought at least to speak of the greatest seer of spirits of all *millenia* [sic: millennia]" (1955: 88).

Schreber never mentions Immanuel Kant's *Dreams of a Spirit Seer*, but that book may well be the source of his own use of the phrase "a seer of spirits." As a young medical student Jung regarded the observations of spiritualists as accounts of "objective psychic phenomena." In this respect, he says that Kant's *Dreams of a Spirit Seer* "came just at the right moment" (1963: 99). According to Kant, a spirit seer is a "visionary" who experiences "wild fantasies" that he projects into external reality. Kant believes that these projections are only a hallucinatory deception of the senses, although he acknowledges that "they may have been produced by a genuine spiritual influence." He elaborates as follows:

> Departed souls and pure spirits can never be present to our outer senses, nor can they be in communication with matter. They can, however, act upon the human soul which belongs with them to one great republic; in doing so, they stimulate certain representations which clothe themselves by dint of the rules of the imagination into analogous images, creating the illusion of external apparitions corresponding to outside objects. This deception can affect each of our senses, but no matter to what extent it may be mixed up with the most absurd hallucinations, this should not prevent us from attributing real spiritual influences to these phenomena.
>
> (Kant 1969: 57)

This deception of the senses, Kant asserts, constitutes a "type of mental derangement which we call neurosis, and in more serious cases, madness." This is a "type of disease," and what is peculiar about it is "the projection by the confused victim of objects outside him which though they exist in his imagination only, are nevertheless viewed by him as existing in reality" (1969: 63). Thus Kant contends that spirits do exist and that they can "influence the soul of a human person." Human souls and spirits have "a similar constitution," and on that basis spirits can "enter into mutual communication with a soul at any time" (1969: 49). When, however, such communications assume the form of hallucinations so that a person believes that he is literally *seeing* spirits, they are evidence of a psychopathological condition.

Schreber believes that there is a correspondence between microcosm and macrocosm, between man and God. Whereas man has soul and finite, temporal, embodied nerves, God has soul and infinite, eternal, unembodied nerves. The soul of man, Schreber says, "is contained in the nerves of the body" (1955: 45). In contrast to man, God consists only of nerves, "not body." There is no body of nerves to contain the soul of God. Schreber says that divine nerves "possess the same qualities of human nerves but in a degree surpassing all human understanding."

The nerves of God have the ability to create the world and all life, including man. Schreber says that "in this capacity they are called rays." God's nerves are qualitatively the same as man's nerves, but as infinite, eternal, unembodied rays, they are the very "essence of divine creation" (1955: 46). On those occasions when the soul of man and the soul of God are in contact, human nerves are under the influence of divine rays. For example, by means of divine rays "God has always been able to infuse dreams into a sleeping human being" (1955: 69). In short, creation of the world, of life, of man, of dreams, and of all else occurs through an irradiation from the nerves of God.

Murdering Schreber's soul

According to Schreber, human contact with divine rays can result not only in creation but also in destruction: a man's soul can be murdered, his body can be unmanned, the world can be ended, even God's very existence can be endangered. His immediate concern is that soul murder was once committed on the Schreber family or might now be committed on him. Schreber defines soul murder by comparing it to demonic possession. He notes that the belief is pervasive "in the folklore and poetry of all peoples that it is somehow possible to take possession of another person's soul" and that "the main role is supposed to be played by the Devil." He dismisses this belief as mere "fable" on the grounds that "the Devil as a power inimical to God does not exist at all." At the same time, however, he says that the ubiquitous "motif of soul murder" gives pause for reflection. He maintains that "it is hardly likely that such ideas could have been formed by so many peoples without any basis in fact" (1955: 55).

What, then, is the factual status of belief in soul murder? Schreber believes that under certain circumstances a man (rather than a demon or the Devil) can murder, or possess, the soul of another man. He wonders whether at some time in the past, perhaps in the eighteenth century, his psychiatrist's family may have perpetrated such a deed on his own family. This genealogical hypothesis is that perhaps one of his psychiatrist's forbears was also a nerve specialist and that this individual "succeeded in *abusing* nerve-contact granted him for the purpose of divine inspiration or some other reasons" (1955: 56). He conjectures that this abuse was an attempt by one of his psychiatrist's ancestors to influence the nerves of the Schreber family "by exerting his will power after the fashion of thought readers" (1955: 57). In effect, soul murder amounts to thought transference, or telepathic influence.

It may be, Schreber says, that there was "something like a conspiracy" against the Schreber family, "perhaps in the direction of denying them offspring or possibly only of denying them choice of those professions which would lead to closer relations with God such as that of a nerve specialist" (1955: 57). Thus Schreber, who is disappointed in his and his wife's futile efforts to have children, imagines that some nerve specialist in some prior generation of his psychiatrist's family, may have plotted, in a jealous feud, familicide against the Schreber lineage by, among other possibilities, murdering the soul of someone by "appropriating his mental powers." He says that he "cannot enlarge on the essential nature of soul murder or, so to speak its technique," except to add – but at this point in Schreber's *Memoirs* there occurs a parenthetical editorial comment: "the passage which follows is unfit for publication" (1955: 58). Whatever Schreber wanted to say further about soul murder is censored.

An alternative hypothesis is that soul murder has been committed or at least attempted not against the Schreber family but against Schreber himself by nerve-contact, or thought transference, by his psychiatrist. Schreber appeals to his psychiatrist to consider whether his nervous illness is the result of "*influences on my nervous system emanating from your nervous system.*" He speculates that his psychiatrist, "like so many doctors, could not completely resist the temptation of using a patient in your care *as an object for scientific experiments* apart from the real purpose of cure" (1955: 34). Of the improper influence that he believes his psychiatrist exerted on him, Schreber says that "in order to stress forcefully that this was a malpractice it was called 'soul murder.'" He asks his psychiatrist three questions in regard to soul murder: whether he ever exerted an influence on Schreber's nervous system by "hypnotic or similar contact," whether he ever experienced supernatural "communications from voices," and whether he ever received "visions or vision-like impressions particularly in dreams" about God, free will, unmanning, and so forth (1955: 35).

How and why would God permit soul murder? According to Schreber, God is not utterly omnipotent. Not only may God's nerves influence man's nerves, but man's may also influence God's. When God's nerves come into contact with man's nerves, the attraction is mutual. Human nerves may exert such an enormous attractive influence on divine nerves as to threaten the existence of God. God knows that "an increase of *nervousness* among men could endanger His realms," and thus Schreber says that asylums for the mentally ill are called "God's Nerve-Institutes" (1955: 56). In this sense, asylums exist to decrease man's nervousness that might imperil God's existence. The dangerous attraction that human nerves can exert on divine nerves and the "precarious position" in which such influence can place God, Schreber confesses, remains to him a mystery, an "unfathomable law" of the universe. He believes that "this forms perhaps the basis of the Germanic saga of the Twilight of the Gods" (1955: 59). Such attraction may be the foundation of the myth of Gotterdammerung.

An increase in man's nervousness is not the only condition that can threaten the existence of God. God can also be endangered by an increase in man's immorality. In this respect, Schreber mentions the myth of Sodom and Gomorrah. When there is "an increase of nervousness or immorality," he says, "the instinct of self-preservation must be aroused in God as in every other living being" (1955: 60). When God's existence is imperiled because His nerves are so attracted by man's nerves, He naturally defends Himself against the influence. The implication is that God countenances soul murder only in the extreme instance when His own existence is threatened. If the nerves of God were so dangerously attracted by the nerves of Schreber's psychiatrist, then God might try to protect Himself by allowing him to commit soul murder on Schreber. In such circumstances God "could be enticed into a kind of conspiracy against human beings who are fundamentally innocent" (1955: 59). Finally – in fact, only in the process of writing his *Memoirs* – Schreber came to the conclusion that "God must have known of the plan, if indeed He was not the instigator, to commit soul murder on me" (1955: 77).

Just as God defended Himself against the threat to His existence, Schreber defended himself against the murder of his soul. He believed that his psychiatrist's nerves were the medium through which God's nerves influenced his nerves. All that Schreber could surmise was that his psychiatrist "in some way knew how to put divine rays to his own use" in order to commit soul murder on him (1955: 69). Eventually, however, Schreber's nerves came under the immediate influence of God's nerves. His psychiatrist was no longer the vehicle for soul murder: Schreber was directly influenced by divine rays. He tried to defend himself against these divine rays by "thinking nothing." He believed that if he could have no thoughts – or at least *seem* to have no thoughts – God would presume that he was "demented" and would withdraw His influence (1955: 47).

The influence of God's nerves manifested itself, Schreber says, "relatively early in the form of *compulsive thinking*." He defines compulsive thinking as "a human being having to think incessantly." According to Schreber, compulsive thinking is a violation of one of the natural rights of man. He says that "man's natural right to give the nerves of his mind their necessary rest from time to time (as occurs most markedly during sleep) was from the beginning denied me by the rays in contact with me." In the form of voices these rays "continually wanted to know what I was thinking about." In an attempt to protect himself against these voices he resorted to "*falsifying my thoughts*" (1955: 70).

This falsification assumed the form of Schreber's deliberately thinking nonsense. Schreber was convinced that the rays were "*able to read my thoughts,*" and to prevent that telepathic influence, he tried to think nothing, to think nonsensical thoughts, or to think thoughts repetitively like a mantra until they meant nothing or made no sense. He acknowledges that thinking absolutely nothing is literally impossible, for "human thinking is inexhaustible." By his thinking a nonsensical thought, however, "the rays were thereby made unreceptive to the power of attraction of such a thought" (1955: 122). Schreber calls this effort, which he considers paradoxical, "the so-called not-thinking-of-anything-thought" (1955: 144).

Lothane notes that "soul murder" is not a neologism that Schreber coined. As early as 1867 Friedrich Krauss employed the term "*Seelenmord*" in a book that was, like Schreber's *Memoirs*, an autobiographical account of psychotic experience (1992: 370n.). Lothane also mentions that Grimms' *Deutsches Worterbuch* defines soul murder "by way of the Italian: '*homicidio spirituale dell'anima*'" (1992: 427). What is unique to Schreber is how he defined the expression. The murder of his soul was synonymous with the destruction of his reason.

Schreber states that although God's rays are "essentially constructive" and "creative," they can also be destructive. In this instance, he says, God had adopted an "irregular policy against me, aimed solely at destroying my bodily integrity and my reason" (1955: 79n.) The apparent rationale for this policy was that, for God to protect Himself against the danger that the attraction of human nerves posed to His very existence, He was trying not only to transform Schreber into a woman (unman his body) but also to render him into a dement (destroy his reason, or murder his soul). Schreber believed that he could defend himself against compulsive thinking and the destruction of his reason if he could deceive God into believing that he had "succumbed to dementia" (1955: 154). Thus Schreber says: "Every time my thinking activity ceases God instantly regards my mental powers as extinct, the desired destruction of my reason (the 'dementia') achieved and the possibility of a withdrawal thus brought about" (1955: 166). Finally Schreber came to another realization about an ultimate limitation on God's omnipotence. He concluded that not even God has powers superior to the Order of the World. Schreber says that his experience has demonstrated to him that "the Order of the World does not provide even God with the means to destroy a human being's reason" (1955: 198).

Schreber believes that in this conflict with God he will ultimately "emerge, albeit not without bitter sufferings and deprivations, victorious, because the Order of the World is on my side" (1955: 79). He acknowledges that in this respect "'the Order of the World' may appear as something impersonal and higher, more powerful than God or even as ruling God." The relation between God and the Order of the World may be a paradox, but it is not a contradiction in terms. "'*The Order of the World*,'" Schreber says, "is the lawful relation which, *resting on God's nature and attributes, exists between God and the creation called to life by Him.*" According to Schreber, "God cannot achieve what contradicts His own attributes and His powers in relation to mankind or, as in my case, to an individual human being who had entered into a special relation with Him." In short, God is not above and beyond the law of the Order of the World. It is perhaps an "oxymoron," Schreber says, that "God Himself was on my side in His fight against me" (1955: 79n.).

Schreber interprets the "divine miracles" that happened to him as "signs of an abnormal state of affairs, which arose because the Order of the World was out of joint" (1955: 183–4). The idea of a "World Order" is not original with or idiosyncratic to Schreber; nor is it an intrinsically psychopathological notion. It is an idea with a considerable history (even an archetypal dimension) as well as a contemporary application. For example, in preparation for Operation Desert Storm, the war that the United States and the United Nations waged against Iraq in defense of Kuwait, President George Bush invoked the idea of a New World Order in an address to a joint session of Congress on September 11, 1990:

> We stand today at a unique and extraordinary moment. The crisis in the Persian Gulf, as grave as it is, also offers a rare opportunity to move toward an historic period of cooperation. Out of these troubled times, our fifth objective – a new world order – can emerge: a new era – free from the threat of terror, stronger in the pursuit of justice, and more secure in the quest for peace. An

era in which the nations of the world, East and West, North and South, can prosper and live in harmony.

(Bush and Scowcroft 1998: 370)

The New World Order that Bush envisions is, of course, a political idea – not, as with Schreber, a religious idea.

In *The New World Order*, Pat Robertson, a television evangelist, criticizes this "vision of the new world order" (1991: xii) as a vast political conspiracy against Christianity. According to Robertson, the New World Order constitutes a plot by a transnational elite that historically includes Cecil Rhodes, the Federal Reserve Board, the US Treasury Department, the Export-Import Bank, J. P. Morgan and Company, the Chase Manhattan Bank, First National City Bank, the Rothschilds, the Warburgs, the Rockefellers, the US State Department, the Council on Foreign Relations, the Carnegie Foundation, the Rockefeller Foundation, the Ford Foundation, Harvard University, Columbia University, Yale University, the University of Chicago, the *Washington Post*, the *New York Times*, the *Los Angeles Times*, the United Nations, Henry Kissinger, the Trilateral Commission, Jimmy Carter, George Bush, and others. This conspiratorial notion has had a major impact on ideological extremists – among them, "militia" members, one of whom ends radio broadcasts with the exclamation "Death to the new world order!" (Rich April 27,1995: A25). For these reactionary malcontents, the adversary is "the 'N.W.O.' – the New World Order" (Egan April 30, 1995, sec. 4: 1). According to them, the Federal Building in Oklahoma City was not bombed in 1995 by Timothy McVeigh but "was destroyed as part of a plot by the United States Government, acting on behalf of a secret international cabal, the New World Order" (Johnson April 30, 1995, sec. 4: 5).

Robertson, who has fomented fanaticism and in the process perhaps even incited terrorism, asserts that "for the past two hundred years the term *new world order* has been the code phrase for those who desired to destroy the Christian faith" (1991: 92). As an alternative to this secular humanist New World Order, Robertson proposes a Christian fundamentalist New World Order. He says: "I have an undeniable sense that we are witnessing the unfolding of a historic age, 'a time of troubles,' if you will, of biblical proportions, and the end of the age will truly bring the revelation of a new world order to justify the hopes and dreams of all mankind and the divine will of God" (1991: xvii). Robertson promises to "place the origin, meaning, and ultimate destiny of the new world order within the clear purview of Bible prophecy" (1991: 14). The New World Order that he prophesies is thus a religious idea – although Robertson, a former presidential candidate, is also an activist who propagandizes and proselytizes in an effort to mobilize Christians to exert political influence.

Robertson is not, like Schreber, a paranoid schizophrenic, and his idea of a religious New World Order is not inherently psychopathological, but his notion of a political conspiracy against Christianity is a version of what Richard Hofstadter calls the "paranoid style in American politics." As Hofstadter defines the paranoid style, "the feeling of persecution is central, and it is indeed systematized in grandiose theories of conspiracy." Although the clinical paranoiac and the political paranoiac are both stylistically suspicious and apocalyptic, the former sees the conspiracy "directed specifically *against him*," whereas the latter sees it "directed against a nation, a culture, a way of life whose fate affects not himself alone but millions of others" (1965: 4). Such is the decisive difference between Schreber and Robertson.

Unmanning Schreber's body

At first Schreber feared that his unmanning was to serve a meretriciously human purpose, not at all the miraculously divine purpose of beginning a new world. He believed that his psychiatrist had nefariously plotted to hand him over, both soul and body (that is, after his soul had been murdered and his body unmanned), to a "human being for sexual misuse" (1955: 75). This, Schreber says, was an "abominable intention," against which he protested with "my whole sense of manliness and manly honour." He felt that he had "to prove my manly courage" (1955: 76). Eventually he realized that all attempts to murder his soul and unman his body "for the sexual satisfaction of a human being" were impossible because they were contrary to the Order of the World (1955: 78).

For a while, however, Schreber seriously entertained the notion that his body could be unmanned and "prostituted like that of a female harlot" (1955: 99). He believed that "my body, after the intended transformation into a female being, was to suffer some sexual abuse, particularly as there had even been talk for some time of my being thrown to the Asylum attendants for this purpose" (1955: 101). What Schreber feared was not transsexual intercourse with God but sexual abuse by men, including members of the asylum staff. He says: "I myself felt the danger of unmanning for a long time as a threatening ignominy, especially while there was the possibility of my body being sexually abused by other people." In an effort to prevent such an atrocity, he "suppressed every feminine impulse by exerting my sense of manly honour" (1955: 120). For Schreber, what was at issue was nothing less than his manhood.

It is difficult to imagine that it was Schreber's psychiatrist who had talked about throwing him to the attendants for sexual abuse. This would have been sadistic treatment indeed. It may be, of course, that the attendants themselves bruited that possibility about. It would not be the first time that attendants in an asylum threatened to abuse a patient sexually or actually did so. Schreber says that the attendants made "all sorts of rude jokes" to him and about him (1955: 77). Alternatively, it may be that the voices of souls that spoke to Schreber talked to him about sexual abuse. Schreber does not say from whom he heard such talk. It may be that he experienced it as a threat of homosexual rape by anal intercourse in a way that would be consonant with Freud's interpretation of his *Memoirs*. This is not, however, the context in which Schreber describes the threat of sexual abuse. The word that Schreber uses is "prostituted," not "raped." The sexual abuse would occur not while he had a man's body but only after he had a woman's body – that is, by vaginal intercourse after he had experienced a sex change. The transformation of his body into a woman's body precedes the possibility of sexual abuse. The sexual abuse that he feared was transsexual intercourse with men. This was what was intolerable to him.

From the perspective of psychopathology, the threat of sexual abuse is perfectly consistent with Schreber's delusion of persecution. His alternative notion that the purpose of his unmanning was to enable him to have transsexual intercourse with God, be impregnated by divine rays, and be delivered of a new world would be an extreme attempt by his unconscious to compensate with a delusion of grandeur. As Freud says, "To express the matter in more formal language, a sexual delusion of persecution was later on converted, in the patient's mind, into a religious delusion of grandeur" (*SE* 12: 18). Schreber has the following thoughts as his nervous illness progresses:

1   It really must be rather pleasant to be a woman succumbing to intercourse.
2   I am being transformed into a woman.
3   I am going to be forced to have intercourse with men.
4   I have been chosen to have intercourse with God.

These thoughts culminate in the conversion of Schreber's delusion from one of persecution into one of grandeur.

Schreber's experience of being unmanned (or transformed into a woman) occurs in stages. First, the thought occurs to him that for a woman to succumb to intercourse must be pleasant. Second, after he *thinks* this, he then begins to *sense* it – that is, to experience female voluptuousness. He begins to experience certain sensations. Third, through those sensations he becomes "aware of the presence of female nerves" in his male body. This experience reduces him to "a human being trembling with feminine anxiety" (1955: 120). The voluptuous sensations, he says, are so intense that, "especially when I am in bed, it requires only a little exertion of my imagination to attain such sensuous pleasure as gives a pretty definite foretaste of female sexual enjoyment in intercourse" (1955: 201). In short, female nerves are what produce voluptuously pleasurable female sensations. Schreber says that "my whole body is filled with nerves of voluptuousness from the top of my head to the soles of my feet." He believes that female sexuality is more diffuse than male sexuality. According to Schreber, nerves of voluptuousness are dispersed throughout the whole of the female body. In contrast, they are concentrated in only a part of the male body, "in and immediately around the sexual organs" (1955: 204). Female sexuality is polymorphous; male sexuality, exclusively genital. Since Schreber has nerves of voluptuousness within his entire body, he concludes that he must therefore be a woman, at least internally. He also believes that women experience more sensuous pleasure than men because female sexuality "involves the whole body" (1955: 205).

In this sense, Schreber is a contemporary Teiresias, who in Greek mythology was not only a prophet but also a transsexual. According to Robert Graves, "Teiresias had seen two serpents in the act of coupling." Graves recounts the consequences as follows: "When both attacked him, he struck at them with his staff, killing the female. Immediately he was turned into a woman, and became a celebrated harlot; but seven years later he happened to see the same sight again at the same spot, and this time regained his manhood by killing the male serpent" (1957 2: 11). Like Schreber, Teiresias was unmanned, or transformed into a woman. Whereas Schreber feared becoming a harlot, Teiresias actually became a famous one. He experienced sexual intercourse not only as a man but also as a woman. He was therefore in a unique position to compare male and female sensuous pleasure. Then an opportunity arose for Teiresias, on the basis of his transsexual experience, to resolve a controversy between Hera and Zeus over that very issue. Graves says:

> Hera began reproaching Zeus for his numerous infidelities. He defended them by arguing that, at any rate, when he did share her couch, she had the more enjoyable time by far. 'Women, of course, derive infinitely greater pleasure from the sexual act than men,' he blustered.
>
> 'What nonsense!' cried Hera. 'The exact contrary is the case, and well you know it.'
>
> Teiresias, summoned to settle the dispute from his personal experience, answered:
>
>> 'If the parts of love-pleasure be counted as ten,
>>
>> Thrice three go to women, one only to men.'
>
> Hera was so exasperated by Zeus' triumphant grin that she blinded Teiresias; but Zeus compensated him with inward sight.
>
> (Graves 1957 2: 11)

Thus, by gaining insight after losing sight, Teiresias becomes a prophet. After being transformed into a woman, he, like Schreber, declares that women experience more sensuous pleasure than men. For Schreber, the voluptuous superiority of women over men is a result of the pervasive distribution of nerves in the female body. In contrast, Teiresias offers no such explanation. He merely rhymes poetically the mathematically exact nine-to-one ratio through an appeal to his personal experience of transsexual intercourse.

Schreber's transformation into a woman begins internally, in terms of thoughts and sensations and nerves. Only then does it begin to manifest itself externally. In this respect, Schreber mentions two brief unmannings in the asylum. "I have myself," he says, "twice experienced (for a short time) the miracle of unmanning on my own body" (1955: 74). When he is unmanned, his male genitals are not castrated but retracted and transformed into female genitals – or they are merely malformed. He says that on at least one occasion "I had a thing between my legs which hardly resembled at all a normally formed male organ" (1955: 77n.). Although Schreber's unmanning entails "especially the various changes in my *sex organ*" – among them, numerous occasions when "there were marked indications of an actual retraction of the male organ" – it also includes much more than just that part of his body. His unmanning is a transformation of the whole of his body. His skin is softened; hairs from his beard and moustache are removed; his stature is diminished six to eight centimeters to approximately the height of a woman (1955: 132). "I myself," he says, "received the impression of a female body, first on my arms and hands, later on my legs, bosom, buttocks and other parts of my body" (1955: 148). Schreber believes that he is not just a part man with female genitals but a whole woman both internally and externally – that he is undergoing a radical sex change, nothing less than a total transsexual reembodiment.

Sex and gender

Was Schreber a homosexual who would, were he alive now, lead a gay life? Was he a transsexual who would now consult a plastic surgeon for a sex change operation? According to Robert J. Stoller, Schreber was not a transsexual. In this respect, Stoller distinguishes between "delusion" and "illusion" (1976 2: 30). A delusion is a false belief that replaces external reality with an internal reality. In contrast, an illusion is also a false belief, but it merely misrepresents external reality; it does not replace it with an internal reality. Although transsexualism "is not exactly an illusion," it is more an illusion than a delusion. "Those who believe transsexuals are psychotic," Stoller says, "should contrast these patients with those like Schreber, who felt God was changing his body to female: transsexuals cannot manage to hallucinate body change; that is why they must take hormones and seek 'sex change' surgery" (1976 2: 31).

Presumably, if transsexuals could hallucinate body change as psychotics like Schreber can, then they would remain content and never pursue such a radical operation. A true transsexual knows that his sexual identity is male but believes that his gender identity is feminine. It is on that basis that he hormonally and surgically changes sex. Plausible as this distinction between transsexuals and psychotics may be, it is not unproblematic. Is it not possible for both transsexualism and psychosis to exist simultaneously? Hormones and sex change surgery were not an option for Schreber; the procedures were technologically unavailable to him as a medical specialization at that that time. Under these circumstances if Schreber was a transsexual, what alternative did he have but a hallucination?

Why does Schreber's encounter with the anima in the second half of life assume the specific form of his imagining that he is literally being transformed into a woman? Why does he become possessed by, or unconsciously identified with, the anima, instead of becoming effectively related to it? Why does he literalize it as a transsexual reembodiment? Why does he not just empathically experience the feminine? Why does he imagine that he is literally *becoming* a female? Why does he conflate anima and body, feminine and female, gender and sex? Why is he finally so *unpsychological* – that is, so literal, so "physical?" It is, of course, simply a fact that he just does so, that he just is so.

Jung says that all people are "contrasexed." For example, a person who is dominantly male is recessively female – and vice versa. Jung commits what might be called the "sex/gender fallacy." He does not adequately and consistently distinguish sex from gender – male from masculine and female from feminine. Maleness and femaleness are physical terms; masculinity and femininity are psychological terms. Persons physically sexed either male or female may be psychically gendered either masculine or feminine. Stoller notes that "one can speak of the male sex or the female sex, but one can also talk about masculinity and femininity and not necessarily be implying anything about anatomy and physiology." He says that "the two realms (sex and gender) are not at all inevitably bound in anything like a one-to-one relationship, but each may go in its quite independent way" (1968 1: ix). Thus it would be more accurate and more precise for Jung to say that all people, however they may be sexed, are "contragendered," either actually or potentially.

Sex and gender constitute a matrix of four factors:

Male	Masculine
Female	Feminine

Logically, the sex/gender matrix permits only four permutations, as follows:

1   A male may be masculine.
2   A male may be feminine.
3   A female may be feminine.
4   A female may be masculine.

A person may have a male sexual identity and either a masculine or a feminine gender identity; a person may have a female sexual identity and either a feminine or a masculine gender identity. A male, however, cannot be a female; nor can a female be a male. Likewise, the masculine cannot be the feminine; nor can the feminine be the masculine. Such permutations are impossible because they would be contradictions in terms. (An additional complication is that the gender identity of a person may be *consciously* or *unconsciously* masculine or feminine.)

Schreber is a person who defies the logic of this sex/gender matrix. He is a man who *imagines* that he is *literally* a woman. He is a male who hallucinates that he is a female. He violates the law of contradiction that stipulates that "A" is "A" and "B" is "B" and that "A" is therefore *not* "B." Instead, he obeys the law of participation, which insists that "A" is "B": that a man is a woman. "Anatomy," Freud declares, "is destiny" (*SE* 11: 189) – and Schreber imagines that he is, quite literally, an anatomically (and physiologically) correct female destined to be impregnated by God and delivered of a new world. He hallucinates, as he says, "the impression of a female body, first on my arms and hands, later on my legs, bosom, buttocks and other parts of my body." The law of participation, which states that

"A" is "B," is the poetic logic of metaphor. With Schreber, it becomes a psychotic logic, because he literalizes the metaphor. For schizophrenics like Schreber to have any opportunity to recover from their nervous illnesses, they would have to metaphorize what they have literalized. Schreber would have to acknowledge that he is only metaphorically, not literally, a woman. He would have to psychologize what he has physicalized. In short, he would have to realize that he has an anima, or feminine soul, but that he most certainly does not have a female body.

In spite of his insistence that his experience is not a psychopathological delusion (and hallucination) but a divine revelation, Schreber does attempt by artificial means to enhance what he himself, like Stoller, occasionally calls the "illusion" that he has been transformed into a woman. For example, he appears "with a clean-shaven face" in an effort "to support my imagination of being a female." He notes that "a moustache would naturally have been an insurmountable obstacle for this illusion" (1955: 160). He also visualizes himself "standing in front of a mirror in the adjoining room in female attire" (1955: 181). That is, he imagines cross-dressing as a woman. Apparently, however, this was not just a fantasy but a reality. "I venture to assert flatly," Schreber says, "that anybody who sees me standing in front of a mirror with the upper part of my body naked would get the undoubted *impression of a female trunk* – especially when the illusion is strengthened by some feminine adornments" (1955: 207). A medical expert testifies against Schreber's discharge from the asylum on the grounds that "in the tendency to undress more or less and to look at himself in the mirror, to decorate himself with gay ribbons and bows, etc., in a feminine way, the pathological direction of his fantasy is manifested continually" (Weber 1955: 273). In an appeal to the court, Schreber acknowledges that "at times I was seen standing in front of the mirror or elsewhere with some female adornments (ribbons, trumpery necklaces, and suchlike), with the upper half of my body exposed" (1955: 300). He promises, however, that on his release from the asylum, he will "spare my wife any painful sight." He will cause no distress for his wife by making a spectacle of himself. He states that he "showed her my female ornaments only with some reluctance when out of forgivable feminine inquisitiveness she insisted upon it" (1955: 305). Whether or not Schreber was a latent homosexual or a latent transsexual in the strict sense, he definitely became a manifest, if a rather discreet, transvestite.

Schreber is by no means the only patient ever to have experienced being unmanned, or transformed into a woman. In *Psychopathia Sexualis* Richard von Krafft-Ebing reports just such a case, which he diagnoses as "METAMORPHOSIS SEXUALIS PARANOIA" (1965: 261). The patient was a physician with a wife and five children. What precipitated his experience of being transformed into a woman was not, as with Schreber, either a half-asleep or a fully-awake thought of female voluptuousness but "extract of Indian hemp." The patient consumed "three or four times the usual dose of it and almost died of hashish poisoning." Suddenly he saw himself "a woman from my toes to my breast." He felt that "the genitals had shrunken, the pelvis broadened, the breasts swollen out." The next morning he experienced "himself completely changed into a woman," with "vulva and breasts"

(1965: 267). He felt "like a woman in a man's form," and even when he was "sensible of the man's form," he always experienced it "in a feminine sense." He experienced "penis as clitoris," "urethra as urethra and vaginal orifice," and "scrotum as *labia majora*." Occasionally he felt "fetal movement" (1965: 269). He also felt the "physiological desire for procreation" (1965: 270). He experienced sexual intercourse in a feminine way and always felt that "I am impregnated" (1965: 271). Like Schreber, he too engaged in cross-dressing, wearing such "female attire" as "gloves" or "a veil" (1965: 272) or "a bracelet above the cuff" (1965: 273). He liked "female drawers and petticoats" and "crinolines" (1965: 274).

Both Krafft-Ebing's patient and Schreber experience the illusion of being transformed, or "metamorphosed," into a woman. They both feel that their male bodies have been changed into female bodies and that they have been impregnated. They both cross-dress. The only difference between them is that Schreber believes that his unmanning is the result of divine intervention to serve a supernatural purpose, the renewal of mankind.

If Schreber was a schizophrenic, he was a schizophrenic with what the American Psychiatric Association in the fourth edition of the *Diagnostic and Statistical Manual of Mental Disorders* [*DSM-IV*] diagnoses as "gender identity disorder." The *DSM-IV* says that individuals with a gender identity disorder "are preoccupied with their wish to live as a member of the other sex." They exhibit "an intense desire to adopt the social role of the other sex or to acquire the physical appearance of the other sex through hormonal or surgical manipulation." (As I have said, Schreber had no access to those technologies.) "In varying degrees, they adopt the behavior, dress, and mannerisms of the other sex," the *DSM-IV* says. "In private, these individuals may spend much time cross-dressed and working on the appearance of being the other sex" (1994: 533). There is no necessary connection between schizophrenia and gender identity disorder. In exceptional instances, however, an individual with schizophrenia may also have a gender identity disorder. As the *DSM-IV* says:

> In *Schizophrenia*, there may rarely be delusions of belonging to the other sex. Insistence by a person with a Gender Identity Disorder that he or she is of the other sex is not considered a delusion, because what is invariably meant is that the person feels like a member of the other sex rather than truly believes that he or she is a member of the other sex. In very rare cases, however, Schizophrenia and severe Gender Identity Disorder may coexist.
>
> (American Psychiatric Association 1994: 537)

Schreber seems to have been just such a rarity.

Catastrophe theories

According to Schreber, God has the means to end the world – and then to begin it again. As an example, he cites the destruction of Sodom and Gomorrah, although that is a myth of the end of two cities, not the end of the world. Schreber evidently believes that in the vast universe the earth is not the only world on which God has created human beings. When human beings become too immoral or too nervous on any of these worlds, God intervenes miraculously to destroy them – and then to recreate them.

This destruction and recreation of human beings is in accordance with what Schreber calls "the basic plan on which the Order of the World seems to rest." When "world catastrophes" require "the destruction of mankind" on any world, Schreber says, "the human race can be renewed" (1955: 72). Because of "moral decay ('voluptuous excesses')," "nervousness," or "a dangerous increase of attraction on God's nerves" such destruction might happen "either spontaneously (thought annihilating epidemics, etc.) or, being decided on by God, be put into effect by means of earthquakes, deluges, etc." (1955: 72–3). It is also possible that "God was also able to withdraw partially or totally the warmth of the sun" from a world, and Schreber conjectures that this may explain "the problem of the *Ice Age* which, as far as I know, has not yet been solved by science" (1955: 73). He mentions various world catastrophes: "glaciation," "earthquake," a "wizard" in the person of his psychiatrist who caused "general nervousness and immorality," "leprosy," and "plague" (1955: 97). In effect, Schreber develops a *catastrophe theory* in an attempt to account for his experience of the end of the world.

"Catastrophe theory" is the name that Rene Thom has given to a branch of applied mathematics, a topology that attempts to describe how stable structures, or forms, abruptly change from one state to another state. These abrupt changes Thom calls "catastrophes." For Thom, the term does not necessarily have a negative connotation. A castatrophe is simply a *transformation*. In this sense, *Transformations and Symbols of the Libido* could just as well have been entitled *Catastrophes and Symbols of the Libido*, for both Jung and Thom are interested in the precise point at which (and the exact way in which) one state abruptly changes to another state – for example, a normal state to an abnormal state or vice versa.

Thom says that "the Universe is not chaos, and we can observe the recurrence of typical forms to which we give names" (1975: 15). Although he occasionally mentions Freud but never even once Jung, he acknowledges that such a typical form in biology might be called an "archetype if the word did not have a finalist connotation" (1975: 291). He says that "a finalist process is characterized by the existence of an aim, a final state toward which the organism tends," and he concedes that "most finalist processes in biology show this behavior." He insists, however, that such "behavior can appear structurally stable in a natural way and therefore does not automatically characterize a finalist process." A process, he says, "is called finalist if its observation sets up, by resonance," an archetype "in the mind of the observer" (1975: 295).

Although Thom applies catastrophe theory mostly to biology, he also applies it to other disciplines, among them psychology. He postulates that "there are coherent systems of catastrophes" that are "organized in archetypes." These archetypes "exist as abstract algebraic entities independent of any substrate," although "the substrate does have a part fundamental in the dynamic of these forms." Thom says that "normal mental activity" involves "a large number of relatively independent substrates." In this sense, "mental activity is only simulating the dynamic of the external world." That is, normally an archetype in the mind, or internal world, is a simulation of the external world. When an archetype becomes independent of any substrate in "a unique functional system" such as "the nervous system," however, a previously stable structure can become unstable. The catastrophic result is then an abrupt change to another stable but now abnormal or "more primitive" mental activity, "what is usually called *delirious thinking*" (1975: 316). Delirious thinking may not be exactly delusional thinking, but Thom does note that when forms have no "external cause we say that there is a *hallucination*" (1975: 303). In just this way, Schreber experiences an archetypal psychological catastrophe when he abruptly – and irreversibly – becomes a paranoid schizophrenic.

E. C. Zeeman has been most active in advocating the application of catastrophe theory to the social sciences, among which he includes psychology. He has, for example, applied it to anorexia and bulimia. Zeeman models the catastrophic change from normal eating to abnormal eating (fasting or gorging and purging). He mentions a psychotherapist who induces trances in anorexic and bulimic patients in an effort to cure them. He describes how, when a patient emerges from a trance, "she discovers that she has regained access to a normal state, and is able to eat again without fear of gorging." The patient, he says, "speaks of this moment as a 'rebirth'" (1977: 44) – as if the abnormal state were a "death." According to Zeeman, patients in trance therapy experience themselves "as a double person-ality." He says that "one personality is usually described as the 'real self' and the other is called by various names by different patients such as 'the little one, the imp, the demon, the powers, the spirit, the voice' or merely 'it.'" Zeeman never mentions Jung, but, like him, he notes that dissociated aspects of the psyche are often personified by patients as "subpersonalities." He says of one patient that her gorging aspect is personified as the "monster within" and her fasting aspect as the "thin beautiful self" (1977: 50). After trance therapy, "the 'monster' and 'thin self' recede in importance, and are replaced by the 'real self' and the 'little one.'" In contrast, the abnormal state, Zeeman says, is "interpreted as 'prohibitions' by the voice or as 'malignant possession' by the little one" (1977: 51). Like Jung, Zeeman says that a patient may, in effect, be catastrophically possessed by a subpersonality – just as Schreber was schizophrenically possessed by the anima, or identified with the feminine.

Alexander Woodcock and Monte Davis provide an example of how catastrophe theory might be applied to schizophrenia. They cite the distinction between *reactive* schizophrenia, which "appears in response to a particular stress or traumatic event in adult life," and *process* schizophrenia, which "begins early in life and becomes progressively more severe." By this definition, Schreber's experience is a case of reactive schizophrenia. Woodcock and Davis specify "genetic predispo-sition and stress" as the two factors that interact to produce the catastrophe of schizophrenia (1978: 136). According to this model, Schreber would have been genetically predisposed to schizophrenia, and when stressed by the demands of service as president of the panel of judges at the supreme court of Saxony abruptly suffered a catastrophic nervous illness. In contrast, Freud emphasizes a developmental fixation, a latent homosexual wish, rather than a genetic predisposition, as the decisive factor. Possible alternative factors would be a transsexual predisposition or a transvestic fixation. Jung would presumably emphasize a contrasexual compensation by the anima.

From the perspective of psychopathology, Schreber does experience an abrupt change from one state to another: from sanity to insanity (paranoid schizophrenia), from reality to fantasy (delusion and hallucination). As he describes this catastrophe, it is a change from reason to dementia (his soul is murdered), and from male to female (his body is unmanned). He explains it as Jung might, purposively and prospectively, from the perspective of eschatology. The old world has ended, and God has transformed him from a man into a woman in order to begin a new world. According to Schreber, the possible explanatory factors for this world catastrophe are not personal but collective – "moral decay among mankind or a general spread of nervous over-excitement in consequence of over-civilization" (1955: 140). A general catastrophe has occurred, and Schreber is simply the particular victim and hero (or "heroine") of a divine intervention and a divine revelation.

Schreber contextualizes his catastrophe theory by reference to Georges Cuvier. "It is possible," he says, "that in this sense Cuvier's theory of periodically recurring world catastrophes contains some truth" (1955: 73). Schreber appeals to science and specifically to the theory of recurrent geological catastrophes (and concomitant zoological extinctions) that Cuvier proposed in the nineteenth century. The most probable source of Schreber's reference is the "Preliminary Discourse" to Cuvier's famous four-volume *Researches on the Fossil Bones of Quadrupeds*, published in 1812. The "Preliminary Discourse," Martin J. Rudwick says, "was easily accessible to any educated person" and "was immensely influential in the intellectual life of the Western world for the rest of the century." It was published as a separate book, reprinted in many editions, and "translated into all the main scientific languages of the day." Rudwick says: "In addition to its arguments for geological 'castastrophes' in the distant past, its treatment of extinction and adamant rejection of 'transformist' explanations of the origin of species were vital components of the evolutionary debates that continued throughout the century" (1997: x).

Although Cuvier based his theory on scientific evidence from the geological and fossil record, he also mentioned mythological accounts of catastrophes in one section of the "Preliminary Discourse." That section was subtitled "All Known Traditions Make the Renewal of Society Reach Back to a Major Catastrophe." Cuvier noted that the Jewish myth of the flood is the record of "a general catastrophe, an irruption of the waters, an almost total regeneration of mankind" (1997: 240). He also mentioned Chaldean, Egyptian, Greek, Indian, Persian, and Chinese myths of a deluge. Of the Greeks, he said: "If a somewhat violent inundation occurred, under one of their princes, they described it subsequently with all the circumstances vaguely remaining in their memory of the great cataclysm; and they had the earth repeopled by Deucalion." In spite of the "incoherence" of all these myths, they were "strong evidence of a major catastrophe" (1997: 241). Cuvier concluded: "Thus all the nations that can speak to us testify that they have been renewed recently, after a great revolution of nature" (1997: 246). He asked: "Would the ideas of peoples who have had so little connection with each other – whose language, religion, and laws have nothing in common – be in accord on this point, unless they were based on the truth?" (1997: 245). As a scientist, Cuvier argued that this most recent major catastrophe, as well as all previous catastrophes, had been the effect of natural causes – not of immorality or nervousness, either man's or God's.

That catastrophes have had a profound influence on the world is not just a notion from the nineteenth century. In the twentieth century, Immanuel Velikovsky (who among other professional activities was a psychoanalyst) proposed a catastrophe theory that provoked radical controversy. Velikovsky speculates that these catastrophes have been forgotten because, like traumas, they have been dissociated, with the result that humanity suffers from "Collective Amnesia." He offers the following analogy:

> The task I had to accomplish was not unlike that faced by a psychoanalyst who, out of dissociated memories and dreams, reconstructs a forgotten traumatic experience in the early life of an individual. In an analytical experiment on mankind, historical inscriptions and legendary motifs often play the same role as recollections (infantile memories) and dreams in the analysis of a personality.
>
> (Velikovsky 1950: viii)

Like Cuvier, Velikovsky asks: "What caused the legend of the Flood to originate in all the countries of the world? Is there any adequate meaning to the term 'antediluvian'? From what experiences grew the eschatological pictures of the end of the world" (1950: 4)? Like Schreber, he cites the precedent of Cuvier as a scientist who believed that the world had experienced "great catastrophes" in the past (1950: 17). According to Velikovsky, however, these catastrophes were not just geological but cosmic – the consequence of collisions between worlds and the impact of comets. Velikovsky amasses an enormous amount of evidence from mythology, including the flood myths of Noah and Deucalion and Pyrrha and others, in an attempt to prove this catastrophe theory. Finally he mentions Jung and the theory of the collective unconscious and wonders "to what extent the terrifying experiences of world catastrophes have become part of the human soul" (1950: 383). Contemporary scientists protested this catastrophe theory and subsequently utterly discredited what they called the "Velikovsky affair" (De Grazia, Juergens, and Stecchini 1966).

Theories of cosmic catastrophes are not necessarily pseudoscientific, as is the case with Velikovsky. In 1980 Luis W. Alvarez, a Nobel laureate in physics, proposed that the impact of an asteroid on the world caused the extinction of the dinosaurs. The geological evidence for this catastrophe is the presence of the rare element iridium in a one-centimeter layer of clay with a uniform distribution in the crust around the world. This layer exists at the K/T boundary between the Cretaceous and Tertiary periods, which coincides precisely with the extinction of the dinosaurs 65 million years ago. According to Alvarez, the impact of an asteroid with a ten-kilometer diameter produced sufficient dust in the atmosphere to obscure the sun, suppress photosynthesis, and starve the dinosaurs. When the dust settled, it deposited the layer of clay that contained the iridium. Alvarez says that the impact of the asteroid rendered "the sky dark as midnight for several years" (1987: 256) and reduced "the temperature to zero degrees Fahrenheit for six to nine months" (1987: 257). It discharged "an energy of some one hundred million megatons of TNT equivalent." Alvarez remarks that even the worst nuclear war scenario "would be a disaster four orders of magnitude less violent that the K/T asteroid impact." He summarizes the effect as follows: "It was quite simply the greatest catastrophe in the history of the earth of which we have any record" (1987: 259). The theory by which Alvarez explains the extinction of the dinosaurs is a scientific account that infers a strictly natural cause for the catastrophe.

In contrast, Schreber's catastrophe theory is a supernatural explanation. Like Cuvier and Velikovsky, Schreber presents evidence from mythology – from Christian, Jewish, Greek, and Roman mythology. He speculates that whenever the world was ended by such a catastrophe in the past, it may be that, "in order to maintain the species, one single human being was spared – perhaps the relatively most moral – called by the voices that talk to me the '*Eternal Jew*.'" The name "Eternal Jew" has for Schreber a significance different from "that underlying the legend of the same name of the Jew Ahasver" (1955: 73). In Christian legend, Ahasver is the "Wandering Jew" who mocked Jesus on the way to the crucifixion and was therefore condemned eternally to wander. George K. Anderson summarizes the legend of the Wandering Jew as "the tale of a man in Jerusalem who, when Christ was carrying his Cross to Calvary and paused to rest for a moment on this man's doorstep, drove the Saviour away (with or without physical contact, depending on the variants), crying aloud, 'Walk faster!' And Christ replied, 'I go, but you will walk until I come again!'" (1970: 11).

In a discussion of the "Eternal Roamer," Henry Meige cites the case of a man by the name of Klein whom Jean-Martin Charcot at the Salpêtrière Hospital in Paris described as "a true descendant" of the "Wandering Jew." Charcot diagnosed the man as one of many "compulsive (neurotic) travelers." He said that the man "is constantly driven by an irresistible need to move on, to travel, without being able to settle down anywhere." According to Charcot, "That is why he has been crisscrossing Europe for three years in search of the fortune which he has not yet encountered." Similarly, Meige mentions "cosmopolitan Israelites who stop at the Salpêtrière" after wandering incessantly (1986: 191). He says that these patients suffered "painful peripeteia" in the diaspora (1986: 192).

In contrast, Schreber's "Eternal Jew" is not an "Eternal Roamer" but an eternal survivor, saved by God from destruction because of his relative morality and chosen by God as an instrument for the recreation of the world. Any relatively moral human being might under such catastrophic circumstances become an "Eternal Jew." In this respect, Schreber says that he is "automatically reminded of the legends of Noah, Deucalion and Pyrrha, etc." (1955: 73). Thus he cites the Jewish and Greek myths of floods that ended the world and mentions Noah and Deucalion and Pyrrha as examples of the relatively moral survivors who functioned as "Eternal Jews" on those catastrophic occasions.

The pregnant virgin

Then Schreber mentions a Roman myth. "Perhaps," he says, "the legend of the founding of Rome belongs here also, according to which Rhea Sylvia conceived the later kings Romulus and Remus directly of Mars the God of War, and not of an earthly father" (1955: 73). This myth, however, is an account not of catastrophe but of creation. Why does Schreber cite it? Apparently he does so because Rhea Sylvia was not a man (like Noah and Deucalion) but a woman who was selected to be impregnated through sexual intercourse with a god and delivered of, if not a new world, at least a new civilization.

Michael Grant says that in the myth "perpetual chastity as a Vestal Virgin" was imposed on Rhea Sylvia, but then "she was raped – it was said by the god Mars – and gave birth to twin sons, Romulus and Remus" (1971: 98). According to Grant, the myth of Rhea Sylvia is "a prestige myth, to invest the birth and deeds of a popular hero with an aura of mystery and wonder." The myth deals with the "ambiguous borderline" between the divine and the human. "Direct divine interventions," Grant says, "are rare in the myths of the Romans, who found them embarrassing." He notes that various writers attempted to rationalize Mars's rape of Rhea Sylvia "on the familiar grounds that Rome's greatness warrants the assumption that supernatural circumstances attended its origins" (1971: 100).

At the very beginning of his *Memoirs* Schreber also discusses the Christian myth of Mary. He does not compare the myth of the Immaculate Virgin Mary to the myth of the Vestal Virgin Rhea Sylvia, but both myths are about virginal conceptions of a woman by a god. He comments on the myth of Mary: "The Christian teaching that Jesus Christ was the Son of God can be meant only in a mystical sense which but approximates the human sense of these words, because nobody would maintain that God, as a Being endowed with human sexual organs, had intercourse with the woman from whose womb Jesus Christ came forth" (1955: 42). Schreber then compares himself to Mary: "Something like the conception of Jesus Christ by an Immaculate Virgin – i.e. one who never had intercourse with a man – happened in my own body" (1955: 42–3n.) On two occasions in his psychiatrist's asylum, he says, "I had a female genital organ, although a poorly developed one, and in my body felt quickening like the first signs of life of a human embryo: by a divine miracle God's nerves corresponding to male seed had been thrown into my body; in other words fertilization had occurred" (1955: 43n.).

This is not exactly parthenogenesis, nor is it exactly pseudocyesis, but twice

Schreber apparently felt that he was a virginally pregnant woman in some mystical sense as a result of miraculous contact with God's nerves – or God's rays. In a discussion of the conception of the Virgin Mary, Ernest Jones mentions "the legends of virgins that have been impregnated by rays of light" (1951 2: 306). The myths of Rhea Sylvia and Mary are important to Schreber because he believes that they parallel and might possibly explain his own peculiar experience.

By comparing himself to Rhea Sylvia and Mary on the basis of the common denominator "intercourse with a god," Schreber invokes the archetypes of "miraculous conception" and "virgin birth." Although Schreber believes that after he has been transformed into a woman he will be literally impregnated by God and delivered of a new world, Jung says that such phenomena constitute not a physical but a "psychic genesis" in which "everything must happen non-empirically, e.g., by means of a virgin birth, or by miraculous conception," etc. (*CW* 9,1: 166, par. 282). For Schreber, his experience is the physical effect of a metaphysical cause.

In contrast, Jung regards such experiences as psychic facts. This psychological perspective, he says, "is exclusively phenomenological, that is, it is concerned with occurrences, events, experiences – in a word, with facts." What interests Jung is *psychological truth*, which he defines phenomenologically as the reality of psychic facts, or the existence of psychic ideas: "When psychology speaks, for instance, of the motif of the virgin birth, it is only concerned with the fact that there is such an idea, but it is not concerned with the question whether such an idea is true or false in any other sense. The idea is psychologically true inasmuch as it exists" (*CW* 11: 6, par. 4).

According to Jung, as science demythologizes miracles like "virgin birth," it aestheticizes them as "pretty stories, but none the less untrue." Jung, however, cautions against such devaluation by putative falsification: "Do not overlook the fact that these ideas which millions of men carried with them through generations are great eternal psychological truths." Rather than physicalize the miracle of virgin birth, as both Schreber and the scientists do, Jung psychologizes it: "Let us look at this truth as the psychologist sees it. Here is the mind of man, without prejudice, spotless, untainted, symbolized by a virgin. And that virgin mind of man can give birth to God himself' (1977: 72).

In this respect, M. Esther Harding notes that the phenomena that traditionally attend virgin birth "would form a flagrant contradiction or require an impossible miracle, if they were taken as true on the objective plane." Although such phenomena may be objectively false, Harding says, they may be subjectively true: "If, however, we recognize religious concepts as symbolic and interpret these contradictions psychologically we realize that the term 'virginity' must refer to a *quality*, to a subjective state, a psychological attitude, not to a physiological or external fact" (1955: 102). In short, what is at issue is not physical but psychic (mental or attitudinal) virginity.

What for Schreber is physically and metaphysically true is for Jung only psychologically and phenomenologically true. Such is the difference between a paranoid schizophrenic and a psychoanalyst. In discussing "virgin conception" or "supernatural conception," Jung says that it "can, of course, be taken as a meta-physical fact, but psychologically it tells us that a content of the unconscious ('child') has come into existence without the natural help of a human father (i.e., consciousness)." The idea of a miraculous conception "in psychological language means that a central archetype, the God-image, has renewed itself ('been reborn') and become 'incarnate' in a way perceptible to consciousness" (*CW* 5: 323, par. 497).

Schreber believes that with the supernatural help of a divine father a new world will come into existence through him. Thus he imagines himself as the woman, the virgin, the mother who by a miraculous conception will be the vehicle for a rebirth and incarnation of all mankind. According to Jung, "The 'mother' corresponds to the 'virgin anima.'" (*CW* 5: 323, par. 497). Psychologically, Schreber's trans-formation into a woman is a transformation into a virgin anima, pregnant with meaning.

Because Schreber is a paranoid schizophrenic, however, he is in no position to understand what his "pregnancy" means as a strictly psychic fact. Whereas Jung interprets such a "conception" as nothing more (nor less) than a *concept* in the unconscious – that is, as an archetypal idea – Schreber reifies the experience. He commits the fallacy that Jung calls "hypostatizing a metaphysical assertion" (1963: 70). Schreber experiences the virgin anima not as the feminine but quite lit-erally as a female and pregnancy quite literally as "a human embryo." His nervous illness is a reification, a hypostatization, a literalization of his experience of being unmanned in order for the world and all mankind to be reborn and incarnated through him.

Creation myths

Although Schreber does not explicitly say so, he implies quite definitely that he considers himself an "Eternal Jew" who has been selected by God to be the medium for world recreation after world destruction. The problem for Schreber is that he is, like Noah and Deucalion, a man – and God is also a "man." In order for him to have intercourse with God for the express purpose of procreation, Schreber has to be unmanned.

As Freud interprets Schreber's experience, to be unmanned is to be castrated. Only once, however (and then not in Schreber's *Memoirs* but in a pre-discharge report by Schreber's psychiatrist), is there any mention of castration. In that docu-ment his psychiatrist states that Schreber believed "that his penis has been twisted off by a 'nerve probe'" (Lothane 1992: 472).

In contrast, what Schreber emphasizes in his *Memoirs* is not a castration but a retraction and transformation of the genitals. He describes the process of unman-ning as follows:

> The Eternal Jew (in the sense described) had to be *unmanned* (transformed into a woman) to be able to bear children. This process of unmanning consisted in

the (external) male genitals (scrotum and penis) being retracted into the body and the internal sexual organs being at the same time transformed into the corresponding female sexual organs.

(Schreber 1955: 73)

That is, in order to be in the same position as Rhea Sylvia and Mary in relation to a god, Schreber has to experience a sex change. The only way that he can have intercourse with God is transsexually. His unmanning is, in this sense, really a "womanning." It is not simply a negative experience but a positive one whose purpose is the beginning of a new world.

Ida Macalpine and Richard A. Hunter, the translators of Schreber's *Memoirs*, note that the question of "procreation as a man" was converted into the possibility of procreation as a woman – and "eventually superseded by fantasies of divine impregnation like the Virgin Mary and Rhea Sylvia." They argue, against Freud, that Schreber's unmanning, or transformation into a woman, was not a "castration" as a result of "homosexual wishes" but a necessary precondition for "procreation" (Macalpine and Hunter 1955: 389). Schreber's experience, they say, was "a reactivation of unconscious, archaic procreation fantasies concerning life, death, immortality, rebirth, creation, including self-impregnation, and accompanied by absolute ambisexuality expressed in doubt and uncertainty about his sex." If there was any homosexual wish at all, it was "secondary to the primary fantasy of having to be transformed into a woman to be able to procreate." In effect, procreation was a metaphor for creation, "sexually or parthenogenetically" (Macalpine and Hunter 1955: 395).

In this respect, Schreber says that the eight years that he spent with his wife between his first nervous illness and his second were "on the whole quite happy ones, rich also in outward honours and marred only from time to time by the repeated disappointment of our hope of being blessed with children" (1955: 63). That is, just before Schreber begins to discuss his thoughts about divine creation, he mentions his personal disappointment about human procreation. In all probability this juxtaposition of concerns about human procreation and divine creation was hardly coincidental. Schreber was not impotent, nor his wife infertile. His wife had at least six pregnancies, all of which ended either in stillbirths or in miscarriages.

Not only manhood but also fatherhood was a serious issue for Schreber. Apparently he conflated masculinity with paternity. From the perspective of psychopathology, his unmanning was an elaborate rationalization that Schreber contrived in order to excuse his failure to father children. (Technically, of course, it was not Schreber but his wife who had "failed" – either by not being able to carry pregnancies to full term or by not giving birth to live children.) Being transformed into a woman was a convenient solution to the problem. Thus Freud says that Schreber "may have formed a phantasy that if he were a woman he would manage the business of having children more successfully." Such a delusion would "be designed to offer him an escape from his childlessness" (*SE* 12: 58). If Schreber was not a man but a woman, that fact would instantaneously render irrelevant any notion that Schreber had not been man enough to become a father. By being transformed into a woman in order to have intercourse with God, Schreber could now mother all mankind. If his wife could not bear children, he would.

Such was the beginning of Schreber's own, ad hoc "creation myth." This is a particular instance of what George Lakoff and Mark Johnson call "the general metaphor CREATION IS BIRTH" (1980: 75). Schreber imagines divine creation metaphorically in terms of human procreation – or, to be exact, parturition. What is distinctive about his cosmogony is that it is not a masculine but a feminine, even a "feminist" creation myth.

Eventually Schreber concluded "beyond doubt that the Order of the World imperiously demanded my unmanning, whether I personally liked it or not, and that therefore it was *common sense* that nothing was left to me but reconcile myself to the thought of being transformed into a woman." The only plausible explanation that occurred to him was that his being unmanned would enable "fertilization by divine rays for the purpose of creating new human beings" (1955: 148). From that moment Schreber "wholeheartedly inscribed the cultivation of femininity on my banner." He resolved to "continue to do so as far as consideration of my environment allows, whatever other people who are ignorant of the supernatural reasons may think of me." He challenged others to consider whether, in identical circumstances, they would accept the alternative: "I would like to meet the man who, faced with the choice of either becoming a demented human being in male habitus or a spirited woman, would not prefer the latter. Such and *only such* is the issue for me" (1955: 149).

In this respect, Schreber's cosmogony is an exception to the rule of the vast majority of creation myths (which tend to be androcentric, or phallocentric, rather than gynocentric) that Marta Weigle surveys in *Creation and Procreation* (1989). Schreber's mythopoeic experience of being unmanned, transformed into a woman, or "womanned" in order to have transsexual intercourse with God is an example of what Stith Thompson calls the motif of miraculous conception. As Thompson classifies the variations on this theme, Type 518 is "*Conception from divine impregnation*" (1955 5: 393). Schreber believed that he was becoming neither the son nor the father but the very mother of all divine creation.

Schreber's creation myth is a "deist" cosmogony. Schreber believes that as soon as God had miraculously created the world, all life, and man, He withdrew from His creation and only in extraordinary circumstances ever again intervened. "God," he says, "exercised His power of miracles on our earth – as probably on any other celestial body which had reached the same degree of development – only until the ultimate aim of His creation was attained with the creation of the human being." Schreber states: "From then on He left the created organic world as it were to itself, and interfered by miracle only very rarely, if at all, in very exceptional cases." After the creation of man, "He Himself retired to an enormous distance" (1955: 191). Schreber rejects Darwin's theory of "blind accident as the cause of evolutionary development." Rather, creation is the result of God's "conscious will." That creation is divinely purposive, Schreber declares, "must be granted even by scientists otherwise inclined to attribute the 'tenacity of deistic notions' to the lack of intellect of the majority of people" (1955: 192). Thus Schreber explicitly identifies himself as a deist and what would now be called a "creationist" rather than an evolutionist.

"The essential secret of creation," Schreber acknowledges, "remains a closed book even for me; I have only an inkling which I will try to set out." He believes that life "did not come into existence as Darwin postulated by new species developing through gradual evolution from earlier forms, but in a series of single acts of creation" (1955: 184). Creation occurs by "direct genesis," which is equivalent to "*spontaneous generation*" (1955: 185). Spontaneous generation only now occurs "since conditions contrary to the Order of the World have arisen." Otherwise, it probably has not occurred "for thousands of years." Schreber then defines the phrase: "'Spontaneous generation' is basically nothing other than a literal term for what I have called – in accordance with the language of the Bible and other religious sources – creation through divine miracles" (1955: 191). In this sense, for Schreber to be unmanned, or transformed into a woman, in order to have transsexual intercourse with God, be impregnated by divine rays, and be delivered of a new world, was for mankind to be miraculously renewed or spontaneously regenerated in a single act of creation.

According to Freud, notions about a "world-catastrophe" often occur to paranoid schizophrenics who experience destruction internally (*SE* 12: 69). "The end of the world," he says, "is the projection of this internal catastrophe" (*SE* 12: 70). The paranoid schizophrenic then replaces external reality with an internal reality – that is, with a delusion. The formation of this delusion, Freud says, "*is in reality an attempt at recovery, a process of reconstruction.*" This effort at recreation, however, is always at least partly a failure. Thus Freud says, rather pessimistically: "Such a reconstruction after the catastrophe is successful to a greater or lesser extent, but never wholly so" (*SE* 12: 71).

In *Creation Myths*, Marie-Louise von Franz is more optimistic than Freud. She asks, "Where do we see creation myths nowadays, or elements, or typical motifs of creation myths in our practical analytical work and in dreams?" She answers that they appear most conspicuously "in *schizophrenic material*, where a schizophrenic episode is often prepared by dreams of world destruction." Contemporary variations on the catastrophe theme, especially during the Cold War between the United States and the Union of Soviet Socialist Republics, between capitalism and communism, often include "an atomic explosion, or the end of the world." Such dreams contain "absolutely apocalyptic images" (1995: 13). These images, von Franz says, indicate that "the unconscious of this human being is in a state of explosion or is going to explode." The schizophrenic's destructive images presage psychic disintegration. They herald the fact that "his subjective world will actually go to pieces." Frequently, however, other, creative images subsequently emerge from the unconscious to facilitate a possible psychic reintegration. Von Franz says that "very often when a schizophrenic episode begins to fade, or to pass out of its acute phase, then in fantasies and dreams the motifs of creation myths come up and the world is recreated from a very small germ, just as it is in creation myths." According to von Franz, a psychoanalyst who is able to "understand these rebuilding symbols" and to "support them adequately" may be able to "help in the rebuilding of a new conscious personality" (1995: 14). Schreber, of course, had no access to such an analyst – Freudian, Jungian, or otherwise.

Similarly, Perry contends that "visions of the end of the world and of its new beginning" assume special prominence at decisively critical junctures of disorganization in the experience of both individuals and cultures. Such visions illustrate the destructive and recreative dynamic "of the psyche's world image in the turmoils of drastic change." In this respect, Perry asserts that "psychotic ideation" is often an instance of the "myth-making process" (1987: 39). Psychohistorically, he says, the "world renewal" motif has undergone a transition from an external "form in myth and ritual traditions" expressed culturally to an internal "counterpart in the spontaneous myth-making process" expressed individually (1987: 56). Perry says that when "profound and acute reorganization" of either an individual or a culture becomes necessary, certain persons "who have the aptitude for visionary encounters with the archaic affect-images – by which he means archetypal images – "experience an activation of the world image" (1987: 57). He describes this mythopoeic process as follows:

> The opposites are rent asunder, that is, opposing forces clash, and disorder vies with order. The previously predominating pattern is broken up, or at least such a catastrophe is threatened. There follows its transformation in the image of world regeneration as the seed of a new culture form in mythic expression. This suggests that a transformed culture arises out of transformed persons.
>
> (Perry 1987: 57)

According to Perry, the experience of an individual may be a truly prophetic vision of a vast, very fast transformation of the world-view of a culture:

> It is imperative for us constantly to remind ourselves that the horrific vision of world destruction is part and parcel of the mythic imagery of rapid culture change and of world views in transition, as we have observed already. Beholding the world coming to its end amid storm, earthquake, flood, and fire we have found to be a typical experience of a prophet whose psyche is registering the emotional impact of the end of an era. The ensuing world regeneration is then the picture of the ushering in of a new age, meaning by this an innovative cultural effort whose configuration is outlined in a fresh myth and ritual form.
>
> (Perry 1987: 192)

Whereas von Franz emphasizes the mythopoeic process on the individual level, Perry extends it to the cultural level through visionary experience on the individual level.

In this sense, Schreber's experience of the end of the world was also an experience of the end of the nineteenth century, the fin de siècle, and the beginning of the twentieth century. Was he a prophet as well as a paranoid schizophrenic, and, if so, what did he prophesy? Was his individual vision, his "creation myth," not also a cultural prophecy of the possibility, for men, of a new experience of the feminine and a new empathic relation to it? Was it not also even a "feminist" manifesto, no longer a male insistence on masculinity, or "manliness," that would negatively equate femininity with effeminacy or unmanning with emasculation (or, as Freud would say, "castration") but a *Weltanschauung* that would positively regard Schreber's experience as a "womanning" – an invagination, an invulvation, a feminization of man? This would be a new dispensation – a new world indeed. Perhaps the time has come for feminists to inscribe Schreber on *their* banner.

Anima and androgyny

In *A Room of One's Own*, Virginia Woolf asks the question that Jung asked about the relation between sex and gender, between men and the feminine (or anima) and women and the masculine (or animus). Nor Hall quotes Woolf as wondering "whether there are two sexes in the mind corresponding to the two sexes in the body, and whether they also require to be united in order to get complete satisfaction and happiness" (cited in Hall 1980: 30–1). Woolf recounts how she proceeded "amateurishly to sketch a plan of the soul so that in each of us two powers preside, one male, one female." She speculates that "in the man's brain, the man predominates over the woman, and in the woman's brain, the woman predominates over the man" (cited in Hall 1980: 31). Woolf elaborates as follows:

> The normal and comfortable state of being is that when the two live in harmony together, spiritually cooperating. If one is a man, still the woman part of the brain must have effect; and a woman also must have intercourse with the man in her. Coleridge perhaps meant this when he said that a great mind is androgynous. It is when this fusion takes place that the mind is fully fertilised and uses all its faculties. Perhaps a mind that is purely masculine cannot create, any more than a mind that is purely feminine, I thought. But it would be well to test what one meant by man-womanly, and conversely by woman-manly.
>
> (cited in Hall 1980: 31)

Schreber literalizes this possibility. Rather than remain male and become more feminine, he becomes literally female. He is the very embodiment of what James Joyce has one of the characters in *Ulysses* say ironically of Leopold Bloom – that he is "a finished example of the new womanly man" (1961: 493). Like Schreber, Bloom is "about to have a baby" (1961: 494). As Jung says, the anima "frequently gives rise in dreams to the symbol of psychic pregnancy" (*CW* 6: 469, par. 806). Apparently the same could be said of at least some masterpieces of modern literature.

At the end of his *Memoirs*, Schreber entertains a radical solution to the "opposite sex" problem – that is, to the ostensible duality between male and female. What he proposes is an imaginative experience of androgyny. Schreber says that "when I speak of my duty to cultivate voluptuousness, I *never mean any sexual desires towards other human beings (females) least of all sexual intercourse*, but that I have to imagine myself as man and woman in one person having intercourse with myself or somehow have to achieve with myself a certain sexual excitement etc. – which perhaps under other circumstances might be considered immoral – but which has nothing whatever to do with any idea of masturbation or anything like it" (1955: 208). Schreber believes that "God would never attempt to withdraw" from him but "would follow my attraction without resistance permanently and uninterruptedly" if only he could attain an androgynous unity – "if only I could *always* by playing the woman's part in sexual embrace with myself" (1955: 210).

This is not exactly the uroboric image of a snake biting its own tail, but it is an androgynous image of a man clasping his own femininity. Is this image an individual delusion, just an autoerotically perverse fantasy, or is it a cultural prophecy? The image might merely be an example of the influence of the "unconscious anima," which Jung says is "an autoerotic being whose one aim is to take total possession of the individual" (*CW* 16: 295, par. 504). Hillman, however, characterizes Schreber as a prophet of "the feminist movement," "the psycho-religions of matriarchy and the Goddess," and "bisexual androgyny" (1988: 56).

In *Androgyny*, June Singer imagines masculine and feminine "clasped together in a well-fitting embrace" (1976: vii). She discerns in contemporary culture a collective psychic transformation that "is preparing the way for a new age" that might eventually be called the "Age of Androgyny" (1976: 18). According to Singer, "Androgyny is an *archetype* inherent in the human psyche." It is perhaps "the oldest archetype of which we have any experience" (1976: 20). She defines it as "a specific way of joining the 'masculine' and 'feminine' aspects of a single human being" (1976: 22).

Singer notes that the image of the androgyne first appears in Greek philosophy (which in this instance is really a mythology) in Plato's *Symposium*. She quotes a passage in which Aristophanes recounts a creation myth that purports to explain the origin of human beings: "The sexes were not two, as they are now, but originally three in number; there was man, woman, and a union of the two, having a name corresponding to this double nature, which once had a real existence, but is now lost, and the word 'Androgynous' is only preserved as a term of reproach" (1976: 118). According to Aristophanes, the subsequent division of the androgynous unity into the duality of the opposite sexes accounts for "the desire of one another which is implanted within us, reuniting our original nature, making one of two, and healing the state of man." As a result of this separation, human beings have "one side only." Not only physically but also psychically male and female are one-sided. Aristophanes says: "For the intense yearning which each of them has for the other does not appear to be the desire of lovers' intercourse, but of something else which the soul of either evidently desires and cannot tell, and of which she has only a dark and doubtful presentiment" (1976: 119). Singer concludes that "Plato's Androgyne suggests, from a psychological point of view, why human beings seem to need each other in a way that goes beyond the demands of pure sexuality or reproduction" (1976: 120).

What Singer calls the archetypal idea of androgyny Jung also calls "the archetypal idea of the syzygy, or conjunction of male and female" (*CW* 9,1: 67, par. 138). Jung says that "the syzygy does indeed represent the psychic contents that irrupt into consciousness in a psychosis (most clearly of all in the paranoid forms of schizophrenia)" (*CW* 9,2: 33, par. 62). In this respect, he notes that Schreber's case is "classic" (*CW* 9,2: 33, par. 62n.). Because Schreber literalizes the archetype of the syzygy, he ultimately imagines the conjunction of male and female as voluptuously androgynous intercourse with himself (not transsexual intercourse with God). According to Schreber, "Voluptuousness is permissible for human beings if sanctified in the bond of marriage it serves the purpose of reproduction" (1955: 210). He himself, however, is apparently an exception to this rule – at least to the extent that he imaginatively experiences androgynous intercourse with himself exclusively for the purpose of cultivating voluptuousness (however different that may be from mere masturbation).

Hillman interprets Schreber's experience in terms of the myth of Eros and Psyche in *The Golden Ass*. "Unmanning did not intend the love of men, homoeros in the literal homosexual sense," Hillman says. "Its intention was not effeminization so much as anima, soul, and it proceeded by voluptuousness, an ever-developing *voluptas*; Voluptas, the child in the belly of pregnant Psyche in Apuleius' tale" (1988: 21). Eros is love; Psyche, soul; Voluptas, pleasure. Female voluptuousness, or sensuous pleasure, evokes in Schreber such love that "she" literally embodies soul, or anima, so that he then literally embraces it in androgynous intercourse. Love of soul so voluptuously animates Schreber that "she" gives birth to pleasure. What Freud calls the "pleasure principle" is for Schreber the "voluptuousness principle."

Schreber ends his *Memoirs* on an unsure but triumphal note as he contemplates the future:

> And so I believe I am not mistaken in expecting that a very special palm of victory will eventually be mine. I cannot say with any certainty what form it will take. As possibilities I would mention that my unmanning will be accomplished with the result that by divine fertilization offspring will issue from my lap, or alternatively that great fame will be attached to my name surpassing that of thousands of other people much better mentally endowed.
>
> (Schreber 1955: 214)

Schreber failed to have children, or offspring in that literal sense, with his wife; he imagined having offspring with God; finally he did succeed in having one child – a "soul-child" – the book that he created, the *Memoirs* that he wrote. Such were the mythopoeic forces of mankind as they became so voluptuously, so fertilely embodied, or "womanned," in Schreber. If Schreber did not exactly achieve "great fame," he at least published "great thoughts," which he hoped readers would eventually regard as much more than merely "a pathological offspring of my imagination."

Analytic indications

Neither Freud nor Jung ever met Schreber, nor did they attempt to do so, although at the time he was still alive – not alive and well but alive and still nervously ill. Freud knew that "the man is still alive." He considered "asking him for certain information (e.g., when he got married) and for permission to work on his story." He worried, however, that "perhaps that would be risky." He asked Jung: "What do you think?" (Freud and Jung 1974: 358). There is no record of any reply from Jung to the question. The risk, of course, was that Schreber might prefer that Freud *not* work on his story. Whether Freud should have sought permission from Schreber is an ethical issue. There is also a practical issue. Freud's interpretation of "Schreber" is an interpretation *not of a person but of a text*. The practical issue is whether any analyst should attempt to analyze any person in absentia.

Psychoanalysis is not only a "talking cure." It is also a "listening cure" and a "talking back cure." The patient talks, and the analyst listens; the analyst talks, and the patient listens – and then the patient has an opportunity to talk back. In short, psychoanalysis is not a monologue but a dialogue. It is what Walter Bonime calls a *"collaborative process"* between analyst and patient (1989: 60). Analysis is an interpersonal dialogue that, when effective, facilitates an intrapsychic dialogue between the ego and the unconscious. An interpretation of a text is not, in that sense, an analysis. A text may "talk," but it cannot listen, nor can it talk back.

Psychoanalysis entails interpretation, but it is not just interpretation *of a text* – it is interpretation *of a person* and *to a person*, and that person may either accept the interpretation or reject it. The patient may reject an interpretation for good reason when it is an inaccurate interpretation. A patient may, of course, resist an interpretation even though it is accurate. The patient may be defensive because an accurate interpretation is emotionally intolerable. Psychoanalysis is not only an interpretative exchange but also a relational encounter. In this respect, the emotional dimension of the relation between patient and analyst in the transference is, if not decisive, at least very important for the success or failure of the analysis. Whether a patient is receptive or not is to a considerable extent a function of whether the transference is emotionally negative or positive (or whether the analyst is able effectively to manage both the negative and positive aspects of the transference in the analytic process). A positive transference can facilitate receptivity, while a negative transference can increase resistance.

Neither Freud nor Jung ever discusses in this sense what an *analysis* of Schreber might have entailed. I do not pretend to know what might have "cured" Schreber. I, too, have at my disposal only the text, not the person. In spite of this liability, what interests me is whether there are, in Schreber's *Memoirs*, any *analytic indications* (material that would indicate how to analyze Schreber effectively). What, if anything, does the text indicate about how an analyst might have analyzed Schreber the person? Although von Franz says that an analyst who "understands" and "supports" the creation myth of a schizophrenic may facilitate the reconstruction of a personality that has experienced "end-of-the-world" destruction, she does not specify what "understanding" and "supporting" would entail in a practical sense.

Paranoid schizophrenics are notoriously difficult, if not impossible, to analyze. Many analysts would say that they are simply "unanalyzable" – that the psyche of a paranoid schizophrenic is utterly impenetrable. For example, Freud says that because with paranoid schizophrenics the transference is essentially negative, "there ceases to be any possibility of influence or cure" (*SE* 12: 107). In this respect, Schreber's *Memoirs* indicates just how difficult it would be for analysis to influence, let alone "cure," Schreber.

According to David Shapiro, the essence of the "paranoid style" is rampant, pervasive suspicion (1965). Paranoid schizophrenics are suspicious that someone might "influence" them. In just this way, Schreber suspects that his psychiatrist's nerves (or God's rays) might influence his nerves – that is, murder his soul or destroy his reason. Schreber believes that his psychiatrist has exerted this influence by telepathy. He assumes that his psychiatrist is attempting to read his thoughts for the purpose of, as he says, "appropriating his mental powers." In order to defend himself, Schreber pretends that he is demented – that he has no thoughts that his psychiatrist might read. This is what Schreber means by "the so-called not-thinking-of-anything-thought."

Schreber is not the only one who considers telepathy to be a distinct possibility. For example, Freud says:

> One is led to a suspicion that this is the original, archaic method of communication between individuals and that in the course of phylogenetic evolution it has been replaced by the better method of giving information with the help of signals which are picked up by the sense organs. But the older method might have persisted in the background and still be able to put itself into effect under certain conditions.
>
> (*SE* 22: 55)

According to Freud, "All this is still uncertain and full of unsolved riddles." Schreber is frightened by the possibility of telepathy, while Freud says that "there is no reason to be frightened by it" (*SE* 22: 55).

That Schreber is so frightened by and so defended against any thought-reading by his psychiatrist (because he is so suspicious of being influenced) indicates that a negative transference would complicate and perhaps contravene any treatment by an analyst. Analysts are, in a certain sense, "thought readers." I do not mean that they are telepaths. I merely mean that an analyst attempts to "read" the thoughts of a patient as they emerge from the unconscious and then, if and when appropriate, interprets them to the patient. The very success of analysis is a function of what I would call the *hermeneutic literacy* of the analyst and the emotional receptivity of the patient to this "thought-reading."

Because Freud emphasizes the essential negativity of the transference in the case of paranoid schizophrenics, he is prognostically extremely pessimistic. He states that paranoid schizophrenics are incapable of a positive transference and that therefore it is not just difficult but impossible to influence or "cure" them by analysis. Is there any reason for optimism in Schreber's case? There is one indication that Schreber might be amenable to analytic influence: he is receptive to penetration and impregnation by God. In spite of what Freud says, Schreber is a paranoid schizophrenic who is evidently capable of a "positive transference" – at least to God.

Actually, Schreber has not only a positive transference but also a negative transference to God – at least to the extent that he believes that God might influence his thoughts, destroy his reason, and murder (or, like a demon, possess) his soul. The form that the transference assumes in this instance is an apparently irreconcilable conflict of opposites. The implication is that Schreber would tend in the positive transference to "deify" the analyst and in the negative transference to "demonize" the analyst. In such a situation, an analyst should avoid in the countertransference any induction that would reproduce this oppositional tendency in the analytic process. The analyst should manage both the positive and negative aspects of the transference so that a patient like Schreber might be better able to tolerate the tension of the opposites and perhaps even eventually achieve a reconciliation of the opposites. The ultimate purpose of the analytic process is neither a "deification" nor a "demonization" of the analyst but rather a *humanization* of both the analyst and the patient.

Jung notes that in certain instances a transference onto the analyst produces an excessive valuation, with the result that to the patient the analyst seems like a "god" (*CW* 7: 130, par. 206). In effect, such a patient projects onto the analyst the archetypal "God-image." Jung quite properly cautions against any inflationary identification by the analyst with the God-image through an induction in the countertransference. It is essential that analysts not believe that they are God or that they are like a god. Analysts need to bear constantly in mind that they are not "gods" but only analysts. It is equally important, however, that the analyst not immediately disabuse the patient of a transference, even if that transference is a projection of the God-image onto the analyst. (The analysis should not "resolve" the transference but tolerate the transference until it "dissolves" of its own accord, in its own good time.)

Von Franz says that the analyst should not only tolerate the transference but also even *actualize* it, at least temporarily. It is appropriate, she says, "if, for example, a mother transference is present, to the extent that one feels it, actually to be motherly until the projection has become ripe for talking about" (1993c: 241). Analogously, it might be appropriate when an archetypal "god transference" is present, for the analyst actually to be "godly" at least until the time is right and the patient is ready to discuss the projection and retract it. In such a situation, it would be essential for the analyst not to identify with the God-image unconsciously but to act on it consciously in the analytic process.

How might an interpretation influence Schreber? How might it eventually penetrate and impregnate him? How might an analysis be as creative as a creation myth? If Schreber had had access to an analyst whom he could temporarily have regarded as a god, as god-like, or godly, he might have regarded analytic interpretation (in the "theologico-psychological" terminology that Schreber employs) not as "demonic possession" (or insidious, telepathic influence) but as "divine revelation." Schreber might have been able to regard the interpretations of such an analyst as examples of what Jung calls the "*logos spermatikos*" (*CW* 13: 40, par. 59), the spermatic word that has the potency (or potential) spiritually to fertilize the psyche so that it becomes pregnant with meaning.

As von Franz says, for an analyst to actualize a transference is only a temporary measure. It is not a permanent solution to the problem. The only indication that Schreber is at all amenable to influence is the receptivity that he exhibits in relation to the notion that God will penetrate him and impregnate him. In this instance, an archetypal transference of the God-image onto an analyst who would, for a time, actualize that transference might effectively diminish the resistance and at least incrementally enhance the possibility of a "cure," however remote that prospect might be in the case of a paranoid schizophrenic. In Schreber's case, if such an actualization did not produce a "cure," it might at least promote a more effective integration of the feminine. (Such an actualization would be a necessary but temporary prelude to the gradual dissolution of the archetypal transference and an eventual humanization of both the analyst and the patient.)

This is, of course, speculation. We will never know whether such an analytic strategy and tactic would have been effective. As refractory as paranoid schizophrenia is to treatment, the only hope for a patient in Schreber's condition might be the toleration and actualization of an archetypal transference. The analyst would not unconsciously succumb to inflation (and "play God") but would consciously empathize with the "god transference" in hopes that such an attitude would enable the patient eventually to be emotionally receptive to analytic interpretation and amenable to analytic influence.

Schreber may have been a paranoid schizophrenic, but he was not utterly inaccessible to contact. He did form a transference of sorts to his psychiatrist. This transference he called "nerve-contact." What was problematic about this transference was Schreber's suspicion that his psychiatrist was abusing that nerve-contact. Schreber suspected that his psychiatrist, "like so many doctors, could not completely resist the temptation of using a patient in your care *as an object for scientific experiments* apart from the real purpose of a cure." The implication is that Schreber would not have objected to nerve-contact if he could have believed that the intent was curative. What he protested against was being "objectified." He did not want someone to "experiment" on him; he needed someone to *empathize* with him.

If the schizophrenic Schreber had had an analyst who was empathic in the transference and who could have effectively managed both the positive and negative aspects of the transference, then he might have been less paranoid. He might eventually have been more receptive to interpretations that might have penetrated and impregnated him (for example, an interpretation that Schreber's "womanning" was not a literal transformation into a female but a "feminization," a metaphorical transformation of the masculine by the anima). With an empathic analyst Schreber might ultimately have been delivered of a "new world" – a new world-view – which, if it did not result in a "cure," might at least have resulted in what would have been, for him, a psychically fertile integration of the feminine.

Chapter 6

Dreaming of the Ku Klux Klan

"Race," culture, and history in psychoanalysis

In the summer of 1994, I spent a month in Britain, where I delivered a series of lectures at the Psychoanalytic Studies Programmes at the University of Kent and Middlesex University, the Psychoanalytic Forum of the History and Philosophy of Science Programme at Cambridge University, the London Convivium for Archetypal Studies, and the Society of Analytical Psychology. These occasions were an opportunity for me to present portions of research that I eventually included in my book *The Multicultural Imagination: "Race," Color, and the Unconscious* (Adams 1996).

On the day of my lecture at the Society of Analytical Psychology (SAP) a friend of mine informed me, in a joking way, that the Jungians whom I would encounter at the SAP would all be "closet Kleinians." He meant that they would hear my lecture with developmental object relations ears. After my lecture I conducted a clinical workshop exclusively for SAP analysts. In that less formal, more intimate format, in which I presented case material, I had an opportunity to receive comments, criticisms, and questions. The consensus among the SAP analysts in attendance was that we become racists quite literally at the breast, when, in the "paranoid–schizoid position," we split object relations into "good" and "bad." From that perspective, "white–black" racism is just a particular application of a general, infantile "good–bad" extremism.

Although I had been told to expect a Kleinian reaction to my lecture, I must say that I was still surprised. I responded to the SAP analysts by saying that I believe that racism is a *cultural* formation in a *historical* context and that it is not conveniently and simply reducible to a *personal* (or *interpersonal*) formation in a *biographical* context. I argued that "culture" and "history" are factors in their own right, with their own, often profound influence. Although cultural and historical factors do ultimately converge in certain personal (or interpersonal) and biographical experiences, these factors exist on an irreducibly collective level. As Andrew Samuels, one SAP analyst who does not reduce the cultural to the personal, says:

> The problem of reductionism does not stem from having a therapeutic *attitude* to the pathologies of culture as these are expressed in political issues. Rather,

the problem stems from approaching an entire culture, or large chunks of it, *as if it were an individual or even as if it were a baby*. In this infantilization of culture, depth psychology deploys a version of personality development couched in judgmental terms to understand a collective and political process.

(Samuels 1993: 9)

(In this context, it is well to recall that Jung objected to the reduction of psychic reality not only to the "sexual" but also to the *infantile*.) We do not become racists because we have sucked "bad milk" from the breast of the mother and have suffered an arrest and a fixation short of the "depressive position." Developmental object relations theory, Kleinian or otherwise, cannot account in practice for why we so illogically regard as *psychically inferior* to us those who are simply (and superficially) *physically different* from us – those who happen to have, say, a different skin color than we have. We become racists because we have a culture with a history that includes the atrocities of slavery and segregation – that is, because culturally and historically we have exploitatively "inferiorized" the other.

I do not know to what extent my response was persuasive. What I had to say seemed so at variance with the conventional theoretical wisdom of the SAP that I may merely have managed to dumbfound most of the analysts. I want to state emphatically that I do not mean to deprecate the SAP. I remain immensely grateful for the opportunity to lecture there and the gracious reception that I was accorded on that occasion. I respect the analysts of the SAP, as well as the theoretical position that they espouse, however much I may beg to differ with some of them on certain points regarding the significance of cultural factors. The very fact that the SAP would invite me to lecture on such a topic indicates that they are amenable to a consideration of other ideas and opinions and a conversation about them. To me, the willingness of the SAP analysts to engage in dialogue on controversial issues is the very epitome of the analytic attitude.

Now, what is the relevance of this anecdote? I do not assume that psychoanalysts are utterly oblivious to culture and history, but I do wonder to what extent certain theoretical preferences prevent them from dealing adequately with such issues as racism. I do not believe that mere sensitivity to patients of different "races" suffices, valuable as it may be. Nor do I propose a novel technique for working with patients for whom "race" is an important issue. We do not need yet another technique. Rather, we need to appreciate that culture and history are *independent variables* in the psychoanalytic equation.

In recent years, psychoanalysis has experienced a paradigm shift to what Jay R. Greenberg and Stephen A. Mitchell call "the relational model" (1983). (Many, if not most, contemporary analysts have become what I call "psycho-relationists.") Psychoanalysis has moved from what Arnold H. Modell calls a "one-person" psychology to a "two-person" psychology (1984). As important as this shift from a monadic to a dyadic model may be, it nevertheless falls far short of what I believe is necessary. Just because we now explicitly acknowledge that analysis is a process that involves two persons, not just one person, and just because we now recognize that object relations are so developmentally significant, this paradigm shift does not mean that we have produced the ultimate theory about which we deserve to be complacent.

Mitchell does briefly discuss culture. Although he mentions what he calls "cultural relations" (1988: 17–18), he seems to reduce them to interpersonal relations – that is, to relations between one person and another person, not to relations between persons and *culture* as an independent variable. Like other analysts with an interest in developmental object relations psychology, he gives short shrift to culture as an autonomous factor with a quite specific history. Mitchell was a faculty member at the William Alanson White Institute where Harry Stack Sullivan, Erich Fromm, and Clara Thompson established the interpersonal school of analysis. Historically, another name for the interpersonal school was the cultural school. As Thompson says: "The contributions of Sullivan and Fromm have come to be called the 'cultural school,' because of the great emphasis of both on the interpersonal factors in personality formation and personal difficulties" (1964: 99). I would note that Thompson, like Mitchell, equates the "cultural" with the "interpersonal." The William Alanson White Institute is one of the great analytic institutes, but I believe that it is accurate to say that the reputation that it currently enjoys is more as the interpersonal school and less as a cultural school – at least as I define "culture."

Karen Horney was perhaps the first psychoanalyst to emphasize the importance of culture. What interests Horney is "the problem of normal and neurotic structures in a given culture." She insists that "we cannot understand these structures without a detailed knowledge of the influences the particular culture exerts over the individual" (1937: 20). Horney criticizes Freud for emphasizing biological factors to the exclusion of cultural factors. "Freud's disregard of cultural factors not only leads to false generalizations," she says, "but to a large extent blocks an understanding of the real forces which motivate our attitudes and actions" (1937: 20–1). It is now over 65 years since Horney wrote these words – and, unfortunately, few psychoanalysts have acquired the extensive cultural knowledge that she considered indispensable. If psychoanalysis is no longer the biological psychology it once was, it still tends to be a personal (or interpersonal) psychology, not a cultural psychology.

I do not mean to reify, or hypostatize, culture, as if it existed utterly above and beyond any personal or interpersonal level, but I do mean to emphasize that it cannot be reduced to that level. In an exhaustive survey of concepts and definitions of "culture," A. L. Kroeber and Clyde Kluckhohn state that individuals "who still deny the autonomy (in some respects) of the cultural level" fall into two categories. They are either "stubborn reductionists" or "such as find it impossible to deal satisfactorily with their own particular interests by a purely cultural approach" (1952: 368). I would recommend Kroeber and Kluckhohn to anyone with any curiosity about what "culture" means and about how analysts might find it possible to deal satisfactorily with their particular interest, the psyche, by a cultural approach. I would also note that one of the most dynamic contemporary academic fields is "cultural studies." The study of culture is suddenly a topic of intense intellectual interest. Analysis, however, remains more or less inattentive to the cultural level. It is as if analysis is uncertain how – or even whether – to take it into account.

Neil Altman's book *The Analyst in the Inner City: Race, Class, and Culture through a Psychoanalytic Lens* is one recent attempt to rectify this situation. Altman asserts that, historically, analysis has tended to ignore or neglect "the specifically cultural context" of therapy (1995: 100). He notes that, even as analysis has moved from a one-person psychology to a two-person psychology, it has still more or less excluded the cultural level from consideration. He advocates what he calls a "three-person," or triadic, psychology. The third "person" in this psychology is culture. Although I do very much appreciate the expansive intent of this gesture, to call culture a "person" seems to me an infelicity that confuses the issue. Culture is *culture*, not a third "person" in the analytic dialogue between a first person and a second person. There are not just two persons with biographies present in the analytic dialogue. A culture with a history is also present.

In *The Multicultural Imagination*, I cite two dreams that employ an image from American culture and history: the Ku Klux Klan. In those dreams, members of the Ku Klux Klan carry either signs and firebrands or burning crosses (Adams 1996: 1, 127–8). The Ku Klux Klan is, of course, one of the most notorious images in American culture and history. Consider, in this respect, the following dream of a white man, a Jewish man. In this dream, 12 men, who are similar to the Ku Klux Klan, are leading a black woman somewhere:

> An entourage walks into the scene. It's like the Ku Klux Klan but not that severe or hostile-looking. Twelve people are in the procession. They're all white. But there's one black person. Her face is covered. They're leading her along. I have a feeling of mild unease; I'm slightly uncomfortable. I turn around. Two doors are behind me. I lock them both.

I asked the dreamer what the Ku Klux Klan is. He replied:

> The Ku Klux Klan is a bunch of racist idiots. White supremacists. Their garb is white hoods, sheets, torches. It's their identity, their dress code, making known their affiliation: "white-on-white." It masks their real identity. They're potential trouble-makers. They have a dislike, a distaste, for blacks. They'd like to get rid of blacks and Jews. I think of crossburnings, hangings, terrorizing.

I should emphasize that I did *not*, like a Freudian, ask the dreamer to "free associate" to the image of the Ku Klux Klan. As a Jungian, I asked him to *stick to the image* and to tell me what it essentially implied to him. What, I wondered, did he consider the "essence" of the Ku Klux Klan to be? I wanted him to provide as precise a description of the phenomenon as he could, as if I had no idea what the Ku Klux Klan is, and, in the process to define what the image meant to him. This is the method that I call *phenomenological essentialism* (or, as I now prefer to say, *imaginal essentialism*).

I do not assume that the issue of "race" in the dream is simply a manifest content, or defensive "derivative," of a more basic, latent content. As I say in *The Multicultural Imagination*, the effect of such an assumption "is to deny the specific reality of 'race' as a content of the unconscious and to deflect attention from it as a serious issue for the dreamer" (Adams 1996: 39). Altman also criticizes the tendency of psychoanalysis, even one with a two-person psychology, to regard "a concern with racial issues on the part of the patient (or analyst) as defensive, or otherwise derivative of nonracial concerns" (1995: 90). This is what I call the Freudian "derivative–reductive" method of interpretation. The method derives a manifest content from a latent content and then reduces the former to the latter – and ultimately to a wish that the dream ostensibly fulfills. In contrast, we need a *non-derivative, non-reductive, phenomenological psychoanalysis* (that is, an *imaginal psychoanalysis*) that will not regard racial concerns merely as distortive allusions to nonracial concerns (for example, "sexual" concerns).

Nor do I assume that the motivation of the dream is a wish that is the expression of a drive in relation to an object: that, for example, the image of the Ku Klux Klan is a distortive allusion to a bad object relation to the mother or the breast in the infantile biographical experience of a dreamer who has never developed further than the paranoid–schizoid position. Such an assumption seems to me utterly inadequate because it is so derivative and so reductive. As John Rowan says of "subpersonalities" in the psyche (an example would be the image of the Ku Klux Klan), developmental object relations psychology "does not really do justice to the complexity of these internal objects, which are much more in reality than internalized mothers, or good or bad breasts" (1990: 57). (I would say that the Ku Klux Klan is *not at all* a "mother" or a "breast"; it is just what it is: the *Ku Klux Klan*.)

It seems to me that this dreamer has a "Ku Klux Klan complex." I also have one – and not just because when my father would take me as a child to visit one of his brothers in Dallas, my uncle used to pull out of his wallet a souvenir from the years immediately after he had returned to Texas from fighting in France during World War I: his old, faded, worn Ku Klux Klan membership card from the 1920s; my uncle meant to impress me, when all he did was embarrass me – as well as my father. Many years later, while living in Illinois, I learned that the Ku Klux Klan had selected Kankakee for its headquarters in the state because of the three "K's" in the name of that city, where, while driving on the highway, I happened to notice a billboard with the following message: "God, Guns, and Guts Made This Country Free. Let's Keep All Three." I believe that all Americans – white, black, and otherwise – have a Ku Klux Klan complex. How could any American not have one, for we all have a culture with a history that includes white supremacists?

The dreamer has no direct personal or biographical experience of the Ku Klux Klan; like most of us, he has only an indirect, cultural and historical experience of them. He has an *image* of them. This image is, in a sense, a "bad object," but I would argue that it can neither be derived from nor reduced to some infantile split. The dreamer elaborated on the dream as follows:

> The people in the entourage are not wearing hoods, not wearing white. They're dressed in normal clothes – jeans and sport jackets. There's no impression of their faces. The black girl is blindfolded. That's something that the Ku Klux Klan might do, with an intent to do malice. They're very calm about it; they do it as though it's normal to them, routine. They make an example of her, they display her. One of them has a hand around her arm. The intent is not to kill, rape, or torture. It's almost as if she's done something wrong in school, been a "bad girl" in front of the class. Embarrassment is being directed toward her. She's done something that they didn't like. The feeling is that she won't change; she's like that: "The blacks are the blacks. They have their way of life." The Ku Klux Klan is going to intimidate blacks, but the blacks are not going to change. She's not numb, but she's going along with it. She's not distressed, not resistant. She's going to take her embarrassment but not change. I wonder what else might happen. I'd better lock the doors because something might come up from behind me. I don't feel a direct threat from the group. I'm just reminded that something might happen. I lock both doors for double protection.

What do we gain – and what do we lose – by attempting to interpret this dream from a developmental object relations perspective? Object relations psychology assumes that an image like the Ku Klux Klan is one bad object in a series of bad objects that originate in and date from a "bad breast" in the first few months of life. There is certainly no "milk of human kindness" in the Ku Klux Klan, but it is difficult for me to appreciate what we gain if we regard the bad breast, in any sense, as an infantile, paranoid–schizoid prototype of that hate group. What we lose if we reduce the hate group to the bad breast is an exact *phenomenological (that is, imaginal) description* of the cultural and historical qualities that define the Ku Klux Klan and that constitute the specific psychic reality of this particular dreamer.

What purpose does the image of the Ku Klux Klan serve for the dreamer? As a Jew, the dreamer knows very well that culturally and historically the Ku Klux Klan is not only racist in the white–black sense but also anti-Jewish. The dreamer observes a group that resembles, in behavior, the Ku Klux Klan. The white men in the group do not look like the Ku Klux Klan – they do not wear white hoods – but they behave like them. (It is perhaps especially insidious that the white men wear "normal clothes," for that implies that they themselves are "normal," not pathological.)

To the white men, the black girl is a "bad girl," a bad object. (It is not just intentional racists like the Ku Klux Klan who equate "black" with "bad." In the year 2000, the theme of the conference of the National Association for the Advancement of Psychoanalysis was "Culture and Psychoanalysis at the Millennium." I was a member of the program committee that chose that topic. There were four keynote speakers at the conference. One of them, an African-American psychoanalyst, spoke on the cultural and psychoanalytic aspects of relations between blacks and whites in America. Then a discussant, a white man, an economist with a special interest in psychoanalysis, offered comments on the presentation from an object relations perspective. Almost immediately, he committed a slip of the tongue: "The black object … I mean, the *bad* object." In fact, the discussant committed this slip not just once but *twice* – and none of the psychoanalysts in attendance even noticed, much less remarked.) Evidently, the white men in the dream regard the black girl as a "bad girl" because she has not "learned her lesson" in school, or in class. As a result, they want to make an object lesson, an example, of her, through intimidation. Apparently, they intend to "teach her a lesson." The implication is that they could do to others – for example, to Jews – what they are doing to her, if others do not learn their lesson.

Although the dreamer says that the black girl does not resist, it would be more accurate to say that she does not *actively* resist. She engages in passive resistance: she refuses to change. She is not just an internal object; she is an image of the capacity to resist change. She is an internal "resister." It is important to emphasize that only from the perspective of the Ku Klux Klan, or the school of racism, is the black girl a bad object; from the perspective of the dreamer, she is a good object, with whom he both empathizes and sympathizes.

Although the dreamer says that he does not feel a direct threat from the group, he does wonder what else might happen – the group reminds him that something might happen. Specifically, he feels that he had better lock both doors for double protection "because something might come up from behind me." (I would note that, directionally, "behind" is often an image of the unconscious.) The psychic reality of the dreamer has within it both an internal "terrorist" in the image of white men (the Ku Klux Klan) and an internal "resister" in the image of a black girl. There is in the psyche of the dreamer a split, a "white–black" dichotomy, or diametrical opposition, but it is not, I would argue, a derivative of some infantile, paranoid–schizoid split.

If, as I have advocated in *The Multicultural Imagination* (Adams 1996: 46), we were to articulate an object relations terminology that would be more adjectivally specific – that is, more adjectivally adequate to the varieties and complexities of psychic reality – then we would expand the terms far beyond "good" and "bad" objects, even far beyond what W. R. D. Fairbairn (1990c) calls "exciting," "rejecting," or "persecuting" objects. We would be much more attentive to the specific images that the unconscious employs – that is, to the quite distinctive, quite precise *phenomenal qualities* of these images and the cultural and historical context that circumscribes and delimits them.

We might invoke Fairbairn and say that, in this case, the "terrorist" is a variation on the theme of the "persecutor," but I would argue that terrorizing is, in the immediate context of this particular dream, a more specific image than persecuting is. A terrorist, Walter Laqueur says, is an individual who attempts "to further his views by a system of coercive intimidation" (1987: 11). Jerrold M. Post has introduced the term "terrorist psycho-logic" in an effort to develop a psychological profile of terrorists. He argues that terrorists *are driven to commit acts of violence as a consequence of psychological forces*" and that they apply a special psycho-logic in an attempt to rationalize "*acts they are psychologically compelled to commit*" (1998: 25). As he diagnoses the situation, he believes that terrorists disproportionately employ "externalization" and "splitting" – defense mechanisms characteristic of "borderline or narcissistic personality disorders" (1998: 27). According to Post, "Political terrorism is not simply a *product* of psychological forces; its central *strategy* is psychological, for *political terrorism, is, at base, a particularly vicious species of psychological warfare*" (1998: 39–40). Terrorism is primarily a psychological weapon. The objective is to induce terror, both personally and collectively.

If we had a more adjectivally specific object relations terminology, we would immediately notice that the psyche of this particular dreamer includes "terrorizing" and "resisting" objects. (From a Jungian perspective, the Ku Klux Klan and the black girl are images of the archetypes of the "terrorist" and the "resister.") Even such attention to detail would, however, be too abstract to suit me. I would want to emphasize, quite concretely, what *specific variety* of "terrorizing" object and "resisting" object they happen to be in this particular instance, in the psychic reality of this one patient. In short, it makes a decisive difference that it is a *Ku Klux Klan* terrorist and a *black girl* resister.

Rhetorically, the Ku Klux Klan terrorist and the black girl resister are "personifications" of aspects of the psyche of the patient – what Rowan calls "subpersonalities." In this instance, the dreamer has a specific relation to the subpersonalities of the "terrorist" and the "resister." The dreamer sees something and then, as a result, does something. He observes the white men leading a black girl, intending to intimidate her. Then he locks two doors. This is an ego-defensive strategy and tactic against some indeterminate, potential danger from "behind," or from the unconscious. The double protection that the dreamer hopes this ploy will afford him seems to indicate that he imagines that the danger is quite considerable.

Of what danger is the dreamer apparently so unconscious? I would hazard a guess that the danger is an ego-affect that is inappropriate, or incongruous. Modell emphasizes that "affects are the medium through which defenses against objects occur" (1984: 23). Although the dreamer may empathize, even sympathize with the black girl, he is curiously unaffected by the scene. As he says, "I have a feeling of mild unease; I'm slightly uncomfortable." It is not just that another dreamer might have tried to protect or even rescue the black girl; rather, it is that this dreamer, who not so incidentally happens to be a Jew who knows what the Ku Klux Klan does to both blacks and Jews, seems to have a minimal emotional reaction to the scene – as the words "mild" and "slightly" indicate.

What are we to make of the disparity between what the dreamer feels about what he sees and what he subsequently does, when he locks the two doors? How are we to explain this discrepancy? I would say that the dreamer has an ego that minimizes the very definite danger in front of him and maximizes an indefinite danger behind him. From what he knows culturally and historically about the Ku Klux Klan, blacks, and Jews, he should feel *great* unease and be *very* uncomfortable about the scene that he observes in front of him. Perhaps he should lock the front door rather than the back doors.

Jungians note that, in the unconscious of whites, blacks are frequently images of the archetype of the "shadow" – that is, images of those aspects of the psyche that whites consider inferior. From this perspective, whites tend to repress or dissociate these ostensibly negative qualities and then to project them onto blacks, who serve them as convenient scapegoats. Such whites are racists – at least unconsciously. What interests me about this particular dreamer, however, is that the black girl is a positive image of a resister, while the white men are a negative image of the terrorist. For this dreamer, "white" is not supreme but inferior, while "black" is superior. The dream indicates to me that if the ego of the dreamer could relate more effectively – that is, more *affectively* – to the black girl, or to the subpersonality of the resister, then the dreamer would be more *appropriately* defensive than he is. The dreamer could then resist any effort by the Ku Klux Klan, or the subpersonality of the terrorist, to force a change that would be an abject capitulation. The resolute dignity of the black girl in this encounter with racism would serve the dreamer – a white man, a Jewish man – as an example of appropriate resistance to terrorism.

In analysis, "resistance" – perhaps especially resistance to change – has had a pejorative connotation as a defense mechanism. Culturally and historically, however, certain varieties of resistance – for example, "passive resistance," from Henry David Thoreau to Mahatma Gandhi to Martin Luther King, Jr. – have had an altogether more noble connotation. In *Gandhi's Truth: On the Origins of Militant Non-Violence*, Erik H. Erikson says that "passive resistance" is an "unsuitable rendition" of *satyagraha*, which literally means "truth force" (1969: 198). In the dream, the black girl quite properly resists change through intimidation by the Ku Klux Klan. An analyst who disregarded the cultural and historical context of this variety of resistance, might well misinterpret the "truth force" of the dream. Not all resistance to change – and certainly not resistance to change through terror – is negative.

A Jungian interpretation of the dream would interpret the black girl as a non-ego image of the "anima," the opposite-sex archetype of "feminine" aspects in the psyche of a man, and the Ku Klux Klan as a non-ego image of the "shadow," the same-sex archetype of ostensibly "inferior" or "negative" aspects in the psyche of an individual. (The dreamer, as he appears in the dream, is an ego-image of the archetype of "identity." The ego-image is who or how "I" imagine myself to be. It is those aspects of the psyche that "I" am identified with, in contrast to other aspects – such as the "anima" and the "shadow" – from which "I" am disidentified.)

In this respect, Jungian psychology is not an object relations psychology but an *image relations psychology*. This dream delineates the relations that obtain between the images of identity, femininity, and inferiority or negativity in the psyche of the dreamer. To be more phenomenologically precise, I would say that the image of femininity is an image of "resistance," and the image of inferiority or negativity is an image of "terrorism." (The anima-image of the black girl is an image of the archetype of the resister, and the shadow-image of the Ku Klux Klan is an image of the archetype of the terrorist.) That is, the psyche of this dreamer includes inferior or negative aspects that relate to feminine aspects by terrorizing them, and those feminine aspects relate to those inferior or negative aspects by resisting them.

What of the ego-image? What of the image of the identity of the dreamer? How does it relate to the anima-image and the shadow-image? The ego-image does not participate or contribute in any way, let alone intervene, but merely passively observes the scene. If the shadow-image is a terrorist, and if the anima-image is a resister, the ego-image is an "observer" of the relation between them. This ego-image does *not* relate to either the shadow-image or the anima-image. It is just a bystander and an onlooker. The ego-image of this dreamer is identified with what Alfred Adler calls a "spectator complex." Adler says that this complex "shows up in people who arrange their life so that they are always spectators without taking any active steps" (1979: 78–9). If the ego-image "relates" at all to the non-ego images, it relates to them defensively. It locks the doors of the unconscious (represses or dissociates these images).

From a Jungian perspective, this dream is a parody of an archetypal "rite of passage" dream. When individuals applied to become members of the Ku Klux Klan, they had to pass an initiation ritual. Candidates were forced to play what I might call a "see-the-donkey-in-the-mirror" game. J. C. Lester and D. L. Wilson say that members blindfolded the candidate and led him "around the rooms and down into the cellar, now and then placing before him obstructions, which added to his discomfort, if not to his mystification." (This is, of course, a variation on the archetypal theme of the descent of the hero into the underworld – or the ego into the unconscious.) The candidate was asked questions, some "grave," others "absurd." He was then crowned, Lester and Wilson say, with "a huge hat bedecked with two enormous donkey ears" (1971: 63–4). Finally, the candidate was positioned before a mirror, and the blindfold was removed, so that he could see how others saw him and reflect on what an "ass" he was. In the dream, the Ku Klux Klan blindfolds the black girl in order to lead her somewhere. The dream is not a rite of initiation, but a *rite of intimidation*. The shadow-image (the Ku Klux Klan) attempts ritualistically to intimidate the anima-image (the black girl).

Jung says that the function of the unconscious in dreams is to compensate the partial, prejudicial, or defective attitudes of the ego. In dreams, the unconscious presents potentially valuable alternative perspectives that the ego has repressed, dissociated, ignored, neglected, or otherwise excluded from consideration. What attitudes of the ego does the unconscious attempt to compensate in this dream? I would say that the dream presents the ego with an opportunity to engage the images of the terrorist and the resister, rather than repress or dissociate them. A certain "Jewish" ego-image that was culturally and historically conscious of the terrorism

of the Ku Klux Klan and of resistance to it by blacks, Jews, and others might intervene and not just observe. It might participate and contribute "heroically." It might
confront and challenge the Ku Klux Klan (the shadow-image) and attempt to rescue the black girl (the anima-image).

This dream is a "mythological dream." It is a dream from what I call the *mythological unconscious* (Adams 2001). The relevant myth in this instance is the myth
of the "white knight," who fights and defeats the "black knight" and rescues the
"damsel in distress" from the "dragon." The complete name of the Ku Klux Klan
is "The Knights of the Ku Klux Klan." Although these "knights" are white men
who wear white hoods and robes and who terrorize black men and women, they
are, in fact, *black knights* – and anyone (*of whatever color*) who heroically confronts and challenges them is, in effect, a *white knight*. (Perhaps it is not irrelevant
to note that one of the offices in the Ku Klux Klan is that of the "Grand Dragon."
The only higher office is that of the "Imperial Wizard.") The Ku Klux Klan is a
parody of the romances of chivalry – of wizards, dragons, knights, and damsels in
distress. (Of course, from the racist perspective of the Ku Klux Klan, the damsels
in distress are white women whom black men might rape, not black women whom
white men might terrorize.)

What do we know (or what should we know) culturally and historically about the
Ku Klux Klan? The organization was founded in the South immediately after the
Civil War, sometime between December 1865 and June 1866. During the period of
Reconstruction, which lasted from 1870 to 1877, the Ku Klux Klan terrorized black
"freedmen," as well as white "scalawags" and "carpetbaggers." After the end of
Reconstruction, the Ku Klux Klan declined into relative inactivity. When, however, D. W. Griffith's *The Birth of a Nation* appeared in 1915 (the movie was an
adaptation of Thomas Dixon's novel *The Clansman*), the organization experienced
a spectacular popular revival, which lasted into the 1920s (Chalmers 1987; Wade
1987).

The second part of *The Birth of a Nation* (Griffith 1992) begins with a dis-
claimer: "This is an historical presentation of the Civil War and Reconstruction
Period, and is not meant to reflect on any race or people of today." In spite of this
caveat, the silent movie also includes a quotation from Woodrow Wilson's *History
of the American People*: "The white men were roused by a mere instinct of self-
preservation ... until at last there had sprung into existence a great Ku Klux Klan,
a veritable empire of the South, to protect the Southern country." A Princeton
University professor, eventually to become president of the United States, apolo-
gizes for the existence of a terrorist organization. In order to sensationalize "racial"
conflict, the movie sexualizes it. A mulatto lieutenant governor lusts after a white
girl and proposes to her on the grounds of equal rights of intermarriage (in one
scene he perversely sniffs her dress), and a black soldier runs after another white
girl who jumps off a cliff in order to avoid rape. At the end of the movie, after these
attempts at miscegenation, whites unite "in common defence of their Aryan
birthright," and Jesus Christ suddenly appears on screen in a special effect.

Were the Ku Klux Klan not a hate group, it would simply be a comical secret society – grown men wearing robes and pointy, conehead hoods like dunce caps. Arnold S. Rice describes the costume in the 1920s as follows:

> The robe of the rank and file of the secret order was of white cotton, girdled with a sash of the same color and material, and with a white cross upon a red background stitched below the left shoulder. The headdress was a white cotton peaked hood from which a red tassel hung. The entire outfit cost $5.
>
> (Rice 1972: 17–18)

Other items were available for purchase. "Any member of the order," Rice says, "was able to obtain a 'Kluxer's Knifty Knife' for $1.25, a bargain indeed, considering the fact that the little instrument was a 'real 100 per cent knife for 100 per cent Americans'" (1972: 18–19).

The Ku Klux Klan is not just a hate group – it is a secret society. The basic "secret" is the identity of the members. That is the reason why members wear hoods, or masks. As Jungians define the archetype of the "persona," it is the appearance that the ego presents in deference to conventional social expectations. (*Persona* means "mask.") In this respect, the image of the hood is a perversion of the persona, for it is an "outlaw" mask. Members of the Ku Klux Klan wear hoods in order to disguise their identities and to preserve their anonymity, so that they may commit crimes of terrorism with impunity.

The very name "Ku Klux Klan" is utterly ludicrous. Lester and Wilson recount how a committee proposed several names:

> They explained that they had been trying to discover or invent a name which would be, to some extent, suggestive of the character and objects of the society. They mentioned several which they had been considering. In this number was the name "Kukloi" from the Greek word *Kuklos* (Kuklos), meaning a band or circle. At mention of this some one cried out: "Call it Ku Klux." "Klan" at once suggested itself, and was added to complete the alliteration. So instead of adopting a name, as was the first intention, which had a definite meaning, they chose one which to the proposer of it, and to every one else, was absolutely meaningless.
>
> This trivial and apparently accidental incident had a most important bearing on the future of the organization so singularly named. Looking back over the history of the Klan, and at the causes under which it developed, it is difficult to resist the conclusion that the order would never have grown to the proportions which it afterwards assumed, or wielded the power it did, had it not borne this name or some other equally as meaningless and mysterious – mysterious because meaningless.
>
> (Lester and Wilson 1971: 55–6)

No organization has ever been as alliterative. In addition to "Ku Klux Klan," the organization employs the following "K-words," among others:

Klankraft: Practices and beliefs of the Klan.
Cyclops: Head of a Klavern (local chapter).
Kligrapp: Secretary.
Klaliff: Vice president.
Klokard: Lecturer.
Kludd: Chaplain.
Klabee: Treasurer.
Kleagle: Organizer.
Klonsel: Supreme attorney.
Klectoken: Initiation fee.

(Forster and Epstein 1965[?]: 40)

In addition, John Moffat Mecklin says that the name of the publication that contains the ritual of the Ku Klux Klan is the "Kloran" (1963: 68) – apparently an allusion to the Koran!

What Mecklin has to say about the Ku Klux Klan is especially valuable, because he attempts a psychological analysis. His book *The Ku Klux Klan: A Study of the American Mind*, was originally published in 1924, when the organization was at the height of its popularity. Mecklin says that members of the Ku Klux Klan have no cosmopolitan curiosity, only "provincial fear of all things foreign" (1963: 101). The Ku Klux Klan appeals, he says, "to imaginations starved by a prosaic and unpoetic environment" (1963: 106). He quotes a Texan who diagnoses the Ku Klux Klan: "There is a great 'inferiority complex' on the part of the Klan membership – due in part to lack of education – Dallas and Fort Worth (where the Klan is especially strong) being largely populated by men and women reared in obscure towns and country places where public schools are short-termed and scarce" (1963: 107).

It was, of course, Adler who introduced into psychoanalysis the term "inferiority complex," as well as the term "superiority complex" (1939). He notes that individuals often if not always develop a sense of inferiority. In the case of the Ku Klux Klan (at least as the Texan diagnoses it), the sense of inferiority is the result, at least in part, of ignorance. According to Adler, individuals with an inferiority complex attempt to compensate – that is, to attain a sense of superiority. In this respect, the Ku Klux Klan provides such an individual with instantaneous compensation. As Mecklin says:

Here is a large and powerful organization offering to solace his sense of defeat by dubbing him a knight of the Invisible Empire for the small sum of ten dollars. Surely knighthood was never offered at such a bargain! He joins. He becomes the chosen conservator of American ideals, the keeper of the morals of the community. He receives the label of approved "one hundred percent Americanism." The Klan slogan printed on the outside of its literature is "an urgent call for men." This flatters the pride of the man suffering from the sense of mediocrity and defeat. It stimulates his latent idealism. It offers fantastic possibilities for his dwarfed and starved personality. Membership in a vast mysterious empire that "sees all and hears all" means a sort of mystic glorification of his petty self. It identifies his own weak incompetent will with the omnipotent and universal will of a great organization. The appeal is irresistible.

(Mecklin 1963: 108)

In effect, when inept individuals become members of the Ku Klux Klan, they immediately develop a compensatory superiority complex.

"The problem of the Klan," Mecklin says, "is the problem of stubborn, uncritical mental stereotypes" (1963: 116). He attributes the popularity of the Ku Klux Klan in the 1920s to "disturbed post-war conditions" (1963: 121). In the aftermath of World War I, Mecklin says, "hates kindled by the war and to which the nation had become habituated during years of bloodshed were suddenly set adrift because stripped of the objects and the ends around which they had been organized by the experience of the war." The Ku Klux Klan simply provided other objects to stereotype, hate, and fear: blacks, Catholics, Jews, and foreigners. In short, Mecklin says, the Ku Klux Klan took advantage of "the irrational fear psychology that followed on the heels of the war" (1963: 122). Immigration, he says, furnished a convenient opportunity to indulge in anti-Jewish prejudice:

The Jew, who has recently been coming to this country mainly from Russia and Southeastern Europe by hundreds of thousands and who, true to his urban traits, has crowded into New York and other large cities where his alien characteristics are thrust into the face of the native American on the street, in the hotel or department store, has also come in for his share of the prevalent fear psychology. Henry Ford in the anti-Semitic publication he has fathered, *The International Jew*, has voiced the fears of the native American brought into close contact with the unassimilated and disagreeably alien Jewish population of our large centers. The Klan has simply capitalized this situation with tremendous success.

(Mecklin 1963: 125)

Jews were "foreigners" with an ethnic style different from that of "natives," and the Ku Klux Klan exploited this difference to incite anti-Jewish prejudice. William Loren Katz notes that when Franklin Roosevelt became president during the Great Depression, members of the Ku Klux Klan said that "his name was really 'Rosenfelt' and his New Deal was really a 'Jew Deal'" (1986: 123).

During the 1920s, the Ku Klux Klan was not only just as racist in the white–black sense as it had always been but also became increasingly anti-Jewish (as well as anti-Catholic and anti-immigrant). The organization has continued to exist as a hate group since that time, although with nothing like the membership it once had. Ironically, in recent years, liberal (sometimes black) civil liberties lawyers have argued that individuals have the legal right to wear hoods, operate a Ku Klux Klan museum, and burn crosses, however racist such activities may be. (In addition, that same period has witnessed a proliferation of "White Identity" or "Christian Identity" hate groups that are just as racist and anti-Jewish as the Ku Klux Klan. Examples include "The Aryan Nations," "The Order," and "The Cross, the Sword, and the Arm of the Lord," whose abbreviation "C.S.A" deliberately invokes "Confederate States of America.")

In 1990, the Ku Klux Klan in Georgia challenged a 1952 law against wearing masks or hoods in public. An article in the *New York Times* reports that although the law did not "name the Klan" specifically and although it included "numerous exceptions, like holiday masks or masks for sports or occupational safety," the intent was obvious: "to unmask Klan members and thus take away their ability to inflict anonymous terror." Police received a telephone call informing them that the Ku Klux Klan would protest the law at a county courthouse. The next day, a member "drove up in his pickup truck, put on his mask and hood and was arrested by waiting policemen and charged with violating the law against wearing masks or hoods in public." The man pleaded not guilty and entered a motion to dismiss the charge on grounds that the law infringed both his First Amendent right of free speech and his Fourteenth Amendment right to equal protection. State officials argued that the issue was not free speech but terrorism. "It's a matter of historical fact," the attorney general of Georgia said, "that people have gone out as members of the Klan for the purpose of terrorizing people, most particularly to keep them from exercising their constitutional rights such as voting and assembly" (Applebome April 15, 1990, sec. 1: 12).

In 1996, a white man in South Carolina opened "The World's Only Klan Museum" and "The Redneck Shop" in a defunct movie theater. An article in the *New York Times* reports that the shop had for sale such souvenirs as "Klansman miniatures, Confederate windbreakers, 'White Power' sweatshirts and racks of T-shirts that read, 'It's a White Thing. You Wouldn't Understand.'" Exhibits in the museum comprised "some 50 robes, with documents and photographs," including one that depicted "a young black man being branded by men in robes" (Bragg November 17, 1996, sec.1: 16). When the city council denied the proprietor, a former member of the Ku Klux Klan, a business license, he protested that they had violated his civil rights, and he hired an attorney to file a federal lawsuit.

In 1998, a black attorney defended a white member of the Ku Klux Klan (whose last name, ironically, was "Black"), who had been arrested for burning a cross in Virginia. An article in the *New York Times* reports that the white man was charged with violating a 1930s law that "made it illegal for anyone with the 'intent of intimidating' another person to burn a cross on another person's property or on a highway or in a public place, which includes private property that can be viewed by the public." The cross had been burned after the Ku Klux Klan had held a rally on private property with the permission of the owner. At the trial, witnesses testified that "the burning cross was about 30 feet tall and was clearly visible from a nearby state highway" and that "the sight of the burning cross caused a car with black occupants to flee the area and some white local residents to seek protection from sheriff's deputies." The black attorney argued that the law against burning crosses infringed his client's First Amendment right of free speech. A representative of the National Association for the Advancement of Colored People commented: "We think it's really an aberration for a person of African descent to represent a Ku Klux Klan person, in particular for burning a cross, which we don't consider a free speech issue. This is an act that has been used historically to terrorize and intimidate African people" (Holmes November 20, 1998: A20).

In 2003, the US Supreme Court finally ruled that states may outlaw the burning of crosses provided they can prove that the intention is intimidation, not free speech protected by the First Amendment (Greenhouse April 8, 2003: A1 and A16). When the case was argued, Justice Clarence Thomas asserted that a burning cross is a symbol unlike any other in America, because the purpose is simply to terrorize people.

Of what relevance is all of this information to a man who dreams of 12 white men similar to the Ku Klux Klan leading a black woman somewhere? The dreamer has never "studied" the Ku Klux Klan culturally and historically. He "knows" none of these details. Such specific knowledge is "in" neither his conscious nor what Jungians would call his "personal unconscious." Where is it then? I would argue that it is in the *cultural unconscious*. The "cultural unconscious" is a concept that Joseph L. Henderson introduced into Jungian analysis. Henderson says that "what Jung called personal was actually always culturally conditioned" (1990: 104). In addition, I have noted that what Jung called collective was also culturally conditioned. In *The Multicultural Imagination*, I have redefined the collective unconscious to comprise two dimensions, one that includes "natural" factors (archetypes and archetypal images) and another that includes "cultural" factors (stereotypes and stereotypical images). The latter is what I mean by the cultural unconscious (Adams 1996: 40, 46; Adams 2001: 106–7). I would also mention that Samuel L. Kimbles has recently introduced into Jungian analysis another important concept – the "cultural complex" (2000). The "cultural unconscious" and the "cultural complex" are potentially very valuable concepts for all psychoanalysts, not just Jungians. We might also consider whether it would be advantageous to employ such terms as the "cultural psyche," the "cultural ego," "cultural projection," "cultural transference," "cultural countertransference," and so forth. Such terms might make us more conscious of and attentive to the constant presence and pervasive, often profound influence of cultural factors in each and every analysis.

As psychoanalysts, we have a responsibility to make the cultural unconscious conscious – that is, to inform the uninformed, which in the first place is ourselves (we, too, have probably never studied the Ku Klux Klan) and in the second place, our patients. To be effective analysts with patients who dream of the Ku Klux Klan (or of other issues, including other "racial" issues, on the cultural level), we need systematically to acquire much more cultural knowledge. In short, we need to become *culturally knowledgeable analysts*, so that we are then in a position consciously to impart this knowledge to patients who are unconscious of it, or uninformed about it. Psychoanalysts would thus have, as facilitators, an informative function. Even if we were to assume that "culture" is a mere epiphenomenon and that the "person" is ultimately the only authentic phenomenon – that is, even if we were to assume that the unconscious of the dreamer simply employs a cultural conflict opportunistically in order graphically to illustrate a personal conflict – quite specific knowledge of the details of that cultural conflict would be an indispensable resource for a meticulously accurate interpretation of the personal conflict (in this instance, terrorism and resistance).

If the dreamer had much more than a cursory knowledge of the Ku Klux Klan, then it would be much more difficult, even impossible, for him not to be profoundly affected by the image of the white terrorists trying to change the black resister. Cultural and historical information would provide the dreamer with an opportunity to ponder the incongruously minimal affect that he experiences as he observes this scene of racist intimidation. The assumption, of course, is that it would be "normal" for a Jewish man like the dreamer emotionally to relate to – perhaps even emotionally to identify with – the black girl as a good object. Knowing what we know, or ought to know, culturally and historically about the Ku Klux Klan as a bad object, I do not believe that this is too much to expect – or too much, for us as analysts, to expedite. It is in this respect that I advocate a school of analysis that would include an appreciation of the cultural and historical dimensions of the psyche.

In conclusion, I would pose some questions to analysts in order to encourage critical reflection about the cultural level.

1   How would you define "culture?"
2   How prominent is culture on your list of priorities that you consider especially important in analysis, and how often does it occur to you to take culture into account during sessions with patients?
3   Do the concepts "cultural unconscious" and "cultural complex" have any value for you?
4   Do you restrict yourself exclusively to personal associations in order to interpret material, or do you also avail yourself of cultural information?
5   Do you regard furnishing cultural information to the patient as one of your responsibilities?
6   Do you believe that analysis does or should include a culturally informative function, or would you consider that an inappropriately "non-analytic" intervention?
7   After a session in which a patient has mentioned some cultural topic, do you make any extra effort to research, or "study," the issue further and acquire additional cultural information?

Jung says that for the practice of psychotherapy "long and thorough training is necessary, and a wide culture which very few possess" (1963: 137). I could not agree more, but from this perspective, training is one thing, culture quite another thing.

Presumably, analytic institutes provide training, while culture is something that analysts simply either possess or do not possess. Culture is hardly integral to the training that analytic institutes currently provide. I would say that institutes might seriously consider whether they should assume responsibility for what I would call the "cultural widening" of analysts, for it is arguable that today, more than ever, only widely cultured analysts are adequately prepared to practice psychoanalysis, however long and thorough a "training" they may have had. The question is: How are analysts to acquire the wide culture that Jung says so very few possess? At present, analysts have to acquire culture on an ad hoc basis. Since institutes apparently believe that they are under no obligation in this respect, the unconscious communication from the profession is that culture is an incidental, not an essential, factor in analysis. I do not presume that analytic institutes will suddenly "reform," but I do believe that they could do much more than they currently do, if they only would, to widen the culture of analysts.

The analytic emphasis on the personal (or interpersonal) and the biographical rather than on the cultural and the historical is, as Alan Roland says, a product of the ideology of "individualism." (I would say that it is also a product of the ideology of "developmentalism" – that is, "infantilism." Rather than infantilizing our patients by reducing their experience developmentally to good and bad "mothering" or "breasting," we could "culturalize" and historicize both their and our experience.) Roland posits a "cultural self" that he says "is invisible unless one has lived in a radically different culture" (1996: xiv). I do not believe that one has to *live in* a different culture to render visible the cultural self; I believe that one can *learn about* the vast variety of cultural selves by an assiduous (if necessary, autodidactic) effort. It is true, as Roland says, that analysis "largely ignores the influence of the cultural world" (1996: 84). To remain ignorant of the cultural world (and the cultural self) is to remain unconscious – and how, I wonder, can any analyst or any analytic institute countenance that?

Chapter 7

Jung, Africa, and the "geopathology" of Europe

Psychic place and displacement

In the year 2000, I received an invitation from the African Studies Program at Baylor University and the Friends of Jung in Waco, Texas, to be a speaker in the John N. Jonsson Peace and Justice Lecture Series. The theme of the lecture series that year was "Black Africa in the White Psyche: Jung's Contribution to Multiculturalism." This chapter, with some revisions, is the presentation that I delivered on that occasion.

It is impossible for us to understand "Black Africa in the White Psyche: Jung's Contribution to Multiculturalism" unless and until we understand "White Europe in Jung's White Psyche." The one simply cannot be understood without the other. On the two occasions when Jung traveled to Africa, he carried with him quite specific psycho-geographical baggage. It was a load that no African bearer could carry for Jung. As Jung traveled from his own place, Europe, to another place, Africa, and from place to place within Africa, his psychic bags were packed with his own place, as well as a diagnosis of that place. His placement in and his diagnosis of Europe informed both his attitude toward Africa and his experience of it.

Una Chaudhuri has introduced a provocative concept in her book *Staging Place: The Geography of Modern Drama*. That concept is "geopathology," and it is applicable to both Europe and Jung. As Chaudhuri defines the term, it means "the idea of ill placement" (1995: 17). Pathology is illness. Geopathology is illness of place. We may feel that a certain place itself is ill. We may feel that we ourselves are ill in that place.

According to Chaudhuri, we desire "both place and displacement" (1995: 157). We may also fear them – or feel a variety of other ways about them. I would say that we feel ambivalent (or even multivalent) about both place and displacement. While we are in a certain place, we may feel "out of place" and feel that if we could only displace ourselves to another place we would not feel ill. We may feel ill because we have been forcibly displaced, against our will, as Africans were by the Europeans who enslaved them. We may feel ill because we have been "kept in our place." There are many varieties of geopathology. The question is: Where, if anywhere, would we, could we, feel well?

Jung suffered from geopathology, and his suffering profoundly influenced his experience of Africa. He felt that Europe was sick – or, more specifically, that the soul of Europeans was sick – and he himself felt sick in Europe. Jung's geo-pathology is evident in his negative attitude toward another European, Albert Schweitzer, the Christian missionary and medical doctor who was awarded the Nobel Peace Prize in 1952. Whereas Jung traveled in Africa for only a few weeks, Schweitzer lived and worked in Africa for many years. Jung did not know Schweitzer personally, but in the 1950s he wrote a number of letters that include derogatory, sometimes sarcastic remarks about him.

In the first of these letters, Jung says that he could not, "like Albert Schweitzer, seek suitable refuge far away from Europe and open a practice there" (1975 2: 40). Thus he characterizes Schweitzer as a refugee and compares him invidiously with himself. In the second letter, Jung chastizes Christian clergy for indulging in "a general *flight outwards*." What they flee, he says, is experience of the inward – experience of the psyche and psychology. "Instead," he says, "one goes in for missions to the heathen." As an example of this fleeing tendency, Jung mentions Schweitzer, "who is urgently needed in Europe but prefers to be a touching saviour of savages and to hang his theology on the wall" (1975 2: 85). According to Jung, Schweitzer ought not to have lived in Africa and tried to save the bodies of Africans but should have remained in Europe and tried to cure the souls of Euro-peans. Then Jung discusses what I would call the "theopathology," or religious ill-ness, of Europe:

> We have a justification for missionizing only when we have straightened our-selves out here, otherwise we are merely spreading our own disease. How is it with God's kingdom in Europe? Not even savages are stupid enough not to see our lies. Shamelessly and childishly we parade our irreconcilable schisms before the wondering eyes of our black "brethren" and preach peaceableness, brotherliness, neighborly love, etc. etc. through the mouths of Evangelists, Lutherans, High Church, Nonconformists, Baptists, Methodists, Catholics, all of whom are resolved to the death *not* to communicate with their brother. Is this fulfilling God's will?
>
> (Jung 1975 2: 85)

Europe has a disease, and in this case it is the many Christian denominations, which are just so many psychic dissociations. Symptomatically, the schismatic condition of European Christianity is an example of "splitting." Instead of curing their own disease, Europeans – and especially Christian missionaries – spread it to Africans. The question is: How can Europeans pretend to be their African brothers' keepers when they cannot even keep themselves? According to Jung, the fraternal altruism of Europeans in Africa is not just displaced but *misplaced*.

What exactly did brotherly love mean to Schweitzer in the context of Africa? In discussing "the relations between the whites and the blacks," Schweitzer wonders what "the general character of the intercourse between them" must be. (He means, of course, "social intercourse," not "sexual intercourse.") The question, he says, is: "Am I to treat the black man as my equal or my inferior?" As a European,

Schweitzer must visibly demonstrate to Africans that "I can respect the dignity of human personality in every one." Schweitzer says that "the essential thing is that there shall be a real feeling of brotherliness." Immediately, however, he issues a caveat. The extent to which the feeling of brotherliness can be implemented in Africa is strictly circumstantial. "How far this is to find complete expression in the sayings and doings of daily life," Schweitzer says, "must be settled by circumstances" (1924: 130). Thus, in practice, the principle of brotherly love is considerably qualified.

Schweitzer infantilizes Africans. "The negro is a child, and with children nothing can be done without the use of authority," he says. "We must, therefore, so arrange the circumstances of daily life that my natural authority can find expression." The circumstances are not given; they are conveniently "arranged" by Schweitzer so as to sustain the white European's "natural authority" over black Africans. Such is his answer to the question of whether his "brothers" are his equals or his inferiors. Schweitzer concludes: "With regard to the negroes, then, I have coined the formula: 'I am your brother, it is true, but your elder brother'" (1924: 130–1). The image of the black African in Schweitzer's white European psyche is the image of a child. Schweitzer is not so much a brother, elder or otherwise, as he is the white father of black children. In this image, fraternalism and equalitarianism are utterly compromised by paternalism and authoritarianism.

"The combination of friendliness with authority," Schweitzer says, "is therefore the great secret of successful intercourse" between whites and blacks in Africa. As evidence of the irrefutable truth of this claim, he mentions the example of a missionary who "left the staff some years ago to live among the negroes as their absolute equal." The missionary built a house near an African village and "wished to be recognised as a member of the village." According to Schweitzer, the experiment by the missionary was a total failure. "From that day his life became a misery," Schweitzer says. "With his abandonment of the social interval between white and black he lost all his influence; his word was no longer taken as the 'white man's word,' but he had to argue every point with them as if he were merely their equal" (1924: 131). "Mere equality" is unimaginable to Schweitzer, for it would mean that he and other white Europeans could no longer rely on authority but would have to engage in argument. White Europeans might not win the argument – they might lose it. In a real give-and-take, black Africans would no longer have to take the "white man's word" for it. How miserable! Thus Schweitzer opposes what he calls "unsuitable freedom" for black Africans (1924: 132). For black Africans to be really free just does not suit him.

As Schweitzer says, white Europeans would risk losing their influence over black Africans. In discussing the issue of influence, Tzvetan Todorov distinguishes between imposition and proposition. As a form of influence, persuasion is ethically acceptable; coercion is not. Todorov says that "it is possible to establish an ethical criterion to judge the form of influences: the essential thing, I should say, is to know whether they are *imposed* or *proposed*" (1984: 179). From this perspective, Schweitzer's appeal to the authority of the "white man's word" is an unethical form of influence, for it deprives black Africans of the opportunity to get a word in edgewise – much less to have the last word.

In a third letter, Jung disparages Schweitzer's efforts as "his African romance, which any little doctor could take care of just as well without being made into a saint." In contrast to Jung's own placement, Schweitzer's displacement "is a mere escape from the problem called Europe" (1975 2: 125). In a fourth letter, Jung belittles Schweitzer for "becoming a white saviour to the natives." He then criticizes Schweitzer for relativizing Christ in his book *Quest of the Historical Jesus*. Jung says: "Anyone who relativizes him is in danger of becoming a saviour himself. And where can that best be done? Well, in Africa. I know Africa and I also know how the white doctor is worshipped there, how touchingly and how seductively!" The implication is that a relativization of Christ induces in Schweitzer and other Christian missionaries an unconscious identification with the archetype of the savior. "Should we all," Jung asks, "following Schweitzer's banner, emigrate to Africa and cure native diseases when our own *sickness of soul* cries to heaven?" (1975 2: 141). Europeans ought not to flee or escape to Africa, Jung contends, but should stay in place, in Europe, for if anything needs curing, he asserts, it is the sick European soul. Schweitzer is "an eminent scholar and researcher, a brilliant organist, and a medical benefactor to the natives in Lambarene," Jung acknowledges, but in removing himself to Africa, instead of remaining in Europe, Schweitzer displaced the problem of his own place onto another place where he could conveniently play savior (1975 2: 142). In a fifth and final letter, Jung simply says that Schweitzer "ran away from the European problem" (1975 2: 324).

If Schweitzer had only been Jung! Then, presumably, he would have been perfect! The ungenerous tone and content of these letters suggest that Jung was envious of the acclaim that Schweitzer received and the fame that he achieved. The Nobel Peace Prize! Saint Schweitzer! Savior Schweitzer! Jung was not just irked – he was infuriated. Just who did Schweitzer think he was? Jesus Christ? *Jesus Christ*! Why was Jung so captiously contemptuous of Schweitzer? Such hypersensitivity indicates the presence of what Jung calls a "complex." Did Schweitzer have a Christ complex that he unconsciously identified with, or did Jung have a Christ complex that he unconsciously projected onto Schweitzer? Or did they both have Christ complexes?

James Hillman recalls an occasion in the 1950s when, as an analyst in training at the Jung Institute in Zurich, he heard Jung indulge in a diatribe against Schweitzer. "Someone," Hillman says, "must have set him off by asking a question about Schweitzer at one of our little discussions at his house, and Jung just couldn't stop" (1983b: 104–5). Once Jung got started, he went on and on about Schweitzer. Hillman says that "Jung couldn't abide the piousness, and Schweitzer's escape from the European predicament by retreating into the white man's colonial jungle where it is easy to do 'good works.'" The moment is so memorable for Hillman because it demonstrates that "Jung had his peeves, his rages, and it came out over a rival senex figure." As Hillman interprets the incident, it illustrates not only Jung's identification with the archetype of the "wise old man" in hostile, senile competition with Schweitzer but also Jung's relation to the archetype of the "shadow," all of those ostensibly negative, inferior, or primitive qualities that the ego repudiates as intrinsic aspects of the psyche and then tends to project onto others. (I say "ostensibly," because it is the ego that regards those qualities as negative, when they may actually be, from another perspective, quite positive.) To witness such a tirade was an important educational experience for Hillman. "I mean," he says, "it's instructive to see how one old wise man hates another old wise man, and that the hatred and showing it is exactly what distinguishes Jung from Schweitzer." For Hillman, Jung evinced more psychic acumen than Schweitzer because he did not suppress or repress the shadow but expressed it so spontaneously. "It is great to see that when you are a student and trying to hide your shadow," Hillman says. "It may have been in that same meeting that someone asked Jung about the shadow, and he said 'It shows right here, in your face'" (1983b: 105). Jung did not attempt to conceal his shadow; he revealed it – and, according to Hillman, that was the decisive difference between Jung and Schweitzer.

Schweitzer went to Africa in 1913, just after he had earned a medical degree. "I gave up my position of professor in the University of Strasbourg, my literary work, and my organ-playing," he says, "in order to go as a doctor to Equatorial Africa" (1924: 1). Schweitzer had not just been an "organ-player"; he had been the organist for the Johann Sebastian Bach Society, and he had published an important book on Bach. He was able to travel to Africa and to set up a hospital there because he contributed "what I had earned by giving organ concerts, together with the profits from my book" (1924: 3). He was not only a physician but also a philanthropist and a successful fund-raiser.

What attitude did Jung have toward all this? He was, in a word, dismissive. Schweitzer's displacement was, Jung says, nothing more than an abdication of his responsibility for curing the sickness of the European soul:

> Faced with the truly appalling *afflictio animae* of the European man, Schweitzer abdicated from the task incumbent on the theologian, the *cura animarum*, and studied medicine in order to treat the sick *bodies of natives*. For the native this is very gratifying, and I am the first to laud those doctors in the tropics who risked their lives, and frequently lost them, on lonely outposts and under more dangerous circumstances. Yet none of these dead who rest in African earth is surrounded by the halo of a Protestant saint. Nobody speaks of them. Schweitzer is doing no more than his professional duty, like any other medical missionary. Every doctor in the tropics would like nothing better than to build his own hospital on his lonely outpost, but unhappily he hasn't Schweitzer's talent for using money-making lectures and soul-stirring organ recitals for this purpose.
>
> (Jung 1975 2: 140)

Thus Jung damns Schweitzer the Protestant saint for wearing a halo that Jung believes rightfully belongs to others.

Why did Schweitzer go to Africa in the first place? He had "read about the physical miseries" of Africans, and he had "heard about them from missionaries." It seemed incomprehensible to him that "we Europeans trouble ourselves so little about the great humanitarian task which offers itself to us in far-off lands" (1924: 1). It is, of course, precisely this displacement, this "far-offness," that is so off-putting to Jung. What motivated Schweitzer to go "off" to Africa? Schweitzer says that the Biblical parable of Dives and Lazarus inspired him to do so:

> The parable of Dives and Lazarus seemed to me to have been spoken directly of us! We are Dives, for, through the advances of medical science, we now know a great deal about disease and pain, and have innumerable means of fighting them: yet we take as a matter of course the incalculable advantages which this new wealth gives us! Out there in the colonies, however, sits wretched Lazarus, the coloured folk, who suffers from illness and pain just as much as we do, nay, much more, and has absolutely no means of fighting them. And just as Dives sinned against the poor man at his gate because for want of thought he never put himself in his place and let his heart and conscience tell him what he ought to do, so do we sin against the poor man at our gate.
>
> (Schweitzer 1924: 1–2)

I would emphasize that, according to Schweitzer, Dives sinned against Lazarus because *he never put himself in Lazarus's place*. By this definition, sin is a lack of empathy. Empathy means to displace ourselves psychologically – to put ourselves in another's place. When we empathize with another person, we may then sympathize with that person, and we may even respond with action. When we displace ourselves psychologically, we may decide to displace ourselves geographically, which is what Schweitzer did.

Schweitzer considered it his "life's task to fight on behalf of the sick under far-off stars." He regarded "the work that needs doing for the coloured folk in their misery, not as a mere 'good work,' but as a duty that must not be shirked." It was not mere benevolence, or Christian charity, but an obligation. "Ever since the world's far-off lands were discovered," Schweitzer asks, "what has been the conduct of the white peoples to the coloured ones?" (1924: 171). The Europeans, "who professed to be followers of Jesus," had behaved abominably toward Africans. The atrocities that Africans had endured were so brutal as to be all but indescribable. "Who," Schweitzer asks, "can describe the injustice and the cruelties that in the course of centuries they have suffered at the hands of Europeans?" Along with a hypocritical Christianity, the Europeans had brought death, alcohol, and disease to Africans. "If a record could be compiled of all that has happened between the white and the coloured races," Schweitzer says, "it would make a book containing numbers of pages, referrring to recent as well as to early times, which the reader would have to turn over unread, because their contents would be too horrible" (1924: 172).

Jung also displaced himself both psychologically and geographically – but, in contrast to Schweitzer, who displaced himself more or less permanently, Jung displaced himself only temporarily. For Jung, the journey to Africa was a *sojourn*. In his autobiography *Memories, Dreams, Reflections*, written when Jung was over 80 years old, he recounts how he traveled twice to Africa – once to North Africa (Algeria and Tunisia) in 1920 and once to Central Africa, or "Black Africa" (Kenya and Uganda), in 1925–26. Whereas what consciously motivated Schweitzer was empathy and sympathy for black Africans, what consciously motivated Jung was an interest in psychological reflection on white Europeans outside Europe. Thus, in reference to his first trip to Africa in 1920, Jung says that he "had often wished to be able for once to see the European from outside, his image reflected back at him by an altogether foreign milieu" (1963: 238). On that trip he "learned to see to some extent with different eyes and to know the white man outside his own environment" (1963: 239). In short, for Jung, Africa was metaphorically a mirror. The mirror of Africa would reflect the image of the white European, and that would present an opportunity for Jung, another white European, to reflect psychologically on that image. That is why he sought "a psychic observation post outside the sphere of the European" (1963: 244).

Again and again, Jung uses the word "outside." He could have stayed inside Europe, in his own place, but he displaced himself from Europe to Africa, all in order to arrive at a place from which he could, as an outsider, observe Europe at a distance, from an objective perspective. Had he simply remained in Europe, he would have had no such point of view and therefore no basis of comparison for an objective observation. He would have had only a subjective experience of what it was to be a European. "I understand Europe, our greatest problem," Jung says, "only when I see where I as a European do not fit into the world." For Jung, Africa is the place where he does not fit in. It is the place of displacement that functions as a mirror that reflects much more than his own subjective, narcissistic white European image. Thus when Jung "contemplated for the first time the European spectacle from the Sahara," he discovered just how much he continued to be "imprisoned in the cultural consciousness of the white man" (1963: 247). I prefer to say that from that vantage point in the desert of Africa Jung became aware of how much he was still subjectively confined in the *cultural ego* of Europe.

Joseph L. Henderson introduced into Jungian analysis the term "cultural unconscious" (1990). The definition that Henderson provided, however, seemed to me inadequate, so I redefined the term. To me, *the cultural unconscious is a dimension of the collective unconscious*. More specifically, *the collective unconscious includes two dimensions: a "natural" dimension, which consists of archetypes and archetypal images, and a "cultural" dimension, which consists of stereotypes and stereotypical images*. What I call the cultural unconscious is the dimension that comprises those stereotypes and stereotypical images (Adams 1996: 40 and 46; Adams 2001: 106–7). Recently, Samuel L. Kimbles has introduced the term "cultural complex" (2000). I now believe that we need to extend, elaborate, and refine this terminology, if we are to develop a cultural (or multicultural) psychology, rather than just an individual psychology. We require several terms: "cultural psyche," "cultural ego," "cultural unconscious," "cultural complex," "cultural projection," "cultural transference," "cultural countertransference," and so forth. Not only individuals but also cultures have psyches, egos, unconsciouses, complexes, projections, transferences, and countertransferences. In this respect, individuals are psychologically conditioned by the cultures in which they happen to be "placed," just as Jung was by Europe. As I define the European unconscious, it is all that the European ego is culturally unconscious *of*. The European unconscious comprises various, distinctively European complexes that manifest as specifically European projections onto other "places," including Africa.

Toward the end of his second trip to Africa in 1925–26, Jung realized that a different and a much more personal interest than psychological reflection on Europeans had motivated him unconsciously to travel to Africa. "To my astonishment," he says, "the suspicion dawned on me that I had undertaken my African adventure with the secret purpose of escaping from Europe and its complex of problems, even at the risk of remaining in Africa, as so many before me had done, and as so many were doing at this very time." It gradually occurred to Jung that he had been secretly – that is, unconsciously – motivated by the very same escapism that he eventually imputed to (or perhaps projected onto) Schweitzer. He, too, could remain in Africa and not return to Europe and its psychologically problematic *cultural complex*. He had gone on an expedition to Africa less to conduct psychological research and more to attempt to answer "the rather embarrassing question: What is going to happen to Jung the psychologist in the wilds of Africa?" (1963: 273). Jung had to admit to himself that he had also been motivated by a question other than the apparent one and that his ostensible purpose had served him as a convenient excuse for an evasion of the real question:

> This was a question I had constantly sought to evade, in spite of my intellectual intention to study the European's reaction to primitive conditions. It became clear to me that this study had been not so much an objective scientific project as an intensely personal one, and that any attempt to go deeper into it touched every possible sore spot in my own psychology.
>
> (Jung 1963: 273)

Unconsciously at least, he had decided to travel to Africa because "the atmosphere had become too highly charged for me in Europe" (1963: 273). For Jung to confess that the question had "touched every possible sore spot in my own psychology" was for him to acknowledge that Africa had activated a complex of geopathological issues that he had previously excluded from consideration and relegated to the unconscious because he had felt that they were just too painful to address consciously.

Jung had not expected that Africa would affect him so personally. He had assumed that he could go to Africa and remain fundamentally untouched by the experience. He had not anticipated that Africa would challenge his very identity as a European, but that is exactly what it did. He had not believed that Africa could so radically displace him psychologically. Africa posed the question: What is my place, and what is my identity? What is the relation between where I am and who I am? The answer was: I could be anyone, I could be anywhere, I could be here or I could be there, I could return to Europe or I could remain in Africa, I could stay white or I could, as Jung says, "go black."

In Africa Jung suffered from an identity crisis that was a "place crisis." Schweitzer says that the better educated a Christian missionary is, the better mentally and intellectually developed he is, the better "he will be able to hold out in Africa." Hold out against what? "Without this safeguard," Schweitzer says, "he is soon in danger of becoming a nigger, as it is called here" (1924: 164). To Schweitzer, Africa is an unsafe place for Europeans, who have to be on guard against becoming "niggers." Even as he calls the missionary who is unable to hold out in Africa a "nigger," he attempts rhetorically to displace responsibility for what he apparently knows very well is an offensively racist epithet. Schweitzer acts as if the phenomenon is not called "becoming a nigger" by *him* but is called that in this *place* (or, as he says, "here"), almost as if it is called that *by* the place.

I have previously noted that Leo Stone has written a psychoanalytic essay on what he calls "the principal obscene word" in the English language (1984). That word, according to Stone, is the "F-word." I have said, however, that what seems most obscene is relative to who one happens to be: "To a Freudian analyst, with sex on the theoretical brain, 'fuck' seems more obscene than any other word in the English language. To an African-American, however, 'nigger' is the most obscene" (Adams 1997b: 90).

Randall Kennedy has recently written a book about the "N-word." Kennedy observes that "nigger" has historically been a racist epithet when whites have applied it to blacks (or to other whites) but that it is not necessarily an obscenity when blacks apply it to other blacks. According to Kennedy, whether "nigger" is obscene or not is circumstantial. Thus he distinguishes between "nigger" as a term of "insult" and as a term of "affection" (2002: 174). On at least one occasion, Jung employs the term "affectionately," when he compares himself to black Africans, in solidarity with them as a fellow primitive. He says that, unlike black Africans, modern white Europeans presume to "know" without any guidance from the unconscious in dreams. In contrast, Jung says: "I am as primitive as any nigger, because I do not know" (*CW* 18: 286, par. 674). Like a black African, Jung believes that the unconscious knows what the ego does not know and that dreams guide us if we interpret them accurately. The editors of Jung's *Collected Works* have this to say about his use of the N-word: "This offensive term was not invariably derogatory in earlier British and Continental usage, and definitely not in this case" (*CW* 18: 286, par. 674n.). I have previously noted that "the word functions in this instance as a means for Jung to associate himself with black Africans and to dissociate himself from white Europeans" (Adams 1996: xxi). Some contemporary African-Americans have begun to employ the N-word subversively. In this respect, Kennedy says that "there is much to be gained by allowing people of all backgrounds to yank *nigger* away from white supremacists, to subvert its ugliest denotation, and to convert the N-word from a negative into a positive appellation" (2002: 175). For Schweitzer in the 1920s, however, "nigger" is a term not of approbation but of opprobrium, with a definitely pejorative connotation.

What Schweitzer calls "becoming a nigger," Jung calls "going black." To go black is to "go unconscious." For Jung, Africa is an image of the unconscious. For example, in his psychological commentary on a European alchemical text, *Symbola Aureae Mensae Duodecium Nationum*, published in 1617, Jung notes that the author Michael Maier's "mystic peregrination" is a fantastic journey to all four directions – Europe, America, Asia, and Africa – in that order. Jung says that "the darkest and the most unconscious" is the fourth direction, the final destination. "'Africa,'" he says, "is not a bad image for this" (*CW* 14: 210, par. 276). Jung then presents an interpretation of the text:

> Maier gives a description of Africa which is very like a description of hell: "uncultivated, torrid, parched, sterile and empty." He says that there are so few springs that animals of the most varied species assemble at the drinking-places and mingle with one another, "whence new births and animals of a novel appearance are born," which explained the saying "Always something new out of Africa." Pans dwelt there, and satyrs, dog-headed baboons, and half-men, "besides innumerable species of wild animals." According to certain modern views, this could hardly be bettered as a description of the unconscious.
>
> (*CW* 14: 211, par. 277)

This Africa is not a lush tropical jungle but a damnably hot desert with only a few watering-holes where feral creatures, mythic, monstrous, and composite animals and men gather together for the teeming, frenzied, cross-species breeding of a veritable bestiary of new hybrids. Such is the hellish, chaotic, orgiastic image of Africa that Jung cites with approval as an apt image of the unconscious. Although Jung did not interpret this image of Africa as an image of the unconscious until the 1950s, 30 years after his trip to Central Africa in 1925–26, it is nevertheless geopathologically symptomatic of the white European imagination from the seventeenth century to the twentieth century. Africa is not, I would emphasize, *the* unconscious. It is a place – a psycho-geographical Rorschach, an inkblot onto which Europeans displace, or project, *their own* unconscious.

Jung first uses the expression "going black" in reference to his trip to North Africa. Just as Schweitzer refers to "the danger of becoming a nigger," Jung refers to the "danger that my European consciousness would be overwhelmed." Overwhelmed by what? By the unconscious, Jung says. Thus he refers to "'going black under the skin,' a spiritual peril which threatens the uprooted European in Africa to an extent not fully appreciated" (1963: 245). The white European would not become physically black in Africa – his skin would not change color – but he could become spiritually black. That is, he could become unconscious. His European consciousness could be overwhelmed by the spirit of Africa.

According to Jung, black Africans have a special "talent for mimicry." They can, he says, "imitate with astounding accuracy the manner of expression, the gestures, the gaits of people, thus, to all intents and purposes, slipping into their skins" (1963: 259). Jung says that black Africans mimic people, not just white Europeans. Although he says that it is dangerous for white Europeans to go black under the skin, Jung evidently believes that it is perfectly safe for black Africans to slip into the skins of people, including the skins of white people, apparently because they can slip right out again. The difference between imitating people and going black is that the one is reversible, the other not.

The second time that Jung uses the expression "going black" he does so in reference to his trip to Central Africa, in a discussion of relations between white European men and black African women. He says that he never once spoke to a black African woman, for to do so "signifies love-making" (1963: 261). Verbal intercourse implies sexual intercourse. The white European man who engages in conversation with a black African woman, Jung says, "not only forfeits his authority, but runs the serious risk of 'going black'" (1963: 262). What Schweitzer calls the "natural authority" of white Europeans over black Africans is evidently also an issue for Jung.

Jung uses the expression "going black" a third time when he recounts a dream from his trip to Central Africa. In the dream, Jung says, an African-American barber "was holding a tremendous, red-hot curling iron to my head, intending to make my hair kinky – that is, to give me Negro hair." He interprets the dream as "a warning from the unconscious." According to Jung, the dream meant that "the primitive was a danger to me." He says: "At that time I was obviously all too close to 'going black'" (1963: 272). For Jung, to go black is to "go primitive." Jung concluded that "my European personality must under all circumstances be preserved intact" (1963: 273).

In *The Multicultural Imagination*, I reinterpret Jung's dream. I note that Jung interpreted the dream in a manner inconsistent with his own theory and method of dream interpretation. According to Jung, the basic function of the unconscious in dreams is compensatory. What the unconscious compensates are the partial, prejudicial, or defective attitudes of the ego. The unconscious presents to the ego potentially valuable alternative perspectives that have been repressed, dissociated, ignored, or neglected – or otherwise excluded from consideration. If the ego is receptive rather than defensive, it then has an opportunity seriously to entertain and critically to evaluate these perspectives and consciously to accept, reject, or otherwise engage them. I argue that Jung's interpretation of his dream is ego-defensive, rather than ego-compensatory. As I reinterpret his dream, it is a compensation for the too "straight" attitude of his white European ego. The dream is not warning Jung to "stay white" but is inviting, encouraging, or challenging him to "go black" or to "go kinky" – that is, consciously to consider and perhaps to adopt a different "style" of identity (Adams 1996: 78–80). As Jung experiences his dream, however, his very identity may become so geopathologically displaced as to be utterly *replaced* by another identity.

In a commentary on the relation between "mind" and "earth" (or psyche and place), Jung says that demographically in Africa "the white man is a diminishing minority and must therefore protect himself from the Negro by observing the most rigorous social forms, otherwise he risks 'going black.'" According to Jung, if the white European "succumbs to the primitive influence, he is lost" (*CW* 10: 47, par. 97). The white European who loses himself when he "goes black" loses his white identity, or his white ego. Although Jung is referring to white Europeans who live in Africa, not to those who, like him, merely travel to Africa, he, too, fears that he may experience loss of identity, or loss of ego. That is what Jung means when he says that his "European personality must under all circumstances be preserved intact."

Jung notes that "primitive pathology recognizes two causes of illness: loss of soul, and possession by a spirit" (*CW* 8: 309, par. 587). What Jung calls loss of soul in "primitives" is equivalent to loss of identity, or loss of ego, in "moderns." On the issue of pathology or the causes of illness, the opposition between African primitivity and European modernity is merely a superficial terminological distinction. What Africans call "soul," Europeans call "identity," or "ego." The phenomenon of "loss" is identical; only the terms are different. Likewise, white Europeans may be possessed by "spirits" just as black Africans may be. In psychological terminology, "possession" by a "spirit" is tantamount to "unconscious identification" with a "complex." Again, it is the same phenomenon merely by another name. In this respect, I would emphasize that there is a *spirit of place*. When we are in a certain place, we may lose our identity, or our ego, and we may be possessed by the spirit of that place. In just this way, Jung feared that he would lose his modern white European identity, or his modern white European ego, be possessed by the primitive spirit of Africa, and "go black."

Jung's fear of Africa was ultimately a fear of his own unconscious, which he projected onto Africa. Jung both feared and desired place and displacement. His geopathological fear was the immediate consequence of his desire. Had he not been so attracted by the spirit of Africa, he would not have been so scared of it. What was the attraction? According to Jung, the psyche exists in "layers." Historically, he says, the white European psyche has more layers than the black African psyche. The layers of the black African psyche are "primitive." Underneath the "modern" layers of the white European psyche are also "primitive" layers. Once, not so very long ago, Europeans were "Africans" – that is primitives. Now, however, they are moderns, at least on the surface. At a depth, they are also still primitives. As a result, Jung says, contact with primitives exerts "a strong suggestive influence upon those historical layers in ourselves which we have just overcome and left behind, or which we think we have overcome" (1963: 244).

For Jung, modernity is equivalent to rationality; primitivity, to vitality. The European who thinks that he has overcome and left behind the primitive layers of the psyche "prides himself on this without realizing that his rationality is won at the expense of his vitality, and that the primitive part of his personality is consequently condemned to a more or less underground existence" – that is, to a more or less unconscious existence (1963: 245). Contact with primitives evokes "an archetypal memory of an only too well known prehistoric past which apparently we have entirely forgotten," Jung says. "We are remembering a potentiality of life which has been overgrown by civilization, but which in certain places is still existent" (1963: 246).

One of those places where this potentiality of life continues to exist, at least in the white European imagination, is Africa. The attraction of Africa is a desire for what white Europeans think they have overcome and left behind, once and for all – but what they know only all too well, have only apparently forgotten, and can immediately remember again under the suggestive influence of the primitive. What white Europeans experience in Africa is intense nostalgia. Geopathologically, the desire that they feel for that place is a displacement of their own unconscious, a projection of it onto Africa. No wonder they fear that they will be possessed by the primitive, vital spirit of Africa and lose their modern, rational identity, or ego.

For white Europeans, the only geopathological alternatives would seem to be to remain in Africa and "go black," to remain in Africa but "stay white" (that is, oppress black Africans – or deny them "unsuitable freedom" – just as white Europeans repress what they desire and fear), or to return to Europe and "stay white." There is, however, another alternative, which Jung advocates. This alternative is what Jung calls a "modus vivendi" (1963: 244). A modus vivendi is a practical compromise. Jung says that if white Europeans were uncritically to relive the potentiality of life that they have apparently forgotten, they would, in effect, "go barbaric." He says:

> If we were to relive it naively, it would constitute a relapse into barbarism. Therefore we prefer to forget it. But should it appear to us again in the form of a conflict, then we should keep it in our consciousness and test the two possibilities against each other – the life we live and the one we have forgotten. For what has apparently been lost does not come to the fore again without sufficient reason.
>
> (Jung 1963: 246)

Rather than simply either relive the primitive or forget it, Jung proposes that we remember it, test it against the modern, and test the modern against it. What has apparently been lost still exists in the unconscious, and the reason it comes to the fore again is because the unconscious functions to compensate the partial, prejudicial, or defective attitudes of the ego. The compensatory function of the unconscious offers us an opportunity for a modus vivendi, a practical compromise between the ego and the unconscious – and, by extension, between the modern and the primitive.

"Compensation" is perhaps the most important concept in Jungian psychology, for it problematizes the complacent, presumptuous attitudes of the ego and recognizes the potential value of the alternative perspectives of the unconscious. If we substitute "modernity" and "rationality" for "ego," if we substitute "primitivity" and "vitality" for "unconscious," the implications are radically subversive. No longer is the modern "superior" and the primitive "inferior." Jung does say that in Africa he "could not help feeling superior because I was reminded at every step of my Europeanism" (1963: 245). Historically, Europeans have had a superiority complex – a white supremacy complex – toward Africans. The concept "compensation" implies that they could, if they only would, have an *equality complex*. Such an attitude transformation need not entail a facile cultural relativism that denies the existence of significant differences between Europeans and Africans. It would, however, oblige Europeans to regard any significant differences not as "racial" differences but as ethnic differences, not as natural differences but as cultural differences – among them, technological differences.

Europeans would have to consider seriously what they, as moderns culturally different from primitives, have lost even as they have gained an identity, or ego. Jung says of the European that "time and its synonym, progress, have crept up on him and irrevocably taken something from him." What compensates the European for this loss is "the illusion of his triumphs, such as steamships, railroads, airplanes, and rockets" (1963: 240). However inventive and innovative these technologies may be, they are only an illusory compensation. In this case, the unconscious does not compensate the ego. Rather, the ego futilely attempts to compensate, with rational conceit, a loss of vital contact with the unconscious. Ultimately, modern rationality is merely a rationalization for the loss of primitive vitality. Such is the "technopathology" of Europe.

There may be demons in Africa, but Europe, Jung says, is the "mother of all demons." The demons of Europe are modern communication and transportation technologies, and Europeans are possessed by, or unconsciously identified with, them. For Jung, Africa is that place where he can get away from those technological demons and receive "no telegrams, no telephone calls, no letters, no visitors" (1963: 264). This respite provides him with an opportunity directly to experience the spirit of another place, Africa, without constant interference from the demons of Europe. (This is, however, the very same Jung who also travels within Africa by Ford trucks, narrow-gauge railroads, and paddle-wheel steamers.) Jung might seem merely to have an anti-technological bias, but perhaps it is more than that. Perhaps it is a necessary precondition for a reconsideration of cultural differences and a deconstruction of any racist notions about natural differences (for example, skin color), about white European superiority, and about black African inferiority. Technology does confer a certain material advantage on those who possess it, but if they are possessed by it, it dispossesses them, and it redounds much to their spiritual disadvantage. Although in some respects Europeans may have superior technology, it does not follow that they have superior humanity.

What, finally, is Jung's contribution to multiculturalism? I would note that "multiculturalism" was not a concept available to Jung when he traveled to Africa in the 1920s. Without it, he could not really conceive, as we now attempt to do, what it might mean to "go multicultural." Jung did have an interest in different cultures and in cultural differences – although, as we still tend to do, he conceived of

Africa in terms of continental homogeneity rather than cultural heterogeneity. (Africa is a continent, a unity in that sense, but it also comprises many nations that include a vast diversity of cultures and ethnicities, which we do not adequately differentiate.)

As significantly different as Europeans and Africans might be culturally (or technologically), Jung did not frame that issue in terms of "racial" differences. He did not consider Europeans to be superior simply because they were "white" and Africans to be inferior simply because they were "black." He did believe that the European psyche had more historical layers than the African psyche and therefore that Europeans were, at least to some extent, more conscious than Africans. Thus he could say of Africans: "What goes on in the interior of these 'simple' souls is not conscious, is therefore unknown, and we can only deduce it from comparative evidence of 'advanced' European differentiation" (1963: 263). Or he could say: "The situation is not so different with the European; but we are, after all, somewhat more complicated" (1963: 242). Jung did not believe that black Africans were less *"racially" evolved* than white Europeans; he believed that they were less *historically layered, differentiated, or complicated*. In this sense, he was not a racist but a historicist. What interested him was the history of consciousness.

If Jung was, in any sense, a racist, it was to the extent that he uncritically adopted the expression "going black" and thereby color-coded what were not "racial" differences but only historical differences. "Going black" is not just a neutral, innocent figure of speech. Had Jung been more conscious, he could, for example, have exclusively and consistently employed the expression "going primitive" as an alternative to "going black." In *The Multicultural Imagination*, I discuss just how problematic the word "primitive" is (Adams 1996: 51, 143), but it does seem to me preferable to the word "black" as an epithet in the history of consciousness. To color-code putative differences in the history of consciousness is not only unnecessary but also pernicious. Had Jung been *much* more conscious – had he been much more pluralistic and particularistic – he could have subtly differentiated among a variety of national, cultural, and ethnic *consciousnesses* in Africa, in comparison with the variety of national, cultural, and ethnic *consciousnesses* in Europe. As it was, however, he simply applied the grossly oppositional psycho-analytic terms "conscious" and "unconscious" continentally to Europe and Africa, respectively, and color-coded the one "white" and the other "black."

Not only whites like Jung but also some contemporary "Afrocentric" blacks, even with the best of intentions, perpetuate the "continentalist" fallacy. They continue to act as if there is one continental psyche *of* Africa rather than many national, cultural, and ethnic psyches *in* Africa with quite specific – and quite different – histories. For example, a recent book by an African-American psych-ologist is entitled *The African Unconscious* (Bynum 1999). In contrast, "going multicultural" would entail "going multiconscious." That is, it would require us to analyze the multiplicity of consciousnesses in the multiplicity of cultures from a global psycho-geographical perspective.

Although Jung distinguished between modernity and primitivity, he did not privilege the one over the other. In fact, for him, the rationality of the modern tended to have a negative connotation and the vitality of the primitive a positive connotation. Europeans had gained something ("progress"), but in the process they had also lost something ("potentiality of life"). That thing was not, however, irretrievably lost. It had only been forgotten, might still be remembered, and might be tested to determine whether and, if so, to what extent it could and should still be experienced. Jung himself both desired and feared that thing. He believed that dreams warned him not to succumb to it. Thus he mentions with approval "our ability to bring the unconscious urges to consciousness with the aid of warning dreams" (1963: 245). In principle, Jung believed that through compensation a modus vivendi, or practical compromise, was possible between the ego and the unconscious, between the modern and the primitive. In practice, however, he himself proved personally incapable of that, at least in Africa. He panicked at the prospect of "going black," "going unconscious," "going primitive," or "going barbaric." Others might "go native," but Jung would "stay white" and go back to Europe. We might diagnose Jung as suffering from a case of geopathological paranoia. We might wonder whether the cure for such an illness would be to "go multicultural."

Jung also believed that before Europeans tried to save Africans they should try to cure themselves. According to Jung, Europeans were suffering from a geo-pathological sickness of the soul. Africans might have sick bodies that Schweitzer would treat, but Europeans had sick souls that Jung would treat. Jung was not just a tourist in Africa; nor was he, like Schweitzer, an emigrant (or, as Jung preferred to call him, a refugee or an escapee). He was what I would call a sojourner. Jung displaced himself to another place to reflect psychologically on the image of the European in the mirror of Africa. What he saw was himself. "I had wanted to know how Africa would affect me," he says, "and I had found out" (1963: 274).

I have not yet traveled to Africa – except in my imagination, in my dreams. A few months after the publication of *The Multicultural Imagination*, I had the following dream:

> I'm taking the examination with other candidates at the institute where I'm training to become a Jungian analyst. The Jungian analyst who is administering the examination tells us that there are five questions. The last question, number 5, is: "Tell about Lake _____." This is a reference to a lake in Africa. It is not Lake Victoria, however. I do not understand the question – the intent of it. Where on the African continent, I wonder, *is* this lake? On Jung's two trips, he visited North Africa and Central Africa. This lake seems to be in Southern Africa. But Jung did not go there. Am I to give a literal description of this lake? I do not know *what* to say about this lake. Finally, I decide, what the hell, I will just go ahead and write something. I will regard this as an imaginal lake, a lake of the imagination. I will satisfy myself and in the process write a Jungian answer.

This is an examination dream, in which I am expected to demonstrate and apply my knowledge of Jungian psychology as part of my training to become a Jungian analyst. The dominant image in the dream is a lake – not just any lake but a lake in Africa, not Lake Victoria where Stanley is reputed to have extended his hand in greeting and said, "Doctor Livingstone, I presume," when they discovered the source of the Nile, and not a lake that Jung ever visited on his trips to Africa. I am asked to tell about a lake in Africa, a lake below where Jung traveled in Africa, a lake lower down than he ever traveled. I am asked to tell about a lake that neither Stanley nor Livingstone nor Jung ever discovered or visited. I am asked to tell about a place where Jung never went.

Although this dream explicitly refers to the examination that a particular Jungian institute requires of all candidates, it also implicitly refers to the possibility – in fact, the necessity – of self-examination. In the dream, I examine how I should answer Jungian questions. In this sense, the dream is about what it means to be a Jungian. The dream indicates that if I or, for that matter, any of us are to become Jungians we must go to places where Jung never went, that these are imaginal places, places in the imagination, and that, if we do not satisfy ourselves in this process of self-examination, being a Jungian will not be a meaningful experience for any of us. Marie-Louise von Franz cautions us against the notion of going beyond Jung: "When you are full of would-be ideas, then you feel you will go far beyond whatever Jung said; you will bring out an idea that will revolutionize our whole age, and so on" (1995: 129). Such a notion may, of course, be just a conceit, a grandiose inflation of the ego. Jung did not, however, explore the entire psyche. I believe that he would have welcomed other analysts going places where he never went. Jung was afraid to "go black." We, however, now have an opportunity – and a responsibility – to go beyond Jung, to "go multicultural," to go where he never went, to displace ourselves to that place, and to tell about it. We do not have to be geopathological; we can be multicultural.

To illustrate what I mean by "going multicultural," I now want to displace us from Africa to America. In the year 2000, relief pitcher John Rocker, who was then a member of the Atlanta Braves baseball team, uttered certain controversial remarks. In a magazine interview Rocker was quoted as having referred to an African-American teammate as a "fat monkey" and having indulged in a diatribe of bigotry, especially about New Yorkers. From the geopathological perspective of Rocker, New York City is a place where he might have to sit on the subway next to "degenerates." For example, he said, the passengers might include "some kid with purple hair next to some queer with AIDS right next to some dude who just got out of jail for the fourth time, right next to some 20-year-old mother with four kids" (McKinley January 9, 2000, sec. 4: 5). The subway is, of course, a classic image of the "subconscious," or of what psychoanalysts call the unconscious. For Rocker, the subway in New York City is an underground, an underworld, a hell full of sinners. Rocker apparently believes that he is, in comparison, a saint.

Major league baseball responded by ordering Rocker to undergo psychological testing and sensitivity training, suspending him from play for the first month of the

2000 season, and fining him $20,000. Were his comments "sick?" Was Rocker "mentally ill?" One social psychologist said that Rocker "just didn't have his mental editor turned on" (McKinley January 9, 2000, sec. 4: 5). Freud says that we all have a "censor" that represses what we might otherwise impulsively or compulsively express. An editor is not exactly a censor, but this social psychologist seems to believe that the problem was not Rocker's attitude but his behavior. From this perspective, if Rocker had "edited" his attitude and "behaved" himself, then there would have been no problem. Presumably the social psychologist would recommend "behavior modification." In contrast, a Jungian analyst would offer the possibility of *attitude transformation*.

Although it is true enough that there was an ineffective relation between Rocker's ego and his "mental editor," what is much more important is that there was an ineffective relation between his ego and his "shadow" – those negative, inferior, or primitive aspects of his own psyche that were dissociated (or, I would say, "segregated") from his ego and that were consequently projected onto others who were conveniently scapegoated. For Rocker to "turn on" his mental editor would be for him merely to attempt to deal with his problem as a function of what Jungians call the "persona." A persona is the appearance that the ego presents in deference to social expectations. At its best, the persona demonstrates respect for propriety, conventionality, and civility. At its worst, it countenances duplicity and hypocrisy. (*Persona* means "mask.") To "edit" the shadow, to mask it may be a "politic" expedient, but it is not an *analytic* solution. In Jungian analysis, Rocker would not be advised to adopt a prudently discreet persona and to modify his "politically incorrect" behavior, for his vulgar and offensive attitudes would remain intact. They would just be private rather than public. In Jungian analysis, Rocker would be presented with the opportunity to develop an effective – that is, an empathic – relation to his shadow and, in the process, to transform the partial, prejudicial, and defective attitudes of his ego.

It is in this sense that I have said that, for whites, an authentically multicultural imagination would require "*desegregation of the white ego*" (Adams 1997b: 100) and the integration of all those aspects of themselves that whites have historically repressed and projected onto others, especially onto blacks. We all – white, black, or otherwise – have a "John Rocker" inside us. That is, we, too, have a shadow. Therefore it is essential that we not "out-Rocker" Rocker, scapegoat him, and righteously imagine that we are different in kind from him. Even at our very best, we are merely different in degree from John Rocker. As I have said: "We all have our biases, by no means all of which are 'racial.' The value of psychoanalysis – and especially of Jungian analysis – is that it offers a theory and a method for exposing them, confronting them, and transforming them" (Adams 1997b: 102).

In the magazine interview Rocker said that "the biggest thing I don't like about New York are the foreigners" (McKinley January 9, 2000, sec. 4: 5). Foreigners are those who come from another place (in this case, from all around the world to New York – and to America). Thus Rocker suffers from a global version of geopathology. Certain aspects of his psyche are so foreign to his ego that he displaces them onto "aliens" who serve him as a convenient excuse not to analyze the alienation that he experiences. In this respect, Jung says in "The Spiritual Problem of Modern Man":

> We used to regard foreigners as political and moral reprobates, but the modern man is forced to recognize that he is politically and morally just like anyone else. Whereas formerly I believed that it was my bounden duty to call others to order, I must now admit that I need calling to order myself, and that I would do better to set my own house to rights first.
>
> (*CW* 10: 81, par. 162)

Setting our own house to rights, getting our own house in order, recognizing that we are just like everyone else, entails acknowledging that the only real "foreigners" are those who are housed in that place that we call our own psyche. To "go multicultural," we need not literally go to Africa, to New York, or to any other place in external reality. We need to go imaginally into our own internal reality, into that place that we call, for lack of a better word, the "unconscious."

James Hillman

Drawing by Michael Vannoy Adams (after a photograph by Harry Heleotis)

Chapter 8

Refathering psychoanalysis, deliteralizing Hillman:

Imaginal therapy, individual and cultural

This chapter is a revised and expanded version of a paper that I presented at the conference of the London Convivium for Archetypal Studies at Cumberland Lodge in 1994. The topic of that conference was James Hillman and Michael Ventura's provocative book *We've Had a Hundred Years of Psychotherapy – and the World's Getting Worse*.

At the conference of the International Association for Analytical Psychology in Paris in 1989, Hillman announced that he had "ceased practicing private analysis." Although he continued "to practice psychology with large groups, in public speaking and teaching, publishing and writing," he no longer practiced psychotherapy with individuals (1991b: 95). Three years later, Hillman and Ventura published *We've Had a Hundred Years of Psychotherapy – and the World's Getting Worse* (1992).

According to Hillman, a century of psychotherapy has made the world worse than it once was. It would be easy to take Hillman literally – and to mistake him. One of Hillman's favorite words is "deliteralizing." As Hillman defines it, it is to "see through" literal realities to metaphorical realities (1975: 136). It may be that we now need to deliteralize Hillman. If psychotherapy is not only a talking but also a listening cure, we need to "hear through" what he has said – or we need to "read through" what he has written – rather than take him at his apparent word, to the letter, imitate him, and repudiate psychotherapy.

What has Hillman said, what has he written? According to Hillman, as individuals in psychotherapy have become more "sensitive" (1992: 3), they have become more "passive" (1992: 5). Making people "better" has made the world "worse" (1992: 5). Although Ventura says, "I'm not sure it's causal" (1992: 5) – that is, he is uncertain that there is a direct, cause-and-effect relation between psychotherapy and the worsening of the world – Hillman says, in no uncertain terms, that "we're disempowering ourselves through therapy" (1992: 6). To Ventura he says, "Our job is to show how *psychology* contributes to making the world worse" (1992: 151). How does psychology or psychotherapy do this, according to Hillman?

Psychotherapy makes the world worse, Hillman says, because it normalizes us. It reduces the abnormal, the deviant, to a norm to which we conform. Hillman advocates an alternative form of therapy. "The goal," Hillman says, "of my therapy" – in explicit contrast to others' therapy – "is eccentricity" (1992: 35). An eccentric therapy would evidently be a therapy that decenters our conventional notions about normality. Our eccentricity, Hillman contends, is the source of our activity and of our political activism. Psychotherapy, he asserts, normalizes us by personalizing all issues and thereby depoliticizing them. It has promoted a form of subjectivism tantamount to solipsism, an orientation so inward as to be virtually oblivious to the world. Rather than becoming extraverted and "outraged" at the worsening of the world, through psychotherapy we merely remain introverted and "enraged" (1992: 11) – or, I might say, "in-raged." Psychotherapy reduces us to passivity and devalues what Hillman calls "the *valuable* madness in our society" (1992: 152), when it induces us to "cope" rather than "protest," to "adapt" rather than "rebel" (1992: 156). People are mad in both senses of the word – not only crazy but also angry – and so is Hillman. If *We've Had a Hundred Years of Psychotherapy – and the World's Getting Worse* is not only Hillman's book but also his complex, the dominant emotion is anger. Hillman is mad because he believes that the world we inhabit is worse than the world we inherited, that it has gone from good to bad to worse, that it is getting worse and worse, and that psychotherapy contributes to this worsening of the world.

We have had a hundred years of psychotherapy, and we have had more than seventy years of Hillman. Is Hillman simply indulging in an aged, tired harangue as the end of a century, the end of a millennium, and the end of a career and a life approach? Is he merely rambling, ranting, and raving about the worsening of the world? Is this ennui or anomie? If we were to imitate Hillman, would we preserve for posterity equally profound or superficial opinions? Where is that Hillman who is so suspicious of ego inflation and of instant analysis "out of the top of my head" (1983b: 3)? Should that Hillman who avoids "the panel discussion, the talk show, and the interview" (1983b: 4) also avoid the tape recording and letter writing that provide him and Ventura with the material for their book about the worsening of the world? Will bookstores now have a special section for "world-help" books next to the "self-help" books? I ask these questions in the belief that Hillman is the most important (I might even say, the only really original) Jungian analyst since Jung. He has certainly been the most important to me personally.

Hillman suggests that we should "entertain the idea that the world is *in extremis*, suffering an acute, perhaps fatal, disorder at the edge of extinction" (1992: 151). This is, of course, an end-of-the-world fantasy. It is, in fact, the typical, or archetypal, fantasy of psychotics, especially paranoid schizophrenics. Hillman acknowledges that *We've Had a Hundred Years of Psychotherapy* has no prophetic, or predictive, value. He cautions that "we can't predict, we can't say the world is going to hell in a basket, it's too easy." Such a facile prophecy entails "the risk of being caught in an archetypal fantasy" (1992: 233). Hillman says that not only the archetypal fantasy that the world is getting better but also the archetypal fantasy that the world is getting worse are equally problematic because they both are myths that comfort us – that reassure us that we know how and where the world is going. Hillman notes that the fantasy that the world is going to hell or that the world is coming to an end is not only archetypal but also apocalyptic:

> The Apocalypse is the myth of our culture, it's *the* book of our culture, it's the last chapter of the holy book, of the writ. And what it is is the destruction of the entire world. If you take that literally you get that book called *The Late Great Planet Earth*, which is one of the only books Ronald Reagan ever read, and which was the largest-selling book in the United States in the 1970s.
>
> (Hillman and Ventura 1992: 239–40)

If you take it literally, I might also add, you get Daniel Paul Schreber or Charlie Manson or David Koresh or Shoko Asahara – all of whom fantasize an end to the world. Hillman suggests that we should take it metaphorically. If we do that, perhaps we get Tony Kushner and *Angels in America: Millennium Approaches*. In this sense, *We've Had a Hundred Years of Psychotherapy* is a quite typical, if not quite an archetypal, book for the end of the century and perhaps for the end of the millennium. If we "read through" what Hillman has written, do we need to deliteralize him, or has he already deliteralized himself?

When Noel Cobb, who was then editor of *Sphinx: A Journal for Archetypal Psychology and the Arts* (which advertised itself as a "fin-de-siècle journal for the turn of the Millennium"), invited me to present a paper at the conference of the London Convivium for Archetypal Studies, I suggested the title "Imaginal Technique in Individual and Cultural Therapy." Cobb dissuaded me from using the word "technique" because he said that it was like "a stone in the shoe." There is, of course, nothing more uncomfortable than that. I confess, however, that I did, momentarily, have a rather perverse fantasy of re-entitling my talk, "A Stone in the Shoe: Imaginal Technique in Individual and Cultural Therapy." One of the reasons I value Hillman is that he has never hesitated to make us all feel uncomfortable. Whatever else a "Hillmanian" psychotherapy does, it does not comfort us. What if the stone in our shoe should happen to be the philosopher's stone? If our shoes are, as Jungians like to say metaphorically, our "understandings" (Young-Eisendrath and Wiedemann 1987: 173), then what about those stones that somehow get between us and our innersoles/innersouls?

Although I acceded to Cobb's request that I not deliver a technical presentation on "Hillmanian" psychotherapy, what continued to concern me about Hillman's apparent repudiation of psychotherapy was the possibility of an all too comfortable misunderstanding. After talking to Cobb and then reading through Hillman again, I was struck by the following sentence in *We've Had a Hundred Years of Psychotherapy*: "There's rocks in the psyche" (1992: 9). According to Hillman, the rocks in the psyche are the things that remain the same, that do not change. Hillman says that it is the rocks in the psyche (I might say, the stones in the shoe) "that make for character, for the peculiar idiosyncrasy that you are" (1992: 30). In this sense, our character is a certain idiosyncratic discomfort that we feel, and to the extent that psychotherapy exists to remove the stones from our shoes, the rocks from our psyches, it is non-Hillmanian or even anti-Hillmanian psychotherapy that constrains one not to "live one's oddity" (1983b: 161). For Hillman, individuation is eccentricity, idiosyncrasy, oddity.

As I read through Hillman, I do not believe that he is literally advocating an end to psychotherapy. He even says "I want to defend therapy" (1992: 50) – but only, I would add, as he redefines it. What he proposes is a psychotherapy that would (to employ another jargon) "deconstruct" such oppositions as subject and object, inner and outer, private and public, personal and political, psyche – or if you prefer (as I do not), "soul" – and world. As I have noted (Adams 1985), there are important similarities (and differences) between what Jacques Derrida calls "deconstructing" and what Hillman calls "re-visioning." In *We've Had a Hundred Years of Psychotherapy*, Hillman is not always consistent in deconstructing – or as he says, re-visioning – these oppositions. Sometimes he seems to privilege the object over the subject, the outer over the inner, the public over the private, the political over the personal, and the world over the psyche. Sometimes he seems to imply that we should do what he has done and quite literally quit practicing individual therapy because it necessarily disempowers people. Sometimes he seems to offer himself as psychotherapist to the world at large. In spite of these occasional tendencies, I believe that a proper "reading through" of Hillman would emphasize just how arbitrary these oppositions are, would emphasize the inextricability of subject-and-object, inner-and-outer, private-and-public, personal-and-political, psyche-and-world.

I would also note that Hillman is by no means the only Jungian who is well aware of the world. In this regard, I would mention in particular the work of Andrew Samuels and Robert Bosnak, both of whom practice individual as well as cultural therapy. Both Samuels and Bosnak are personally and politically active. In *The Political Psyche* (1993), Samuels presents the results of a survey that he conducted internationally to determine whether – and, if so, to what extent – psychotherapists consider political issues to be relevant material in therapy. The percentage of psychotherapists who say that they do already regard political issues as relevant material – and not merely a defensive avoidance of strictly personal issues – surprises and pleases him. Samuels has recently published another book, *Politics on the Couch*, in which he argues that "psychotherapy can contribute to a general transformation of politics" (2001: 1). Bosnak is also politically active. He has organized three international conferences on the theme of apocalypse – the first, on nuclear war; the second, on environmental catastrophe; the third, on charisma and holy war. In *Dreaming with an AIDS Patient* (1989), Bosnak has engaged one of the dominant personal and political issues of our time. I could, of course, mention other Jungians – such as Ginette Paris in *The Sacrament of Abortion* (1992) and Michael Perlman in *The Power of Trees* (1994) – for whom issues of gender and ecology are decisively significant topics. I admire and respect these efforts. I myself have employed psychoanalysis to address a political issue in *The Multicultural Imagination: "Race," Color, and the Unconscious* (Adams 1996).

Why, then, do I also feel a certain ambivalence about these efforts? I am ambivalent about Hillman and ourselves being caught, all too literally, in a meliorist fantasy – a judgmental (in the sense of a "last judgment") fantasy of betterment, in which we presume to know better and to do better than others. It is in this sense that I believe that we must deliteralize Hillman – and ourselves. Freud was right to caution us against the notion that psychoanalysis – whether Freudian or Jungian – is, could be, or should be a *Weltanschauung* (*SE*: 22), or "world-view." Psychotherapists who uncritically imagine *anima mundi*, the world-soul, may delude themselves that they have a world-view politically superior to, or more politically correct than, the world-views of others. Freud says that "there are no indications of reality in the unconscious" (1985: 264). I would emphasize that there are also no indications of political correctness in the unconscious. Similarly, we need to be wary of an ego psychology that imagines that it knows political reality – and a superego psychology that imagines that it knows political morality.

We live in a world in which God is dead but the "gods" and "goddesses" are alive. There is no one God who intervenes to reveal to us what is unambiguously true or false, good or bad. There are many gods and goddesses (archetypal images), with a variety of foibles (Hillman would say, "pathologies"). To imagine that the world is getting worse and that we have repressed, neglected, or ignored it is to imagine that we might suddenly become saints rather than sinners and save the world – and a salvationist psychotherapy is merely another variation on the theme of what Hillman disparages as "Christianism" (1983b). What attracts me to "Hillmanian" psychotherapy, what appeals to me about it, is that analyzing is neither ego-realizing nor superego-moralizing but image-metaphorizing. Who are we to say that the world is not both good enough and bad enough? Are "good" and "bad," "better" and "worse," the only adjectives in our psychotherapeutic vocabulary? (These words are not even concrete images but abstract concepts.) Are our descriptive and evaluative capacities – our imaginations – so restrictive and so oppositional?

What distinguishes Hillman is his ability to discern precisely where we are most unconscious – that is, where our egos are most complacent. In a sense, for Hillman, the ego *is* the unconscious. The ego is that sense of "I-ness" that imagines it knows when it does not know. What the "I" does not know is that it, too, is an image – what I call the "ego-image" – a figment of the imagination, a fiction, a fantasy – and not "reality." (As I define the ego-image, it is who or how "I" imagine myself to be.) There are institutional as well as individual egos, as in the institution of psychotherapy. As Hillman redefines psychotherapy, it is not the translation of fantasy into reality but the translation of reality into fantasy (1985: 95–7). That is, by this definition, psychotherapy is a demonstration that what the ego takes – or mistakes – for reality is always already a fantasy, a rhetorical device, a poetic conceit, a metaphor. A "Hillmanian" psychotherapy is based not on any putative reality principle but on what I call the *fantasy principle*.

Where is the ego of psychotherapy today? Where is psychotherapy complacently egocentric – egoistical and egotistical – and therefore unconscious? Hillman asserts that the ego of psychotherapy as an institution is fixated on interiority and introversion. He advocates a return of the repressed, dissociated, neglected, or ignored: a psychotherapy of exteriority and extraversion. Hillman urges us to get out of our egos in order to get into the world.

Rather than psychotherapy for the "inner child," Hillman would presumably recommend psychotherapy for the outer child in the inner city. From my experience as a psychotherapist with African-American and Latino children in the East New York section of Brooklyn, however, I must say that translating the reality of the outer child in the inner city into the fantasy of an inner child in the outer city is hardly an activity without value. I am entirely in sympathy with Hillman's position that a strong ego rather than a weak ego is not the ultimate purpose of psychotherapy. "The strong ego," Hillman says, "is also an imaginal figure" (1983b: 68) – although it does not realize that it is merely one image among many others in the psyche. As Hillman defines the strong ego, it is the imaginal figure that "doesn't lose control, doesn't give over to what comes in" (1983b: 68–9) – that is, to the other imaginal figures that come in. The strong ego, he says, is "the suppressive master of the psyche" (1983b: 69). It is defensive rather than receptive.

Hillman thus defines the strong ego differently – and more restrictively – than many other psychoanalysts do. Heinz Hartmann declares that the strong ego "cannot be defined solely" in terms of conflict – for example, with the id or the superego (1958: 15). For Hartmann, the strong ego includes many other functions than the defensive function that Hillman emphasizes. Most psychotherapists in New York City would believe that they should strengthen what might be called the "ghetto-ego." They would assume that such children have weak egos, if they have any ego at all. In my experience, these children have strong egos (at least according to Hillman's definition) that are exteriorized and extraverted. What these children do not have is an interiorized, introverted appreciation of imaginative possibilities. Outer reality is all too "real" to them. It is an all too adult reality of sex, drugs, and guns – of "shooting off," "shooting up," and "shooting down."

In 1991, when I was a clinical social work intern at New Hope Guild in East New York (a section of Brooklyn), I proposed conducting a psychotherapy group for African-American and Latino boys, seven and eight years old, on the topic of "Fathers and Sons." Colleagues of mine at the agency were enthusiastic about my theme but skeptical about my method – which was quite deliberately (although I did not use the word) "Hillmanian."

One of my favorite books by Hillman is *Healing Fiction* (1983a). My idea was to use fiction to heal, to read stories about fathers and sons to the group of boys. My colleagues doubted that the boys would sit still. (One of the most popular diagnoses was "oppositional defiant disorder.") My own son was the same age as the boys in the group, however, and I knew how eagerly he looked forward to my reading stories to him.

With one exception, the boys in the group had either abusive or absent fathers. I did more than read stories – I served cookies and juice and sometimes popcorn, and I helped the boys draw and color pictures, model clay, assemble toy gliders, and stitch coin purses in the shape of baseballs, but mostly I read stories – and the boys did sit still. I went to a multicultural bookshop in Brooklyn and selected stories (such as Tolowa Mollel's *The Orphan Boy*, John Steptoe's *Daddy Is a Monster*, and Ruth Sonneborn's *Friday Night Is Papa Night*) about African, African-American, and Latino fathers and sons, but I also read a version of the *Odyssey* to the boys. We had lively discussions about the stories – and about that other, contemporary Homer and his son Bart Simpson, as well as the "Black Bart" variation so popular among African-Americans.

I suppose that one could regard this psychotherapy group as one more example of the men's movement – or the "men-and-boys' movement." Was this political or personal psychotherapy, cultural or individual psychotherapy? Inextricably both, I would argue. I would also insist that psychotherapy need not be a process that normalizes people and renders them apathetic in relation to the world but can be a process that enables people actively to reimagine psyche-and-world.

In *The Father: Contemporary Jungian Perspectives*, Samuels says that "an imaginative experience of 'father' can be available to some extent to a child who grows up in a home which has no father in it" (1985: 40). I would pluralize this proposition and say that imaginative experiences of "fathers" can be available to boys who grow up in homes that have either absent or abusive fathers. I do not mean the "archetypal" father but *imaginal* fathers, plural. As Hillman emphasizes, we never experience archetypes in the abstract – we only ever experience images in the concrete.

A father–son fiction, the Laius–Oedipus myth, is the very foundation of psychoanalytic theory. As Hillman notes, Freud placed "the complex of the absent father" at the very center of both the psyche and psychoanalysis (1972: 16). The Laius–Oedipus myth, however, imaginally exemplifies not only the complex of the absent father but also the complex of the abusive father. (It is not a healing fiction but a "wounding fiction.") It is a story of infanticidal–patricidal, intergenerational conflict: if the father does not kill the son, then the son will kill the father. Even if we deliteralize this myth and acknowledge that for a son to be father to the man, he must metaphorically "kill" the father or "be killed" by him, this myth provides only one, very particular, father–son image. In emphasizing the Laius–Oedipus myth, Hillman says, "Freud told us less which myth was the psyche's essence than that the *essence of psyche is myth*" (1972: 16). It is not so much that the Laius–Oedipus myth is the wrong myth, but that, for psychoanalysis, it has been the one and only myth rather than, as Hillman says, merely one myth among many equally important myths (1991a).

There are many father–son myths besides the Laius–Oedipus myth. For example, in the Shiva–Ganesh myth the abusive father decapitates the son, just as in the Laius–Oedipus myth the abusive father impedes the son. (I have often joked – quite seriously – that the Laius–Oedipus myth is an "anti-pedestrian" myth: Laius drives a nail through the foot of Oedipus and later drives a chariot over the foot of Oedipus. The name "Oedipus" means "swollen-foot.") Unlike Laius, however, Shiva reheads the son that he has beheaded. In the Abraham–Isaac myth, the father prepares to sacrifice the son, and in the Abraham–Ishmael myth, the father exiles the son. In the Odysseus–Telemachus myth, the father rescues the son – and then, after being an absent father for 20 years, finally returns to initiate the son that he had to leave.

It is Heinz Kohut who confronts Freud with the pertinent question: What would psychoanalytic theory have been like if it had been founded on Odysseus–Telemachus rather than on Laius–Oedipus? If Freud had conceived a Telemachus complex rather than the Oedipus complex, Kohut says, psychoanalytic theory – and practice – would have been radically different. According to Kohut, it is the intergenerational continuity that Odysseus and Telemachus exemplify between father and son that "is normal and human, and not intergenerational strife, and mutual wishes to kill and destroy – however frequently and even ubiquitously, we may be able to find traces of those pathological disintegration products of which traditional analysis has made us think as a normal developmental phase, a normal experience of the child" (1991 4: 563). Two Greek, one Hindu, one Jewish, and one Islamic father–son myth hardly exhaust all of the imaginative possibilities. A vast, perhaps infinite number of alternative images of father–son relations are available both actually and potentially (we need to acknowledge not only the existence of a variety of old father–son images but also the continuous emergence of a variety of new ones).

As I was preparing for my fathers-and-sons psychotherapy group, an article entitled "Beliefs: The Story Calls for Fathers, But Too Many Have Written Themselves Out of the Script" happened to appear in the *New York Times*. The author, Peter Steinfels, reported that David Blankenhorn, president of the Institute for American Values, a research organization in New York City, was advocating what was, in effect, an imaginal story of fatherhood. Steinfels quotes Blankenhorn as having said, "Never before in our nation's history have so many children grown up without a father's presence and provision" (June 20, 1992, sec. 1: 11). He continues:

> Homes without fathers can be models of love and courage, but homes without fathers are also among the likeliest to be visited by poverty, domestic violence, juvenile crime and teen-age pregnancies. "If current scholarship proves anything," Mr. Blankenhorn has written, "it is that children who grow up without their fathers are worse off – economically, educationally, psychologically, every way we can measure – than children who grow up with their fathers."
>
> (Steinfels June 20, 1992, sec. 1: 11)

Then Steinfels says: "Yet in all the comedy and commentary inspired by Vice President Dan Quayle's recent speeches on 'family values,' the bulk of attention has been focused on 'single mothers' rather than on the real issue of absent fathers" (June 20, 1992, sec. 1: 11). According to Steinfels, Blankenhorn's argument is similar to Quayle's:

His favorite metaphor in talking about fatherhood is a "cultural script" – a social story, a set of cues, an ideal character and a classic plot line that shapes, guides and at times pressures men into a certain sense of who they are and how they should act. Like the Vice President, Mr. Blankenhorn emphasizes the role of opinion leaders and cultural elites in telling or reshaping the "prevailing story of fatherhood."

(Steinfels June 20, 1992, sec. 1: 11)

There is nothing objectionable in Blankenhorn's motivation. Like Hillman, he believes that the world has gotten worse, and he advocates a form of cultural therapy that utilizes a healing fiction. Unlike Hillman, however, he appears to propose a single cultural script – a rather abstract, archetypal social story – one with "an ideal character and a classic plot line that shapes, guides and at times pressures men" (or boys) into being (and acting) a certain way. The emphasis on "idealism" and "classicism" seems to me conservative, nostalgic, sentimental, perhaps even reactionary. The word "script" seems to me too prescriptive. It suggests a text that specifies a particular performance, a model that requires imitation in the service of normalization.

In spite of these reservations, I believe that what Blankenhorn has to say about the topic of fathers merits serious consideration. In *Fatherless America*, Blankenhorn champions (in a style reminiscent of D. W. Winnicott) the "good-enough" father (1995: 18). He criticizes what he calls the dominant "cultural story" that characterizes fathers as (1) "superfluous," (2) "part of the problem" (not the solution), and (3) in need of transformation from "gender-specific male roles" to "gender-neutral human values" (1995: 67). According to this script, the ideal father is the "like-a-mother father" (1995: 99). Blankenhorn never once mentions Jung, but rather like a Jungian he describes several typical images of the father in contemporary America: the "Unnecessary Father," the "Old Father," the "New Father," the "Deadbeat Dad," the "Visiting Father," the "Sperm Father," the "Stepfather," and the "Nearby Guy." All of these (but especially the New Father) he contrasts with the typical image of the "Good Family Man," who is "a loving husband and committed father" (1995: 223).

According to Blankenhorn, the typical image of the New Father entails "an androgynous rejection of all traditional masculinity" (1995: 224). Blankenhorn would presumably abjure what Samuels calls "the father of whatever sex" (1993: 133), for the concept suggests that the function of the father is not "given" biologically but is "constructed" socially. Although Blankenhorn believes that cultural stories are crucially important to the extent that they constrain or even determine how we characterize fathers, it is ultimately not imaginal fathers but "real" fathers – that is, flesh-and-blood fathers – men, not women, that interest him. In contrast to Samuels, he does not believe that women can perform the function of the father as well as men can.

Where I differ from Blankenhorn is in my belief in the importance of multiple, concrete, imaginal stories of fatherhood and sonhood, manhood and boyhood (the more stories, the more imaginative possibilities, the better) to stand these boys in effective stead as they become men – and not only ideal, classic, normal stories but also abnormal, deviant, psychopathological stories, coping and adapting stories as well as protesting and rebelling stories, as comprehensive an array of narrative options, or scenarios, as possible, in all the modes that Northrup Frye enumerates: mythic, romantic, high and low mimetic (or realistic), and ironic (1957: 33–4).

Blankenhorn is by no means the only man in New York City with an interest in fathers and sons. A "Father's Day" article by Susan Chira in the *New York Times* mentions Blankenhorn (and includes a photograph of him, his wife, and their four-year-old son in Central Park) but also cites Wade F. Horn, director of the National Father Initiative, and James Levine, director of the Fatherhood Project. The title of the article provocatively declares that there is a "war" over the role of American fathers, as if the controversy over fathers and sons (or fathers and children) is merely a variation on the theme of the war between the sexes – between men and women, fathers and mothers. Blankenhorn, Horn, and Levine all insist that they are not attacking single mothers or attempting to reinstate an anachronistic stereotype of fathers and mothers and a traditional division of labor. For example, in criticizing what he calls the "new father paradigm," Blankenhorn says that he is merely arguing that nurturance is not the only role for the contemporary father but that provision and pedagogy are also equally important roles. According to Chira, these men who would revision 1990s fatherhood maintain that they are "not trying to revive the 1950s father nor redraw traditional sexual roles" but are trying instead "to curb what they saw as excesses of feminism and to reward fathers for their contributions" (June 19, 1994, sec. 1: 22).

Fatherhood is an issue not only for "white" men but also for "black" men in America. In an op-ed piece in the *Wall Street Journal*, Michael L. King argues that African-American men all too often have "fathered" children out of wedlock and abandoned them to single, frequently teen-age mothers. He notes that more than 50 per cent of African-American children are now born out of wedlock (more than 90 per cent to teen-age mothers.) This statistical pattern is not, of course, unique to the African-American community but is a trend in the general population. If there is a cultural script to all this, it is the quest as conquest. Too many African-American fathers, King says, are not men but boys who continue to believe that "sexual irresponsibility is a rite of manhood." Rather than a masculine rite of passage that results in marriage and family, this scenario all too often merely results in intercourse and pregnancy. According to King, this is an indulgence that demonstrates "utter indifference to the dignity and feelings of other human beings." It is a ritual that has not initiated boys as men, or fathers, but that has simply taught them "that it was acceptable to use women like whores" – and then to abandon those women and, of course, the children, too. What King advocates instead is for African-American men, especially "highly visible black professionals" (of whom he as an attorney for the Federal Trade Commission is one), to assume a special responsibility. They must "lead by example," he says, and affirm the benefits of marriage and family (June 6, 1988: 20).

Samuels is right to say that an imaginal father "is not the same as one of flesh-and-blood" (1985: 41). We know, however, that even a flesh-and-blood father who is neither absent nor abusive is never enough of a father for any son. Every son needs more than one father, needs many fathers – and not only a flesh-and-blood one, but also mythic ones, fantastic ones, fictional ones. As James Joyce demonstrates in *Ulysses*, that modern *Odyssey* in the ironic mode, the most important father to Stephen is not the material father, Dedalus, but the spiritual father, Bloom. Joyce irrevocably dissociates the flesh-and-blood father from the imaginal father. Imaginal fathers in myth, in fantasy, in fiction may be just as "real" – and are just as necessary – to the son as any flesh-and-blood father.

"I have found," Hillman says, "that the person with a sense of story built in from childhood is in better shape than one who has not had stories." An early familiarity with stories provides the child with knowledge of imaginative possibilities. The child discovers that stories create alternative, imaginal worlds and "transpose existence into these worlds" (1983a: 46). According to Hillman, stories are a form of active imagination: "The person having had his stories early has had his imagination exercised as an activity. He can *imagine life*, and not only think, feel, perceive, or learn it. And he recognizes that imagination is a place where one can be, a kind of being." Imaginal therapy, Hillman says, "re-stories life" (1983a: 47).

It was with this sense of therapeutic purpose – of "being-as-imagining" – that I originally proposed the fathers-and-sons group. I did so in the conviction that the induction of active imagination through stories can also be a form of personal and political activism. I do not believe that this effort saved the world – or saved the lives of even a few boys, but I do believe that more "realism" (and egoism or egotism) is not what the boys in the group needed. They needed not to "get real" but to "get imaginal." They needed to begin to appreciate the relation between actual worlds and possible worlds, appreciate that the actual world of East New York, with actual fathers and sons, is not the only "real" world but that there are many possible, equally "real" worlds available to them through the imagination. They needed to begin to deliteralize the reality – and the psychopathology – of their everyday lives. They needed not to be limited to the one story that they are apparently "really" living but to be exposed to many other stories that they might live imaginally.

Paul Ricoeur says that when we read a story, we enter "a *proposed world* which I could inhabit and wherein I could project one of my ownmost possibilities" (1981a: 142). Through imaginative projection, we entertain propositions about our own possibilities in other, alternative worlds. What Ricoeur says is very similar to, if not identical with, what Hillman says. According to Ricoeur, the world of the story "is real only insofar as it is imaginary." We are, he says, "potentialised" by stories. (I might also add that we are "potentiated," or empowered, by them.) Reading stories, Ricoeur says, "introduces me into the imaginative variations of the ego" (1981a: 144). He concludes that "some new perspectives" are needed "on the old problem of the imagination." He poses the following very "Hillmanian" question: "Are we not ready to recognise in the power of imagination, no longer the faculty of deriving 'images' from our sensory experience, but the capacity of letting new worlds shape our understanding of ourselves?" Like Hillman, Ricoeur believes that with such recognition "a new link would appear between imagination and metaphor" (1981b: 181).

One form of imaginal therapy, with both personal and political consequences, would thus entail the metaphorical experience of multiple stories, a multitude of multicultural stories. The result would be not a single ego, one realist "I" with no variations, but a "multi-individual" with a potentializing, potentiating capacity continually to deliteralize and then reimagine – or re-story – the world throughout life. I do not know whether the world is literally getting worse or getting better – perhaps it is always ambiguously both bad enough and good enough – but I do know that the outer children in the inner city, the boys in East New York, those sons who will soon enough become fathers, will be among the ones who will tell whatever stories get told about it. It is their views of the world, their stories – and not ours – that will ultimately be "telling," in every sense of the word, for better or for worse.

Addendum

Luigi Zoja has recently published an impressive Jungian book entitled *The Father: Historical, Psychological and Cultural Perspectives*. Western civilization, he says, "at least unconsciously, remains patriarchal." This patriarchal unconscious entails what Zoja calls *"the paradox of the father"* (2001: 4). Traditionally, he says, the mother "interacts with her child," whereas the father both "interacts with his child" and "interacts with society" (2001: 4–5). According to Zoja, these dual, paradoxical functions are expectations that complicate the role of the father.

"Do we truly live in an epoch of the absent father?" Zoja asks. "Numerous studies have already sounded the alarm and declared the missing fathers to be a malady that knows no precedents" (2001: 9). He says of the father: "His erosion as a psychological figure is by now accompanied by physical disappearance." Statistics, Zoja notes, calculate that American fathers "spend an average of seven minutes a day with their children" (2001: 225). The father, he says, is now a "vanishing father" (2001: 233).

What interests Zoja is not, however, only the absence of the father but also the presence – and the performance – of the father. As a Jungian, he analyzes the father mythologically in order to analyze the father psychologically. He discusses three myths of the father – those of Hector, Ulysses (Odysseus), and Aeneas.

Hector is the Trojan hero who fights the Greek hero Achilles to the death in single combat. Before the battle, Hector visits his wife Andromache and his son Astyanax. Zoja notes that Hector is a man who "is tempted by the warmth and reasonability of women" (2001: 83). Andromache pleads with him not to fight outside the walls of Troy but to stay inside and defend the walls where they are weakest. Interaction with society, however, supersedes interaction with family, with wife and son. The temptation of a warm and reasonable woman may be great, but, if Hector does not fight Achilles, the shame of a man before the men and women of Troy will be greater. Hector says that although he knows that Achilles will kill him, he will still fight him. Zoja then describes a poignant scene: "Having spoken these words, Hector extends his arms to his son. But the boy seeks refuge and, emitting a cry, clings to the bosom of his nurse: the child has been frightened by his father's armor and helmet, which is topped by a formidable horsehair crest" (2001: 87). Zoja continues:

> At this point, the father and mother exchange a smile. Hector removes his hel-met and places it on the ground, and can then embrace his son. Reawakened by this little incident, the hero now grows aware of the danger of sealing him-self up in a melancholy in which everything has already happened. Shaping good wishes for the future, he lifts his son above him, both with his arms and in his thoughts. This gesture, for all times to come, will be the hallmark of the father.
>
> Hector prays for the boy, challenging the laws of epic for the sake of his child:
>
> "Zeus and ye other gods, make this child of mine strong. And one day, on seeing him return from battle, may one of you say, 'He is far stronger than his father.'"
>
> (Zoja 2001: 87)

Zoja concludes: "Hector is the image of the father we would like to have" (2001: 90).

What appeals to Zoja is that Hector is a father who does not wish his son ill (as, for example, Laius, who tries to kill Oedipus, does) but wishes him well. I, how-ever, am not so certain that Hector is what I would like to have as *the* image of the father. What is the well-wishing that this father bestows on his son? It is to wish his son well in battle – that he will be strong enough to kill rather than (like Hector in the battle with Achilles) be killed. The image of the father remains the image of the absent father who ultimately decides to interact with society rather than continue to interact with his son. The image is of a father who prefers to go to war (and die in battle) rather than stay with his son. (Hector's wish that his son be stronger than his father does not come true. In fact, Zoja notes that it is Achilles's son Neottolemus who kills Hector's son Astyanax.)

When Zoja discusses Ulysses, he does so in terms of what Homer recounts in the *Odyssey*. That is, he emphasizes Ulysses's return to his wife and son after the Trojan war. There is more to the myth, however, than his return to Ithaca. Zoja hardly mentions Ulysses's departure for the Trojan war. Had he done so, he would have had to describe Ulysses as yet another absent father who goes to war. Unlike Hector, Ulysses does *try* to continue to interact with his son rather than interact with society by going to war. An oracle prophesies that if Ulysses goes to war, he will not return to Ithaca for 20 years. In effect, the prophecy is that he will be an absent father. At the time of the Trojan war, his son Telemachus is less than one year old. In an attempt not to be an absent father, Ulysses tries to avoid going to war. When Agammemnon, Menelaus, and Palamedes come to Ithaca to conscript him, he feigns insanity. Ulysses tries to be a "draft dodger." He wears a peasant's cap, plows his field with an ox and an ass, throws salt over his shoulder, and pretends not to recognize his visitors. Palamedes snatches Telemachus from his mother's arms and places him on the ground in front of the plow. To avoid killing his son, Ulysses reins in his team – and, in doing so, reveals that he is perfectly sane and fit to go to war.

At least in intent, Ulysses is very different from Hector as a father. Like Hector, he does ultimately leave his son and wife, but only after he has done his utmost to avoid doing so. Unlike Hector, Ulysses is *not* a father who prefers to go to war rather than stay with his son. Not only is he a father who prefers to continue to interact with his son rather than interact with society, he is a father who (in contrast to Laius, who tries to kill his son Oedipus) avoids killing his son Telemachus – and he is a father who finally returns to his son after 20 years. Ulysses is an absent father but not because he prefers society over his son. Zoja says of Ulysses: "The father is the figure who abandons the home and goes off into combat, and who then combats to return to it" (2001: 114). I would not say that Ulysses "abandons" his son and wife. He leaves them reluctantly, only after an attempt at deception and under duress.

The third father whom Zoja discusses is Aeneas. During the night when the Greeks emerge from the Trojan horse and set fire to Troy, Aeneas is sleeping. In a dream, the shade of Hector appears to Aeneas and urges him to flee. Zoja notes, however, that "Aeneas forgets his role as a father and regresses to the state of the male who lives the life of a warrior" (2001: 137). Aeneas insanely seizes his sword. All that he desires is death in defense of Troy. Then, however, he remembers his father Anchises, his wife, and his son Ascanius. Suddenly, Venus appears to him and, like the shade of Hector, urges him to flee with his family. Aeneas does flee, carrying his father on his back and holding his son by the hand, while his wife follows at a distance. After Aeneas escapes with his father and his son, he looks back, but his wife has disappeared. He returns to search for her, only to encounter her shade – she has been killed.

In this flight after the fall of Troy, Zoja says that Anchises, Aeneas, and Ascanius "constitute a genealogical tree that makes its way into the future." This lineage is, he says, "the transmission of fatherhood from one generation to the next." According to Zoja, "The image of Aeneas in flight with his father and his son is the central link in the chain of fathers that held society together" (2001: 142). The prophecy is that the destiny of Aeneas and the Trojans who flee Troy is eventually to arrive at Italy where they, through the line of Aeneas, are to found the Roman Empire.

Aeneas is not an absent father (nor is he an absent son). He does not abandon either his son or his father. He does go to war, but when the Trojan war is lost – in spite of a momentary regression to the state of the warrior (when he expresses a desire to die in defense of Troy) – he flees with both his son and his father. He chooses to continue to interact with his son and father rather than interact with society, at least when that social interaction is a war that has obviously been lost. (Ironically, it is the shade of Hector, a father who does abandon his son to die in battle, who urges Aeneas not to abandon his son and father but to flee with them.)

The three myths of Hector, Ulysses, and Aeneas demonstrate a progressive transformation of the image of the father from a definition of the father exclusively as a warrior. Ulysses tries to dodge the draft in an effort to stay with his son, and Aeneas flees with his son (and father) rather than futilely and fatalistically fight to the death. In contrast to what Zoja says, I would say that Ulysses and Aeneas are much more than Hector "the image of the father we would like to have."

On a personal note, Zoja discusses his own father and his father's father – and he does so in terms of war. He compares his father to Telemachus: "Like Ulysses's son, my father had just been born when his father departed for the Great War" (2001: 184). Zoja's grandfather served as a medical officer in World War I and after the armistice remained in the army for some time. He was an absent father until his son was four years old. As a result, Zoja's father was raised among women – his mother, sisters, maids, and a nursery school mistress. Like Ulysses, Zoja's grandfather eventually returned home after the war. There was a celebration for the stranger, but Zoja says that his father, as a little boy, was at first bored by it:

> It was only when dinner was served that he too brightened, owing partly to the fact that the table was finally laden with good things to eat, and partly to his need to return to his place at center stage, perhaps as well in hopes of winning a new admirer.
>
> Halfway through the meal he had passed from lively to boisterous, and my grandfather, who was still a man of the nineteenth century and still in military uniform, banned him to the kitchen. Here the child gave vent to protest, since he couldn't understand such treatment. But what first of all burst out with his tears was the question, "Who is that man?" And the maids replied, while making a sign for him to be quiet, "Don't you know? That's the master."
>
> (Zoja 2001: 185)

Zoja does not say so, but the contrast between his grandfather and Hector is evident. Whereas Hector removes his helmet when his son cries and then embraces his son, Zoja's grandfather still wears his military uniform and banishes his son to the kitchen, where he cries. No wonder that Zoja says that Hector is "the image of the father we would like to have!"

What sort of father (or grandfather) we have had (if we have had a father at all) obviously influences the image of what sort of father we would like to have. Zoja does not say whether his own father went to war. My father did not (neither did my grandfathers). He was born in 1900 and just happened to be too young for World War I and too old for World War II. In addition, he was a man of very slight build – five-foot-four-inches in height and never more than 125 pounds in weight, hardly the image of the father as a warrior. I was always proud that my father had not fought in either war. I suppose that another son might have experienced other emotions (perhaps, for example, shame), but I was not born until after World War II, in 1947, when "patriotism" was not such an issue. My father was not ideologically a "pacifist" (he had no ideology), but neither was he psychologically a warrior. He was not a fighter. He was always gentle, never violent. He never abused my mother or me either verbally or physically. (I do not mean that he never disciplined me. Occasionally he did, but I always understood perfectly well why – it was usually because I had spoken rudely to my mother – and the discipline was always in proportion to the deed.) He was the sort of father who awoke before my mother and me at 5:00 a.m., went to the barn to milk the cows with me, had breakfast with us, at 8:00 a.m. went to work at the post office where he sold stamps until 5:00 p.m., and then returned home to milk the cows again with me and have dinner with us. He cultivated a vegetable garden and a fruit orchard (his own father had owned a nursery). He was the very epitome of fidelity and responsibility. He owned one suit and tie. He was a kind, generous, honest man with a genial sense of humor. At the age of 57, he became a father again – he and my mother adopted two Korean-American war orphans, four and five years old, as a brother and sister for me. He raised them in the same reliable way that he raised me, until he died at the age of 70. Everyone should be so fortunate to have such a father.

Of course, as I have said, no one father is ever enough for any son. I have had other "fathers" who have inspired and initiated me. I am also a father – I have a 20-year-old son and a 14-year-old daughter. The father and "fathers" I am fortunate to have had now serve me as an image of the father I myself would like to be.

Chapter 9

A baby is being eaten

A case of cannibalistic malpractice and suicide

The original version of this chapter was a presentation that I delivered at the conference of the International Federation for Psychoanalytic Education in New York in 1999. In deciding what to entitle that presentation, I vacillated between "A *Child* Is Being Eaten" and "A *Baby* Is Being Eaten." "A Child Is Being Eaten" would have been an almost verbatim allusion to Freud's "A Child Is Being *Beaten*." Finally, however, I decided on "A Baby Is Being Eaten," because I wanted to discuss a dream from Joyce McDougall's *Theaters of the Body* (1989) – a dream in which a baby is being eaten. After I had proposed the presentation for the conference and had submitted that title, I happened to notice that in McDougall's *Theaters of the Mind* (1985) one of the chapters, the subject of which is an entirely different case, bears the subtitle "A Child Is Being Eaten." Had I, by cryptomnesia, been subliminally prompted to plagiarize from McDougall? Or had McDougall and I independently felt an urge to indulge in an identical pun?

McDougall is an object relations analyst. She is, in fact, a "scientific member" of the Object Relations Institute for Psychotherapy and Psychoanalysis, where I am a faculty member and supervisor. (At the Object Relations Institute, I teach two courses – "Dream Analysis: Object Relations and Jungian Perspectives" and "Freud's *The Interpretation of Dreams*.") As an object relations analyst, McDougall has a special interest in the dynamic relations between "internal objects" in the psyches of patients. Prominent among these internal objects are the "mother" and "child." Object relations theory, especially in the version espoused by Melanie Klein, emphasizes the "good mother" and the "bad mother" in relation to the "child." (In a modification of this theory, D. W. Winnicott emphasizes the "good enough mother.") According to object relations theory, the mother as an external object is internalized by the child. Thus the "mother" becomes an internal object, which is experienced as either "good" or "bad," as either nurturing or depriving. (By extension, object relations theory advocates that the psychoanalyst should be a "good mother" – or at least a "good enough mother" – who nurtures her patient as a "child.")

McDougall presents the case of a psychiatrist, a 40-year-old man, married with two children. In the fifth year of his analysis with McDougall, he dreamed of cooking and eating a baby. He recounted the dream to McDougall as follows:

Last night I had a horrible nightmare. I had a newborn baby in my hands and I was getting ready to roast it. I put it on a spit and watched over the cooking carefully, without a trace of concern or guilt. Then I began to eat it, starting with its hand. And I offered its arm to someone, maybe my wife. At that moment I became suddenly aware of the tiny stump of an arm and I began to feel afraid. The thought came to me in the dream, "My God, you've committed a crime! It's forbidden to eat children. When he grows up he'll be crippled. I've damaged him for life." I was flooded by a feeling of horror and my mounting panic woke me up in the middle of the night. I was sweating and trembling and couldn't get back to sleep again for thinking about the dream.

(McDougall 1989: 60–1)

The psychiatrist had entered analysis with McDougall after a severely delusional patient of his had committed suicide. The patient, a woman, married with three children, had set herself on fire and burned herself to death. As McDougall says, the psychiatrist "felt extremely guilty, as though this tragedy were due to some irresponsibility on his part" and "wondered whether his patient's unexpected and fatal act was linked to his own state of perpetual anxiety" (1989: 57). I would put it more bluntly: the psychiatrist was worried that his own disturbed psychic condition either had rendered him incapable of preventing his patient's suicide or had perhaps even caused it.

McDougall says that the psychiatrist immediately associated his own dream with a dream that "his *psychotic patient had made* shortly before her suicide." (Unfortunately, McDougall does not quote the patient's dream in its entirety; she merely paraphrases the gist of it. I would also say that it is an infelicity for her to say that the patient "made" the dream. No one makes dreams; they emerge spontaneously and autonomously from the unconscious.) McDougall says of the patient: "She dreamed that she took her youngest child (the third) and boiled it until there was nothing left 'but its little heart beating in her hand.' In the dream she rushed to her psychiatrist for help, asking him to make the child whole again" (1989: 61). The common denominator of the psychiatrist's association is apparently that in both dreams a child is being cooked – boiled in the one and roasted in the other. The psychiatrist says that the very thought that he could dream of cooking and eating a baby "makes me feel ill" (1989: 62). He continues: "I'm as psychotic as my patient. I understand now why she committed suicide! I feel such hatred for myself. I can't tolerate this dream" (1989: 63).

What I propose is to take very seriously the psychiatrist's feeling that he was somehow responsible for his patient's suicide. It is not enough, however, just to say – as the psychiatrist does – that a baby-cooking, baby-eating dream proves that he is just as psychotic as his patient and that therefore we now understand why she committed suicide. Simply *that* the dream is so sickening to the psychiatrist is not an "understanding" of any "why." The psychiatrist enters analysis with McDougall because he desperately wants to know whether he did anything that caused his patient to commit suicide or whether he could have done anything to prevent her from committing suicide. Although neither McDougall nor the psychiatrist names it as such, the issue is, in a word, malpractice – in this case, cannibalistic malpractice.

McDougall theorizes that "there is a rejecting and death-bearing image of the mother with whom the child, once he has become an adult, will identify, consequently behaving in similar manner to his own child-self" (1989: 58). In this respect, she interprets the psychiatrist's baby-cooking, baby-eating dream in terms of what she characterizes as his fantasies about an "unwanted child." The psychiatrist had been, to his own mother, an unwanted child; his wife currently wanted another, third child, but the psychiatrist did not want one; and evidently the psychiatrist's patient had not wanted her third child. According to McDougall, not wanting a child (or not being a wanted child) amounts to an unconscious identification with the "bad mother" who would kill her child – in this case by cooking it and also eating it. In spite of the fact that in the dream it is no mother but a father, the psychiatrist, who cooks and eats a baby, McDougall says: "The dream-script reads: 'Look, mothers cook and eat their babies.'" She wonders to what extent the psychiatrist was "identifying with a 'killer-mother'" (1989: 62).

I propose to interpret the patient's dream transferentially and the psychiatrist's dream countertransferentially in an attempt to answer the question that the psychiatrist asks McDougall: Did he commit malpractice that unconsciously induced (or at least did not deter) a suicide, and, if so, could the result have been otherwise? I believe that the psychiatrist's dream addresses quite specific, extremely serious issues of both consciousness and conscience. If these issues were not interpreted accurately and confronted directly, the psychiatrist would continue in peril of committing malpractice again and again. I shall interpret both the psychiatrist's and the patient's dreams, discuss technical and ethical considerations in this case, and present very particular cautions about radically unconscious psychic states that countertransferentially may result in malpractice and such disastrous consequences as suicide.

Traditionally, the term "countertransference" had a negative connotation. If transference was what the patient projected onto the analyst, then countertransference was, conversely, what the analyst projected onto the patient. Analysts defined both transference and countertransference as neurotic or psychotic distortions. To rectify these distortions, the countertransference, no less than the transference, had to be analyzed. The analyst who experienced countertransference was advised to undergo additional analysis and supervision. Over the years, some analysts have radically redefined countertransference, so that to them it no longer means at all what it once meant – in fact, it means quite the opposite. For them, countertransference now has a positive connotation. It means not a distortion that the analyst neurotically or psychotically projects onto the patient but a communication that the unconscious of the patient transparently transmits to the unconscious of the analyst. (I would note that countertransference is now, ironically, similar to telepathy, or "thought transference," although presumably the communication from the unconscious of the patient to the unconscious of the analyst is not extrasensory but only subliminal.) I consider this redefinition of countertransference deplorable. Against the contemporary trend, I continue to define countertransference exclusively as a neurotic or psychotic projection by the analyst onto the patient.

Jung notes that "the patient's premises are to some extent pathological, whereas a so-called 'normal' attitude is presupposed of the analyst" (*CW* 16: 329, par. 544). He then discusses countertransference:

> "Normal" is a somewhat vague concept which simply means that the analyst at least has no neurosis and is more or less in full possession of his mental faculties. If, on the contrary, he is neurotic, a fateful, unconscious identity with the patient will inevitably supervene – a "counter-transference" of a positive or negative character. Even if the analyst has no neurosis, but only a rather more extensive area of unconsciousness than usual, this is sufficient to produce a sphere of mutual unconsciousness, i.e., a counter-transference. This phenomenon is one of the chief occupational hazards of psychotherapy. It causes psychic infections in both analyst and patient and brings the therapeutic process to a standstill. This state of unconscious identity is also the reason why an analyst can help his patient just so far as he himself has gone and not a step further.
>
> (*CW* 16: 329–30, par. 545)

According to Jung, the countertransference of a neurotic analyst, in combination with the transference of a neurotic patient, does not increase consciousness but, on the contrary, merely produces "mutual unconsciousness." There is no communication from one unconscious to another unconscious, just a conflation of unconsciouses.

I believe that the material that a patient presents in an analysis comprises important diagnostic and prognostic information, including indications about appropriate and inappropriate interventions (what the analyst should say or not say to the patient), even indications of whether a patient should be in analysis at all. Is the patient analyzable? Is analysis appropriate for a particular patient? Analysis may be strictly contraindicated by the material that the patient presents, and to attempt to analyze an unanalyzable patient is to commit malpractice. In short, I believe that the material communicates valuable (indeed, indispensable) unconscious information about a patient. If analysts are able accurately to interpret that information, then they are in a position to know *how* – or, indeed, even *whether* – to proceed with the analysis.

McDougall concludes her presentation of the case of the baby-cooking, baby-eating psychiatrist by minimizing the importance of interpretative accuracy. "Whether my interpretations were accurate or not," she says, is incidental. She states that "perhaps other interpretations of his underlying fantasies would have worked as well" (1989: 66) – that is, perhaps *inaccurate* interpretations would have worked just as well as accurate ones! McDougall thus adopts the position of a pragmatist. It matters not to her whether an interpretation is accurate or not. What matters is what "works." According to McDougall, an interpretation might be inaccurate but still be effective. (She never, however, explains why such an interpretation would "work.") In contrast, I believe that for an interpretation to be effective it must be an accurate interpretation of the unconscious communications from the psyche of the patient. Interpretations do not "work" (they do not increase consciousness) unless they are accurate.

First, the baby-cooking dream of the psychiatrist's patient. In the dream, the patient boils her youngest child until nothing remains but "its little heart beating in her hand." She then rushes to her psychiatrist, presumably heart-in-hand, and asks him to make her child whole again. From a Jungian perspective, the patient in the dream is the "ego-image" (who or how "I" imagine myself to be) and the psychiatrist, the child, and the heart are "non-ego images" from the unconscious. According to Jung, *the communications from the unconscious in dreams are compensations.* He says that the function of the unconscious in dreams is to present alternative perspectives that compensate the partial, prejudicial, or defective attitudes of the ego. These alternative perspectives, which have been repressed, dissociated, ignored, neglected, or otherwise excluded from consideration, manifest in dreams as non-ego images that emerge from the unconscious in an effort to compensate the maladaptive, dysfunctional, or pathological attitudes of the ego-image. If the ego-image is receptive rather than defensive, it is in a position effectively to engage these non-ego images – to entertain them seriously, evaluate them critically, and either accept or reject them.

Although McDougall is an object relations analyst, not a Jungian analyst, she does at least implicitly have some notion of the compensatory function of the unconscious. She mentions that "because of certain ways of mental functioning" the emotional experience of certain events may be "excluded not only from consciousness, but also from the symbolic chain of meaningful psychic representations." As a result, McDougall says, such experience "goes *uncompensated*" (1989: 52). I would emphasize that in the patient's dream "meaningful psychic representations" – or what I, as a Jungian analyst would call meaningful psychic *images* – emerge from the unconscious so that her emotional experience will *not* go uncompensated.

Jung interprets dreams on two levels – what he calls the *objective level* and the *subjective level*. When he interprets a dream on the objective level, he regards the images in the dream as references to objects in external reality. In contrast, when he interprets a dream on the subjective level, he regards those images as correlatives of factors in the internal reality of the subject, the dreamer – or, as Jung says, "subjective factors entirely belonging to the subject's own psyche." Jung notes that "the psychic image of an object is never exactly like the object" (*CW* 6: 472, par. 812). He cautions that the image "should not be assumed to be identical with the object." As a result, it is preferable, he says, "to regard it as an image of the subjective relation to the object" (*CW* 6: 473, par. 812). According to Jung, "Even where the objective interpretation is advisable, it is well to consider also a subjective possibility." He says that "it is exceedingly valuable and wise to see how far the object that is to be taken objectively is also a subjective factor in yourself" (1984: 31).

The image of the child in the patient's baby-cooking dream is a reference to an object in external reality – her youngest child. This is the objective level of interpretation. On the subjective level of interpretation, the image is also, however, a correlative of a factor in the internal reality of the dreamer. This factor is what Jung calls the "child archetype." Jung interprets this archetype as follows: "One of the essential features of the child motif is its futurity. The child is potential future. Hence the occurrence of the child motif in the psychology of the individual signifies as a rule an anticipation of future developments, even though at first sight it may seem like a retrospective configuration" (*CW* 9, 1: 164, par. 278). That is, the child is a *prospective configuration*. Rather than say, as Jung does, that the child is an *archetype*, I prefer to say that the child is an *image of the archetype of the potential future*. (The "potential future" is the archetype, and the "child" is an especially apt image of that archetype.) From a Jungian perspective, the child in the patient's baby-cooking dream is an image of the patient's own potential future.

In the dream, the patient boils the child until nothing remains but the heart. As I would interpret the dream, it is about "what it all boils down to." The dream states that the potential future of the patient all boils down to nothing but the heart of a child. Like the child, the heart is also an image, but what is the heart an image *of*? "The human heart is first and foremost," Robert Romanyshyn says, "a psychological reality" (1982: 133) – but what, exactly, is this psychological reality? The heart is a quite specific organ. McDougall says that the heart is "the essential organ of affect, the metaphor of love, grief, and nostalgia, as well as of hatred, rage, and violence" (1989: 119). Hillman notes that it is also the organ of "courage," "strength," "passion," "loyalty," "boldness," and "compassion" (1981b: 5). Psychologically, the heart is not only the organ of emotion but also the organ of life (death occurs when the heart stops beating). In the dream, the heart is not just any heart but quite specifically the heart of a child. In this respect, the heart of the child is an *image of the archetype of emotion and life in the potential future*. As the image configures this prospect, it indicates, both diagnostically and prognostically, that the situation is extreme indeed.

From a transferential perspective, this dream is an image of the relation between patient and psychiatrist. The dream describes the patient's condition and her prospects for a "cure" (or, as Jungians would say, a transformation). In the dream, the ego-image subjects a non-ego image, the youngest child (an image of what has most recently been "born" and what, under the rubric of the archetype of mother-and-child, should now be "nurtured"), to a cooking process that reduces it to nothing but a part of the whole – "its little heart beating in her hand." The dream is about "partness" and the possibility of "wholeness." In effect, the ego-image commits against the non-ego image what I would call "inner child abuse" (which, of course, is revulsively offensive to traditional notions of maternal instinct). That is, the partial, prejudicial, and defective attitude of the ego-image is an *abusive, "bad mother" attitude* toward the "child," the non-ego image of the potential future. In fact, the dream indicates that this is a *fatally, infanticidally abusive attitude*. The heart (emotion and life) of the child (potential future) is still beating. At least for the time being, it remains viable. Making the child "whole again" (as the patient asks the psychiatrist to do) would entail reintegrating that part into the whole (reimplanting the heart into the body). Nothing, however, remains of the body of the child but the heart. The rest of the body is dead. There is no body in which to reimplant the heart, and without a body it is just a matter of time until the heart stops beating and dies.

In the dream, the patient rushes to the psychiatrist for help and asks him to make the child whole again. There is a sense of urgency, a sense of emergency. With such a plaintive, poignant gesture, with such a desperate plea, what psychiatrist could refuse such a patient? I would say, however, that the dream indicates that, in this case, that is exactly what the psychiatrist should have done – contrive some convenient excuse not to continue the analysis and perhaps provide a referral for some alternative therapy. This patient asks the psychiatrist to do the impossible. To make the child whole again would violate the laws of nature. It would be a miracle – a reintegration tantamount to a resurrection:

> Clearly, the patient's dream of boiling her baby had made as lasting and per- haps as traumatic an impact on her psychiatrist as the horror of learning later that she had deliberately burned herself to death. It is not surprising that he subsequently found himself unable to use the dream and to further his patient's insight into her own deep conflict.
>
> (McDougall 1989: 62)

Whether a patient's dream of boiling her baby should traumatize a psychiatrist as much as learning that his patient has burned herself to death (I confess that, to me, such a notion seems quite peculiar, if not perverse), the decisive issue is not that the psychiatrist was unable to "use" the dream to increase his patient's conscious- ness about her condition but that he was unable to interpret the dream accurately so that he would have realized that psychoanalysis was utterly inappropriate in this case.

What the dream demonstrates is that this patient is in extremis, in such a state of disintegration that a "cure" (or transformation) is beyond the capacity of this psychiatrist – in fact, of any psychoanalyst. Had the psychiatrist had the ability to interpret the dream accurately, he might then have been in a position to act in a different and better way toward the patient – perhaps, for example, to obtain for her an alternative therapy, some extraordinary care so intensive that it might have pre- vented her suicide (even if it had not increased her consciousness). The technical and ethical error that the psychiatrist commits is to continue to attempt to engage the patient analytically, when the dream indicates that this is an exercise in futility. After the fact – that is, after his patient's suicide and after his own baby-cooking, baby-eating dream – the psychiatrist concludes that he is just as psychotic as his patient. Had he been a proficient interpreter of dreams, he could – well before the fact – have discerned from such atrocious images that his patient was too fatally psychotic for analysis to be effective in this case.

I am reminded, in this respect, of one of Jung's cases. A doctor who wanted to become an analyst came to Jung, who describes him as a "'normal' pupil." Jung says: "Now he had a normal practice, normal success, a normal wife, normal children, lived in a normal little house in a normal little town, had a normal income and probably a normal diet" (1963: 134). The man told Jung that he had "no problems." He also said that he had "no dreams." Jung replied: "You will soon have some."

Jung says that after two weeks the man had "an impressive dream" (1963: 135). In the dream, the man entered a building. Jung recounts the rest of the dream as follows:

> At this moment he discovered that he was lost, and no longer knew where the exit was. He started in alarm, and simultaneously realized that he had not met a single person in this building. He began to feel uneasy, and quickened his pace, hoping to run into someone. But he met no one. Then he came to a large door, and thought with relief: That is the exit. He opened the door and discovered that he had stumbled upon a gigantic room. It was so huge and dark that he could not even see the opposite wall. Profoundly alarmed, the dreamer ran across the great, empty room, hoping to find the exit on the other side. Then he saw – precisely in the middle of the room – something white on the floor. As he approached he discovered that it was an idiot child of about two years old. It was sitting on a chamber pot and had smeared itself with feces. At that moment he awoke with a cry, in a state of panic.
>
> (Jung 1963: 135)

According to Jung, the dream was obvious evidence of a "latent psychosis." Jung felt that, under the circumstances, he had no choice but to employ a dishonest strategy and tactic: "I must say I sweated as I tried to lead him out of that dream. I had to represent it to him as something quite innocuous, and gloss over all the perilous details" (1963: 135). The shit-besmeared idiot child in the center of the room was "a sinister symbol." Jung realized that the man's "normality was a compensation" for his latent psychosis. He had "caught him in the nick of time, for the latent psychosis was within a hair's breadth of breaking out and becoming manifest." He finally "succeeded in finding an acceptable pretext for ending the training analysis." Both he and the man were, he says, "very glad to stop." Jung did not inform the man of his diagnosis, but he says that the man "had probably become aware that he was on the verge of a fatal panic." The man returned to his normal existence and, Jung says, "never again stirred up the unconscious." Jung summarizes the incident as follows: "His emphatic normality reflected a personality which would not have been developed but simply shattered by a confrontation with the unconscious." He states that "latent psychoses are the *bêtes noires* of psychotherapists, since they are often very difficult to recognize" (1963: 136). In effect, as Jung interprets the dream, the shit-besmeared idiot child was an image of the latently psychotic potential future of the man, and that is why Jung abruptly terminated the analysis. The image indicated to Jung that the man should not be in analysis, much less become an analyst.

Now the baby-cooking, baby-eating dream of the psychiatrist. The psychiatrist's dream is even more gruesome, even more grisly, even more grotesque than his patient's dream. Like his patient, the psychiatrist cooks a child, in this case a new-born baby. Unlike his patient, he roasts rather than boils the child, and then begins to eat the child – or cannibalize it. For Freud, the earliest developmental stage is "the so-called 'cannibalistic' or 'oral' phase" (*SE* 17: 106). In discussing "privations which affect everyone" and the "instinctual wishes that suffer under them," he mentions "incest, cannibalism and lust for killing" (*SE* 21: 10). He comments: "Cannibalism alone seems to be universally proscribed and – to the non-psychoanalytic view – to have been completely surmounted" (*SE* 21: 11). When the primal horde killed the father, Freud says, the sons did not pause to cook him, but (Freud says with prehistoric certitude), "as was the custom in those days, devoured him raw" (*SE* 23: 81). Freud interprets "the cannibalistic act as an attempt to ensure identification with him by incorporating a piece of him" (*SE* 23: 82).

In the "culinary triangle" of Claude Lévi-Strauss, the raw is transformed either naturally by rotting or culturally by cooking. In modestly proposing that babies be eaten in Ireland, Jonathan Swift satirically expresses no preference for any one mode of cooking them:

> I have been assured by a very knowing American of my acquaintance in London, that a young healthy child, well nursed, is at a year old a most delicious, nourishing, and wholesome food, whether *stewed, roasted, baked,* or *boiled*, and I make no doubt that it will equally serve in a *fricassee*, or a *ragout*.
>
> (Swift 1984: 493–4)

In contrast to Swift, Lévi-Strauss privileges two modes of cooking among the many different modes available. "There are certainly two principal modes," he asserts, "attested in innumerable societies by myths and rites which emphasize their contrast: the roasted and the boiled" (1966: 587–8). He contends that "the roasted is on the side of nature, the boiled on the side of culture" (1966: 588). That is, the natural process of roasting a child is a more rudimentary mode of cooking than the cultural process of boiling a child. From this perspective, the psychiatrist's mode of cooking a child is anthropologically – and, I would argue, psychologically – even more primitive than his patient's mode.

The psychiatrist roasts the baby "without a trace of concern or guilt." The dream indicates that he is not merely, as he says, as psychotic as his patient but that he is psychopathic – that he is not only unconscious but also conscienceless. He does not just cook a baby; he begins to eat it, or cannibalize it. Lévi-Strauss says that cannibalism "ordinarily employs boiling rather than roasting" and that in those exceptions to the rule, when cannibals roast rather than boil those whom they eat, they tend to roast and eat their enemies and boil and eat their relatives. "It would be interesting," he says, "to carry out statistical research on this point" (1966: 589). In carrying out psychoanalytic research on cannibalism, Eli Sagan similarly distinguishes between two varieties – "aggressive" cannibalism toward one's enemies and "affectionate" cannibalism toward one's relatives. William Arens mentions three varieties: "(1) gastronomic cannibalism, where human flesh is eaten for its taste and food value; (2) ritual or magical cannibalism, identifying an attempt to absorb the spiritual essence of the deceased; and (3) survival cannibalism, indicating a resort to this normally prohibited behavior in crisis conditions" (1979: 18). Anthropologically and psychologically, these practices amount to what Arens calls "the 'cannibal complex'" (1979: 161).

Scientists have argued that evidence from DNA indicates that cannibalism was probably a rather pervasive practice prehistorically. "Deep in the recesses of the human heart, lurking guiltily beneath the threshold of consciousness, there may lie a depraved craving – for the forbidden taste of human flesh," a recent article in the *New York Times* reports. "The basis for this morbid accusation, made by a team of researchers in London, is a genetic signature, found almost worldwide, that points to a long history of cannibalism" (Wade April 11, 2003: A20). People who have the genetic signature are protected against infection from prions, proteins that can be transmitted when people eat meat (diseased animal flesh and, even more easily, diseased human flesh – hence the probability of prehistoric cannibalism).

"It is time," Sagan says, "to look at the most degrading thing one human being can do to another, even if we risk finding feelings in ourselves that we wish were not there" (1974: xx). This is precisely what the psychiatrist does in his cannibalistic dream, and he does find feelings in himself that he wishes were not there. After the psychiatrist begins to eat the hand of the baby that he has roasted, after he offers the arm of the baby to someone, perhaps his wife, he suddenly becomes aware and begins to feel afraid. He realizes that he has committed a crime, that it is forbidden to eat children. From what Michael Eigen would call the "psychotic core" of his personality (1986) – or what I would call the *psychopathic core* of his personality – he becomes conscious of the enormity of what he has been doing so unconsciously, so consciencelessly, to the newborn baby. Then it occurs to him that when the baby grows up, it will be crippled, that he has damaged the baby for life. This thought, however, is a quite curious non sequitur, for the psychiatrist has not just crippled or damaged the baby – he has put the baby on a spit and *roasted* it. The dream, it is true, does not explicitly say that he has cooked the baby to death. Unless, however, we assume that the baby has survived being roasted in this primitive way and has suffered only severe burns, we have to conclude that the psychiatrist has, as he says, "watched over the cooking carefully," that he has cooked the baby until it is "done" – that is, until it is *dead*. Such a baby, even a medium rare one, will *never* grow up. (If the baby has somehow survived the roasting, that means that the psychiatrist then begins to eat the baby alive – which is perhaps an even more detestable and repugnant cruelty.)

Whatever the case may be, the baby in the psychiatrist's dream has been just as abominably and irreparably abused as the child in his patient's dream. Although the psychiatrist becomes less psychopathic in his horror and panic when he becomes aware of his criminality, he remains incompletely conscious of the drastic, dire, deadly consequences of his actions. In the dream, the psychiatrist is so unconscious as to be absolutely oblivious to what is forbidden, to what Freud designates as the most universally proscribed of the three privations that he enumerates. Even more than incest or the lust for killing, cannibalism is for this psychiatrist the fulfillment of what I might call a "self-devouring prophecy."

If I were to interpret the psychiatrist's dream on the subjective level, I would say that it is another case of "inner child abuse." The dream indicates that, like his patient, the psychiatrist has an ego-image with an abusive attitude toward the non-ego image of the child. In this case, it is a *criminally, cannibalistically abusive attitude* toward his potential future. If the image of the child is a prospective configuration – or, as Jung says, "an anticipation of future developments" – then the dream demonstrates that, developmentally, the psychiatrist can anticipate *no* future as a psychoanalyst. A psychiatrist who has an ego-image with a baby-roasting, baby-eating attitude – or countertransference – would be unable to empathize with a patient who has an ego-image with a baby-boiling attitude. The result would be not empathy but what Jung calls "mutual unconsciousness" – a *folie à deux*, in which psychiatrist and patient share virtually the same "insanity."

As I have said, Kleinian and Winnicottian object relations theory advocates that the analyst should be a "good mother" or a "good enough mother" who nurtures the patient as a "child." This is a bias that has serious consequences in analytic practice, for it arbitrarily privileges the maternal over the paternal. In this case, the psychiatrist is, in fact, not a mother but a father. I would emphasize that in the psychiatrist's dream the ego-image is not a "mother" but a "father." It is an ego-image with an *abusive, "bad father" attitude* toward the "child."

One of the Jungian techniques of interpretation is *amplification*. When Jung "amplifies" an image in a dream, he compares it to the same or similar images in other sources – among them, myths – in order to establish archetypal parallels. In this case, an archetypal parallel would be the myth of Cronus. In Greek mythology, Cronus is one of the Titans. Cronus fathers on Rhea several children, goddesses and gods: Hestia, Demeter, Hera, Hades, Poseidon. As soon as they are born, he swallows them, one by one. Finally, Cronus fathers Zeus. When Zeus is born, Robert Graves says, Rhea hides him and gives Cronus "a stone in swaddling clothes" (1957 I: 40). Cronus swallows the stone instead of Zeus. When Zeus becomes a man, he mixes mustard and salt with the mead (honey and water) that Cronus drinks. Cronus vomits up first the stone and then all the children that he has swallowed. The myth of Cronus is not an exact parallel to the dream of the psychiatrist – Cronus does not cook his children and eat their parts, as the psychiatrist does; he swallows them raw and whole. Nevertheless, the myth does provide a motive for why a father might devour a child – and that is defensively to eliminate the potential future before it has an opportunity to develop. To swallow the non-ego image of the child is to attempt a priori to eliminate any compensatory competition, or rivalry, to the status quo of the ego-image of the father.

The myth of Cronus is a myth about the archetype of "time," about *how the actual present attempts to eliminate the potential future*. In this respect, Jung mentions "Chronos, the god who ate his own children, the word having the meaning of time" (1984: 429). Although William McGuire notes that Jung erroneously conflates "Kronos (or Cronus)," the Titan in Greek mythology, with "Chronos," a god in Orphic tradition, and that "Kronos is unrelated to the word *chronos*, 'time'" (1984: 428n.), when Cronus eats his own children, he does attempt, in effect, to stop time, to prevent the "birth" of a future that would competitively rival the present. In this sense, the myth of Cronus is, psychologically, an anti-developmental myth. The "unwanted child" is unwanted precisely because it is a non-ego image that, if permitted to develop, would eventually pose a threat to the ego-image – and this is a prospective configuration that just cannot be allowed (but must be "swallowed") by the "father."

After ten years of what the psychiatrist describes as "a typically Lacanian analysis" that was "entirely an intellectual adventure" (1989: 56), and after five years of analysis with McDougall, he finally has a dream that discloses just how psychopathic he is and how countertransferentially responsible he was for his patient's suicide. I would say that the psychiatrist's own diagnosis and prognosis are almost as pessimistic as his patient's. McDougall, of course, was his analyst, not his supervisor – she says that his supervisor was "an analyst experienced in the psychoanalysis of psychotic patients" (1989: 57) – but I would argue that an accurate interpretation of his own and his patient's dreams and a confrontation with him over his technical and ethical defects as an analyst would have been necessary in order to prevent him, in his state of perpetual anxiety, from continuing unconsciously to commit cannibalistic malpractice. In this respect, I would say that not only did the psychiatrist fail *his* patient but also his own analysts and supervisor failed *him*.

I know a psychoanalyst who in addition to his practice of conventional analysis specializes in an unusual variety of "career counseling." He counsels analysts and therapists who experience profound, persistent anxiety with patients to take "early retirement" and change careers. In short, he assists them in getting out of the business. This seems to me an indispensable public service. Whether from naiveté, excessive optimism, hubris, or simple interpretative or relational incompetence, some individuals are technically, ethically, or characterologically incapable of practicing analysis – or knowing how or even whether to analyze another individual. This particular analyst is a one-man "consumer protection agency." He is convinced that somewhere in the deep or even shallow recesses of the psyche these analysts and therapists "know" that they have no business analyzing anyone, or at the very least anyone who is severely disturbed. He has established for himself a certain reputation, and he receives a considerable number of referrals that have as their singular aim a conscious, conscientious withdrawal from the field, on the principle that not everyone is fit to be an analyst. I have no doubt that had he been either the analyst or the supervisor in this case, he would have recognized a cannibal when he saw one and helped the psychiatrist acknowledge how inept, even catastrophic, his countertransferential propensity was. The last thing that a severely delusional, suicidally psychotic patient needs is a perpetually anxious, psychopathic, baby-cooking, baby-eating psychiatrist.

After I delivered my presentation at the conference, a psychoanalyst asked me for a copy. Joyce McDougall, he said, was a friend of his. He thought that she might be interested in reading my presentation, and he wondered what she would think of it. Later, he told me that she had informed him that the entire case "history" was a *fiction*! According to him there was no patient who had dreamed of boiling a baby and who had then committed suicide, and there was no psychiatrist who had dreamed of roasting and eating a baby. McDougall, he said, had made the whole thing up. The psychoanalyst reported that McDougall had said to him that the fictional status of the case invalidated all that I had said about "cannibalistic malpractice" in my presentation. There had been no case; hence there had been no malpractice.

If it is true that this case is a fiction, I am personally pleased (and relieved) that there is evidently one less case of grossly egregious malpractice than McDougall's chapter had led me to believe existed. I would say, however, that the apparently fictional status of the case does not necessarily render invalid what I or anyone else might say about it. Surely, McDougall did not make up a case that she considered utterly implausible. At the very least, the case illustrates how she would have analyzed such a psychiatrist had he existed exactly as she describes him. In this respect, the case provides an opportunity for a critical evaluation of a hypothetical analysis as McDougall would presumably have conducted it. (I should perhaps say that I have nothing against an analyst's making up a case, as long as her fiction is plausible. I myself, however, do not engage in this practice. When I present a case, it is always factual, never fictional. The ethics code to which I subscribe as a Jungian analyst requires me to obtain written permission from any patient whose material I wish to present or publish, and I adhere strictly to that code. Whenever I present or publish such material, I do alter certain details in order to preserve the anonymity of the patient and respect the confidentiality of the analysis, but only to that extent do I ever "fictionalize" a case.

Later, the same psychoanalyst who had asked me for a copy of my presentation said to me that someone had told him that Jung had declared that he never tried to prevent patients from committing suicide. The psychoanalyst was appalled at what seemed to him an utterly irresponsible attitude, and he wondered whether it was true that Jung had actually said such a thing. I replied that Jung had, indeed. Subsequently, I gave the psychoanalyst a copy of the relevant passage from Jung's *Collected Works*. "I never hinder people," Jung says. "When somebody says, 'I am going to commit suicide if –,' I say, 'If that is your intention, I have no objection'" (*CW* 18: 96, par. 207).

This is not the only comment by Jung on suicide. He also discusses the issue in letters to various individuals. For example, in a letter to an 80-year-old man with high blood pressure, he says:

> The idea of suicide, understandable as it is, does not seem commendable to me. We live in order to attain the greatest possible amount of spiritual development and self-awareness. As long as life is possible, even if only in a minimal degree, you should hang on to it, in order to scoop it up for the purpose of conscious development. To interrupt life before its time is to bring to a standstill an experiment which we have not set up. We have found ourselves in the midst of it and must carry it through to the end.
>
> (Jung 1973 1: 434).

In this instance, Jung advocates prolonging life as long as possible. As a psychoanalyst, what he values about life is the opportunity it presents to increase consciousness. To commit suicide is summarily to terminate that project. Therefore, Jung does not personally recommend killing oneself.

In another letter, Jung discusses the terminal illness of a Jungian analyst, Kristine Mann:

> It is really a question whether a person affected by such a terrible illness should or may end her life. It is my attitude in such cases not to interfere. I would let things happen if they were so, because I'm convinced that if anybody has it in himself to commit suicide, then practically the whole of his being is going that way. I have seen cases where it would have been something short of criminal to hinder the people because according to all rules it was in accordance with the tendency of their unconscious and thus the basic thing. So I think nothing is really gained by interfering with such an issue. It is presumably to be left to the free choice of the individual. Anything that seems to be wrong to us can be right under certain circumstances over which we have no control and the end of which we do not understand. If Kristine Mann had committed suicide under the stress of unbearable pain, I should have thought that this was the right thing. As it was not the case, I think that it was in her stars to undergo such a cruel agony for reasons that escape our understanding.
>
> (Jung 1973 1: 436)

Jung reiterates that it is not his policy to prevent anyone from committing suicide. He never hinders anyone, because suicide in certain instances may be in conformity with the tendency of the unconscious. The individual may freely choose to commit suicide or not. According to Jung, whether it is right or wrong to kill oneself is strictly circumstantial, relative to the specific situation of the individual.

In a letter to a 47-year-old woman who had attempted suicide at the age of 21, Jung says: "The goal of life is the realization of the self. If you kill yourself you abolish that will of the self that guides you through life to that eventual goal." Jung defines the "self" (which Jungians sometimes spell as the "Self," with a capital

"S") as the archetype of the totality of the psyche. According to Jung, the goal of life is self-realization, or what he calls "individuation," which he defines as "wholeness." In contrast to the "Self" (the psyche as a whole), the ego is just a part of the psyche. When the ego individuates in relation to (or under the guidance of) the "Self," the ego as a part of the psyche becomes more whole. In this sense, suicide is the abrupt abolition of any opportunity for individuation. "Therefore," Jung says, "suicide certainly is not the proper answer" (1975 2: 25).

In a letter to a sick old woman, Jung declines to offer any advice about whether suicide might be reasonable in her case:

> How can anybody be expected to be competent enough to give such advice? I feel utterly incompetent – yet I cannot deny the justification of your wish and I have no heart to refuse it. If your case were my own, I don't know what could happen to me, but I am rather certain that I would not plan a suicide ahead. I should rather hang on as long as I can stand my fate or until sheer despair forces my hand. The reason for such an "unreasonable" attitude with me is that I am not at all sure what will happen to me after death. I have good reasons to assume that things are not finished with death. Life seems to be an interlude in a long story. It has been long before I was, and it will most probably continue after the conscious interval in a three-dimensional existence. I shall therefore hang on as long as it is humanly possible and I try to avoid all foregone conclusions, considering seriously the hints I got as to the *post mortem* events.
>
> Therefore I cannot advise you to commit suicide for so-called reasonable considerations.
>
> (Jung 1975 2: 278–9)

Jung was 80 years old when he wrote this letter in 1955. He had previously had a "near-death" experience, to which he alludes when he mentions "a three-dimensional existence" and "the *post mortem* events." Eleven years earlier, in 1944, he had suffered a serious heart attack. In the hospital, Jung had "hung on the edge of death" (1963: 289). During that time, he had what he describes as "visions." They were "out-of-body," "after-death" experiences in which he floated in outer space 1,000 miles above the earth. Jung resisted returning to earth – or to life – for it seemed to him that to do so would be to return to being confined in "a three-dimensional world" (1963: 292). Although Jung says that he is "not at all sure what will happen to me after death," these visions were among the experiences that gave him what he calls "good reasons to assume that things are not finished with death," and it is on that basis that he eschews advising anyone "to commit suicide for so-called reasonable considerations." The very possibility of an "after-life" was, for Jung, reason enough not to commit suicide.

These letters demonstrate that suicide was not a viable alternative for Jung personally. He scrupulously refrained, however, from hindering others from exercising their freedom of choice to commit suicide. The purpose of psychoanalysis is not to prevent anyone from doing anything (or to encourage anyone to do anything) –

and it is certainly not to *induce* anyone *countertransferentially* to do anything (as the psychiatrist in McDougall's apparently fictional case fears he has done). If a patient announces that she is thinking of doing something – even something as extreme as committing suicide – the responsibility of the analyst is simply to do the one and only thing that analysts are uniquely qualified to do, and that is to *analyze* why the patient is having such a thought and what that thought *means* psychologically. Thus James Hillman says that "*the issue is not for or against suicide, but what it means in the psyche*" (1976: 37).

Psychoanalysis does not exist to prevent suicide; it exists to increase consciousness. If a patient thoroughly analyzes her thoughts, whatever they happen to be, consciously assumes responsibility for the consequences of her thoughts, and then consciously decides to do what she has been thinking of doing (even, for example, killing herself), then the analysis has served its purpose. What the psychoanalyst thinks of what the patient is thinking about is (or should be) utterly irrelevant. Analysts should never impose their own opinions either consciously or unconsciously (impulsively or compulsively) – that is, countertransferentially – on their patients. To do so is to introduce extraneous factors that inevitably bias the analysis. The sole responsibility of the analyst is to maintain neutrality and to facilitate and mediate a dialogue between the ego and the unconscious of the patient.

Suicide is not just one thing; it is many things. Hillman differentiates a variety of suicides:

> Petronius, opening and closing his veins at pleasure in the true Eupicurean style, exchanged gossip with his friends as he let out his blood for the last time; Seneca and Socrates, out of favour, were their own executioners; antiquity reports the suicides of Hero in the Hellespont, Sappho from the rock at Neritos, Cleopatra, Jocasta the mother and wife of Oedipus, Portia who would follow Brutus, and Paulina after Seneca; more recently, Hart Crane, Herbert Silberer, Thomas Beddoes, Cesare Pavese, Virginia Woolf, and such men of rank and action as Condorcet, Castlereagh, Forrestal, Winant, Vargas, Hemingway, Bridgman the Nobel Laureate, and Belmonte the matador.
>
> What are we to make of these: a daughter of Karl Marx, a son of Eugene O'Neill, of Thomas Mann, of Robert Frost, of Herman Melville?
>
> (Hillman 1976: 39)

This list is, of course, hardly exhaustive. Hillman says: "The broad conclusion that the analyst can draw from these varied accounts is: suicide is one of the human possibilities. Death can be chosen. The meaning of this choice is different according to the circumstances and the individual" (1976: 41).

What do patients who are contemplating doing something (including committing suicide) want from an analyst? According to Hillman, "The first thing that the patient wants from an analyst is to make him aware of his suffering and to draw the analyst into his world of experience" (1976: 44). Psychopathology is the study of *pathos*, which means "suffering." In this sense, all patients are "pathetic," and they

want analysts to be empathic. (The word "empathy" includes the root "pathos.")
To empathize with patients is *not* to sympathize with them; it is simply to *under-stand* the suffering that they are experiencing and, in the process, to help *them* to understand it (by analyzing what it means psychologically in order to increase their consciousness).

Hillman says that efforts at "suicide prevention" are non-psychoanalytic inter-ventions. They are non-psychoanalytic interventions because they are judgmental rather than empathic. "Because prevention is their goal," Hillman says, "they can-not adequately serve an analyst." According to Hillman, the task of the analyst is not to prevent the patient from doing anything but to take "events as they come without prior judgment" (1976: 48). Theologians may "immoralize" suicide, and politicians may "illegalize" it, but analysts should only *analyze* it psychologically.

Death is an issue that eventually appears in every psychoanalysis. For example, Hillman says:

> The dreamer dies in his dreams and there are deaths of other inner figures; relatives die; positions are lost never to be regained; deaths of attitudes; the death of love; experiences of loss and emptiness which are described as death; the sense of the presence of death and the terrible fear of dying.
>
> (Hillman 1976: 64)

Why does death appear? Hillman says that "*death appears in order to make way for transformation*" (1976: 67). The transformation of what? I would say, the transformation of the ego – or, more precisely, the transformation of old attitudes that need to "die" in order for new attitudes to be "born." It is not so much the patient who fears dying as it is the *ego* that fears "dying." It is not the life of the patient but the "life" of the ego that must come to an end in order for any transfor-mation to occur. "Where the death experience insists on a suicidal image," Hillman says, "then it is the patient's 'I' and everything he holds to be his 'I' which is coming to an end" (1976: 75).

Hillman says that "a suicide impulse is a transformation drive" (1976: 68). From a Jungian perspective, suicidal fantasies and ideas are an extreme, compensatory effort by the unconscious radically to transform the partial, prejudicial, or defec-tive attitudes of the ego. If we take these fantasies and ideas literally, we may commit suicide. If, however, we are able, through psychological analysis, to *de-literalize* these fantasies and ideas – that is, if we are able to take them metaphoric-ally – then we may be able *not* "to experience psychic reality only by acting out concretely our fantasies and ideas" (1976: 77). The patient who literalizes suicide (rather than metaphorizes it) and then acts it out concretely has committed not only suicide but also a rhetorical fallacy.

David H. Rosen has introduced a valuable term, "egocide," into psychoanalytic discourse. Rosen defines egocide as "the letting-go of a hurt and hurting dominant ego-image or identity." In contrast to suicide, he says that egocide "is a symbolic killing of the ego that is experienced as ego death" (1993: xxi). That is, egocide is an alternative to suicide; it is a metaphorical "death" of the ego rather than a literal *death* of the individual.

Hillman says that the soul (I would say, the ego) "must have its death, if it would be reborn." According to Hillman, "If death is deprived in any way of its over-whelming reality the transformation is misbegotten and the rebirth will be abortive" (1976: 87). Hillman insists that the analyst must remain strictly neutral about suicide as one of the human possibilities (or, in at least some cases, one of the human necessities):

> The analyst cannot deny this need to die. He will have to go with it. His job is to help the soul on its way. He dare not resist the urge in the name of preven-tion, because *resistance only makes the urge more compelling and concrete death more fascinating*. Nor can he condemn every wish for suicide as an 'acting out', because again he sets up a prevention ban before he can be sure whether the act is necessary for the experience. He may not favour one mode over another.
>
> (Hillman 1976: 87)

Neither Jung nor Hillman is Jack Kevorkian, "Dr. Death." They do not assist patients in committing suicide. Nor, however, do they prevent them from commit-ting it. Jung simply informs them that he has no objection to their killing themselves if that is indeed their intention. As he says, he hinders no one. Strict analytic neutrality toward suicide communicates to patients that they – and no one else, including the analyst – are ultimately responsible for consciously choosing either death or life. "Death," Hillman says, "can be chosen" – but so can life. I would say that there are also choices about what *kind* of death and what *kind* of life. It may be, as some individuals sincerely believe, that there are worse things (including certain kinds of life) than death.

Analysts who attempt to prevent patients from committing suicide have egos that are countertransferentially identified with the "savior complex." (In a culture that is historically "Christian," such an identification should hardly be a surprise.) According to Jung, there are not only personal complexes (such as the mother complex and the father complex) but also collective complexes (such as the savior complex), which are archetypal. Jung says that patients often transferentially project onto the analyst the savior complex. The analyst should not reject such a projection, Jung says, but should accept it (without, however, countertransfer-entially identifying with it) and then reflect it to the patient: "So, if a patient pro-jects the saviour complex into you, for instance, you have to give back to him noth-ing less than a saviour – whatever that means. But *you* are not the saviour – most certainly not" (*CW* 18: 152, par. 352). In short, analysts should have the discipline to resist any "projective identification" by a patient. (That is, analysts should have the capacity to withstand any effort by a patient unconsciously to project the sav-ior complex not just onto them but *into* them in a manipulative attempt to induce them to identify with it).

The projection of the savior complex onto the analyst is what Jungians call an *archetypal transference*. The savior archetype, Jung says, is an occupational hazard in psychoanalysis:

> Projections of an archetypal nature involve a particular difficulty for the analyst. Each profession carries its respective difficulties, and the danger of analysis is that of becoming infected by transference projections, in particular by archetypal contents. When the patient assumes that his analyst is the fulfilment of his dreams, that he is not an ordinary doctor but a spiritual hero and a sort of saviour, of course the analyst will say, "What nonsense! This is just morbid. It is a hysterical exaggeration." Yet – it tickles him; it is just too nice. And, moreover, he has the same archetypes in himself. So he begins to feel, "If there are saviours, well, perhaps it is just possible that I am one," and he will fall for it, at first hesitantly, and then it will become more and more plain to him that he really is a sort of extraordinary individual.
>
> (*CW* 18: 152–3, par. 353)

Jung says that such analysts cannot "resist the continuous onslaught of the patients' collective unconscious – case after case projecting the saviour complex" (*CW* 18: 153, par. 354). When they identify countertransferentially with the savior complex, they experience a grandiose inflation of the ego, because the "savior" is an archetype. As Jung says, "The saviour complex is certainly not a personal motif; it is a world-wide expectation, an idea which you find all over the world and in every epoch of history" (*CW* 18: 154–5, par. 358).

When a patient informs the analyst that she is contemplating suicide, the analyst who is countertransferentially identified with the savior complex will immediately attempt to "save" her. Is the analyst attempting to save her *body*? Her *soul* (as in Christianity)? Her *ego*? Her *analysis* (that is, her opportunity to increase her consciousness)?

In Christianity, unless one is "saved," one is *damned*. In a commentary on "Christianism" (the implication is that Christianity is merely one more "ism"), Hillman says that contemporary Jungian psychology is "a path of salvation" (1983b: 83–4). To the extent that Jungian psychology has been "Christianized," it exists to save the ego from the unconscious – that is, from damnation. "Christianity," Hillman says, "has already declared what all the images mean in its language of good and evil." That is, it does not analyze the psyche (the ego and the unconscious) but dogmatizes it a priori, moralizes it into God and devil, good and evil, salvation and damnation, heaven and hell. From the Christian perspective, suicide is always already a sin, whatever the circumstances may be. In contrast, Hillman says: "Psychology can't look at things through the glasses of evil: [because if it does,] you can't see what might be going on in the suicide" (1983b: 87). Psychoanalysis exists not to "save" anyone from the devil, evil, damnation, hell, or sin but simply to "see what might be going on" in the psyche – including the suicidal psyche – in order to increase consciousness.

Easter Sunday baptism in the East Village

Photograph by Michael Vannoy Adams

Chapter 10

The importance of being blasphemous

Profanation versus resacralization

I do still attend church – once every several years when the spirit moves me. The most recent occasion was an Easter Sunday at a church in the East Village of New York City in 1998. One morning a week or two earlier, I had happened to ride my bicycle by the church, had noticed a "Jesus Saves" neon cross on the building, and, in passing, had heard singing. I turned around, went back, and listened from outside. I liked the singing so much that I decided, then and there, to return for the service on Easter Sunday.

Opposite this page is one of the results – a photograph that I took of one of several baptisms that a minister and a missionary performed that day. The image is of a black man between two white men, the minister to his right and the missionary to his left. The black man holds his nose with his right hand as he holds his breath right before the two white men dunk his head under water.

Even though the church had an ethnically diverse, multicultural congregation and in spite of the fact that I had taken the photograph and therefore knew that the subject matter was baptism, when I first saw the image – the black man positioned between two white men with another white man looking at them from behind – the image seemed ambiguously menacing to me, as if the white men might be preparing to commit some act of violence against the black man. The photograph had the same effect on me as images in the Thematic Apperception Test. It evoked from me a fantasy that I projected onto the scene. Whatever that projection may say about my unconscious, as I imagined the scene it was not religious but racist – not sacred but profane.

In *Politics on the Couch*, Andrew Samuels advocates a political transformation that would produce what he calls "a resacralization of culture" (2001: 97). Samuels first mentions resacralization in *The Political Psyche*. There he defines it as "the contemporary drive to render the secular holy." Samuels says that resacralization may be "a return to religion" in the traditional sense, although it need not be (1993: 13). It is more a contemporary experience of the sacred.

Samuels has identified a very real cultural phenomenon. It is, however, a phenomenon that induces a certain ambivalence in me. From a Jungian perspective, I regard the profane as the indispensable shadow of the sacred and blasphemy as a necessary compensation for the holy (and, at worst, for the religiosity of a holier-

than-thou attitude on the part of true believers). Leonard W. Levy defines blasphemy as "an intolerable profanation of the sacred" (1993: 3). As I define it, it is
an act that is offensive to the religious sensibilities of believers.

On the issue of religion, I confess to utter disbelief. (Perhaps I should emphasize
that I have no interest whatsoever in the conversion of anyone else to this position.
I would not proselytize either belief or disbelief.) Personally, I am not at all religious. I was raised a Christian, but if Freud was a "godless Jew," I am a "godless
Christian" (if I am now a Christian in any sense of the word). Freud, a "Jew," did
not believe in God, and I, a "Christian," do not believe in God. Some true believers,
of course, would regard such a confession as blasphemous per se.

A few years ago, while in psychoanalytic training, I had tea one afternoon with a
friend, a historian of Jungian psychology who had delivered a lecture the previous
evening at a meeting that I had been unable to attend. One of my fellow analysts in
training had asked him what he considered the decisive difference to be between
Jungian analysts and other psychoanalysts. On reflection, he had replied: "I've
never known a Jungian who was an atheist." "Well, what about me?" I said. "I'm a
Jungian, and you know me."

I regard all religions as manifestations of what I call the *mythological unconscious* (Adams 2001). "All talk of God," Jung says, "is mythology" (1975 2: 255).
Or, as I would say: *Religions are simply mythologies that adherents "believe in."*
What I believe is what James Hillman believes: "Psychology can do very well
without the category of belief" (1981a: 129).

The stereotype is that Freud was an atheist who emphasized sexuality, while
Jung was a mystic who "desexualized" psychoanalysis and emphasized spiritu-
ality. In short, the cliché is that – at least theoretically – Freudians are sexual and
Jungians spiritual. Jung says, however, that although Freud "always made much of
his irreligiosity," for Freud sex *was* "God" (or at least a demiurge). The irony is that,
in effect, Freud "deified" sex and "worshipped" it. Thus Jung says of Freud that "in
the place of a jealous God whom he had lost, he had substituted another compelling
image, that of sexuality." According to Jung, "the 'sexual libido' took over the role
of a *deus absconditus*, a hidden or concealed god." This substitution conveniently
enabled Freud to regard sexuality "as scientifically irreproachable and free from all
religious taint." Nevertheless, only the name of "God" had changed. In this respect,
Jung says that "the psychological qualities of the two rationally incommensurable
opposites – Yahweh and sexuality – remained the same" (1963: 151).

Jung protests that it is "a widespread error to imagine that I do not see the value
of sexuality." He declares that sexuality "plays a large part in my psychology as an
essential – though not the sole – expression of psychic wholeness." In contrast to
Freud, what interested Jung most about sexuality was the opportunity "to investi-
gate, over and above its personal significance and biological function, its spiritual
aspect" (1963: 168). That is, Jung did not, like Freud, oppose sex and spirit but
recognized the spiritual dimension of sexual desire.

In two interviews, Jung was asked whether he believed in God. At the time of
the first interview with the *Daily Mail* in 1955, Jung was 79 years old; at the time

of the second interview with BBC television in 1959, he was 83 years old. On the first occasion, Jung said: "All that I have learned has led me step by step to an unshakable conviction of the existence of God. I only believe in what I know. And that eliminates believing. Therefore I do not take His existence on belief – I *know* that He exists" (1977: 251). On the second occasion, he said: "I *know*. I don't need to believe. I know" (1977: 428).

That was how Jung answered the question toward the end of his life. For most of his life, however, he protested that he was a mere psychologist, and in that capacity he scrupulously eschewed any metaphysical assertions about the existence of God. In this respect, Jung distinguishes between God, "God-images," and the "God-concept." All cultures, without exception, have God-images; this is simply an empirical fact. The universality of these God-images does not, however, prove the existence of God. All that these God-images prove is the existence of a God-concept. (In this sense, a strictly psychological perspective cannot provide an ontological proof.)

The God-concept is an abstract theme, and God-images are concrete variations on that theme. From an empirical perspective, Jung says, "'God' can just as well mean Yahweh, Allah, Zeus, Shiva, or Huitzilopochtli" (*CW* 11: 303, par. 454). That is, different cultures – for example, the Jewish, Islamic, Greek, Hindu, or Aztec cultures – may have very different God-images. This is what Jung calls the relativity of God-images. Specific God-images are relative to the particular culture – or what I call the "cultural unconscious" – from which they derive. The God-concept is the *archetype* of God. The archetype of God is a strictly psychic reality, not a metaphysical reality. In contrast to theology, psychology is an empirical science, and, as such, it is incompetent to answer any metaphysical questions about the existence of God. According to Jung, such questions are simply beyond the proper purview of the discipline. Religion is about belief; science is about knowledge. In short, as a psychologist, Jung was an agnostic. Only in his old age (or perhaps in his dotage) did Jung depart from this position and indulge in a personal affirmation of the existence of God. Otherwise, he espoused the strict separation of religion and science.

Freud regards "God" as a psychological projection. According to Freud, religion is an "illusion," and the motive for this illusion is a wish-fulfillment. In this respect, he says that "we call a belief an illusion when a wish-fulfillment is a prominent factor in its motivation" (*SE* 21: 31). From this perspective, "God" is simply a projection of the earthly father as a heavenly father – a projection of the natural father as a supernatural father. This projection, Freud asserts, is an illusion with no future. He contends that "in the long run nothing can withstand reason and experience, and the contradiction which religion offers to both is all too palpable" (*SE* 21: 54). It is only a matter of time, Freud predicts, until reason and experience dispel faith and illusion (that is, until science inevitably supersedes religion and renders it obsolete). Belief in God is merely a temporary expedient. For Freud, religion is not only an illusion but also a disease, "the universal obsessional neurosis of humanity" (*SE* 21: 43) – and science is the cure. Perhaps even more damning, belief in God is a consolation comparable to "a narcotic" (*SE* 21: 49). The implication is that religion is an addiction.

For Jung, too, "God" is a psychological projection. A retraction of that projection is possible – that is, it is possible to recognize that "God" is a projection of the "God within" (*CW* 11: 58, par. 101) – but the utter eradication of the projection is impossible, for "God" is an archetype. In contrast to Freud, Jung considers "God" a permanent fixture in the collective unconscious. If belief in God is in certain respects an "illusion," it is a still a psychic reality, and, for Jung, a psychic reality is no less real (at least in the effects it produces) than any other reality. From this perspective, the God-concept is a psychic factor that (in spite of reason and experience that contradict it) will continue autonomously and spontaneously to generate God-images. This is what Jung means by the "religious function" of the psyche (*CW* 16: 46, par. 99).

I grew up in a small town in Texas. In my hometown, there were few Catholics, very, very few Jews, and no Muslims (not to mention Hindus, Buddhists, or members of other religious traditions). Almost everyone was a Protestant of one denomination or another. A railroad divided my hometown in two, and on "the wrong side of the tracks" there were holy rollers who talked in tongues, but most of the Protestants in my hometown were rather conventional Baptists. I was raised a Methodist. One of my great-grandfathers had been a minister (not a Methodist but a Presbyterian, although in my experience there was not much difference between Methodists and Presbyterians). One of my grandmothers had been the pianist and organist for the Methodist church in my hometown. For many years, my father, who had a beautiful tenor voice, had sung in a church quartet. One of my mother's fond memories was of my baptism as a baby. As she had held me in her in arms, the minister had dipped the petals of a long-stemmed rose in holy water and had then sprinkled the top of my head. (Among Protestants, Methodists are "sprinklers," not, like Baptists, "dunkers.") As my mother loved to tell the story, I had turned around, looked toward the congregation, and, with a big smile on my face, beamed in absolute delight.

One of my very first memories is of a Bible story. At the time, I must have been about four years old. One afternoon, I awoke from a nap in an anxious reverie about the "Judgment of Solomon." In that story, God appears to Solomon in a dream and grants him the wisdom to judge between good and bad. Shortly thereafter, two harlots approach Solomon. Both women live in the same house, and both have recently given birth. One of the women says that the other woman's baby died one night and that the mother of the dead baby then switched babies with her, taking the living baby and leaving the dead baby with her. The dilemma for Solomon is that two different women each claim to be the mother of the same baby. Solomon declares that he will divide the baby in two with a sword and give half to one woman and half to the other woman. One of the women begs Solomon to give the baby to the other woman and spare the life of the baby. The other woman urges Solomon to divide the baby. In this way, Solomon wisely judges who the real mother is (I Kings 3). Someone, perhaps my own mother, had apparently read the story to me – and it must have had a big impact on me. (In a sense, this Bible story was my introduction to what object relations psychology calls the "good mother" and the "bad mother.")

Later, another Bible story, "Isaac as the Child of Abraham and Sarah's Old Age," made an impression on me. In that story, Yahweh promises that a child will be born to Abraham when he is 100 years old and Sarah 90 (Genesis 16). My own parents had delayed getting married because of the Great Depression and had then delayed having a child because of World War II. Like Isaac, I was a child of their "old age." When I was born, my father was 47 years old and my mother 41, which in the 1940s was a late age for having a child. If Herman Melville's Great American Novel begins with "Call me Ishmael," my life began, in a sense, with "Call Me Isaac." My actual name is, of course, "Michael," one of the commonest names in America. It is a Biblical name, the name of the archangel who slays the dragon (the devil) with a sword. When, before my birth, my mother considered what to name me, this religious association was not uppermost in her mind. What most concerned her, she joked in a letter to her sister, was that "Mike" sounded to her like the name of a professional wrestler.

My mother lovingly collected the pencil and crayon drawings that I made as a child and glued them into a scrapbook. Among them, the only religious image (which I drew when I was five years old) is of a blond, blue-eyed, beardless Jesus in an apocryphal orange and gold chariot.

My parents were not particularly religious. They did not attend church regularly. As a child, however, I attended Sunday School. My first memory of Sunday School is of a teacher, a woman, telling us children (we must have been about five years old) that if we were not good, God would punish us, and we would go to hell. Why, I wondered, would one would not simply be good for the sake of being good? Why was the threat of eternal damnation necessary? (I should perhaps note that this woman was an aberration, a real exception to the rule. None of the other teachers whom I had in Sunday School ever emphasized the image of a punitive God.)

What I liked best about Sunday School were the Bible stories that the teachers told us. The Methodists in my hometown were not at all "fundamentalists." The teachers who told us Bible stories in Sunday School did not take those stories literally; they took them metaphorically. What they emphasized was the "moral" of the stories. To them, the value of the Bible stories was not whether they were historically accurate (or literally true) but whether they were morally instructive (or metaphorically apt). That is, what were valuable were the *metaphorical implications* of the Bible stories. In retrospect, I now realize, with great gratitude, that this experience was precious preparation for me, as a psychoanalyst, eventually to interpret the images in dreams, fantasies, and other material as metaphors. What Hillman calls "deliteralizing" (1975: 136) has never been difficult for me, thanks in large part to those teachers in Sunday School so many years ago. Hillman says: "Nothing is literal; all is metaphor" (1975: 175). I would say that whether anything is literal is simply beside the psychoanalytic point (I would also say that it is beside the religious point). "An archetypal content," Jung says, "expresses itself, first and foremost, in metaphors" (*CW* 9,1: 157, par. 267). As I have previously argued, what is of decisive importance psychoanalytically are the specific "constitutive" metaphors that the unconscious employs in particular patients (Adams 1997c). These are the metaphors that constitute the distinctive psychic realities of those patients. Such metaphors are the very basis of any interpretation that purports to be definitively valid.

As a child, I avidly collected baseball cards. I had thousands. A few of them, especially dear to me, were cards that my father had collected at the turn of the century. They were Colgan's Mint Chips cards, small and round with black-and-white photographs of baseball players, in a tiny dark green tin. I also inherited from my father a set of religious cards, which the Methodist church in my hometown had awarded to children for attendance at Sunday School. These were larger, more or less square cards, beautifully printed Bible stories illustrated with color drawings – "The Flood," "The Child Moses Saved from Death," "Crossing the Red Sea," "Israel Enters the Land of Promise," "David and Goliath," "Jesus' Death and Burial," "Christ Risen," and so forth. The earliest was from 1904, when my father was four years old.

One afternoon, the doorbell rang at our house. I was alone at the time. A man was standing there. He asked to come in, and I made the mistake of letting him. He was a Jehovah's Witness. He sat down on the sofa in our living room and proceeded to offer me irrefutable proof of the existence of God. "Do you know," he catechized me, "those scenes in cowboy movies when the bad guy in the black hat is hanging by his fingertips from a cliff?" Yes, I said. "Well, what does he always say when he finally loses his grip and falls to his death?" I don't know, I said, what? With a look of immense satisfaction, the Jehovah's Witness replied: "Oh, God!" *Quod erat demonstrandum.* Many years later, I wondered whether even Anselm could have contrived a more parsimonious proof.

My mother was an amateur artist who taught private classes in drawing and painting. One day, she was teaching a class of teenagers. One of the teenagers, a girl, enthusiastically reported a religious experience that she had recently had in a youth group at the Baptist church. The boys and girls in the group had formed a circle, had shut their eyes, and had held one another's hands. The girl had felt the "holy spirit" move around the circle. My mother sardonically remarked, in words that Freud would have appreciated, "Sounds like sex to me." I knew what my mother meant. For two summers as a teenager, I attended a church camp. I had much less interest in God, I now publicly confess, than in the pretty girls who attended that camp from other towns. What I looked forward to most eagerly was the opportunity to sneak over with other boys to the girls' cabins at night for clandestine parties, which were, of course, against the rules of the camp. There was no actual sex as such, but we boys kissed the girls, and they kissed us back.

Like my father, I sang in a church quartet as a teenager. We four boys had a repertoire of exactly one hymn, which we sang on numerous occasions. One Sunday afternoon, we sang it at "Brush Arbor Day" in a community center that had once been the school auditorium of Cotton Center, a nearby rural village. We were among several "acts" to entertain the few elderly people who still lived there. A quartet of adults, three men and a woman, also sang. I remember how surprised I was to realize that the woman was singing the bass part, with the deepest voice I had ever heard. She sounded like a bullfrog. That same woman introduced the main attraction. "We're proud to have Jerry Lewis's cousin with us today," she announced. "His cousin Jerry sings for the devil, but he sings for the Lord." At that, a young man bounded on stage, sat down at the piano, and began to sing and shout, pounding the keys with his fingers and fist and keeping time by stomping the floor with his foot. It was quite a sight – and quite a sound.

Not until we four boys were on our way home did I suddenly realize that the young man had not been Jerry Lewis the comedian's cousin but Jerry *Lee* Lewis the rock-and-roller's cousin. "Great Balls of Fire!" On the stage that day, there had certainly been a whole lot of shakin' goin' on. Not until many years later did I learn that Jerry Lee Lewis's cousin was Jimmy Swaggart. Eventually, Swaggart became famous as a television evangelist (in the late 1980s with an audience of 2.1 million in America and 500 million in 143 other countries) – and then notorious, when, weeping and confessing his sins, he begged forgiveness after having been arrested for soliciting a prostitute, as Ann Rowe Seaman so ably documents in her biography *Swaggart*. Seaman even interprets Swaggart's sexual fall from spiritual grace in Jungian terms, as an ego inflation both angelic and demonic and as a conflation of the sacred and the profane (1999: 390).

Our quartet eventually evolved into a folk group and then a rock-and-roll band. We four boys continued, however, to sing in the youth choir at the Methodist church on Sunday nights. The service would begin with the choir singing several hymns. Then, before the minister delivered the sermon, he would invite us to join the congregation (a few little old ladies, spinsters and widows, in the front pew). We had to exit through a door into a music practice room behind the choir and then enter the congregation through another door. One Sunday night, however, when the minister invited the choir to join the congregation, we four boys exited through the door into the music practice room behind the choir – and then we exited down the hallway and all the way out the back door of the church into the street, where we got into a car and drove as fast as we could to the nearest television set. It was February 9,1964, and the Beatles were on the Ed Sullivan Show, and like millions of other teenagers in America, we enthusiastically watched them sing "I Want To Hold Your Hand." Later, when John Lennon said that the Beatles were more popular than Jesus, we knew exactly what he meant.

When I mentioned to one Jungian analyst that I had been raised a Methodist, she burst out laughing. I had to grin, because in many ways my religious upbringing *was* ludicrous.

In high school, I played football on a team that won the district championship my junior year. In the playoffs, we lost to the eventual state champions. Then an incident occurred that I have previously recounted as follows:

> After the season, at the banquet where we received our varsity letter jackets, the professional football player who delivered the usual inspirational speech

also presented each of us with a small book of religious testimonials by members of the Fellowship of Christian Athletes. A few weeks later, a fan of some rival team (may he burn eternally in hell) anonymously reported the gift to the Texas Interscholastic League, which ruled that we had technically exceeded the monetary limit on the value of awards and that we would therefore be ineligible for the playoffs the next season no matter how many games we might win. As the newspapers erroneously inflated the story, we had been penalized for accepting Bibles.

(Adams 1997b: 88)

This was, for me and my teammates, a most unhappy "religious experience."

As a teenager, I assumed that I would eventually attend Southern Methodist University in Dallas. This assumption had nothing to do with religion and everything to do with football. I was a fan of the SMU team, the "Mustangs." (Early in the century, one of my uncles had attended SMU and had played football for the Mustangs. He had kicked the winning field goal in one game.) When I did go to college, however, I went to Texas Christian University in Fort Worth. I did so not because I had any interest whatsoever in religion. On a visit to the campus, I had won a gold medal in a journalism competition that the Texas Interscholastic League had sponsored at TCU, and the professors whom I met on that occasion had expressed appreciation for my skill as a student writer. Had they not been so friendly to me, I would surely have gone to college elsewhere, for it had never occurred to me to attend TCU. At that time, TCU required all students to take one religion course. In the course that I took, the professor had written a book about religion, and he had us buy that book as the one and only text. He never delivered a single lecture; nor did he invite any discussion. For the entire semester, he read that book to us, line by line, word for word. Needless to say, that experience hardly inspired me to take another religion course.

Baylor University in Waco was much more seriously religious than either SMU or TCU. I was rather envious of the students at Baylor, because they had much more of an excuse than I had to be irreverent. There was a notorious secret society at Baylor. The members of the NoZe Society (Noble NoZe Brotherhood) were students who mocked religion at every opportunity. They all had nicknames that included puns on the word "nose" (for example, "God-Only-NoZe"). Whenever they appeared as an organization in public, they wore masks with enormous plastic noses to disguise their real identities. They literally "thumbed their noses" at any religious authority. At the time, the president of Baylor University was also the president of the Southern Baptist Convention. The students in the NoZe Society satirically called him "Cardinal Lucid" – an insult that simultaneously characterized him as a Catholic (to a Baptist, what could be worse?) and an ignoramus. Baylor finally banned the NoZe Society from campus after the members entered an especially offensive float in the homecoming parade one year. Dangling off the back of the float was a bloody effigy of the beheaded John the Baptist. As juvenile as this behavior was, the compensatory intention was to deflate any religiosity at Baylor.

Many years later, when Attorney General Janet Reno, the FBI, and the Bureau of Alcohol, Tobacco, and Firearms burned down the Branch Davidian compound near Waco (and in the process burned up most of the members of that fundamentalist sect of Baptists), I wondered whether the blasphemies of the NoZe Society, had it still existed, might have prevented that holocaust. What if David Koresh had been a student at Baylor and a member of the NoZe Society? Would he then have had such grandiose prophetic (or messianic) pretensions? Or what if Koresh had had the opportunity to experience a Jungian analysis? As I have previously noted, Jung believes that "an identification with the collective unconscious, or more specifically with the archetypal image of the prophet, is probably a pathological inflation and certainly a dubious proposition" (Adams 1998b: 13). Jung says:

> I would not deny in general the existence of genuine prophets, but in the name of caution I would begin by doubting each individual case; for it is far too serious a matter for us lightly to accept a man as a genuine prophet. Every respectable prophet strives manfully against the unconscious pretensions of his role. When therefore a prophet appears at a moment's notice, we would be better advised to contemplate a possible psychic disequilibrium.
>
> (*CW* 7: 170, par. 262)

Perhaps the Justice Department should have a Jungian analyst on staff (or at least on call) – or perhaps President George W. Bush, who has a ranch near Waco, should have a Jungian analyst in the cabinet to consult during apocalyptic political crises.

One day while I was a graduate student at the University of Texas at Austin, I drove a friend of a friend of mine to the PX of a military base where he had shopping privileges. He was a hippie who liked to take LSD (lysergic acid diethylamide). Suddenly, he said to me, "Have you heard the expression 'God is acid?'" Yes, I said. "Well," he said, "have you heard the expression 'God is love?'" He gave me a significant look, as if he had had a profound, psychedelic revelation and wondered whether I had the acumen to discern what he meant. "Acid is love!"

My father died in 1971. In the parking lot of the funeral home, a man approached me and offered what he considered words of consolation. He said that he knew that the afterlife really existed. He had been in hospital for major surgery. The doctors had given him morphine. He had seen a "glass elevator" that conveyed souls from earth to heaven.

As a graduate student at the University of Sussex, I attended the Guy Fawkes bonfire one November 5 on the hills above the town of Lewes. That night in 1974 I had an opportunity to witness just how persistent anti-Catholic sentiment still was in England almost four centuries after the failure of the Gunpowder Plot to blow up Parliament (an early example of terrorism in the name of religion). On a platform were three men who had apparently volunteered, at considerable risk to life and limb, to pose as Catholic priests for the occasion. The men were dressed in cassocks and miters, and they were solemnly reading aloud from fake religious tomes (perhaps volumes of infallible edicts from the pope). The crowd lighted fire-crackers and zealously hurled them at the three papists. Later, they blew up giant effigies of Guy Fawkes and the pope that the organizers of the event had stuffed with fireworks. Then the crowd blew up an effigy of an Arab sheik (apparently an airplane hijacker) riding a 747 and holding a purse (evidently an image of exploit-ative Arab oil profits at the expense of the West). The scene was not only anti-Catholic but also anti-Islamic (or at least anti-Arabic), as well as anti-royalist (the crowd blew up another effigy of Princess Anne and Mark Phillips riding a horse).

One of my fondest (and funniest) memories of my mother is of a moment when I was driving her back home in Texas from dinner at a restaurant. On the way, we passed a movie theater. My mother suddenly burst out laughing. The marquee read: "OH GOD THE JERK." Two different comedies were showing at the theater, *Oh God!*, starring George Burns, and *The Jerk*, starring Steve Martin. My mother had misread the two titles as one good joke.

One of my favorite memories of my son as a little boy is of my wife trying to explain the story of Adam and Eve to him. She told him that because the serpent had tempted Eve to eat the apple, God had punished the serpent by making him crawl on his belly. "*Whose* belly?" my son asked.

Several years ago, I drove with my wife and son through the American southwest to see Taos Pueblo, Monument Valley, the Grand Canyon, Mesa Verde, and other sites. One of my favorite experiences on that trip was a "roadside attraction." A man, an "outsider artist," had used wet sand to sculpt a life-size "Last Supper." (For this devotion, he had developed arthritis.) Figures of Jesus and the 12 disciples sat around a table. What I liked best about the sculptures was that someone had van-dalized them – had broken the beards off all the figures. Beards (and I myself have one!) are images that convey a certain authority – even a "prophetic" authority. Thus all "prophets" need to have their beards plucked occasionally, lest their prophecies be taken too authoritatively. Jung, who had only a moustache, regarded Freud as just such a prophet. In one of the very last letters that he ever wrote to Freud, Jung says: "For sheer obsequiousness nobody dares to pluck the prophet by the beard and inquire for once what you would say to a patient with a tendency to analyse the analyst instead of himself. You would certainly ask him: '*Who's* got the neurosis?'" According to Jung, Freud was just as neurotic as his patients, because, unlike Jung, Freud had never been *analyzed* but had only "analyzed" himself. Jung declares, with a superstitious gesture: "I am not in the least neurotic – touch wood! I have submitted *lege artis et tout humblement* to analysis and am much the better for it. You know, of course, how far a patient gets with self-analysis: *not* out of his neurosis – just like you" (Freud and Jung 1974: 535).

One of my favorite restaurants in Greenwich Village is the Cowgirl Hall of Fame. Whenever I have a craving for Texas vittles, I go there to eat a chicken fried steak and drink some Lone Star Beer. One Christmas, I was walking by the restau-rant when I suddenly noticed the window display: a crèche scene with life-size cardboard figures. Hovering above was a blond, buxom angel whom I immediately recognized as Dolly Parton. Standing below were the three wise men: Gene Autry,

Roy Rogers, and Hank Williams. Lying in the crib was the "King," a baby Elvis with sideburns. I immediately went inside to compliment the manager of the restaurant. She replied: "We've had death threats."

Three summers ago, I returned to my hometown in Texas to attend a high school reunion. The final event was a barbeque at the football stadium. The speaker for the event was an African-American "ex" who after graduation had played football for the University of Oklahoma and then for the New York Giants. He had subsequently become a missionary in Africa. The president of the high school alumni association introduced him. "Our speaker," he said, "is a professor at Southern Babel ... I mean, *Bible* College." That was just the first slip of the tongue – and how apt that it was an allusion to the Bible story of the "Tower of Babel" and the "confusion of tongues!" The theme that the speaker had selected was "homecoming." We had all come home, he said, for the high school reunion. He then mentioned the Bible story of the "Prodigal Son." He noted that the prodigal son had also returned home. (The speaker was apparently utterly unconscious of the fact that this parallel insinuated that everyone at the high school reunion was guilty of prodigality!) In the Bible story, when the prodigal son returns home, his father immediately forgives him, welcomes him, and says to his servants: "Bring forth the best robe, and put it on him; and put a ring on his hand, and shoes on his feet" (Luke 15: 22). The speaker, however, paraphrased this passage as: "Lord, give him a finger." ("Which finger," I wondered, "might *that* be?" It seemed to me quite probable that the father of the prodigal son *had* felt like praying to God to give his son the finger!) As a psychoanalyst, I interpreted these slips not as innocent accidents but as a symptomatic "return of the repressed." If I were at all religious, however, I might just as well have interpreted them as examples of demonic possession, for it was as if the very devil had humorously intervened to subvert a public display of piety with a compensatory measure of profane irony. (Alternatively, perhaps it was "God" who intervened on this occasion – that is, if "God" has a sense of humor.)

Freudian slips include not only slips of the tongue but also slips of the ears. A few years ago, at a party in celebration of the publication of a new psychoanalytic book, one of the editors recounted how he had misheard "The Bible is the blueprint of God" as "The Bible is the blooper in print of God." A blasphemously unconscious pun worthy of James Joyce!

One of my Freudian friends, Michael Moskowitz, read the Bible, both the Old and New Testaments, for the very first time just before the bar-mitzvah of his first-born son. The experience moved him to write a paper in which he compares Yahweh as a God of law with Jesus as a God of love (Moskowitz, n.d.). He notes that, like Marx, Freud was an atheist. If for Marx religion was like opium, it was for Freud, Moskowitz says, "perhaps more like Prozac." What interests Moskowitz is whether the "cure" in psychoanalysis occurs more through law or more through love. I first heard his paper a few years ago at a conference on psychoanalysis and multiculturalism. Moskowitz and I happened to be on the same panel. Not until recently, however, did I ask him for a copy of his paper. He sent it to me by e-mail as a zip-file attachment. When I downloaded it, a message appeared on my computer screen: "JESUS has been transferred."

One of my favorite greeting cards depicts a Jesus that even Freud would have appreciated. Sometimes a cigar is just a cigar, but sometimes a cigar is a good cigar. The legend on the greeting card reads: "Jesus enjoying a good cigar." We may be able to imagine Freud enjoying a good cigar (or Jung enjoying a good pipe), but are we able to imagine Jesus smoking a stogy?

Over the years, I have had a few "religious" dreams. For example, in 1997, I had a dream that consisted of a single image. In the center were several sticks of wood, some of them on top of others. Around them was a circle of flames, and around that, a square. In the dream, I realized that this was an image of the "Burning Bush." In the Bible story, an angel appears to Moses "out of the midst of a bush." Moses looks and beholds "the bush burned with fire, and the bush was not consumed." Moses turns aside to see "this great sight, why the bush is not burnt." At that, Yahweh calls to him "out of the midst of the bush." Yahweh says to Moses: "Here am I" (Exodus 3: 2–4).

In Jewish tradition, there are many Midrash interpretations of the Burning Bush (Levine 1981). Jung interprets the Burning Bush as an image of "power" (libido, or psychic energy). "In the Old Testament," he says, "the magic power glows in the burning bush" (*CW* 7: 68, par. 108). One Jungian analyst, M. Esther Harding, interprets the Burning Bush as a "numinous" experience (a numen is a "spirit"). She says that the story of the Burning Bush is a variation on the archetypal theme of the "hero myth." According to Harding, Moses "is called to become a hero in the mythological sense of that term" (1971: 2). Out of the Burning Bush, God calls Moses to lead the Chosen People out of Egypt into the Promised Land. Moses first resists this call to heroism but finally accepts it. As Harding recounts the story, Moses "saw in the distance a bush that seemed to his eyes to be on fire." It may have been, she speculates, an optical illusion that Moses interpreted as a miracle: combustion without consumption. "Perhaps the sun," she says, "shone on a desert bush that was in the full flower of spring – whatever it may have been it seemed to Moses to be blazing and yet it was not burned up." Whatever the outer event may have been, Harding says that the story of the Burning Bush is "the account of an inner experience, a psychic happening" (1971: 8). That is, from a psychoanalytic perspective, the voice that speaks to Moses from the Burning Bush (and calls him to heroism) is simply a projection from internal reality (the "voice" of the unconscious) onto an object in external reality.

If I were religious, I might interpret my dream of the Burning Bush as a literal revelation from God. As a psychoanalyst, however, I interpret it as a metaphorical projection from the unconscious. I sometimes say to my patients that unless and until they see a "burning bush" (whether in internal or external reality) they are not really *in* analysis. By this, I mean that they have not yet experienced the projective (or "revelatory") reality of the unconscious. If and when they do see a "burning bush," they suddenly realize just how "miraculously" fraught with psychic significance all of reality, both internal and external, is. (Even as I write this, Ginette

Paris, a core faculty member and research director of the Mythological Studies Program at Pacifica Graduate Institute, forwards to me by e-mail a "Post-Deity Purchase Questionnaire." One of the questions is: "What factors were relevant in your decision to acquire a deity? Please check all that apply." The last option on the checklist is: "My shrubbery caught fire and told me to do it.")

My wife is from India. Her father was a Sikh; her mother is a Hindu. We were married in Bethlehem (Pennsylvania) in the home of Jewish friends who now live in Tel Aviv. A Christian minister conducted the service. Our Jewish friends read passages about love from the Song of Songs in Hebrew. My wife wore a red sari, the wedding dress of Indians. Our wedding march was the Western Swing song "Yearning (Just for You)" by Bob Wills and the Texas Playboys. I wonder whether there has ever been a wedding as oddly – and as happily – multicultural as ours.

In our apartment in New York City, there are many "religious" images: Vishnu, Shiva, Hanuman, Ganesh, Jagannath, Guru Nanak, Buddha, a lingam, a wheel of life, a tree of life, two crucifixes, a priest, two saints, a Black Madonna, the Venus of Willendorf, the sleeping lady of Malta, the snake goddess of Gnossos, a "Jesus Action Figure" ("with poseable arms and gliding action"), a "Hellvis" (a glossy red ceramic bust of Elvis Presley with horns), and a "Kali Smurf" (a multi-armed, multi-weaponed, bright blue sculpture wearing a headband of skulls and holding the bloody, decapitated head of Grandpa Smurf, while standing on his prostrate corpse). At a party in our apartment, a psychoanalyst who surveyed all those images asked me what tradition we were raising our children in. "All of them," I said. "But won't that just confuse them?" he asked. "Shouldn't you raise them in just one?"

If I am a "theist" at all, I am a "polytheist" – but only in the strictly psychological sense that Hillman employs the term (1981a). As a friend, a Jewish psychoanalyst, once said to me: "I have never understood the advantage of monotheism over poly-theism." Jung says that among psychological types, certain individuals have an inclination toward monism, others toward pluralism (*CW* 6: 318, par. 536). I am a pluralist. I do not believe in *one* God (with a capital "G"). I believe in *many* "gods" and "goddesses" (with lower-case initials and within quotation marks to indicate that they are not literal, metaphysical entities, but metaphorical, psychic factors, what Jung calls archetypes of the collective unconscious).

Monotheism is a variety of monism. William James says that the distinction between pluralism and monism is "the most pregnant of all the dilemmas of phil-osophy." James asks: "Does reality exist distributively? or collectively? – in the shape of *eaches, everys, anys, eithers*? or only in the shape of an *all* or *whole*?" (1968: 258). He says that "the attribute 'one' seems for many persons to confer a value, an ineffable illustriousness and dignity upon the world, with which the con-ception of it as an irreducible 'many' is believed to clash" (1968: 267). Jung says that monism "proceeds from the desire to set up one function or the other as the supreme psychological principle." According to Jung, "This psychological monism, or rather monotheism, has the advantage of simplicity but the defect of one-sidedness." It entails, he notes, "exclusion of the diversity and rich reality of life and the world." Perhaps even worse, he says, "it holds out no real possibility of human development" (*CW* 7: 288, par. 482).

I prefer the many-sidedness of polytheism to the one-sidedness of monotheism. This preference is not, however, simply a subjective predilection. I have what I regard as an objective basis for this preference. Because of the obvious, intrinsic diversity of the unconscious, monotheism seems to me utterly untenable psychologically. In my experience as a psychoanalyst, all of the evidence available to me from the dreams, fantasies, and other material of my patients demonstrates conclusively that the psyche is not monistic but, as Samuels says, "plural" (1989). As Jung says, the unconscious is "a Multiple Consciousness" (*CW* 8: 190: par. 388) – or, I would say, the unconscious comprises multiple *consciousnesses*, in the plural. In this sense, "the" unconscious includes a multiplicity of images, or "consciousnesses," of which the ego is (more or less) unconscious. (As I define the unconscious, it is simply all that the ego is unconscious *of*.) Thus Jung emphasizes what he calls "the multitudinous quality of the unconscious" (1988 2: 1404).

Jung also says, however: "The unconscious gives the impression of multiplicity and unity at once" (*CW* 11: 288, par. 440). In this respect, Jung mentions the "dragon" in alchemy. He interprets the dragon as an image of the "Self," which he defines as the archetype of the totality of the psyche. Jung quotes a passage about the genealogical lineage of the dragon, who says: "Many from one and one from many, issue of a famous line, I rise from the lowest to the highest. The nethermost power of the whole earth is united with the highest. I therefore am the One and the Many within me" (*CW* 14: 223, par. 296). From this alchemical perspective, the dragon contains both the one and the many.

In Tibetan Buddhism, Jung notes, the one contains the many. Tibetan Buddhism regards pluralism as a mere illusion, on the assumption that "all separate forms originate in the indistinguishable oneness of the psychic matrix, deep down in the unconscious." Whether it is true that pluralism is really an illusion, Jung says, is questionable:

> The questions naturally arise: "Why should the One appear as the Many, when ultimate reality is All-One? What is the cause of pluralism, or of the illusion of pluralism? If the One is pleased with itself, why should it mirror itself in the Many? Which after all is the more real, the one that mirrors itself, or the mirror it uses?" Probably we should not ask such questions, seeing that there is no answer to them.
>
> (*CW* 11: 498, par. 798)

Sometimes Jung seems to suggest that, in the history of human consciousness, monotheism is a necessary but difficult progression from "polytheism and polydemonism" (*CW* 9,2: 175, par. 271). He also says, however, that "the striving for unity is opposed by a possibly even stronger tendency to create multiplicity, so that even in strictly monotheistic religions like Christianity the polytheistic tendency cannot be suppressed" (*CW* 5: 99, par. 149). That is, when polytheism is suppressed (or repressed), it inevitably returns.

In the controversy over monotheism and polytheism, I would privilege multiplicity over unity and reverse the usual dictum that the one contains the many. In this respect, Rafael Lopez-Pedraza says that "the many *contains* the unity of the one *without losing* the possibilities of the many" (1971: 214). That is, if unity exists, it is merely one of many possibilities that multiplicity contains – or expresses: if there is a oneness, it is the oneness of each of the many ones that constitute the psyche. In short, if there is any illusion, I would say that it is the illusion of monism. This may, of course, merely be the inclination – or bias – of an individual of my particular psychological type, but in my experience as a psychoanalyst, the unconscious invariably manifests in my patients as a multiplicity of images. To affirm the existence of a "Self" as a unity from which these images emanate seems to me to multiply hypotheses beyond the necessary. The "Self" seems to me a gratuitous and superfluous notion to which I would happily apply Occam's razor.

I realize that this position may seem non-Jungian or even anti-Jungian. I would note, however, that Jung acknowledges that "the self is no more than a psychological concept, a construct" (*CW* 7: 238, par. 399). He considers it a necessary construct equivalent to the "God within us." Since, however, the images in dreams, fantasies, and other material from the unconscious demonstrate that there is not just one "God" within us but, on the contrary, many "gods" and "goddesses" within us, I consider the "Self" to be an utterly unnecessary, purely *arbitrary* construct, a mere deus ex machina. That is, the "Self" is a theoretical construct that seems to me untrue to the empirical diversity of the psyche. To me, the "Self" is simply a specious abstraction. In this sense, to posit a "Self" is arbitrarily to derive the multiplicity of *concrete images* in the unconscious from the unity of an *abstract concept* and then to reduce those many images to that one concept. In contrast, I maintain that the imaginal multiplicity in the unconscious is primary and constitutive, while the conceptual unity of the "Self" is secondary and derivative.

Is there an archetype of totality? Yes, I would say – and (for lack of a better word) I might, as Jung does, call it the "Self" – but a "totality" is just a *sum*. In this respect, Jung *infers* the concept of the "Self" by an a posteriori induction from all of the images in the unconscious. By this definition, the "Self" is merely the additive, or aggregative, total of those images. Jung also, however, *posits* the concept of the "Self" by an a priori deduction. That is, he regards the "Self" not just as the archetype of the totality of the psyche (a whole that is simply the sum of the parts) but as a "supraordinate personality" (*CW* 9,1: 187, par. 315), with agency, intentionality, and intelligence – the equivalent, I might say, of "God."

To the extent that Jung privileges this definition of the "Self" as a *personality*, Jungian psychology is a monotheistic, not a polytheistic, psychology. Thus Jung explicitly correlates "the self with monotheism" (*CW* 9,2: 268, par. 427). By this correlation, the "Self" is, in effect, the psychological equivalent of the God (Yahweh or Allah) of the monotheistic religions of the Middle East – Judaism, Christianity, and Islam. From this perspective, the Jewish, Christian, or Islamic

"Self" is a "jealous God" that will have no other "gods" (much less "goddesses") before it – and it is also a "God" that will have no *images* of it (it is iconoclastic because it assumes that images are idolatrous). In traditional Jungian analysis (I would say, also in traditional Freudian analysis), there is a tacit monotheistic tendency – or bias. Since Jung was a Christian (and Freud a Jew) this should hardly be a surprise. If for Freud, sex is "God," then for Jung, the Self is "God."

The purpose of psychoanalysis is to establish an effective relation between the ego and the unconscious. This relation is a dialogue in the service of individuation. For those Jungians who regard the "Self" as a necessary construct, the conversation is between the ego and the Self. For some religious Jungians, however, the dialogue also includes *God* (quite literally). For example, Ann Belford Ulanov maintains that the conversation is "between ego, Self, and that which the Self knows about, God" (1994: 92). I confess that I cringe at this conflation of the psychological and the metaphysical. It is bad enough to posit the "Self" as a psychological construct; it is even worse to posit God as a metaphysical entity. To me, this is to exceed the epistemological limitations of psychoanalysis.

As Hillman notes, Jung defines "individuation" in two ways. One definition emphasizes *integration*, the other *differentiation*. Hillman prefers (as I do) the Jung who defines individuation as "a process of *differentiation*" (*CW* 6: 448, par. 757). *In one model, individuation proceeds from unity to duality (opposition) to unity (integration). In the other model, individuation proceeds from unity to duality (opposition) to multiplicity (differentiation).* In effect, one definition of individuation is psychologically monotheistic, the other polytheistic.

Which is truer to the facts of the psyche? The notion that individuation should culminate in integration privileges unity over multiplicity (wholeness over partness) and tends to "pathologize" differentiation. From the perspective of integration, differentiation seems tantamount to dissociation, or disintegration of the psyche. In this respect, Jung cites a dream as evidence of "dangerous plurality" (*CW* 12: 81, par. 105). Similarly, he mentions the individual who has "great difficulty in uniting his own multiplicity." Such an individual, he says, "will have no defense against his inner multiplicity" (1963: 343). From this perspective, the unity of the "Self" is a necessary defense against the threat that the multiplicity of the unconscious poses to the very integrity of the psyche. This threat is what Jung calls "the dissociation or dissociability of the psyche" (*CW* 8: 173, par. 365).

Differentiation, however, is *not* dissociation. As Jung says: "Differentiation is the essence, the *sine qua non* of consciousness" (*CW* 7: 206, par. 329). As I experience the facts of the psyche in the dreams, fantasies, and other material that my patients present in analysis, "the" unconscious manifests to the ego not as a unity (the "Self") but as multiple consciousnesses (multiple images). These images offer for consideration many-sided alternative perspectives on the one-sided attitudes of the ego. The purpose of psychoanalysis (or the process of individuation) is not an integration of these images *with* the ego but a differentiation of them *by* the ego and thus an increase in consciousness. Psychoanalytically, the decisive issue is *which specific "gods" or "goddesses"* (archetypes) manifest as images in the dreams, fantasies, and other material of *particular patients* – and for *what distinctive (even idiosyncratic) purposes.*

If I believe in any sense in "God," it is "God" as the imagination (or the meta-phorical imagination). I quite deliberately, however, do not spell the word with a capital "I," for, to me, the imagination is not (like the "Self") a monotheistically supraordinate personality with agency, intentionality, and intelligence. As I define the imagination, it is simply the sum of all of the images in "the" unconscious. As I have said, I regard the images in the unconscious as "consciousnesses," and, in this respect, I regard them as "personalities" (at least in the rhetorical sense that they are "personifications" of psychic factors, or archetypes). I might even call them polytheistically "ordinate personalities" (none of them supraordinate or sub-ordinate to any other), in the sense that they all serve to establish principles of "order," on an ad hoc basis, in the psyche. It is *as if* each and every one of these many images is – or has – a "personality" with a qualitatively distinctive, even a unique, "consciousness" (agency, intentionality, and intelligence). That is, the imagination is replete with personifications that I might metaphorically call "gods" and "goddesses."

It is true that some individuals privilege one and only one of the contents of the unconscious over all others. For Jews, this is Yahweh; for Christians, Yahweh (or Jesus as the "son" of Yahweh); for Muslims, Allah; for Freud, sex; for Jung, the Self. This monotheistic preference a priori imputes to the unconscious a dogmatic content, which it "deifies" and "worships." It excludes from consideration (represses or "demonizes") all other contents, which it regards as polytheistic (and idolatrous). In contrast, what I advocate is a psychoanalysis that would not dog-matically presuppose what the unconscious contains. It would not stipulate a definite content in advance. It would not exclude – or, more precisely, *preclude* – any contents. It would be an *inclusive* psychoanalysis, one that would, without bias, equally esteem all of the contents of the unconscious, precisely differentiate them one from another, critically evaluate them, effectively engage them, and explicitly recognize the vast, intrinsic diversity – or, as Hillman says, "inherent polytheism" (1981a: 125) – of the unconscious. To the extent that the very basis of monotheism is a comprehensive repression of polytheism, it is, I would argue, non-psychoanalytic or even anti-psychoanalytic.

According to Hillman, monotheism is pervasively implicit in Western culture. Because, however, Western culture now espouses secularism, this monotheism is not so much an overt theology as a covert ideology. Thus Hillman says that in Western culture monotheism "no longer appears with" – for example – "the devout and fanatic visibility of Islam." Rather, it manifests in "hundreds" of psycho-logical assumptions "about how things are and how they should be" (1981a: 127). As an example, Hillman mentions the very motto of America. "*E pluribus unum*," he says, "is only a tiny manifestation" of the prevalence of monotheism in Western culture (1981a: 127–8). (A recent novelty "sex"-dollar bill, which features the portrait of President William Jefferson Clinton, jokes, "*E pluribus coitus*.") If, as Hillman says, monotheism suffuses Western culture, is it any wonder that it also

profoundly influences psychoanalysis? If this monotheistic tendency is so dominant, is it any wonder that it is so difficult to establish a polytheistic psychology (in
spite of the fact that the psyche is plural)?

The lead article on the front page of a recent issue of the humor newspaper *The
Onion* bore the headline "Judge Orders God To Break Up into Smaller Deities."
Under the headline were a cross, a crescent and star, and a star of David – images
of Christianity, Islam, and Judaism. The article purported to be an account of an
antitrust suit against God for anti-competitive practices. God, the judge said, had
effectively perpetrated "an illegal monotheopoly." Monotheism as monopoly! The
judge had ruled that God was guilty of restraint of religious trade. God had pur-
posely established "a marketplace hostile to rival deities." As a legal remedy, the
judge had ordered God "to divide Himself into a pantheon of specialized gods,
each representing a force of nature or a specific human custom, occupation, or state
of mind." The article quoted a woman who had followed the case. "There will most
likely be a sun god, a moon god, sea god, and rain god," she said. "Then there will
be some second-tier deities, like a god of wine, a goddess of the harvest, and perhaps a few who symbolize human love and/or blacksmithing." The article also
quoted a man who mentioned a number of advantages to the decision: "With polytheism, you pray to the deity specifically devoted to your concern. If you wish to
have children, you pray to the fertility goddess. If you want to do well on an exam,
you pray to the god of wisdom, and so on. This decentralization will result in more
individualized service and swifter response times" (Anonymous, January 30–
February 6, 2002: 1 and 6).

I mailed copies of this article to several Jungian analysts – among them,
Hillman. One Jungian analyst who shares my polytheistic proclivities actually
asked me if I had written the article. (I wish I had.) Hillman responded with a letter,
the last sentence of which read: "Is this *Onion* piece a joke, a scam, or is there such
a judge?" The answer, of course, is that there is indeed such a judge – in the satiri-
cal imagination. The article was clever enough momentarily to induce even James
Hillman, the archetypal deliteralizer, seriously to entertain the possibility that this
was an accurate account of an actual court case against God!

As a little boy, I was fascinated by the image of Thor. I still remember the thrill
I felt when I learned that Thursday is "Thor's day." Thunder and lightning! In my
experience as a little boy, the week comprised seven days that culminated in a
Christian Sunday. How, I wondered, had one of those days been named after a
hammer-wielding Norse god? Was not Thursday a blasphemy?

It is possible to blaspheme against "God" (Yahweh, Jesus as the "son" of God,
or Allah), but it is apparently impossible to blaspheme against Thor. As Jack Miles
says:

> "Try blaspheming against Thor," Chesterton challenged; and if the challenge
> has lost some of its bite, try telling jokes about Thor. God jokes are still
> common. But some even of those who stand regularly in the pews of church or
> synagogue might find it no harder or easier to blaspheme against God than to

do the same against Thor. Similarly, there are some for whom God-humor is as opaque and unfunny as Thor-humor. Impiety seems to require piety as its foil.

(Miles 1992: 22)

For Christians, Jews, and Muslims, it is impossible to blaspheme against Thor or even to joke about him, because they regard Thor as a mere image in a mythology, not in a religion (that is, a mythology that they happen to "believe in"). Levy defines blasphemy as "speaking evil of sacred matters" (1993: 3). I would emphasize that it also includes making fun of sacred matters (what Miles calls "God-humor"). "Monotheism," Hillman says, "cautions us *not* to laugh" (1996: 117). It has no sense of humor about "God" (and "God" has no sense of humor). Catholics are so serious about blasphemy that they define it as a mortal sin, and Dante consigns blasphemers to the seventh circle of hell.

In *After Strange Gods*, T. S. Eliot says that only believers can be blasphemers. He declares that "no one can possibly blaspheme, in any sense except that in which a parrot may be said to curse, unless he profoundly believes in that which he profanes" (1934: 52). It is true that blasphemy requires believers – Levy notes that "blasphemy could not exist in a society of atheists" (1993: 570) – but, contrary to what Eliot says, it is not true that the blasphemer has to be a believer. It is a fallacy to define blasphemy by reference to the individual who commits it rather than by reference to the individuals who are offended by it. What constitutes blasphemy is that believers "take offense." It is no paradox but a contradiction in terms to say that blasphemers must believe in what they profane.

Jung says that as a boy he "felt the strongest resistances to imagining God by analogy with my own ego." The notion, he says, "seemed to me boundlessly arrogant, if not downright blasphemous" (1963: 57). Ironically, it was a blasphemous image that made Jung, at the age of 12, conscious of the fact that there was more to him – or more to his psyche – than his ego. "I saw before me the cathedral, the blue sky," Jung says. "God sits on His golden throne, high above the world – and from under the throne an enormous turd falls upon the sparkling new roof, shatters it, and breaks the walls of the cathedral asunder" (1963: 39). Jung describes this scatological image as "the blasphemous vision which God directly or indirectly (i.e. via the devil) had imposed on my will" (1963: 58). God not only shits but shits on Christianity in the image of the church! In this excremental vision, Jung imagines God (or God "via the devil") by analogy with his own unconscious.

Jung says that the dialogue between the ego and the unconscious is analogous to the dialogue "between patient and analyst, the role of devil's advocate easily falling to the latter" (*CW* 8: 89, par. 186). The implication is that in relation to the ego the unconscious is not "God" but a *devil's advocate*. Imagine the ego as the pope and cardinals sitting around a table in the Vatican and discussing various theological positions. Then imagine the unconscious as a devil's advocate sitting at that same table and complicating and problematizing that discussion by stating different or even opposite opinions. The function of the devil's advocate in relation to the pope and cardinals is identical with the compensatory function of the unconscious in relation to the ego. The purpose of the unconscious as devil's advocate is to present alternative perspectives that have been ignored, neglected, repressed, dissociated, or otherwise excluded from serious consideration by the ego. What the unconscious advocates are alternative perspectives that compensate the partial, prejudicial, or defective attitudes of the ego. To the ego, the advocacy of these alternative perspectives from the unconscious seems "devilish" – or, I would say, blasphemous. That is why the ego tends to be defensive rather than receptive to them.

I personally prefer the notion that the unconscious is analogous to a devil's advocate rather than to God (or God "via the devil"), because the devil's advocate analogy seems to me more accurately to approximate the actual function of the unconscious. All three of these analogies, however, are monotheistic: either the unconscious is a God that functions alone, a God that functions through the devil, or an advocate that functions for the devil. In a sense, of course, the very notion of "the" unconscious is monotheistic. In contrast, I would say that, from a polytheistic perspective, what psychoanalysts call "the" unconscious, as if unconsciousness were unitary, is a misnomer for all of the *multiple consciousnesses ("gods" and "goddesses," or psychic factors) of which the ego is unconscious and that confront the ego and challenge it to become more conscious.*

Levy notes that "monotheistic religions have no monopoly on blasphemy" (1993: 3). I would argue that polytheistic religions do, however, have a certain psychological advantage over monotheistic religions. Because they are pluralistic rather than monistic, they are more inclusive of the virtual infinity of factors in the psyche and, as a result, they have an intrinsic, syncretistic tendency to tolerate and accommodate differences, even radically contrary ones, that monotheistic religions might immediately consider offensive. In short, polytheistic religions are *psychologically more capacious* than monotheistic religions. The monotheistic religions (for example, Judaism, Christianity, and Islam) tend to generalize (and *moralize*) the psyche in terms of "opposites" (good and evil): God is good, the devil is evil. In contrast, the polytheistic religions tend to particularize the psyche in terms of "differences" (a vast diversity of gods and goddesses with a variety of distinctive qualities not conveniently reducible to "good" and "evil").

The ultimate reason why a polytheistic psychology is preferable to a monotheistic psychology is that it is less likely to countenance an ego that regards the images (the "gods" and "goddesses") from the unconscious as evil, offensive, or blasphemous and that then summarily excludes them from consideration. I would say that from the perspective of the ego, the unconscious is intrinsically "blasphemous," because the images that emerge from it continually address the pieties of the ego with irreverence. To these images from the unconscious, the attitudes of the ego are "unbelievable." The ego is a "true believer" with "holier-than-thou" attitudes toward the unconscious, and that is why the profane is the indispensable shadow of the sacred and why blasphemy is a necessary compensation for the holy.

References

Abbreviations

CW: *The Collected Works of C.G. Jung*, 20 vols. (plus 2 supplementary vols.), eds. H. Read, M. Fordham, G. Adler, and W. McGuire, trans. R. F. C. Hull, Princeton, NJ: Princeton University Press, and London: Routledge, 1953–1991.

SE: *The Standard Edition of the Complete Psychological Works of Sigmund Freud*, 24 vols., ed. and trans. J. Strachey with A. Freud, A. Strachey, and A. Tyson, London: Hogarth Press, 1953–1973.

Abrahamsen, D. (1976) *Nixon vs. Nixon: An Emotional Tragedy*, New York: Farrar, Straus and Giroux.

Adams, M. V. (1985) "Deconstructive Philosophy and Imaginal Psychology: Comparative Perspectives on Jacques Derrida and James Hillman," *Journal of Literary Criticism*, 2,1: 23–39. Reprinted in Rajnath (ed.) (1989) *Deconstruction: A Critique*, London: Macmillan, pp. 138–57, and in R. P. Sugg (ed.) (1992) *Jungian Literary Criticism*, Evanston, IL: Northwestern University Press, pp. 231–48.

—— (1993) "Psychoanalytic Studies In British and American Universities: The Kent and New School Programs," *International Federation for Psychoanalytic Education Newsletter*, 3,1: 20–6.

—— (1996) *The Multicultural Imagination: "Race," Color, and the Unconscious*, London and New York: Routledge.

—— (1997a) "The Archetypal School," in P. Young-Eisendrath and T. Dawson (eds.), *The Cambridge Companion to Jung*, Cambridge: Cambridge University Press, pp. 101–18.

—— (1997b) "Desegregating the White Ego: Racism and the Ethic of White Civilization," *Spring*, 62: 87–103.

—— (1997c) "Metaphors in Psychoanalytic Theory and Therapy," *Clinical Social Work Journal*, 25,1: 27–39.

—— (1998a) "For Love of the Imagination," in J. Reppen (ed.), *Why I Became a Psychotherapist*, Northvale, NJ, and London, pp. 1–14.

—— (1998b) "Noll and Void: The Jung Scholarship of Richard Noll," *Round Table Review*, 5, 3: 11–16.

—— (2001) *The Mythological Unconscious*, New York and London: Karnac.

Adler, A. (1916) *The Neurotic Constitution: Outlines of a Comparative Individualistic Psychology and Psychotherapy*, trans. B. Glueck and J. E. Lind, New York: Moffat, Yard, and Company.

Adler, A. (1939) *Social Interest: A Challenge to Mankind*, trans. J. Linton and R. Vaughan, New York: G. P. Putnam's Sons.

—— (1979) "Complex Compulsion as Part of Personality and Neurosis," in A. Adler, *Superiority and Social Interest: A Collection of Later Writings*, ed. H. L. Ansbacher and R. R. Ansbacher, New York and London: W. W. Norton, pp. 71–80.

Altman, N. (1995) *The Analyst in the Inner City: Race, Class, and Culture through a Psychoanalytic Lens*, Hillsdale, NJ, and London: The Analytic Press.

Alvarez, L. W. (1987) *Alvarez: Adventures of a Physicist*, New York: Basic Books.

American Psychiatric Association (1994) *Diagnostic and Statistical Manual of Mental Disorders, Fourth Edition* [*DSM-IV*], Washington, DC: American Psychiatric Association.

Ammer, C. (1992) *Have a Nice Day – No Problem! A Dictionary of Clichés*, New York: Dutton.

—— (1997) *The American Heritage Dictionary of Idioms*, Boston and New York: Houghton Mifflin.

Anderson, G. K. (1970) *The Legend of the Wandering Jew*, Providence, RI: Brown University Press.

Anonymous (January 30–February 6, 2002) "Judge Orders Deity To Break Up into Smaller Deities," *The Onion*: 1 and 6.

Applebome, P. (April 15, 1990) "Klan Challenges Law against Hoods," *New York Times*, sec. 1: 12.

Arens, W. (1979) *The Man-Eating Myth: Anthropology and Anthropophagy*, New York: Oxford University Press.

Arlow, J. A., and Brenner, C. (1964) *Psychoanalytic Concepts and the Structural Theory*, New York: International Universities Press.

Bachelard, G. (1969) *The Poetics of Reverie*, trans. D. Russell, New York: Orion Press.

—— (1983) *Water and Dreams: An Essay on the Imagination of Matter*, trans. E. R. Farrell, Dallas, TX: Dallas Institute of Humanities and Culture.

Baudrillard, J. (1994) *Simulacra and Simulation*, trans. S. F. Glaser, Ann Arbor, MI: University of Michigan Press.

Beebe, J., Cambray, J., and Kirsch, T. B. (2001) "What Freudians Can Learn from Jung," *Psychoanalytic Psychology*, 18,2: 213–42.

Bion, W.F. (1977) *Elements of Psychoanalysis*, in *Seven Servants: Four Works by Wilfred F. Bion*, New York: Jason Aronson.

Blankenhorn, D. (1995) *Fatherless America: Confronting Our Most Urgent Social Problem*, New York: Basic Books.

Bleuler, E. (1950) *Dementia Praecox or the Group of Schizophrenias*, trans. J. Zinkin, New York: International Universities Press.

Boa, F. (1992) *The Way of the Dream: Conversations on Jungian Dream Interpretation with Marie-Louise von Franz*, Boston and London: Shambhala.

Bohm, D. (1981) *Wholeness and the Implicate Order*, London: Routledge & Kegan Paul.

Boison, A. T. (1936) *The Exploration of the Inner World: A Study of Mental Disorder and Religious Experience*, New York: Harper & Brothers.

Bonime, W. (1989) *Collaborative Psychoanalysis: Anxiety, Depression, Dreams, and Personality Change*, Rutherford, Madison, and Teaneck, NJ: Fairleigh Dickinson University Press.

Bosnak, R. (1988) *A Little Course in Dreams*, Boston and Shaftesbury, MA: Shambhala.

—— (1989) *Dreaming with an AIDS Patient*, Boston and Shaftesbury, MA: Shambhala.

—— (1997) *Christopher's Dreams: Dreaming and Living with AIDS*, New York: Delta.

Boss, M. (1963) *Psychoanalysis and Daseinsanalysis*, trans. L. B. Lefebre, New York and London: Basic Books.

—— (1977) *"I Dreamt Last Night ..."*: *A New Approach to the Revelations of Dreaming – and Its Uses in Psychotherapy*, trans. S. Conway, New York: Gardner Press.

Bragg, R. (November 17, 1996) "In a South Carolina Town, a Klan Museum Opens Old Wounds," *New York Times*, sec. 1: 16.

Bulkeley, K. (1996) "Political Dreaming: Dreams of the 1992 Presidential Election," in K. Bulkeley (ed.), *Among All These Dreamers: Essays on Dreaming and Modern Society*, Albany: State University of New York Press, pp. 179–93.

Bush, G., and Scowcroft, B. (1998) *A World Transformed*, New York: Alfred A. Knopf.

Bynum, E. B. (1999) *The African Unconscious: Roots of Ancient Mysticism and Modern Psychology*, New York and London: Teachers College Press.

Casey, E. S. (1976) *Imagining: A Phenomenological Study*, Bloomington, IN, and London: Indiana University Press.

Chabot, C. B. (1982) *Freud on Schreber: Psychoanalytic Theory and the Critical Act*, Amherst, MA: University of Massachusetts Press.

Chalmers, D. M. (1987) *Hooded Americanism: The History of the Ku Klux Klan*, Durham, NC: Duke University Press.

Chaudhuri, U. (1995) *Staging Place: The Geography of Modern Drama*, Ann Arbor, MI: University of Michigan Press.

Chira, S. (June 19, 1994) "War over Role of American Fathers," *New York Times*, sec. 1: 22.

Corbin, H. (1972) *"Mundus Imaginalis*: Or the Imaginary and the Imaginal," *Spring*: 1–19.

Craig, P. E., and Walsh, S. J. (1993) "Phenomenological Challenges for the Clinical Use of Dreams," in G. Delaney (ed.), *New Directions in Dream Interpretation*, Albany, NY: State University of New York Press, pp. 103–54.

Cuvier, G. (1997) "Preliminary Discourse," in M. J. S. Rudwick, *Georges Cuvier, Fossil Bones, and Geological Catastrophes: New Translations and Interpretations of the Primary Texts*, Chicago and London: University of Chicago Press, pp. 183–252.

De Grazia, A., Juergens, R. E., and Stecchini, L. C. (eds.) (1966) *The Velikovsky Affair: Scientism vs. Science*, New Hyde Park, NY: University Books.

Derrida, J. (1981) *Dissemination*, trans. B. Johnson, Chicago: University of Chicago Press.

Eco, U. (1976) *A Theory of Semiotics*, Bloomington, IN, and London: Indiana University Press.

Edwards, A. (1989) "Schreber's Delusional Transference: A Disorder of the Self," in A. Samuels (ed.), *Psychopathology: Contemporary Jungian Perspectives*, London: Karnac, pp. 229–36.

Egan, T. (April 30, 1995) "Inside the World of the Paranoid," *New York Times*, sec. 4: 1 and 5.

Eigen, M. (1986) *The Psychotic Core*, Northvale, NJ, and London: Jason Aronson.

Eliot, T. S. (1934) *After Strange Gods: A Primer of Modern Heresy*, London: Faber and Faber.

Emerson, R. W. (1987) *Representative Men: Seven Lectures, Collected Works of Ralph Waldo Emerson*, eds. W. E. Williams and D. E. Wilson, Cambridge, MA, and London: Belknap Press of Harvard University Press, vol. 4.

Erikson, E. H. (1969) *Gandhi's Truth: On the Origins of Militant Nonviolence*, New York: W. W. Norton.

Fairbairn, W. R. D. (1990a) "Endopsychic Structure Considered in Terms of Object-Relationships," in *Psychoanalytic Studies of the Personality*, London and New York: Tavistock/Routledge, pp. 82–132.

—— (1990b) "Features in the Analysis of a Patient with a Physical Genital Abnormality," in *Psychoanalytic Studies of the Personality*, London and New York: Tavistock/Routledge, pp. 197–222.

—— (1990c) "Steps in the Development of an Object-Relations Theory of the Personality," in *Psychoanalytic Studies of the Personality*, London and New York: Tavistock/Routledge, pp. 152–61.

—— (1994a) "In Defence of Object Relations Theory," in *From Instinct to Self: Selected Papers of W. R. D. Fairbairn*, eds. D. E. Scharf and E. F. Birtles, Northvale, NJ, and London: Jason Aronson, 1: 111–28.

—— (1994b) "Imagination a1nd Child Development," in *From Instinct to Self: Selected Papers of W. R. D. Fairbairn*, eds. E. F. Birtles and D. E. Scharff, Northvale, NJ, and London: Jason Aronson, 2: 195–209.

Ferenczi, S. (1950) *Sex in Psychoanalysis*, trans. E. Jones, in *The Selected Papers of Sandor Ferenczi*, New York: Basic Books, vol. 1.

Firestone, D. (July 19, 2001) "Ailing Statue: Symbol of Industry or Pork Barrel?", *New York Times*: A14.

Fordham, M. (1974) "Technique and Counter-Transference," in M. Fordham, R. Gordon, J. Hubback, and J. Redfearn (eds.), *Technique in Jungian Analysis*, London: William Heinemann Medical Books, pp. 260–88.

Forster, A., and Epstein, B. R. (1965[?]) *Report on the Ku Klux Klan*, New York: Anti-Defamation League of B'nai B'rith.

Fosshage, J. L. (1987) "New Vistas in Dream Interpretation," in M. L. Glucksman and S. L. Warner (eds.), *Dreams in New Perspective*, New York: Human Sciences Press, pp. 23–43.

Fosshage, J. L., and Loew, C. A. (eds.) (1987) *Dream Interpretation: A Comparative Study, Revised Edition*, New York: PMA Publishing Corp.

Freud, S. Except as below, all references are to the *Standard Edition* (*SE*), by volume and page number.

Freud, S. (1985) *The Complete Letters of Sigmund Freud to Wilhelm Fliess, 1887–1904*, ed. and trans. J. M. Masson, Cambridge, MA, and London: Belknap Press of Harvard University Press.

Freud, S., and Jung, C. G. (1974) *The Freud/Jung Letters: The Correspondence between Sigmund Freud and C. G. Jung*, ed. W. McGuire, trans. R. Manheim and R. F. C. Hull, Princeton, NJ: Princeton University Press.

Freud, S., and Pfister, O. (1963) *Psychoanalysis and Faith: The Letters of Sigmund Freud and Oskar Pfister*, eds. H. Meng and E. L. Freud, trans. E. Mosbacher, New York: Basic Books.

Frye, N. (1957) *Anatomy of Criticism: Four Essays*, Princeton, NJ: Princeton University Press.

Giegerich, W. (1999) *The Soul's Logical Life: Towards a Rigorous Notion of Psychology*, Frankfurt am Main: Peter Lang.

Goodstein, L. (June 23, 1998) "Town's Fish Logo Becomes a Battleground on Religion," *New York Times*: A1 and A17.

Grant, M. (1971) *Roman Myths*, New York: Charles Scribner's Sons.

Graves, R. (1957) *The Greek Myths*, New York: George Braziller, 2 vols.

Greenberg, J. R., and Mitchell, S. A. (1983) *Object Relations in Psychoanalytic Theory*, Cambridge, MA, and London: Harvard University Press.

Greenhouse, L. (April 8, 2003) "Justices Allow Bans on Cross Burnings Intended as Threats," *New York Times*: A1 and A16.

Griffith, D. W. (1992) *The Birth of a Nation* [videotape], Kino International.

Grimes, W. (May 9, 1998) "Talk About a Fork in the Road," *New York Times*: B9 and B11.

Gulland, D. M., and Hinds-Howell, D. (1986) *The Penguin Dictionary of English Idioms*, Harmondsworth: Penguin Books.

Guntrip, H. (1961) *Personality Structure and Human Interaction: The Developing Synthesis of Psychodynamic Theory*, New York: International Universities Press.

Hall, N. (1980) *The Moon and the Virgin: Reflections on the Archetypal Feminine*, New York: Harper & Row.

Harding, M. E. (1955) *Woman's Mysteries: Ancient and Modern*, New York: Pantheon Books.

——(1971) "The Burning Bush: An Experience of the Numinosum," in H. Kirsch (ed.), *The Well-Tended Tree: Essays in the Spirit of Our Time*, New York: G. P. Putnam's Sons, pp. 1–13.

Hartmann, H. (1958) *Ego Psychology and the Problem of Adaptation*, trans. D. Rappaport, New York: International Universities Press.

——(1964) "Notes on the Reality Principle," in *Essays on Ego Psychology: Selected Problems in Psychoanalytic Theory*, New York: International Universities Press, pp. 241–67.

Hauke, C. (2000) *Jung and the Postmodern: The Interpretation of Realities*, London and Philadelphia: Routledge.

Henderson, J. L. (1990) "The Cultural Unconscious," in *Shadow and Self: Selected Papers in Analytical Psychology*, Wilmette, IL: Chiron Publications, pp. 103–13.

Hillman, J. (1972) *The Myth of Analysis: Three Essays in Archetypal Psychology*, Evanston, IL: Northwestern University Press.

——(1975) *Re-Visioning Psychology*, New York: Harper & Row.

——(1976) *Suicide and the Soul*, Dallas, TX: Spring Publications.

——(1979a) *The Dream and the Underworld*, New York: Harper & Row.

——(1979b) "Image-Sense," *Spring*: 130–43.

——(1980) "On the Necessity of Abnormal Psychology: Ananke and Athena," in J. Hillman (ed.), *Facing the Gods*, Dallas, TX: Spring Publications, pp. 1–38.

——(1981a) "Psychology: Monotheistic or Polytheistic," in D. L. Miller, *The New Polytheism: Rebirth of the Gods and Goddesses*, Dallas, TX: Spring Publications.

——(1981b) *The Thought of the Heart*, Dallas, TX: Spring Publications.

——(1983a) *Healing Fiction*, Barrytown, NY: Station Hill.

——with Pozzo, L. (1983b) *Inter Views: Conversations with Laura Pozzo on Psychotherapy, Biography, Love, Soul, Dreams, Work, Imagination, and the State of the Culture*, New York: Harper & Row.

——(1984) *Insearch: Psychology and Religion*, Dallas, TX: Spring Publications.

——(1985) *Anima: An Anatomy of a Personified Notion*, Dallas, TX: Spring Publications.

——(1988) *On Paranoia*, Dallas, TX: Spring Publications.

——(1991a) "Oedipus Revisited," in K. Kerenyi and J. Hillman, *Oedipus Variations: Studies in Literature and Psychoanalysis*, Dallas, TX: Spring Publications, pp. 87–169.

——(1991b) "The Yellowing of the Work," in M. A. Mattoon (ed.) *Personal and Archetypal Dynamics in the Analytical Relationship: Proceedings of the Eleventh*

International Congress for Analytical Psychology, Paris, 1989, Einsiedeln: Daimon Verlag, pp. 77–96.

Hillman, J. (1996) "'Psychology – Monotheistic or Polytheistic': Twenty-Five Years Later," *Spring*, 60: 111–25.

Hillman, J., and Ventura, M. (1992) *We've Had a Hundred Years of Psychotherapy – And the World's Getting Worse*, San Francisco: HarperSanFrancisco.

Hofstadter, R. (1965) *The Paranoid Style in American Politics and Other Essays*, New York: Alfred A. Knopf.

Holmes, S.A. (November 20, 1998) "Klan Case Transcends Black vs. White," *New York Times*: A20.

Horney, K. (1937) *The Neurotic Personality of Our Time*, New York: W.W. Norton.

Ipp, H. R. (2000a) "The Dreamer and the Dreams," *Psychoanalytic Dialogues*, 10, 1: 89–101.

——(2000b) "Dreaming to Different Beats," *Psychoanalytic Dialogues*, 10, 1: 159–67.

Isaacs, S. (1952) "The Nature and Function of Phantasy," in M. Klein, et al. (eds.), *Developments in Psycho-Analysis*, London: Hogarth Press: 67–121.

James. W. (1929) *The Varieties of Religious Experience: A Study in Human Nature*, New York: Modern Library.

——(1968) *Radical Empiricism*, in J. J. McDermott (ed.), *The Writings of William James: A Comprehensive Edition*, New York: Modern Library, pp. 134–310.

——(1983) *The Principles of Psychology*, Cambridge, MA, and London: Harvard University Press.

Jaspers, K. (1946) *General Psychopathology*, trans. J. Hoenig and M. W. Hamilton, Manchester and Chicago: Manchester University Press and University of Chicago Press.

Johnson, A. (1952) *Pioneer's Progress: An Autobiography*, New York: Viking Press.

Johnson, G. (April 30, 1995) "The Conspiracy That Never Ends," *New York Times*, sec. 4: 5.

Jones, E. (1951) "The Madonna's Conception through the Ear," in *Essays in Applied Psycho-Analysis*, London: Hogarth Press, 2: 266–357.

——(1955) *The Life and Work of Sigmund Freud: Years of Maturity, 1901–1919*, New York: Basic Books, vol. 2.

Joyce, J. (1961) *Ulysses*, New York: Modern Library.

Jung, C. G. Except as below, all references are to the *Collected Works* (*CW*), by volume, page number, and paragraph.

Jung, C. G. (1916) "Psychology of the Unconscious Processes," in *Collected Papers on Analytical Psychology*, ed. C. E. Long, London: Baillière, Tindale and Cox, pp. 354–444.

——(1963) *Memories, Dreams, Reflections*, ed. A. Jaffe, trans. R. and C. Winston, New York: Pantheon Books.

——(1964) "Approaching the Unconscious," in C. G. Jung and M.-L. von Franz (eds.), *Man and His Symbols*, Garden City, NY: Doubleday, pp. 18–103.

——(1973) *Letters: 1906–1950*, ed. G. Adler with A. Jaffe, trans. R. F. C. Hull, Princeton, NJ: Princeton University Press, vol 1.

——(1974) *Dreams*, trans. R. F. C. Hull, Princeton, NJ: Princeton University Press.

——(1975) *Letters: 1951–1961*, ed. G. Adler with A. Jaffe, trans. R. F. C. Hull, Princeton, NJ: Princeton University Press, vol. 2.

——(1977) *C. G. Jung Speaking: Interviews and Encounters*, ed. W. McGuire and R. F. C. Hull, Princeton, NJ: Princeton University Press.

——(1984) *Dream Analysis: Notes of the Seminar Given in 1928–1930*, ed. W. McGuire, Princeton, NJ: Princeton University Press.

—— (1988) *Nietzsche's Zarathustra: Notes of the Seminar Given in 1934–1939*, ed. J. L. Jarrett, Princeton, NJ: Princeton University Press, 2 vols.

—— (1997) *On Active Imagination*, ed. J. Chodorow, Princeton, NJ: Princeton University Press.

Kant, I. (1969) *Dreams of a Spirit Seer and Other Related Writings*, trans. J. Manolesco, New York, Washington, DC, and Hollywood, CA: Vantage Press.

Katz, W. L. (1986) *The Invisible Empire: The Ku Klux Klan Impact on History*, Washington, DC: Open Hand Publishing.

Kennedy, R. (2002) *Nigger: The Strange Career of a Troublesome Word*, New York: Pantheon Books.

Kermode, F. (1967) *The Sense of an Ending: Studies in the Theory of Fiction*, London, Oxford, and New York: Oxford University Press.

Kerr, J. (1993) *A Most Dangerous Method: The Story of Jung, Freud, and Sabina Spielrein*, New York: Alfred A. Knopf.

Kimbles, S. L. (2000) "The Cultural Complex and the Myth of Invisibility," in T. Singer (ed.), *The Vision Thing: Myth, Politics and Psyche in the World*, London and New York: Routledge, pp. 157–69.

King, M. L. (June 6, 1988) "Fatherhood and the Black Man," *Wall Street Journal*: 20.

Kohut, H. (1991) "Introspection, Empathy, and the Semicircle of Mental Health," in P. H. Ornstein (ed.) *The Search for the Self: Selected Writings of Heinz Kohut: 1978–1981*, Madison, CT: International Universities Press, 4: 537–67.

Krafft-Ebing, R. von (1965) *Psychopathia Sexualis: A Medico-Forensic Study*, trans. H. E. Wedeck, New York: G. P. Putnam's Sons.

Kroeber, A. L., and Kluckhohn, C. (1952) *Culture: A Critical Review of Concepts and Definitions*, New York: Vintage.

Lakoff, G., and Johnson, M. (1980) *Metaphors We Live By*, Chicago and London: University of Chicago Press.

Laqueur, W. (1987) *The Age of Terrorism*, Boston and Toronto: Little, Brown and Company.

Lester, J. C., and Wilson, D. L. (1971) *Ku Klux Klan: Its Origin, Growth and Disbandment*, New York: AMS Press.

Lévi-Strauss, C. (1966) "The Culinary Triangle," *Partisan Review*, 33: 586–95.

—— (1970) *The Raw and the Cooked*, trans. J. and D. Weightman, London: Jonathan Cape.

Levine, E. (1981) *The Burning Bush: Jewish Symbolism and Mysticism*, New York: Sepher-Hermon Press.

Levy, L.W. (1993) *Blasphemy: Verbal Offense against the Sacred, from Moses to Salman Rushdie*, New York: Alfred A. Knopf.

Lifton, R. J. (1985) "The Image of 'The End of the World': A Psychohistorical View," in S. Friedlander, G. Holton, L. Marx, and E. Skolnikoff (eds.), *Visions of Apocalypse: End or Rebirth?*, New York and London: Holmes & Meier, pp. 151–67.

Loewald, H. W. (1980) "On Internalization," in *Papers on Psychoanalysis*, New Haven, CT, and London: Yale University Press, pp. 69–86.

Lopez-Pedraza, R. (1971) "Responses and Criticisms," *Spring*: 212–14.

Lothane, Z. (1992) *In Defense of Schreber: Soul Murder and Psychiatry*, Hillsdale, NJ, and London: The Analytic Press.

Macalpine, I., and Hunter, R. A. (1955) "Translators' Analysis of the Case," in D. P. Schreber, *Memoirs of My Nervous Illness*, London: William Dawson & Sons, pp. 369–411.

Macalpine, I., and Hunter, R. A. (1969) *George III and the Mad Business*, New York: Pantheon Books.

McDougall, J. (1989) *Theaters of the Body: A Psychoanalytic Approach to Psychosomatic Illness*, New York and London: W. W. Norton.

—— (1991) *Theaters of the Mind: Illusion and Truth on the Psychoanalytic Stage*, New York: Brunner/Mazel.

McKinley, J. C. (January 9, 2000) "Weighing Therapy for a Narrow Mind," *New York Times*, sec. 4: 5.

McNamara, E. (1994) *Sex, Suicide, and the Harvard Psychiatrist*, New York: Pocket Books.

Mann, W. E., and Hoffman, E. (1980) *The Man Who Dreamed of Tomorrow: A Conceptual Biography of Wilhelm Reich*, Los Angeles: J. P. Tarcher.

Mecklin, J. M. (1963) *The Ku Klux Klan: A Study of the American Mind*, New York: Russell & Russell.

Medin, D., and Ortony, A. (1989) "Psychological Essentialism," in S. Vosniadou and A. Ortony (eds.), *Similarity and Analogical Reasoning*, Cambridge: Cambridge University Press, pp. 179–95.

Meige, H. (1986) "The Wandering Jew in the Clinic: A Study in Neurotic Pathology," trans. L. Benzinger, in G. Hasan-Rokem and A. Dundes (eds.), *The Wandering Jew: Essays in the Interpretation of a Christian Legend*, Bloomington, IN: Indiana University Press, pp. 190–4.

Meltzer, D. (1984) *Dream-Life: A Re-Examination of the Psycho-Analytical Theory and Technique*, Reading: Clunie Press.

Merton, R. K. (1965) *On the Shoulders of Giants: A Shandean Postscript*, New York: Free Press.

Miles, J. (1992) "In Impious America," *Spring*, 52: 20–6.

Mitchell, S. A. (1988) *Relational Concepts in Psychoanalysis: An Integration*, Cambridge, MA, and London: Harvard University Press.

Modell, A. H. (1984) *Psychoanalysis in a New Context*, New York: International Universities Press.

Moskowitz, M. (n.d.) "Love and Law on the Path to Redemption," unpublished manuscript.

Murray, H. A. (1960) "The Possible Nature of a 'Mythology' To Come," in H. A. Murray (ed.), *Myth and Mythmaking*, New York: George Braziller, pp. 300–53.

Nagy, G. (1994) "The Name of Apollo: Etymology and Essence," in J. Solomon (ed.), *Apollo: Origins and Influences*, Tuscon, AZ, and London: University of Arizona Press, pp. 3–7.

Niederland, W. G. (1974) *The Schreber Case: Psychoanalytic Profile of a Paranoid Personality*, New York: Quadrangle.

Nietzsche, F. (1968) *The Birth of Tragedy*, in W. Kaufman (ed.), *Basic Writings of Nietzsche*, trans. W. Kaufman, New York: Modern Library.

Paris, G. (1992) *The Sacrament of Abortion*, Dallas, TX: Spring Publications.

Perlman, M. (1994) *The Power of Trees: The Reforesting of the Soul*, Dallas, TX: Spring Publications.

Perls, F. S. (1969) *Ego, Hunger and Aggression: The Beginning of Gestalt Therapy*, New York: Vintage Books.

Perry, J. W. (1976) *Roots of Renewal in Myth and Madness*, San Francisco, Washington, and London: Jossey-Bass.

—— (1987) *The Heart of History: Individuality in Evolution*, Albany, NY: State University of New York Press.

Pfister, O. (1917) *The Psychoanalytic Method*, trans. C. R. Payne, New York: Moffat, Yard & Company.

Pine, F. (1990) *Drive, Ego, Object, and Self: A Synthesis for Clinical Work*, New York: Basic Books.

Popper, K. R. (1962) *Conjectures and Refutations: The Growth of Scientific Knowledge*, New York and London: Basic Books.

Post, J. M. (1998) "Terrorist Psycho-Logic: Terrorist Behavior as a Product of Psychological Forces," in W. Reich (ed.), *Origins of Terrorism: Psychologies, Ideologies, Theologies, States of Mind*, Washington, DC: Woodrow Wilson Center Press, pp. 25–40.

Rappaport, D., and Gill, M. M. (1967) "The Points of View and Assumptions of Metapsychology," in D. Rappaport, *The Collected Papers of David Rappaport*, ed. M. M. Gill, New York and London: Basic Books, pp. 795–811.

Redfearn, J. (1992) *The Exploding Self*, Wilmette, IL: Chiron Publications.

Reich, W. (1945) *Character-Analysis*, trans. T. P. Wolfe, New York: Orgone Institute Press.

——(1948) *The Function of the Orgasm: Sex-Economic Problems of Biological Energy*, trans. T. P. Wolfe, New York: Orgone Institute Press.

Rice, A. S. (1972) *The Ku Klux Klan in American Politics*, New York: Haskell House.

Rich, F. (April 27, 1995) "New World Terror," *New York Times*: A25.

Ricoeur, P. (1974) *The Conflict of Interpretations: Essays in Hermeneutics*, ed. D. Ihde, Evanston, IL: Northwestern University Press.

——(1981a) "The Hermeneutical Function of Distanciation," in *Hermeneutics and the Human Sciences: Essays on Language, Action and Interpretation*, ed. and trans. J. B. Thompson, Cambridge: Cambridge University Press, pp. 131–44.

——(1981b) "Metaphor and the Central Problem of Hermeneutics," in *Hermeneutics and the Human Sciences: Essays on Language, Action and Interpretation*, ed. and trans. J. B. Thompson, Cambridge: Cambridge University Press, pp. 165–81.

Robertson, P. (1991) *The New World Order*, Dallas, TX, London, Vancouver, and Melbourne: Word Publishing.

Roland, A. (1996) *Cultural Pluralism and Psychoanalysis: The Asian and North American Experience*, New York and London: Routledge.

Romanyshyn, R. D. (1982) *Psychological Life: From Science to Metaphor*, Austin, TX: University of Texas Press.

Rosen, D. H. (1993) *Transforming Depression: Egocide, Symbolic Death, and New Life*, New York: Jeremy P. Tarcher/Putnam.

Roth, P. (1980) *The Breast*, New York: Farrar, Straus, Giroux.

Rowan, J. (1990) *Subpersonalities: The People Inside Us*, London and New York: Routledge.

Rudwick, M. J. S. (1997) *Georges Cuvier, Fossil Bones, and Geological Catastrophes: New Translations and Interpretations of the Primary Texts*, Chicago and London: University of Chicago Press.

Rycroft, C. (1968) *A Critical Dictionary of Psychoanalysis*, New York: Basic Books.

Sagan, E. (1974) *Cannibalism: Human Aggression and Cultural Form*, New York and London: Psychohistory Press.

Samuels, A. (1985) *Jung and the Post-Jungians*, London: Routledge & Kegan Paul.

——(1989) "Introduction," in A. Samuels (ed.), *The Father: Contemporary Jungian Perspectives*, New York: New York University Press, pp. 2–44.

Samuels, A. (1993) *The Political Psyche*, London and New York: Routledge.

—— (2001) *Politics on the Couch: Citizenship and the Internal Life*, New York: Karnac.

Santner, E. L. (1996) *My Own Private Germany: Daniel Paul Schreber's Secret History of Modernity*, Princeton, NJ: Princeton University Press.

Sass, L. A. (1994) *The Paradoxes of Delusion: Wittgenstein, Schreber, and the Schizophrenic Mind*, Ithaca, NY, and London: Cornell University Press.

Scharfetter, C. (1980) *General Psychopathology: An Introduction*, trans. H. Marshall, Cambridge: Cambridge University Press.

Schatzman, M. (1973) *Soul Murder: Persecution in the Family*, New York: Random House.

Schlochower, H. (1970) *Mythopoesis: Mythic Patterns in the Literary Classics*, Detroit, MI: Wayne State University Press.

Schreber, D. P. (1955) "Grounds of Appeal," in *Memoirs of My Nervous Illness*, eds. and trans. I. Macalpine and R. A. Hunter, London: William Dawson & Sons, pp. 285–313.

—— (1955) *Memoirs of My Nervous Illness*, eds. and trans. I. Macalpine and R. A. Hunter, London: William Dawson & Sons.

—— (1988) *Memoirs of My Nervous Illness*, eds. and trans. I. Macalpine and R. A. Hunter, intro. S. M. Weber, Cambridge, MA, and London: Harvard University Press.

Schwartz-Salant, N., and Stein, M. (eds.) (1992) *Gender and Soul in Psychotherapy*, Wilmette, IL: Chiron Publications.

Schweitzer, A. (1924) *On the Edge of the Primeval Forest: Experiences and Observations of a Doctor in Equatorial Africa*, trans. C. T. Campion, London: A. & C. Black.

Seaman, A. R. (1999) *Swaggart: The Unauthorized Biography of an American Evangelist*, New York: Continuum.

Searles, H. F. (1979) "The Schizophrenic Individual's Experience of His World," in *Countertransference and Related Subjects*, Madison, CT: International Universities Press, pp. 5–27.

Segal, H. (1974) *Introduction to the Work of Melanie Klein*, New York: Basic Books.

Seinfeld, J. (1990) *The Bad Object: Handling the Negative Therapeutic Reaction in Psychotherapy*, Northvale, NJ, and London: Jason Aronson.

—— (1993) *Interpreting and Holding: The Paternal and Maternal Functions in Psychotherapy*, Northvale, NJ, and London: Jason Aronson.

Shapiro, D. (1965) *Neurotic Styles*, New York and London: Basic Books.

Singer, J. (1976) *Androgyny: Toward a New Theory of Sexuality*, Garden City, NY: Anchor Press/Doubleday.

Steinberg, L. (1983) *The Sexuality of Christ in Renaissance Art and in Modern Oblivion*, New York: Pantheon Books.

Steinfels, P. (June 20, 1992) "Beliefs: The Story Calls for Fathers, But Too Many Have Written Themselves Out of the Script," *New York Times*, sec. 1: 11.

Stern, D. (1985) *The Interpersonal World of the Infant: A View from Psychoanalysis and Developmental Psychology*, New York: Basic Books.

Stoller, R. J. (1968) *Sex and Gender: On the Development of Masculinity and Femininity*, New York: Science House, vol. 1.

—— (1976) *Sex and Gender: The Transsexual Experiment*, New York: Jason Aronson, vol. 2.

Stone, L. (1984) "On the Principal Obscene Word of the English Language," in *Transference and Its Context: Selected Papers on Psychoanalysis*, New York and London: Jason Aronson, pp. 323–66.

Swift, J. (1984) "A Modest Proposal for Preventing the Children of Poor People from being a Burthen to their Parents or the Country, and for making them Beneficial to the Public," in *Jonathan Swift*, eds. A. Ross and D. Woolley, Oxford and New York: Oxford University Press, pp. 492–9.

Taylor, M. C., and Saarinen, E. (1994) *Imagologies: Media Philosophy*, London and New York: Routledge.

Thom, R. (1975) *Structural Stability and Morphogenesis*, trans. D. H. Fowler, Reading, MA: Benjamin Cummings Publishing Co.

Thompson, C. M. (1964) "Sullivan and Fromm," in *Interpersonal Psychoanalysis: The Selected Papers of Clara M. Thompson*, ed. M. R. Green, New York and London: Basic Books, pp. 95–9.

Thompson, S. (1955) *Motif-Index of Folk-Literature*, Bloomington, IN, and London: Indiana University Press, vol. 5.

Todorov, T. (1984) *The Conquest of America: The Question of the Other*, trans. R. Howard, New York: Harper & Row.

Tomberlin, M. (June 14, 2003) "Vulcan's Skin Returns to Gray Base," *Birmingham News*: 1A.

Ulanov, A. B. (1994) "Jung and Prayer," in J. Rice-Menuhin (ed.), *Jung and the Monotheisms: Judaism, Christianity and Islam*, London and New York: Routledge, pp. 91–110.

Van den Berg, J. H. (1972) *A Different Existence: Principles of Phenomenological Psychopathology*, Pittsburgh, PA: Duquesne University Press.

Velikovsky, I. (1950) *Worlds in Collision*, Garden City, NY: Doubleday & Co.

Von Franz, M.-L. (1993a) "Profession and Vocation," trans. M. H. Kohn, in *Psychotherapy*, Boston and London: Shambhala, pp. 267–82.

——(1993b) "Self-Realization in the Individual Therapy of C. G. Jung," trans. M. H. Kohn, in *Psychotherapy*, Boston and London: Shambhala, pp. 1–15.

——(1993c) "Some Aspects of the Transference," in *Psychotherapy*, Boston and London: Shambhala, pp. 238–55.

——(1995) *Creation Myths*, Boston and London: Shambhala.

——(1996) *The Interpretation of Fairy Tales*, Boston and London: Shambhala.

Wade, N. (April 11, 2003) "Gene Study Finds Cannibal Pattern," *New York Times*: A20.

Wade, W. C. (1987) *The Fiery Cross: The Ku Klux Klan in America*, New York: Simon & Schuster.

Watkins, M. (1984) *Waking Dreams*, Dallas, TX: Spring Publications.

——(1986) *Invisible Guests: The Development of Imaginal Dialogues*, Hillsdale, NJ: The Analytic Press.

Weber, G. (1955) "Medical Expert's Report to the Court," in D. P. Schreber, *Memoirs of My Nervous Illness*, ed. and trans. I. Macalpine and R. A. Hunter, London: William Dawson & Sons, pp. 267–74.

Weber, M. (1992) *The Protestant Ethic and the Spirit of Capitalism*, trans. T. Parsons, London: Routledge.

Weigle, M. (1989) *Creation and Procreation: Feminist Reflections on Mythologies of Cosmogony and Parturition*, Philadelphia: University of Pennsylvania Press.

Whitmont, E. C., and Perera, S. B. (1989) *Dreams, A Portal to the Source*, London and New York: Routledge.

Winwood, S., Capaldi, J., and Wood, C. (1967) "Dear Mr. Fantasy," on *Mr. Fantasy*, Island Records: ILP961.

Wittgenstein, L. (1967) *Lectures and Conversations on Aesthetics, Psychology and*

Religious Belief, ed. C. Barrett, Berkeley, CA, and Los Angeles: University of California Press.

Wohlgemuth, A. (1923) *A Critical Examination of Psycho-Analysis*, London: George Allen & Unwin; New York: Macmillan.

Woodcock, A., and Davis, M. (1978) *Catastrophe Theory*, New York: E. P. Dutton.

Yoon, C. K. (February 11, 2003) "Fish Evolve and Multiply, but Not in the Traditional Way," *New York Times*, F1 and F7.

Young-Eisendrath, P., and Wiedemann, F. (1987) *Female Authority: Empowering Women through Psychotherapy*, New York and London: Guilford.

Zeeman, E. C. (1977) "Catastrophe Theory: Draft for a *Scientific American* Article," in *Catastrophe Theory: Selected Papers, 1972–1977*, Reading, MA: Addison-Wesley Publishing Co., pp. 1–64.

Zoja, L. (2001) *The Father: Historical, Psychological and Cultural Perspectives*, trans. H. Marin, London and Philadelphia: Brunner-Routledge.

Index

Abraham 209
Abraham–Isaac myth 175
Abraham–Ishmael myth 175
Abrahamsen, D. 11–12
absent father complex 175
abusive father complex 175
Achilles 180–1
active imagination xi, 3, 11, 15–19, 30,
    54–5, 64, 72, 93; definition of 15–16, 55;
    as interactive imagination 15–16; stories
    as a form of 179
Adam 214
Adams, M.V. ix, xii, 18, 37, 39, 58, 62–3,
    67–8, 70–1, 73–4, 82, 93, 131, 134–5,
    137, 141, 146, 155, 157, 159, 163, 166,
    172, 206, 213
adherence 24, 26
Adler, A. x, 9, 25, 140, 143
Aeneas 180, 182–3
Africa: description of 158; as an image of
    the unconscious 158; as a mirror 155,
    164; as a projection of the European
    unconscious 158
Agammemnon 182
Age of Androgyny 124
Age of Myth 93
Age of Reason 22, 93
Ahasver 115
alchemy 31, 158, 218
Allah 207, 219, 221–2
alternative perspective(s) 19, 21–3, 34,
    36–7, 140, 159, 161, 189, 220, 224
Altman, N. 134–5
Alvarez, L.W. 114–15
American Psychiatric Association 12, 44,
    79, 110
American Psychological Association 61
Ammer, C. 74

amplification xi, 15–17, 19, 54–5, 60, 62–4,
    72, 90; as an extension of explication 15;
    definition of 15, 55, 62, 195
analyst-mother 65–6
analytic indications 27, 30–1, 33–4, 36,
    127–30, 188
Anchises 182
Anderson, G.K. 115
androcentric 120
androgyny 124–5
Andromache 180
anima 70, 107, 113, 123; as an abstract
    generalization 50; as a concept 49–53,
    56; contrasexual archetypal image of the
    feminine 84, 92; feminine aspects in the
    psyche of a man 40, 77; femininity 50;
    opposite-sex archetype of the feminine
    aspects in the psyche of a man 139; as
    siren 54; as soul 95, 109, 125; virgin 118
anima-image 50, 140–1
anima mundi 173
anima-possession 92, 95, 107, 112, 124
animus 49, 123; as a concept 50, 56;
    masculine aspects in the psyche of
    a woman 40
animus-image 50
Apollinian 58–9
Apollo 57–9; god of dreams 58; principle
    of individuation 58; maxims of (know
    thyself and nothing in excess) 58
aptness condition 10, 23, 49, 73
Apuleius 125
archetypal: complex(es) 202; images 45,
    56, 58–9, 64, 67, 92, 173, as archaic
    affect-images 122; of Madonna and
    Child 65; of prophet 213; father 175;
    literacy 68, 71; psychology versus
    stereotypical psychology 51;